Secondary Schooling in a Changing World

Secondary Schooling in a Changing World

Susan Groundwater-Smith

Marie Brennan

Mark McFadden

Jane Mitchell

Australia · Canada · Mexico · Singapore · Spain · United Kingdom · United States

102 Dodds Street
Southbank Victoria 3006

Email highereducation@thomsonlearning.com.au
Website http://www.thomsonlearning.com.au

First published in 2001 by Harcourt Australia Pty Ltd.
Reprinted in 2003 by Thomson Learning Australia.
10 9 8 7 6 5 4 3 2
06 05 04 03

Copyright ' 2003 Nelson   Australia Pty Limited.

National Library of Australia
Cataloguing-in-Publication data

   Secondary schooling in a changing world.

   Bibliography.
   Includes index.
   ISBN 0 7295 3614 9.

   1. Education, Secondary - Australia. 2. Education - Effect of
   technological innovations on - Australia. 3. Educational change -
   Australia. 1. Groundwater-Smith, Susan.

373.94

Publishing Services Manager: Helena Klijn
Edited, indexed and project managed by Forsyth Editorial Services
Cover and internal design by Tania Edwards
Typeset by Egan-Reid Limited, Auckland
Rights and Permissions: Debi Wager
Printed in Australia by McPherson's Printing Group

This title is published under the imprint of Thomson.
Nelson Australia Pty Limited ACN 058 280 149 (incorporated in Victoria)
trading as Thomson Learning.

The URLs contained in this publication were checked for currency during
the production process. Note, however, that the publisher cannot vouch
for the ongoing currency of URLs.

Contents

Preface   vii

About the Authors   ix

Acknowledgments   x

Credits   x

Part One   The Challenge of Change   1

Chapter 1   The Challenge of Change   3

Chapter 2   Re-thinking Today's Secondary Schools   15

Chapter 3   Teaching: A Changing Profession   33

Part Two   Changing Times, Changing Students   53

Chapter 4   From Adolescence to Young Adulthood   55

Chapter 5   Accepting and Rejecting Secondary Schooling   67

**Part Three   Learning to Teach in Contemporary
                Australian Secondary Schools**   87

Chapter 6   Communication and Relationships   89

Chapter 7   A Context for Learning   109

Chapter 8   Negotiating the Practicum   127

Chapter 9   Learning, Teaching and Technology   151

**Part Four   New Ways of Understanding
                Curriculum and Assessment**   173

Chapter 10   Literacy Teaching Across the Curriculum   175

Chapter 11   Changing Trends in Curriculum Design   191

Chapter 12   New Ways of Thinking About Assessment
              and Reporting   207

Part Five   **The Workplace Learning of Teachers —**
                A Fresh Orientation   229

Chapter 13   Professional Development: Documenting Teachers'
             Workplace Learning   231
Chapter 14   Documenting the Corporate Learning of the School
             Community for School Improvement   249
Chapter 15   The Full Service School   263

Part Six   **Ethical Accountability**   279

Chapter 16   Ethics and Responsibilities in the Education
             Profession   281

Index   291

Preface

We have conceived of this book as one which serves a multiplicity of purposes. It assumes as its audience both students of teaching and scholars of teaching. In doing so, it acknowledges that each reader will bring to the text different histories and experience. It asks its readers 'what is it to position oneself as a teacher in these times of considerable social, political, economic and technological change?'

The structure of the book provides an interpretative framework for 'reading' today's secondary schools, their focus and their practices. It initially examines the nature of change itself and the ways in which these changes impact upon teachers' work and the organisation of schools. It progresses to pose questions regarding adolescence and the ways in which young people deal with secondary schooling. Following these opening chapters the book attends to more practical matters related to the lived experience of teaching in the context of the school itself as a learning community.

It has been a deliberate choice to address the text to you, the reader. We have used this device to engage you in the complex debates surrounding secondary schooling as a sociocultural practice. While it is not a 'how to' series of recipes it discusses issues in grounded and practical ways. We have drawn upon our own research, which is Australia wide, as well as the salient research and scholarship in the field.

Either at the end of a chapter, or embedded in the chapter, we have incorporated a range of inquiry strategies. Our experience in practitioner research has taught us the merit of engaging you as active agents in teacher research from the very beginning of your teaching careers.

As our next generation of teachers, we believe that you will be facing continuous change, which will be occurring exponentially. Relying uncritically upon old practices will not be sufficient for effective schooling in the twenty-first century. Curriculum is changing, assessment of learning is changing and the uses to which learning is to be put are changing. These are exciting and challenging times. Our hope is that this book will give you assistance and insight into dealing with our new futures.

Susan Groundwater-Smith
Marie Brennan
Mark McFadden
Jane Mitchell
July 2000

About the Authors

Susan Groundwater-Smith is a visiting scholar at the University of Sydney and the University of East Anglia in the UK. She co-directs the Centre for Practitioner Research at the University of Sydney, along with Professor Judyth Sachs. She has been a teacher educator since the 1970s and has particular interests in practitioner research (including students as researchers), educational evaluation and authentic assessment across all school sectors. She is currently researcher-in-residence at a large independent girls' school where she works across the age range supporting teachers in developing evidence-based practice.

Marie Brennan is Professor of Education at the University of Canberra, having also worked at Central Queensland and Deakin Universities. Prior to that she worked in a wide range of positions in the Victorian Ministry of Education, ranging from humanities teaching in technical schools to policy work. Her main interests are in how best to support practitioner research, student participation in schools and school innovation projects.

In 1997 and 1998, **Professor Mark McFadden** was Charles Sturt University's Director, Learning and Teaching. His doctoral research on 'second chance' education for disadvantaged young people gained an award for excellence in educational research from the NSW Institute for Educational Research. He is currently Head, School of Education and Professor of Education at Charles Sturt University, Wagga Wagga, and Director of the Group for Research in Employment and Training (GREAT). He has published and presented nationally and internationally on issues of access to and resistance to education. He has conducted ARC funded research on educational success for Indigenous Australian students. In 1999 he conducted an AusAID consultancy on institutional capacity for distance education delivery in Papua New Guinea.

Jane Mitchell is currently completing her PhD at the University of British Columbia in Canada. Her research interests are located in the field of teacher education, more particularly the practicum and uses of communications technology. Jane is a member of the Faculty of Education at Charles Sturt University in Wagga Wagga. She has also worked for several years in high schools in the ACT and New South Wales.

Acknowledgments

Our thanks to Mr Bob Dengate, Lecturer in Mathematics Education, Charles Sturt University, for the maths and technology classroom ideas (Chapter 9) and to Mr Paul Brown, Head Teacher History, Camden High School, Mr Troy Whitford, Mt Erin High School, Wagga Wagga, and Ms Tamara Jones for the HSE (Human Society and the Environment, a curriculum Key Learning Area) classroom ideas (Chapter 9). Mr Whitford and Ms Jones are both recent graduates from the Graduate Diploma of Education, Charles Sturt University.

We also wish to thank Dr Ralph Lattimore of the Productivity Commission, for assistance in our discussion of 'value adding' (Chapter 12).

The photographers

Gary Lawrence is a Science teacher whose hobby during a 30-year career has been photographing students enjoying learning in many different school environments.

Shae Fleming is a teacher of Design and Technology who has joined him in this project.

Credits

Allen & Unwin, Sydney. Latham, M. (1998). *Civilising Global Capital.* pp. xxii, 216, 246–7, 276. Allen & Unwin, Sydney. Scott, G. (1999). *Change Matters.* pp. 9–10. Allen & Unwin, Sydney. Welch, A. (1996). *Australian Education, Reform or Crisis?* p. 25. AERA Publications Department. Lipman, P., Smith, G., and Wehlage, G., (1992) Restructuring urban schools: the New Futures experience, *American Educational Research Journal*, 29, pp. 85–6. ACT Government (2000) Code of Ethics http://www.act.gov.au/government/publications/psms/1ethics.htm. Australian Centre for Equity through Education (ACEE), Sydney. Muirhead, B. (1996). State and Local Interagency Work in Queensland. In Australian Centre for Equity through Education, *School and Community action for Full Service Schools: Making it Work. The views of education, health, and community service practitioners presented at a national conference on full service schools.* Australian Centre for Equity through Education (ACEE), Sydney. Thompson, P. (1996). An education perspective: cooperation, coordination and collaboration . . . "but for what?" *School and Community action for Full Service Schools: Making it Work. The views of education, health, and community service practitioners presented at a national conference on full service schools.* p. 32. Australian Council for Educational Research (ACER Press), Camberwell, Vic. Freeland, J., 'Quality of what and quality for whom?' in Angus, L., Burke, G. and Chapman, J., (eds) *Improving the Quality of Australian Schools.*(ACER, 1991), p. 65. Australian Early Childhood Association Inc.(AECA). *The Early Childhood Code of Ethics.* Australian Educational Researcher (AARE). Gilbert, P. (1998). Gender and schooling in New Times: The challenge of boys and literacy, 25, 1, April, p. 30. Australian Government Printing Service (AGPS) Canberra. Australian Bureau of Statistics (1998a). Small towns: which ones are in decline. *In Australian Social Trends* (1998). p. 10. Australian Government Printing Service (AGPS) Canberra. Fitzgerald, R. (1978). *Outcomes of Schooling: Aspects of Success and Failure.* Report of the Commission of Inquiry into Poverty. pp. 5–7. Australian Teaching Council: Leichhardt, NSW. National Project on the Quality of Teaching and Learning (NPQTL) (1996). *National Competencies Framework for Beginning Teachers.* Bagnall, N. Dr., (1995). Global culture capital: the global field. In N. Bagnall (ed.) *Tradition and Change.* Proceedings of the Australia New Zealand Comparative and International Education Society, University of Sydney, p. 221, 234. Brennan, M. & Hoadley, R., (1984) *School Self-Evaluation.* p. 13, 15, 18. Cambridge University Press, Cambridge. Wiseman, J. (1998). *Global Nation: Australia and the Politics of Globalisation.* Department of Education, Training and Youth Affairs (DETYA) (1997). *Digital Rhetorics: Literacies and technologies in education — current practices and future directions.* © Commonwealth of Australia, Canberra. (vol 1) p. 20. Department of Education, Training and Youth Affairs (DETYA) (2000). Full service schools for students at risk. http://www.detya.gov.au. Falmer Press: London. Featherstone, D. (1997). Common themes in learning to teach. In D. Featherstone, H. Munby, & T. Russel (eds.), *Finding a Voice While Learning to Teach.* p. 16. Falmer Press: London, New York. Fullan, M. and Hargreaves, A. (eds) (1992). *Teacher development and educational change.* p. 5. Falmer Press: London, New York. Fullan, M. and Hargreaves, A. (eds) (1992). *Teacher development and educational change.* p. 4. Falmer Press: London. Siskin, L. (1994). *Realms of Knowledge: Academic Departments in Secondary Schools.* p. 2. HarperCollins Publishers: Sydney. Smith, S. (1917) A Brief History of Education in Australia (1788–1848). Angus & Robertson Ltd. pp. 32–3, 86. Human Rights and Equal Opportunity Commission (HREOC), (1999) *Bush Talks.* http://www.hreoc.gov.au. Kendall/Hunt Publishing Company, Dubuqe, Iowa. McDonald, J., (1993). Exhibitions: authentic assessment that points but doesn't drive. In J. Bamburg (ed.). *Assessment — How do we know what they know?* p. 68. Kluwer Academic Publishers: Spencer, D. (1997). Teaching as Women's Work. In B. Biddle, T. Good & I. Goodson (eds.) International Handbook of Teachers and Teaching. p. 179. With kind permission from Kluwer Academic Publishers, The Netherlands. Multilingual Matters Ltd, Clevedon, UK. Broadfoot, P., Dockrell, B., Gipps, C., Harlen, W. and Nuttall, D. (eds.) (1992). *Policy issues in national assessment.* BERA Dialogues 7. p. 6. Open University Press: Buckingham, UK. Ball, S. (1994). *Education reform: a critical and post-structural approach.* p. 41. Open University Press: Buckingham, UK. Broadfoot, P. (1996). *Education, assessment and society.* p. 13.

Open University Press: Buckingham, UK. Lankshear, C., with Gee, J.P., Knobel, M., and Searle, C., (1997). *Changing Literacies.* p. 44. Pearson Education Australia. Reproduced from Australian Centre for Industrial Relations, Research and Training (ACIRRT) & Buchanan, *Australia at Work*, 1999, p. 66. Philosophy of Education Society (PES): University of Illinois at Urbana-Champaign. Hansen D. (1994). Revitalizing the Idea of Vocation in Teaching. At, http://www.ed.uiuc.edu/EPS/PEs-Yearbook/94_docs/Hansen.htm pp. 4–5. Queensland Board of Teacher Registration: Toowong. Queensland Board of Teacher Registration (1996). *Report of the working party on the preparation of teachers for the education of young adolescents.* p. 3. Queensland Board of Senior Secondary School Studies (QBSSSS): www.bssssq.edu.au/Assessment/ Sch-based.html. State University of New York Press, New York. Britzman, Deborah. P. (1991). *Practice Makes Practice: A Critical Study of Learning to Teach.* pp. 8,14. Taylor & Francis Ltd, 11 New Fetter Lane, London EC4P 4EE. Black, P. & William, D., Assessment and classroom learning. In *Assessment in education: principles, policies and practices*, (1998), 5/1 pp. 17–18. Taylor & Francis Ltd, 11 New Fetter Lane, London EC4P 4EE. Hargreaves, A., 'The emotional politics of teaching and teacher development', *International Journal of Leadership in Education*, 1/4 (1998), p. 330. Taylor & Francis Ltd, 11 New Fetter Lane, London EC4P 4EE. McWilliam, E., 'Admitting impediments: or things to do with bodies in classrooms', *Cambridge Journal of Education*, 26/3 (1996), p. 368. Taylor & Francis Ltd, 11 New Fetter Lane, London EC4P 4EE. Reid, J., 'Holding firm to the bonds of convention: Primary English, Child Study and the Competent teacher' *Changing English*, 6/2 (1999), p. 197. UNESCO Publishing, Paris. Delors, J., (1996), *Learning: The Treasure Within.* p. 141. University of Chicago Press, Chicago, IL. Egan, K., (1997). *The Educated Mind: How Cognitive Tools Shape Our Understanding.* p. 248. University of Minnesota Press, Minneapolis: Aronowitz, S. & Giroux, H. (1991). *Postmodern Education: Politics, Culture and Social Criticism.* p. 109. University of Newcastle, NSW, Faculty of Education. Barcan, A. (1980). *History of Australian Education.* p. 138, 403–5.

PART ONE

The Challenge of Change

CHAPTER *1* The Challenge of Change

CHAPTER *2* Re-thinking Today's Secondary Schools

CHAPTER *3* Teaching: A Changing Profession

The three chapters which follow provide the context for reading this book. They discuss the ways in which economic, technological, and social change impact upon the public and private lives of us all.

Change is occurring such that many traditional primary and secondary industries are employing fewer and fewer people. The impact of globalisation upon Australia's citizens is only just becoming fully manifest as we move towards an economy which is based far more in service industries and the new knowledge economies. The computer on which this is being written is worth very little in terms of its material parts; it is the knowledge work invested in it which has made it a very expensive commodity indeed.

Technology is not only altering the workplace, it is affecting the ways in which we communicate, entertain ourselves and generally conduct our daily lives. In turn, our social world in both the public and domestic environments is being transformed. Families are changing, roles are being redefined, young people themselves, their values and mores are changing.

These may seem apparent truisms. However, for those who are to become tomorrow's teachers they are matters of critical importance. Teachers are needing to rethink not only the ways in which they work but also the structures within which they work and the ways in which they serve to advantage or disadvantage their students. The transition from the teacher-centred classroom to one in which students more effectively manage and make sense of their own learning in a differentiated fashion is slowly but surely occurring. It has been said that, for more than any other generation, today's teachers are being required to teach in ways which are very different from the manner in which they themselves were taught.

We recognise that many of our readers will have a deep knowledge of these trends; they will have studied them in the context of earlier degrees. However, we believe that by covering the ground, as we do, and providing a number of brief narrative accounts, we have recontextualised these trends within the discourses of schooling.

CHAPTER

The Challenge of Change

The chapters in the opening section of this book are designed to contextualise the work of secondary school teachers in a world remarkable not only for the ways in which it is changing, but for the pace and intensity of those changes.

Were our great-grandparents to reappear today they would find our world a very different place. Each generation knows that it faces changes. Yet the changes to our political, social, economic, technological and knowledge structures are developing today at a rate never before experienced.

Our great-grandparents could have predicted the general shape of the futures their children might have experienced, but this is becoming more and more difficult. Globalisation is upon us and no corner of Australia can be free of it (Wiseman 1998, p. 1):

> An Aboriginal girl in Alice Springs cradles her Pocahontas Barbie while she watches the Winter Olympics on satellite TV. Another factory closes in Newcastle because it can no longer compete with Chinese wages. Another Latrobe Valley power station is sold off to a United States energy corporation. Moody's credit-rating agency warns that Australian governments must keep cutting taxes and services — or else. Australian environmentalists and Aboriginal groups mobilise support from the European Parliament in their opposition to the opening of the Jabiluka uranium mine in the Northern Territory. A public park in Melbourne is taken over for an international car race beamed across the world. A Tasmanian mother frets about her sunburned child and the risk of skin cancer. This is Australia in an age of globalisation.

As one about to enter teaching in secondary schools you are charged with the responsibility not only of developing the discipline knowledge of your students but also for supporting them in the use of that knowledge in complex environments embodying the community, home and work. Indeed even the division between home and work is no longer clear as more and more people engage in work from home. Furthermore, you are expected to be familiar with policies in relation to drugs and alcohol, child protection and a myriad of other social concerns.

This chapter's purpose is to sketch major developments in global social, economic and technological change. It will note that change is occurring in every sphere of our public and private lives. Economic and technological changes interact to produce not only new knowledge but new ways of working, whether in the industrial, agricultural, extractive, service, civic or domestic domains. In turn, these changes influence and interact with social change. The patterns and organisation of work are changing, family structures are changing and well-known institutions are changing. These changes, in turn, impact upon our notions of civil society and the ways in which it may operate.

The chapter is of particular importance because it will examine the ways in which macro change is impacting upon education and the consequences for the schooling of adolescents and young adults. It will concentrate not only upon the implications of education for employment but also upon education for lifelong learning in the domestic and community domains. During your teaching career you will be teaching the adults of the future. This has always been the case but the future is becoming unimaginable as the rate of change and its consequences burgeon exponentially. Our secondary schools are not immune to change. You shall have to think deeply and seriously about current barriers that exist — between disciplines, between practitioners and between cultures and traditions. You will need to reflect upon whether they are any longer viable and what your roles will be in the schools of the future; schools within a knowledge-based society.

Our changing world

Pauline is in her early sixties. She was born in London just before the Second World War. Her school education was in primary and grammar schools in London and the English Midlands. She came to Australia by ship in the mid-1950s, arriving in Melbourne as it prepared for the Olympic Games.

I remember that time on the ship. It was terrific. We were at sea for about six weeks. We were one of the last ships to go through the canal before the Suez crisis. We called in at places like Aden, Bombay and Colombo. Our first port of call in Australia was Fremantle. Nearly everything was single-fronted, single-storey. Melbourne was unbelievable, literally. We arrived on a Sunday and were met at Station Pier and driven to our hotel near the Treasury Gardens. We drove through the city. The streets were so wide and totally empty, not a car, not a person. No wonder Ava Gardner talked about it being the right place to make a film about the end of the world, you know On the Beach.

The whole family had been transferred to Australia, but Pauline was keen to return to England as soon as possible. She had completed her Advanced levels in the English School Certificate but had no intention of going on to tertiary education. Work was plentiful and easy to find. In no time she had a job with a large bank. She earned less than her male colleagues and she was not permitted to handle money as a teller — that was for the young men only. In the end, Pauline did not return to England, but instead went on to Sydney. She flew for the first time in her life. When she wanted to contact her family in Melbourne she could phone. If there was an emergency she could send a telegram.

Pauline had good friends who were from Austria and Hungary. They were regarded as quite exotic. Goulash was cooked minus the garlic, 'because people said it was offensive'. They once took a trip to country New South Wales where they were castigated for not speaking in English. When they went to the delicatessen for lunch, the nearest they could come to finding salami was Devon sausage — a bland luncheon meat of indeterminate origin. Cheese was processed and had the texture of soap.

In her mid-twenties Pauline married. She was expected to leave her job in the bank and she did. She and her husband saved for a deposit on a house in the suburbs. Pauline obtained part-time office work, caring for the books and typing the occasional letter. She entered information into ledgers in black ink. As it was a small office there were no adding machines — she was expected to be able to compute 'in her head' and to be quick and accurate. There was a manual typewriter and any copies of correspondence were made using carbon paper.

She was deeply disturbed by the Vietnam War. She took part in street marches and sit-ins. By her late twenties she had her first child, with another following soon afterwards. Pauline never went back into the full-time paid work force. She was expected to stay at home and care for her family and she did that too.

Pauline's own daughters finished their school education during the eighties. They both went on to complete university degrees. They travelled and each has had several different jobs. They have each completed post-graduate studies and already had a career change. Neither expects that this will be the end of the matter. They assert that they will have to go on to further studies, both in terms of workplace training and tertiary courses. One lives in Sydney, the other in Brisbane. They communicate by the Internet with each other and their friends in Europe, North America and South-East Asia. They are both activists and send on petitions about women's rights and the environment. One of them has recently married, after living with her partner for several years, and is now expecting a child.

Pauline's story is not exceptional. She came to Australia when it was aggressively monocultural; when marriage meant 'until death do us part'; when Aboriginal culture was invisible; when mass media meant radio and newspapers — television was just gearing up. Huge projects such as the Snowy Mountains Hydro-Electric Scheme were underway. Australia, in international economic terms, was seen as the farm and the quarry and its major markets were in Europe. Canberra was still a sleepy country town with some government departments having relocated from Melbourne and Sydney. Transport and communications were changing, but not at such a pace that there couldn't be adjustment and accommodation. Pauline's school education was sufficient to sustain her in her chosen occupations in the paid work force and at home. Her daughters already understand that they are engaged in lifelong education. Her grandchild will occupy a very different world to the one in which she grew up. He or she will need to accumulate knowledge as a form of capital investment, as a member of a knowledge society.

Being a member of a knowledge society

If you were to visit Sydney in the 1950s you would find it hard to miss the Eveleigh Locomotive Workshops. Easily seen from the train as it approached Redfern railway station, the workshops were a landmark, a symbol of an advanced industrial society. They employed up to 3000 people making locomotive equipment ranging from a tiny spring to a 20-ton boiler. When opened in 1887, the workshops were recognised as the largest and most technologically advanced in the Southern Hemisphere; but today there is not a locomotive in sight. The only remnant of the industrial heritage is a forge making wrought iron artworks. Many of the Victorian buildings remain; no longer dedicated to heavy industry, but as the sites of the new knowledge industries. For today, the workshops have been transformed into the Australian Technology Park (ATP), a joint venture between the University of Sydney, the University of New South Wales, and the University of Technology, Sydney.

Cutting edge communications and information technology industries, drug companies, and business consultants are engaged in joint partnership arrangements with the participating universities. There are 'incubators' growing new businesses in biomedicine, telecommunications and software development. The participants in the ATP are inventing our futures. As old jobs disappear, new ones are being created. It is the claim of the ATP that there will be a shortfall of suitably qualified people to fill the positions created by the new knowledge industries. Whereas in earlier years capital and labour were the core factors in production, today and into the foreseeable future knowledge is an increasingly significant component, a commodity to be traded. The students who are now in our schools will need very different skills and competencies than students did in the past, if they are to participate and benefit from the new economies.

Mark Latham (1998), in his provocative book *Civilising Global Capital*, quotes the American writer Larry Letich, who claims (p. xxii):

> It is possible that over the last 100 years, and especially the last 40, we may have created a society that demands more brain power than most people are able to give . . . Until this century, at least 95 per cent of what an adult knew fell into two categories: practical or interpersonal. Both of these types of knowledge are concrete; they involve things one can see, touch and feel. Almost all of the remaining 5 per cent — the abstract knowledge — was comprised of myths, legends and religious beliefs passed down by the culture.

When the Eveleigh Locomotive Workshops were functioning, notions of what was worth knowing were closely associated with the manufacturing of material goods. In the ATP what is worth knowing is know-how: how to communicate faster and more efficiently, how to manipulate a genetic structure such that an agricultural product might be enhanced, how to evolve a more effective organisational culture.

Latham argues that the skills of Australian people are its most important resource in the struggle for competitive advantage, and that those skills can only be enhanced by increased investment in education and training. He says (p. 53): 'In the information age, the public sector needs to invest in the enhancement of knowledge no less fully than the industrial age invested in machines'.

But work is not only changing in the industrial sector, with a concomitant shift from the hands-on worker to the knowledge worker. The service sector is also being transformed. Commercial enterprises, such as banking, insurance and travel, have dramatically changed. Downsizing is the order of the day as the dependence upon electronic funds management increases. Call centres are growing as local facilities disappear. Queries about an account held in Devonport, Tasmania, might be answered in Melbourne. A plane booking made in Cairns might be handled in Adelaide. If you have a problem with your fax machine in Fremantle, you are helped by an operator in Sydney. Employment opportunities in the primary industries, such as agriculture and mining, are being increasingly curtailed as technological advances are made. A forest resource in south-east Queensland may be mapped by computer in an office in Brisbane.

Data show us that a greater and greater proportion of people are employed in particular areas of the service industries, which have been casualised and where the pay is low, specifically those associated with fast food and hospitality. Latham claims that there are now more workers employed by McDonalds than the entire Australian steel industry. The Australian Bureau of Statistics (ABS) (1997a) notes (p. 93):

> Over the past few decades the Australian labour force has changed substantially. The shift in labour demand arising from new technology, microeconomic reforms (such as tariff reductions, industrial relations reforms and changes to standards and regulations) and internationalisation of product markets have all contributed to this change. Another factor affecting the demand for labour has been the adoption of new management strategies that emphasise work force flexibility, particularly increased use of part time and casual employees. Employment has grown significantly in the service sector . . .

The ABS data notes that in 1966, 46 per cent of workers in Australia were employed in the production industries. Thirty years later, that proportion has diminished to 28 per cent. During that period nearly all employment growth has been in the service sector, which has increased from 2.6 million to 6.0 million workers.

Another area of the service industry with high employment growth has been property and business. This division includes services such as property operators, technical, computing, legal, accounting and marketing services. It is in this division that the knowledge workers are to be found. The ABS notes (p. 97): 'Conversely, the majority of occupation groups in which employment shrank over the same period were low-skilled occupations or those that have been affected by the impact of technological and economic change'. The ABS study argues that unless workers receive training the inevitable effect will be that those with low levels of skill will be left out or marginalised.

The emergence of a knowledge-based labour market means that schools and their practices must change. If there is to be an equitable distribution of work so that participation is inclusive and available across the socioeconomic spectrum and across urban and rural regions, then school education must be such that learners are truly intellectually flexible and adaptable.

The knowledge-based work force — winners and losers

There can be no question that where you live (Hunter 1995), who your parents are and what they do will influence your access to the knowledge-based labour market. In New South Wales, teachers working in schools west of the Great Dividing Range talk of the 'Sandstone Curtain' and they are right to do so. Social atlases show us that 'the most reliable guide to someone's employment, health and educational status is their postcode' (Latham 1998, p. 216).

The more remote the schools are from Perth, Adelaide, Brisbane, Melbourne, Sydney, Hobart and Darwin, the greater the challenge to the teachers. Over a ten-year period between 1986 and 1996 nearly a third of small towns declined in population. Those that had declined most were inland (ABS 1998a, p. 10). Those small towns that did grow were coastal and located around metropolitan cities or associated with particular industries, such as wine growing or tourism. The ABS summarises the experiences of those living in declining towns as follows (1998a, p. 10):

(They) risk losing their savings, livelihood and support systems as they confront the break-up of their community, loss of jobs, deteriorating infrastructure and declining property values. In addition, declining towns often lose services through the closure of schools, hospitals, retail establishments and banks. Such closures have direct impact on the health and well being of remaining residents.

Rural families — that is those living on separate properties or in small rural locations — are further disadvantaged. They have limited accessibility to education and health services and to job opportunities (ABS 1998b, p. 42).

Locational disadvantage also works within cities; there is massive social distance between those who live in their poorest communities and those residing in their most wealthy suburbs.

As Gregory has observed (1996, p. 3), 'Australia has always had neighbourhoods that are clearly demarcated by income and socioeconomic status'. However, he goes on to argue that there is a significant increase in the geographic polarisation of household income across Australia; a view supported by other economic commentators (c.f. Apps 1997). Much of the loss of income has arisen because the kind of work that has been available has changed. The transformation of the Eveleigh Locomotive Workshops into a technology park is symbolic of the shift from industrial and agricultural work to knowledge work. The effect is a widening chasm between the winners and losers in the work force. As the Australian Centre for Industrial Relations Research and Training observes (1999, p. 66):

> The gap between Australia's workers is increasing on an annual basis. Between 1982 and 1994, the average Australian took a $67 a week decline in real market income, while the top 10 per cent of earners gained an increase in real market incomes of about $100 per week . . . According to economists like Bob Gregory, these changes amounted to a 'disappearing middle' and are best explained by important developments in the labour market.

It would seem then that, as Richardson and Harding (1998) argue, over the past two decades there has been a decline in income and job opportunities for blue-collar workers (more often than not male) and reduced employment prospects for clerical white-collar workers, sometimes referred to as white-collar factory workers, along with lower rates of pay for other service industry workers (the majority of whom are women). At the same time there has been a new and emerging category of worker — the 'gold-collar worker' — the knowledge worker. Gold-collar workers have been portrayed by *Time* magazine as young, creative, computer literate people. They are not place-bound, either residentially, or in terms of workplace loyalty, they are willing and ready to be on the move (Munk 1998).

The privileged gold-collar workers in the United States are the university graduates. The unemployment rate for this group is 1.9 per cent. In some fields of knowledge work, particularly the information technologies, the labour demands are such that new junior staff earn more than senior people. Munk says (pp. 55–6), 'Gold collar workers expect to be well paid and well fed. But they also think that they're entitled to a job that's fun . . . Loyalty, Gratitude, Fortitude. They're dead man'.

In Australia the participation rate in the post-compulsory years of schooling has increased and larger numbers of students are going on to tertiary level studies (ABS 1997b). But Australia still lags behind international standards. Latham (1998, pp. 246–7) says:

In the OECD, for instance, Australia ranks in the bottom quarter of nations for post-secondary participation with just 23 full time students per thousand population. This compares unfavourably with Canada's 41 students, France's 36, Norway's 32, the United States' 31, Japan's 29 and New Zealand's 28.

While the structural changes in the world of work, outlined thus far, are not the responsibility of teachers it is their responsibility to support their students by encouraging them to continue their studies and see how they are relevant to their life chances.

Of course, the challenge of change is not only related to economic and technological change in the workplace. Students are also living out their lives in domestic, cultural and civic circumstances that are very different from those experienced one or two generations ago.

On the home front

Just as technology has hugely impacted upon the nature of work in Australian society, so too has it had its effects on the home front, most specifically through the impact of television on our cultural mores and values.

A study undertaken for the Australian Broadcasting Authority (Sheldon & Loncar 1996), quotes a Nielsen study that found 55 per cent of Australian homes had two or more television sets (p. 21). Television has become an integral part of family life. Soap opera families are incorporated into the lives of viewers; the clothes that are worn, the body images portrayed, the sexual politics displayed, have all become shaping forces for young Australians. Television viewing is as much an everyday occurrence as eating and sleeping. It is watched in the mornings, in the evenings and on the weekends. It has been estimated that over the school years, students watch television for more hours than they attend school.

Latham observes (1998, p. 276):

> Never before has society left it to a commercial market (and the mass media cannot be properly understood as anything but commerce) to fashion its norms, values and sources of social recognition. Young people in particular no longer take the bulk of their social atlas and role models from family life and community, but from television and other forms of electronic entertainment . . . In the United States it is estimated that the average teenager watches 21 hours of TV per week, while spending 5 minutes per week along with his or her father and 20 minutes along with his or her mother.

Just as the world of work has been transformed by globalisation, so too has the domestic world been changed by global mass media. Not only are the programs developed and marketed for global consumption, but the advertising has become globalised in both ownership and content (Wiseman 1998, p. 76). The effect can be seen on a daily basis in our cities and our country towns. The same popular music can be heard in London, Chicago, Perth and Townsville. Back-to-front baseball caps are worn by adolescent males in Glasgow, Rome and Bathurst. The television soap 'The Bold and the Beautiful' is watched in Tokyo, Toronto and Bacchus Marsh. Graffiti tags are sprayed on walls in Berlin, New York and Brisbane. Nikes are worn, Coke is drunk and McDonald's hamburgers consumed in nearly every country in the world.

While teachers may want to maintain a certain social distance from their students, they also need to understand the forces of popular culture and the ways in which they influence students' lives. Many of you will be separated from your students by only a few years. Popular culture, with all of its problems of cultural derivation and sameness, can be a bridge; a means of developing sound social relations. Knowing the soapies watched by students, being able to name sports stars and having a sense of 'what's in/what's out' in cyberspace may seem trivial, but having no idea of these things is to signal an unbridgeable gap.

Technological changes in the home are manifest in other ways also. The purchase of home computers has increased exponentially. Downes (1999, p. 44) reports that in a two-year period from 1994 to 1996:

- computer usage in private households in Australia increased from 23 percent to 30 per cent;

- the total number of computers in households increased from 1.9 million to 2.5 million;

- the percentage of computer-owning households with printers remained reasonably static, increasing marginally from 80 per cent to 82 per cent;

- the percentage of computer-owning households with CD-ROM equipment increased substantially from 13 per cent to 41 per cent;

- the percentage of computer-owning households with modems increased slightly from 17 per cent to 23 per cent; and

- the use of integrated software packages increased from 32 per cent to 43 per cent in households with a computer.

Students are increasing their use of computers at home at a pace that exceeds the knowledge of their teachers. Downes' study indicated that they are often greater risk-takers than their teachers. They are happy to fiddle around to find solutions and to explore the underlying architecture of software in order to use it to its fullest capability.

Downes' analysis of the distribution of the domestic computer reflects the earlier discussion in this chapter regarding geographic location. Computer technologies are more likely to be found in affluent, metropolitan homes than in those that are less well off and are remote.

While, as yet, access to the Internet has not penetrated the domestic environment to the same extent as television, it will not be long before they are on a par. Access to, and use of, Internet technologies will become easier and more affordable. Murray (1995, p. 3) suggests that the prospective merging of interactive TV, phone pad services and virtual reality with cable and telephone networks will provide entertainment and a host of services that will become the basis of a major evolution of the entire communications and media industries.

Teachers who do not understand such technologies will rapidly become positioned as today's Luddites. Nearly ten years ago Green and Bigum (1993) identified students who were becoming increasingly comfortable in cyberspace as 'Aliens in the Classroom' who navigated their way through and evaluated information in ways quite different from those employed by their teachers. These issues will be taken up at greater length in later chapters in this book. Suffice to say here that as a teacher you cannot ignore change that happens in the home. Outside the school, students are using technologies in new, unanticipated and unpredictable ways.

Rapid change in the domestic environment is not only related to technologies. Youngsters today are facing unprecedented pressures in relation to drugs and alcohol. As more and more families work harder and longer (ACIRRT 1999) in conditions where employment security can no longer be taken as a given, parents and caregivers are finding it difficult to monitor and manage their youngsters' behaviour. The 'consenting-overworked' (as ACIRRT names them) are not only less available to their families, they are so fatigued that, when they do come home, they do not want to engage in stressful family confrontations.

Policy-makers are increasingly targeting schools as the sites for social engineering. They espouse attitudes such as:

- if there is a drug and alcohol problem, the school should tackle it;
- if youth suicide is increasing, and it is, then schools should ensure that the signs are read and understood;
- if young drivers are engaged in disproportionately high accident rates, and they are, then schools should undertake driver education;
- if adolescent girls are suffering eating disorders then schools should teach human nutrition, body shape and bourgeois values;
- if gambling is on the increase, then schools should instruct students on probability statistics;
- if racism and sexism are widely manifest, then schools should draw students' attentions to their consequences;
- if the environment is degraded then schools should teach environmental science; and
- if there is inadequate knowledge of our processes of government, then schools should teach civics.

The curriculum of the secondary school is as much a social curriculum as one that is founded upon the traditional disciplines and it will fall to you to understand its origins and to teach it well.

The challenge of change

The nature of social, technological and economic change in Australia today is such that we cannot wish it away. We are enmeshed in forces that go beyond any nation state. They can be forces that will ultimately enhance our civil society and our sense of wellbeing or they can be forces that contribute to inequity and injustice. Change is both unsettling and exciting. It is not the purpose of this chapter to demonise change, but to ask you, as a beginning teacher, to consider it most carefully in the ways in which you go about your work.

Change can split communities. It can equally mobilise communities to develop mutuality and interdependence. Change can make life harder; it can make life more congenial and comfortable. Change can bring great benefits; it can incur great costs.

We are not asking you to be pessimistic about change, but to be realistic — to be both guarded and excited. Most of all we are asking that you face the challenge of change by being careful and reflective about what Australian schools are and what they do for their citizens. In our next chapters we are going to bring the challenge of change right up to teachers' doors; for we will look at our schools moving from past practices to ones that will take us into the twenty-first century. Furthermore, we will look at teachers' work in those schools and how it, too, has changed.

INQUIRY STRATEGIES

1. Interview two or three seniors. Try to ensure that they have had different life experiences. One might come from country Australia, another might come from overseas. One may still be in the work force, another may have engaged in little paid work. One might be from a wealthier community, another from one that is poorer. Discuss their schooling with them and the ways in which it both prepared them for, and was less helpful in going into, the world.

2. Conduct a discussion with a small group of adolescents. How do they understand social, economic and technological change? How well do they believe their schools are serving them in preparing them for the short-term and medium-term future?

3. With some fellow students, monitor a daily newspaper for a week. Collect articles that are indicators to you about the changing world. What were the positive, negative and interesting points? What surprised you?

4. Find a site, such as the Eveleigh Locomotive Workshops, where the structure and function of the building has changed in response to new times. In what ways is the site symbolic of change?

5. Consider your disciplinary background (mathematics, languages, history . . .). How has the knowledge base and methodology changed? How confident are you that you are 'keeping up'?

References

Apps, P. (1997). *Income Distribution, Redistribution and Incentives*. Discussion Paper 379. Canberra: Australian National University, Centre for Economic Policy Research.

Australian Bureau of Statistics (1997a). Changing industries, changing jobs. In *Australian Social Trends*. Canberra: Australian Government Publishing Service (AGPS), pp. 93–98.

Australian Bureau of Statistics (1997b). Education and employment. In *Australian Social Trends* (1997). Canberra: AGPS, pp. 84–87.

Australian Bureau of Statistics (1998a). Small towns: which ones are in decline. In *Australian Social Trends* (1998). Canberra: AGPS, p. 10.

Australian Bureau of Statistics (1998b). Rural families. In *Australian Social Trends* (1998). Canberra: AGPS, pp. 42–45.

Australian Centre for Industrial Relations, Research and Training (ACIRRT) (1999). *Australia at Work — Just Managing?* Sydney: Pearson Education Australia, pp. 66.

Downes, T. (1999). *Children's Use Of Computers in Their Homes*. Sydney: University of Western Sydney, MacArthur. Unpublished Doctoral Dissertation.

Green, B. & Bigum, C. (1993). Aliens in the classroom. *Australian Journal of Education*, 37 (2) pp. 119–141.

Gregory, R. & Hunter, B. (1995). *The Macro Economy and The Growth Of Ghettos and Urban Poverty in Australia*. The National Press Club Telecom Address. Discussion Paper 325. Canberra: Australian National University, Centre for Economic Policy Research.

Gregory, R. (1996). *Growing Locational Disadvantage in Australian Cities*. 1995 Shann Memorial Lecture. Nedlands, WA: Department of Economics, University of Western Australia.

Hunter, B. (1995). Is there an Australian underclass? In *Urban Futures*, 18, p. 20.

Latham, M. (1998). *Civilising Global Capital*. Sydney: Allen & Unwin.

Munk, N. (1998). Gold collar workers. In *Time*, 23 March, pp. 54–57.

Murray, B. (1995). How can new interactive communication technology enhance harmonious and functional communities. *Report of an Exploratory Aspen Workshop*. LA: California Institute of Technology.

Nevile, J. (ed) (1995). *As The Rich Get Richer*. Sydney: Committee for Economic Development in Australia.

Richardson, S. & Harding, A. (1998). *Low wages and the distribution of family income in Australia*. Discussion Paper 33. Canberra: National Centre for Social and Economic Modelling, Faculty of Management, University of Canberra.

Sheldon, L. & Loncar, M. (1996). *Kids Talk TV*. Sydney: Australian Broadcasting Authority.

Wiseman, J. (1998). *Global Nation: Australia and the Politics of Globalisation*. Cambridge: Cambridge University Press.

CHAPTER

Re-thinking Today's Secondary Schools

Why is it that in spite of ongoing massive social, technological and economic change as outlined in the previous chapter, and some changes to the curriculum and assessment of student learning, as well as changes to teachers' work, the institution of schooling itself has changed so little? In this chapter we shall argue that the institution of schooling is subject to competing agendas which arise out of different purposes for schooling. On the one hand there is the expectation that schools should prepare the citizens of tomorrow, on the other that their principal function is to develop the nation's work force as a form of investment in human capital. Even within these purposes there is great variation; what kind of citizens and what kind of tomorrow; what kind of work and what kind of economy (Hunter 1994)?

These tensions are not new. Ever since European occupation of Australia, debates about the structure and function of schooling have been conducted, with different stakeholders ascending differently within each generation. Settlements are agreed, but they are fragile and temporary. The push and pull of competing interests mean that schooling, as a social institution, changes very slowly overall.

Freeland (1991) suggests that the term 'settlement' is an important one to incorporate into our education lexicon. Too often we unrealistically seek for consensus, with its connotation of cohesion and agreement; settlement connotes (p. 65):

> . . . a potential for ongoing conflicts of interest and ongoing struggle, largely, but not necessarily within agreed limits or parameters . . . The word 'settlement' provides a more accurate description of the historical development of education and the debate about education.

Settlements are always provisional. They form a kind of plateau. There is contestation and disagreement, but there is a kind of truce. The accumulation of various truces in the educational landscape has left much of the terrain relatively undisturbed.

To make our point, take a walk through any major Australian town or well-established city suburb, whether in Tasmania, Western Australia or Queensland. You will find schools: government schools; church schools; independent schools. Many of them will be a hundred years old or more. You will recognise them instantly as schools.

Their layout will be familiar to you: separate classrooms, many with rows of desks, almost all with a blackboard at the front; special purpose laboratories, long corridors; faculty offices; honour boards; asphalted assembly areas; playing fields. Some may have remnants of another age such as carved sandstone boys' and girls' entrances; sepia tinted photographs of students in their serried ranks. They will smell familiar. They will sound familiar. Even those recently built will not depart very far from the model. They may have a carpeted reception area, flowers and well-displayed photographs, but essentially they will be recognisable as schools.

This is not only the case in Australia. Visit schools in England, Canada, the United States, Germany, almost any advanced economy and you will find great similarities in their appearance and organisation. One does not have to look far to find evidence for this assertion. At the conclusion to the last chapter we suggested that you interview some senior citizens and discuss with them their school experiences. We asked three mature adults to think about the secondary schools which they attended.

Barbara is in her late seventies. She went to a Catholic school in Adelaide.

I can't remember a lot love. I left school at fourteen. Me friends were very important to me. I left and went to work in a boot factory. Work was hard to get. The school was run by the nuns. We sat in seats that were bolted to the floor. There wasn't much money around. Not like now. There were big classes. If you had troubles reading and writing and stuff, you just had to wear it. There was some neglect. But we had these subjects, English, arithmetic, geography and stuff. I did cooking and sewing. I still like cooking. It's harder work in schools now. When me grandchildren come and ask me to help them; I don't really know what they're doing.

Sargan is in his early fifties and lives in Melbourne. He is a contractor working on demolitions. He spent his early years in Iraq and came to Australia aged fourteen years.

At my school in Iraq we had large numbers in each class, it was very cramped, like a crowded restaurant. We had to study a lot of subjects, including English. I had to start to learn English in Year 5. At my school we had half day shifts. It was very strict. The discipline was very strict, as the teacher walked in we had to stand up. I remember a maths teacher, he was very good at pointing out when a kid had made mistakes with his homework; this particular kid must have been copying because he couldn't do the homework on the board, but he had it right in his book, so the teacher smacked him right in the face. He was the boss and we knew it. 'The man rules' sort of stuff. There was another teacher, he was blind. He taught us Scripture. He knew the kids well and we liked him. When I came to Melbourne it was hard at first because of the language. I could translate in my head, I knew what was going on, but I couldn't express myself. The school was much more relaxed and there was a set day for sport. The teachers were more flexible and there were girls! I enjoyed that, but I had to get used to it. The kids had less respect for the teachers, a couple of times I witnessed kids making rude gestures to the teachers. But I liked it here, I liked it very much.

When we asked Sargan whether there were more similarities or more differences he added:

Oh well, schools are really the same the world over. The teachers are the bosses and the kids learn.

Ray came to Australia in the early 1970s to help meet a teacher shortage being experienced in New South Wales. He went to school in Yonkers, just out of New York City. It was a large, co-educational Catholic High School.

> *It was nondescript. The desks were all in rows. There were bells every forty-five minutes. You spent most of your time being silent. The nuns did the talking. They delivered the curriculum as though it were the catechism — question/answer, question/answer. They'd bend the kid to fit the curriculum. It suited me. We took subjects and did what the subjects required so that we could get the marks. I wanted success and did what the system required. It was an age of obedience. I was good at science. In the senior years you'd get a monthly report card to keep you up to the mark. I remember the physics textbook. We went to a co-ed school, but the science book was full of 'secret men's business'; the girls hated it.*

Ray's description of curriculum as catechism resonates to an account given by Downing (1950) [quoted in Siskin (1994)] of her experiences teaching in a Vermont school in 1885 where a superintendent came to hear and judge the recitations of her students. The interrogations were designed not only to provide evidence of student learning, but of the efficacy of teaching (p. 2):

> . . . A vast and terrifying audience having assembled, entirely out of proportion to the number of pupils. There were fond parents, and grandparents, and aunts and uncles and cousins thrice removed . . . What I thought was of (devising) a wonderful set of 'Instructive Questions and Answers' suggested by a *New England Primer* that had come down in our family, but I did not limit the field of instruction to matters Biblical, attempting rather to cover the entire realm of knowledge in art, science, history, literature, and what you will.

In relation to Ray's claim that science was 'secret men's business' we can see it borne out by studies cited by Musgrave (1987) who argues that (p. 136):

> Science (taught in Australian school classrooms in the eighties) is often packaged in a masculine way. Textbooks use as examples material connected with cars, guns and football and constantly cite the industrial rather than domestic uses of science. All more central to the male than female subculture in western capitalist societies.

So what is different all these years further on, following Barbara's, Sargan's and Ray's experiences? In our last chapter we indicated the rapid transformations being made in our global society. We wrote of changes in the world of work, in the family, in international transactions. And yet, we reiterate, our schools, which are society's engine rooms for change, in many respects, seem to have barely altered at all. In order to make some sense of this apparent paradox we shall argue that we need first to understand something of the historical provision of school education in Australia in order to better apprehend its shape and force today. We shall propose that changes, forms of settlement, are afoot in our schools, but they are complex, even contradictory. Some are subtle and almost always painfully slow to take hold; others, particularly those associated with school management, are crisis driven, essentially superficial and contribute greatly to teacher stress. We propose that for schools to fulfil their multiple functions in the preparation of tomorrow's citizens and workers, both in terms of individual benefit and social benefit, a more radical and coherent model is required.

Issues raised in this chapter will be discussed in greater detail throughout the book. Our purpose here is to locate some of the roots of current practices and to suggest areas where there are the shadows of the kinds of changes which might arise in the future.

Antecedents to today's schools

In his discussion of history, Hexter (1972) suggested that '. . . "history" means any patterned, coherent account, intended to be true, of any past happenings involving human intention or doing or suffering' (p. 3). A study of the patterns of providing for the education of Australia's young people over the past 200 years of European occupation in this country reveal the emergence of a view that schooling is a means of taming and socialising the young rather than liberating or emancipating them. It was clear that when schools were established in the burgeoning colony of New South Wales it was through the offices of missionary and voluntary societies, with a close nexus being tied between schooling and the church, the church being the principal agency for civilising the uncouth and untutored.

It was argued by Smith (1917) that the history of Australian education entered a new phase with the coming of Governor Macquarie to Sydney on 1 January 1810. He undertook to establish government schools and appoint teachers. It was Macquarie who coined the phrase 'the rising generation'. He expressed a concern that children born and raised in the colony had the potential to become very different citizens to their parents, the majority of whom had been transported as convicts. The curriculum of the day was still strongly linked to basic literacy and numeracy through the study of religiously based material. The teaching methods were allied to the understandings surrounding instruction which were currently prevalent — this included rote learning and a monitorial system in which senior students acted as teachers of their juniors. The emphasis was more upon what the teachers should do than the ways in which the students might learn.

By 1824 there were 12 public schools, two orphan schools and an Aboriginal school in the struggling colony. A new plan was taking place for the provision of churches and schools with the affairs of both being administered by the same body of trustees. In a letter from Scott, Secretary to Darling, it stated (quoted in Smith 1917, pp. 32–3):

> In each parish and near the church a primary school for males and females (being separate) should be erected on a simple and economical plan and contiguous to it a plain residence for the master and mistress. It will be sufficient if at an early age they are well grounded in the common rudiments of reading, writing and the four simple rules of arithmetic with their compounds and afterwards removed to a larger establishment to be instructed in agriculture or trades, or apprenticed out . . . Where the population should require it a Central School may be established for higher attainments; that is, upon an equality with those usually called Academies in England.

During the next several decades, as more schools were formed across the emerging Australian colonies, a struggle between Protestant and Catholic claims to state support emerged. In the former case it was also true that there were differences between various denominations; Anglican, Presbyterian, Baptist and so on. When Governor Bourke, in 1836, first proposed a national system he was strongly opposed by all of the Protestant clergy, but found support among the Roman Catholic clergy and laity (Smith 1917, p. 84). Support and dissent seesawed between the two groups, who finally found unity in their opposition to a national education system — a unity which remains to this day as states and territories jealously guard their autonomy regarding school education policies. Arguments, at the time, were more to do with land and material resources than with the nature of teaching and learning. Indeed, Smith (1917) concludes his brief history with these words (p. 86):

> Practically Australia concerned herself little with these larger questions (methods and practices of teacher, curricula and philosophy underlying these ideas) prior to 1848. Her schools provided for the mere rudiments of literary instruction, her teachers were in the main, untrained, unskilled and incompetent, and but a small proportion of her children received even the modicum of instruction provided by the schools.

The second half of the nineteenth century saw an increased insistence upon schools being the sites for the socialisation of young people as a means of preparing them to become an obedient and compliant work force within an increasingly industrialised society. Barcan (1980) quotes William Wilkins, Secretary of the Council of Education, 1867, who expressed thus the moral qualities and values which teachers should instil in their students (p. 138):

> The formation of habits of regularity, cleanliness, and orderly behaviour; the inculcation of regard for the rights of property, public and private; the growth of a spirit of obedience to the law, and respect for duly constituted authority; the correct practical appreciation of the value of time as an element of worldly success; the implanting of love for patient and sustained exertion in some industrial pursuit; and the development of a character for energy and self reliance . . . Honesty, truthfulness, temperance and other virtues, may be cultivated by school discipline, reverence for sacred things may be fostered . . . a religious spirit may be educed by a teacher who exhibits in the performance of his own duty the prompting of religious influences.

Barcan (1980) went on to identify eight major stages or phases of development in Australian education (pp. 403–5):

1. The early convict settlement, 1788–1815
2. The attempted Anglican monopoly, 1815–1831
3. The denominational period, 1831–1848
4. The period of shared power, 1848–1880
5. The operation of free, compulsory and secular education, 1880–1904
6. The educational ladder, 1904–1938
7. The age of transition, 1938–1967
8. The new era in education 1967 . . . (considerable growth of the Commonwealth's influence upon education policy particularly in the area of teacher professional development and capital resourcing of schools).

The model which emerged was one which mirrored the industrial age; utility and standardisation being the key underpinning concepts. Little attention was paid to alternative pedagogies. There was to be no interruption to the paradigm in spite of another kind of knowledge about teaching and learning which prevailed in the Aboriginal community. Barcan reminds us that Aboriginal education prior to invasion was a complex cultural and factual knowledge mix (p. 2):

> Aborigines had to acquire a detailed knowledge of their social system and social obligations. Secondly they needed a factual knowledge of nature. They had to develop vocational skills. Finally, they needed a knowledge of the laws of the information, skills and beliefs constituting their ideological and cultural inheritance.

The major aim was the wellbeing of the social group as opposed to the kind of education aimed at improving the lot of the individual, especially the wealthy and powerful individual. Differentiation in Aboriginal education was based upon gender, reflecting the division of labour which in turn was based upon sex roles. Welch (1996, p. 25) has further observed:

> Each Aboriginal community was held together not by the economic utility of its members to each other, but because each member of the group shared the same world view and meaning system. Although language and specific forms of mythology differed from one group to another, a generally non-materialistic philosophy was common . . . Economic activity, then was not for personal profit or economic gain, as in Western society, but part of giving and receiving the reinforcement of social bonds and kinship obligations.

It is not the intention or purpose of this chapter to present a digest of educational history in Australia, rather this opening section serves to remind us that it is not by chance that we find the dominant provisions, practices and policies which exist today. What is clear is that for most of Australian history, following European occupation, there has existed a close nexus between religion, class, education and race in the formation of young people in our schools. As well we have depended upon an arrangement of largely age-based, simultaneous instruction, characteristic of the school as factory, delivering a standardised and centrally determined curriculum.

Educating for the future is a recent policy trend; the impetus for this shift from looking backwards to looking forward has been the result of the shock of rapid social, economic and technological change.

What is there to change?

To this point, in the chapter, we have focused upon the relatively static nature of educational arrangements in our schools. Scott (1999) suggests that there are two major areas for change — learning programs themselves and the milieu in which they are developed.

Within learning Scott includes (p. 9):

- learning objectives and content;
- teaching and learning strategies;
- learning resources;
- the sequencing of learning;
- learning procedures;
- learning locations and modes of learning;
- approaches to learner recruitment and participation;
- approaches to evaluation and enhancement;
- administration;
- timing and flexibility of learning; and
- fee structures.

With regard to the educational milieu he includes (pp. 9–10):

- culture and climate;
- staff selection and support;
- leadership;
- approach to identifying and disseminating good practice;
- systems of communication;
- administrative focus and procedures;
- structure;
- approaches to monitoring and enhancing organisational operation;
- documentation and decision making;
- planning and decision making; and
- resource distribution.

Of course, each one of these elements is interrelated and each will be visited, in one way or another, throughout this book. However, we wish to argue in this chapter that the most significant possibilities for change in the institution of schooling will come about when there is simultaneous transformation of the classroom, the work of teachers, the relations between teachers, students and the broader community, and the management of the school itself. This requires more than just a tentative settlement, but one of a major character.

It is clear that there has been a shift in educational focus from what teachers do, to what learners do and what their needs are. To illustrate this maxim we are going to take three instances where change is desirable and possible in terms of preparing our secondary school students for tomorrow's world. These are:

1. changing from teacher-centred classrooms to learner-centred classrooms;
2. shifting the curriculum emphasis from 'knowing that' to 'knowing how';
3. moving from student alienation to student incorporation in the middle years of schooling.

Transforming the classroom

One of us, during the 1970s, taught in a progressive open primary classroom in Sydney. Students returned to the school on visits shortly after they had begun their secondary schooling. Asked how it was for them, one replied: 'Oh, the maths teacher asked which of us had gone to W School, when we put our hands up he said "well let's get this straight, I teach, you learn"; they're mostly like that you know'.

During the 1970s, in common with a number of cultural trends to greater openness in communication, in relationships, even in marriage, there was a brief flirting with changing towards a more progressive mode of education (Rogers 1969). Arguments which were made regarding the oppression of whole peoples were seen to equally apply to the oppression of students in classrooms. Writers such as Illich (1971) and Freire (1972) had spent considerable time in South America; they lamented upon the irrelevance of fixed, mechanical curricula and made a plea for de-institutionalising schooling so that students might come to a redefinition of a world in which they had hitherto been powerless.

Physical classrooms, particularly in primary schools, were altered so that internal spaces could be used more adaptively; students gained greater agency with respect to decision-making about how, when and what they would learn; and teachers moved towards a position where they negotiated with learners through the development of learning contracts (Thibadeau 1995). The direction of the change was from teacher-centred classrooms to learner-centred classrooms.

However, little endures today of the shift which moved the teacher from centre-stage. Partly this can be attributable to the changing conditions of teachers' work, which we shall discuss in Chapter 3. But also there clearly was a hostile climate towards giving students greater agency in the classroom. Freeland (1991) argues that liberal progressive education was not compatible with the emerging economic settlement of the day which was veering towards a post-Keynesian model which was to be based upon an economy at the will of market forces. This was particularly the case with respect to secondary schooling in the United Kingdom and the United States, where some attempts had been made to redefine secondary schooling as a more comprehensive and inclusive institution, with a more relevant curriculum. It was perceived that standards were being eroded, meaning that school leavers would not have the requisite skills to be competitive in a free market economy. In England *The Black Papers* thundered (Cox & Dyson 1971) while in the United States the publication of *A Nation at Risk* (National Commission on Excellence in Education 1983) suggested a significant loss of public confidence in US schools.

While Australian primary schools had briefly flirted with progressive education methods, there is little evidence that secondary schools greatly changed. Hence the quote at the beginning to this section. Secondary teachers preferred that their colleagues in the primary sector prepare their students for a regime of conformity and a lock-step curriculum. Of course there were exceptions to this claim, with the establishment of community managed alternative schools. It is worth noting, however, that few of these schools remain today.

Indeed, it is difficult to offer here some well-tried and sound models of secondary schools which have comprehensively developed student-centred learning practices. Those that do exist, tend not to have been documented. Fragile innovation is often protected from those who may detract and undermine.

Transforming secondary classrooms means transforming secondary school culture. As we can see from the section which follows, this means first re-thinking the ways in which curriculum is organised in secondary schools, itself a difficult and perilous matter.

Curriculum for the future

At a recent conference in Sydney a noted American academic asked his audience of school principals 'Why is curriculum like a graveyard?'. We were struck by one notable response, 'because more and more goes in and generally nothing comes out!'. Curriculum is essentially that which is taught in schools, both intentionally and unintentionally. What goes into, or on those rare occasions comes out of, the official and sanctioned curriculum is a matter of great debate, even more so when considering curriculum for the future. Our argument, in this section of the chapter, is that it is essential that we rethink the emphasis upon curriculum from a dominance of content knowledge, knowing *that*, to a more serious inclusion of process knowledge, knowing *how*. Curriculum needs to cease to be a graveyard of ideas and practices. It needs to take far more interest in the needs of students as learners in our schools.

Connell (1998, p. 84) makes the claim that the 'default option' in curriculum discussions is the Competitive Academic Curriculum (CAC) which is marked by:

- an abstract division of knowledge into 'subjects';
- a hierarchy of subjects (with classics, now mathematics, at the top);
- a hierarchical ordering of knowledge within each subject (fine-grained distinction between elementary and advanced material);
- a teacher-centred classroom-based pedagogy;
- an individualised learning process;
- a formal competitive assessment (the 'exam').

His claim is that in spite of attempts to change from a competitive academic curriculum to one which recognises cultural diversity, honours a range and plurality of knowledge forms and has different powers of utility, there has been little movement from the status quo. Partly, this persistence of the CAC can be attributable to the ways in which current practices become entrenched. Teachers, who are beset by directives to change, but have become accustomed to success with older practices, and those who have limited opportunities to become deeply familiar with proposed changes and their purposes, will resist altering what they do and taking on what may seem to them to be quite risky procedures. Evans (1996) points to teachers feeling loss, confusion, conflict and challenges to their competence.

Elsewhere in this book we shall examine closely the Australia-wide, indeed international, trend to outcomes-based curriculum frameworks; however, at this juncture we shall argue that powerful as these reforms have been they have done little to address the Connell critique. Secondary schooling, particularly in the senior years, continues to focus upon privileged content knowledge, upon knowing *that* rather than upon knowing *how*.

Siskin (1994), in discussing secondary schooling in the United States, points to the persistence of the division of knowledge into subjects, or what she refers to as 'realms of knowledge'. She states (p. 9): 'The organisation of high schools into "realms of knowledge" of subject departments is now a nearly universal feature of the 22,000 secondary schools across the United States'. She goes on to argue that the division of knowledge reaches right into school organisation and modes of teaching. Siskin's study of secondary school subject departments focused principally upon the consequences for the teachers themselves, specifically in relation to boundaries and barriers and difficulties with communication. In writing of secondary schools in England, Ball (1987) referred to subject departments as 'baronies' which vie for wealth and territory. Similarly, Hargreaves and MacMillan (1992) have written of them as 'Balkanised'.[1] All of these writers see the power base of the secondary school lying within subject-based departments in that they are the sites which contribute to the professional identity and practices of the teachers within them. The reification of content knowledge lies in the

---

[1] In the context of the break up of Yugoslavia, Balkanisation is today an even more dramatic term than when used as a metaphor by Hargreaves and MacMillan. They adopted it to connote the ways in which small states can harbour intense rivalries for territory and culture; rivalries which have long histories and vendettas.

ways in which the subject departments are entrenched within the power structures of the school. This holds as much true for Australia as for the United States or Britain.

And yet a curriculum for the future cannot solely stem from content knowledge; which, as we have argued in Chapter 1, has a fluid and changing base as a result of the knowledge explosion. The Delors *Report to UNESCO* (1996) included content knowledge as only one of four foundations of education for the twenty-first century, these being:

1. Learning to know.
2. Learning to do.
3. Learning to live together, learning to live with others.
4. Learning to be.

Learning to do, we argue, is no mere adjunct to content knowledge. It gathers to itself the skills and competencies we need, as human beings, to manage the knowledge we acquire and use it effectively. Learning to do embraces within itself the generic learning-to-learn competencies which students require not only as students, but as future employees, parents, citizens and decent human beings who can live together, live with others and with themselves.

During the early 1990s an Australia-wide educational initiative occurred which attempted to address the issues of learning *how*. Growing out of a conception of a general-vocational education which attempted a convergence of education and work (Marginson 1997, pp. 174–5) an examination was conducted regarding post-compulsory education; that is, education for those beyond the age of 15 years. Known as the Finn review (Finn 1991) an important outcome was the development of key areas of competence which were seen as essential to employability. A second committee (Mayer 1992) was formed to bring the named generic competencies to a point where curriculum development and teacher professional development could follow. The Mayer committee adopted a position where the competencies were to be seen not only as applying to vocational settings, but as a means to lifelong learning, including social learning.

Marginson (1997) suggests that the Mayer aspiration was 'heroic' (p. 176). He took the competencies to act as a normalising device designed to prepare for a flexible and adaptable work force, with the emphasis shifting to economic benefits, rather than the cultural or social good. However, for schools, including primary schools, the naming and describing of what became known as 'the key competencies', which appear below,

Key Competencies

KC 1 — Collecting, analysing and organising information.
KC 2 — Communicating ideas and information.
KC 3 — Planning and organising activities.
KC 4 — Working with others and in teams.
KC 5 — Using mathematical ideas and techniques.
KC 6 — Solving problems.
KC 7 — Using technology.
KC 8 — (Using) cultural understandings.

was seen by many to provide a means of balancing the knowledge and process elements of the curriculum. As well, a number of teachers were appreciative of their responsibilities not only to prepare their students in social and cultural terms, but also, as equitably as possible, prepare them for engagement in paid work and the benefits which flow from it, both individually and nationally.

In 1996 the National Schools Network (NSN 1996)[2] developed a resource for schools, *The Key Competencies Kit*. Taking the eight key competencies identified as essential for lifelong learning the Network investigated with a number of schools across Australia ways in which the curriculum could be managed to ensure that learning *how* took its place alongside learning *what*.

The study worked with schools to systematically enquire into ways in which each of the key competencies might be implemented across the curriculum. In the preparation of teachers for the project the following work trends were discussed (NSN 1996, OHT # 8):

- Globalisation of competition
- Projects not jobs
- Teams not individuals
- Outsourcing
- Capabilities not position
- Employability not permanency
- Multiskilling career planning

It was argued that a new learning paradigm was required for the future. It would need to incorporate the following principles (NSN 1996, OHT # 9):

1. That learning is lifelong, no longer front-ended school learning but continuous across the life cycle to facilitate flexible career paths and enhance personal development.

2. That the curriculum should be learner driven — the learner not the teacher has control of the learning process with the teacher becoming the facilitator of learning and the therapist and diagnostician to achieve optimum learning outcomes.

3. That 'just-in-time' learning opportunities are available from the global learning 'supermarket' when and where the learner needs them to meet their learning needs.

4. That customised products and services are designed to meet different learning preferences and can be appropriately modified by the learner to meet the particular needs of individual groups.

5. That learning is transformative by enabling learners to challenge and change belief systems and behavioural patterns to meet new needs and opportunities, and to overcome disabilities and disadvantage.

---

[2] The National Schools Network is an Australian school reform organisation. It has been instrumental in a number of initiatives aimed at improving student learning outcomes through the reform of teachers' professional work practices. A fuller account of the NSN and its history appears elsewhere in this book.

6. That learning is collaborative, encouraging groups as well as individuals to learn interactively across time and space.

7. That learning to learn is paramount and designed to develop the capability in individuals and in groups to understand and more effectively plan and realise their own learning potential.

8. That learning is contextualised and locates theoretical learning and competencies in different contexts through real-life learning environments and simulations and includes action learning.

Schools in the project showed themselves well able to change and to develop their curriculum from a matrix which intersected key learning areas with key competencies. However, these schools are in a minority and the question remains 'why is it that schools are so slow to change in matters of such substance?'.

Lest you begin to despair that secondary schools will remain essentially as they were when Sargan, Barbara and Ray attended them (see beginning of chapter), we do believe that change is occurring. The wedge is twofold. One is the dramatic burgeoning of information technology and student management of it, a matter which we shall not pursue at this point; the other is the developing interest in altering the arrangements for the middle years of schooling.

The struggle to deal with student alienation during those years when they adjust from primary to secondary schooling, has become a template for the possibility of change.

Middle years innovation

The rift between primary and secondary schools has long been one which has been of interest to educators. A trite saying often heard is that 'primary teachers teach students, secondary teachers teach subjects' and like many sayings of this kind there is a grain of truth in it. If you reflect for a moment upon your transition from primary to secondary school you will probably remember a number of things, among them:

- the shift from having a class teacher (often supported by specialists in areas like music, sport and art) to having a number of subject teachers;
- the change from having your own classroom to moving from one room to another, and perhaps getting lost in the process;
- the adjustment from being considered the most senior and independent in the school to being the most junior and dependent; and
- the anxiety which comes about as you have to make new friends in a new and often alien environment.

While we would want to be careful not to romanticise primary schools and their concern for student welfare it is clearly the case that teachers in primary schools are better positioned to keep track of student achievement and student welfare within one class than is the case where the one student may meet up to 13 or 14 teachers during the first year at secondary school. There is a growing body of research which has drawn attention to changes in the development of measurable student learning outcomes and to the potential for student alienation as the transition is made from primary to secondary school.

Hill's research (1995a, 1995b) indicates a negligible increase in performance levels in English and mathematics between Years 5 and 8, particularly with respect to the bottom ten per cent of students. This data would suggest that many students are not able, or enabled, to derive significant benefit from their schooling during the transition years. Indeed many students, for example low achieving boys, actually regress as they move through high school.

A significant factor in such loss of momentum has been identified by Barratt (1998) — it is the culture of the secondary school. At the very point when young adolescents are establishing their identity and autonomy they are engaged in a schooling process which 'anonymises' them. They cease to be members of a well-known, integrated cohort of learners, as has been the case in their primary schools, and become, instead, faceless, even nameless. The curriculum which they experience becomes fragmented and detached. The school itself is physically more complex with an infrastructure which is more rigid and uncompromising.

A second factor, curriculum constraints, is discussed by Beane (1990) who sees the curriculum as a potential meeting point for rethinking relations between students, teachers and schools. He argues that a middle school curriculum should be based upon three dimensions:

1. a general education program that focuses upon the personal concerns faced by the emergent adolescent;
2. skills required by the adolescent to develop reflective thinking, problem-solving capability and values clarification; and
3. concepts which recognise and emphasise social justice, democracy and cultural diversity.

Beane (1995) goes on to argue that an authentic curriculum for the middle years of schooling needs to be one which is integrated and where the formal subjects become tools for enquiry and learning. He believes that the subject-based curriculum tends to privilege high status knowledge for high status students, an issue we discussed earlier in this chapter, and that such a curriculum effectively marginalises those who do not fall into this category. This view is strongly supported in the Australian context by Cumming (1994, 1996).

A third factor (one which is also curriculum-related) is what we have already referred to as the overcrowded nature of the curriculum. The Coalition of Essential Schools in the United States has been paying particular attention to 'doing less, better' (Cushman 1994). The Coalition, which is paying very close attention to the middle years, is arguing that if students are to develop competence and insight they need to tackle real problems in real time. They need to discuss, to interact, to question, to build a case. This is difficult to achieve in short periods of time, devoted to specific subject areas. It is the middle years initiative which is causing secondary schools to re-examine blocks of learning time and what will occur within them.

Stromlo High School, in the Australian Capital Territory (ACT)[3] described its middle school innovation in this way (1999, pp. 1–2):

Over the past two years (1997–98) Stromlo High School has undertaken a Middle Schooling

---

[3] Stromlo High School recently participated in the Innovation and Best Practice Project (IBPP). It chose to remain identifiable in this description of its work. In the face of this decision we have not anonymised the school.

initiative designed to facilitate and enhance the transition of over 180 students from primary to secondary school. The project has organisational, pedagogical and curriculum features and takes account of the affective and cognitive needs of young people taking their first steps into early adolescence. It is also a project which is concerned with providing professional development opportunities for secondary school teachers as they are positioned to reinvent their practices and engage in dialogue with their primary school colleagues.

Accordingly, the project has the following features:

- regular meetings with the cluster of primary schools which provide the majority of students entering Year 7 at Stromlo High School. The meetings are designed to:
  — identify students' needs and make provision for soundly based class groupings;
  — discuss curriculum decision-making in the context of an outcomes-based education framework;[4] and
  — consider classroom strategies, particularly with reference to assessment of student learning;
- the development of a 7 line timetable which enables maths and science, English and studies of society and environment (SOSE) to be contiguous;
- the appointment, wherever possible, of one teacher to teach both English and SOSE in Year 7;[5]
- the formation of teams (maths, science, English, SOSE) to monitor student progress and plan for curriculum integration; and
- the organisation of a Year 7 camp and peer support program intended to enable the social networks of students to be expanded in a safe and encouraging environment.

The innovation has grown out of two imperatives. The first of these is related to enabling students to be fully participative in secondary school life in the light of current understandings of the potential for student alienation. The second is to do with the organisation of teachers' work, so that teachers may interact more substantially with fewer students.

This is an example of curriculum, organisational and cultural change. The relationships between subject areas such as English and SOSE mean that cross-curriculum teaching and learning can potentially take place; in addition, double periods with more flexible time management can occur. The students meet fewer teachers — teachers who can come to know them rather better than had formerly been the case. Teachers, in turn, can learn something of their students before they come to the High School through their interactions with the feeder primary schools.

Stromlo is not alone in their attention to the middle years of schooling. Indeed their project is quite a modest one. Brennan and Sachs (1998) report on seven schools from the ACT, Victoria, Tasmania, New South Wales and Queensland all of whom have been members of state networks whose objective has been to transform the early years of secondary schooling. Strongly influenced by the work of Anna Ratzki in Germany

---

[4] It should be noted that in the ACT there is still a provision for school-based curriculum decision-making. The outcomes framework is generic and schools have a degree of latitude in deciding upon the actual substance of the curriculum. Unless care is taken, there is a significant likelihood of repetition and overlap between Years 6 and 7.

[5] Achievable in six out of eight classes.

(Monkemeyer et al. 1999) and the Coalition of Essential Schools in the United States, these schools, now numbering hundreds, are making quite dramatic changes to the ways in which teachers teach and students learn.

Conclusion

The middle schooling innovations show that schools can and do change, but in a context in which secondary schooling itself remains wedded to the competitive academic curriculum with students held in subject-oriented, teacher-centred classrooms.

In this chapter we have argued that secondary schools, as institutions, are essentially conservative and that fundamental change is slow to take hold. Moving beyond Barcan's periodisation (1980) we have indicated that at each stage of the development of the institution of schooling there has been a particular settlement, a balancing of different versions of the nature of citizenship and different versions of the nature of work. In many ways the current discourses on schooling overemphasise the work connections. What may be needed is a reinvigoration of students, not as to-be-prepared citizens, who will ultimately vote and have property, but as citizens in a public institution.

We have argued that we should take account of the truism that there are many people with different issues at stake in the schools, some of which conflict with one another. That is what makes it so difficult to change things and the result is that we have a series of temporary settlements. The current settlement is under significant erasure as the conservative forces come to dominate (Freeland 1991).

The institution of school is a very complex thing so voluntaristic, individual action is not going to basically change schooling, because the institutions of schooling are so fixed. Even those trying to change such things as subject associations may change one element, but the effort won't change the organisation or the climate. The middle schooling reform on the other hand is trying to work on all of the aspects at once — organisation, curriculum, assessment, and teachers' work relations including teachers' professional relations with each other.

In spite of these arguments there is evidence that aspects of school management have changed quite dramatically and quickly, particularly in response to the notion that schools themselves constitute a marketplace as part of the current economic settlement. It is these changes which have had great impact upon the ways in which teachers work and how that work, itself, has changed. The next chapter in this book now turns its attention to the changing nature of teachers' work.

INQUIRY STRATEGIES

1. Locate a secondary school which has celebrated its centenary. See if you can identify artefacts which indicate something of the culture of the school. In what ways has the school changed and in what ways has it remained the same? Why do you think this is so?

2. What does student-centred learning mean to you? What evidence do you have that schools are moving towards student-centred learning?

3. Try conducting what Anna Ratzki refers to in her workshops as a 'silent conversation'. Spread large sheets of paper around the room. Everyone writes one positive and one negative statement about the ways in which the secondary school curriculum is arranged. Visit other people's observations and write your responses to them.

References

Ball, S. (1987). *The Micro-Politics of the School.* London: Methuen.

Barcan, A. (1980). *History of Australian Education.* Melbourne: Oxford University Press.

Barratt, R. (1998). *Shaping Middle Schooling in Australia: A Report of the National Middle Schooling Project.* Canberra: Australian Curriculum Studies Association.

Beane, J. (1990). *A Middle School Curriculum: From Rhetoric to Reality.* Columbus, Ohio: National Middle School Association.

Beane, J. (1995). Curriculum integration and the disciplines of knowledge. *Phi Delta Kappan*, April, pp. 616–622.

Beare, H. & Slaughter, R. (1993). *Education for the Twenty-First Century.* London: Routledge.

Brennan, M. & Sachs, J. (1998). *Integrated Curriculum: Classroom Materials for the Middle Years.* Canberra: Australian Curriculum Studies Association in association with the National Schools Network.

Connell, R. (1998). Social change and curriculum futures. In *Change: Transformations in Education*, 1 (1) pp. 84–90.

Cox, C. & Dyson, A. (eds) (1971). *The Black Papers on Education.* London: Davis Poynter Ltd.

Cumming, J. (1994). Catering for the needs of all young adolescents: Towards an integrated approach. In *Unicorn*, 20 pp. 12–20.

Cumming, J. (1996). *From Alienation to Engagement: Opportunities for Reform in the Middle Years of Schooling.* Canberra: Australian Curriculum Studies Association.

Cushman, K. (1994). Less is more: The secret of being essential. In *Horace*, 11 (2), pp. 1–13.

Delors, J. (1996). *Report to UNESCO of the International Commission on Education for the Twenty-First Century.* Paris: UNESCO Publishing.

Downing, L. (1950). Teaching in the Little Red Schoolhouse: A Sketch. In N. Hoffman (ed), *Woman's True Profession.* New York: The Feminist Press, McGraw Hill.

Evans, R. (1996). *The Human Side of School Change: Reform, Resistance and the Real-Life Problems of Innovation.* San Francisco: Jossey Bass Publications.

Finn, B. (1991). *Young People's Participation in Post-Compulsory Education and Training.* Canberra: Australian Government Printing Service.

Freeland, J. (1991). Quality of what and quality for whom? In J. Chapman, L. Angus & G. Burke with V. Wilkinson (eds), *Improving the Quality of Australian Schools.* Hawthorn, Vic: Australian Council for Educational Research.

Freire, P. (1972). *Pedagogy of the Oppressed.* Harmondsworth: Penguin.

Hargreaves, A. & MacMillan, R. (1992). Balkanised Secondary Schools and the Malaise of Modernity. Paper presented at the Annual Conference of the American Educational Research Association. San Francisco.

Hexter, J. (1972). *The History Primer.* London: Allen Lane.

Hill, P. (1995a). Value added measures of achievement. Paper presented to the IARTV seminar, Melbourne, May, 1995.

Hill, P. (1995b). *The Middle Years of Schooling.* Melbourne: University of Melbourne Press.

Hunter, I. (1994). *Rethinking the School: Subjectivity, Bureaucracy, Criticism.* Sydney: Allen & Unwin.

Illich, I. (1971). *Deschooling Society.* London: Calder & Boyars. Ltd.

Marginson, S. (1997). *Educating Australia.* Cambridge: Cambridge University Press.

Mayer, E. (1992). *Employment Related Key Competencies.* Melbourne: Mayer Committee.

Monkemeyer, M. Ratzki, A., Wubbels, H. Neiser, B. Schulz-Wensky, G., Laskey, H. (eds) (1999). *Team Small Group: A Whole School Approach.* Sydney: Hawker Brownlow Education.

Musgrave, P. (1987). *Socialising Contexts.* Sydney: Allen & Unwin.

National Commission on Excellence in Education (1983). *A Nation at Risk: The Imperative for Educational Reform.* Washington, DC: US Government Printing Office.

National Schools Network (1996). *The Key Competencies Kit.* Ryde: National Schools Network.

Rogers, C. (1969). *Freedom to Learn.* Columbus, Ohio: Charles E. Merrill.

Scott, G. (1999). *Change Matters.* Sydney: Allen & Unwin.

Siskin, L. (1994). *Realms of Knowledge: Academic Departments in Secondary Schools.* London: Falmer Press.

Smith, S. (1917). *A Brief History of Education in Australia (1788–1848).* Sydney: Angus and Robertson Ltd.

Stromlo High School (1999). Innovation and Best Practice Project (IBPP). Canberra: Stromlo High School.

Thibadeau, G. (1995). Open education. In L.W. Anderson (ed), *International Encyclopedia of Teaching and Teacher Education.* Oxford: Pergamon, pp. 167–171.

Welch, A. (1996). *Australian Education, Reform or Crisis?* Sydney: Allen & Unwin.

3
CHAPTER

Teaching: A Changing Profession

In our previous two chapters we outlined issues associated with global change and the changes which have happened in mass schooling. Here we examine the changing nature of teaching itself.

What is a teacher?

A beginning teacher recently asked her students the question 'What is a teacher?'. She did so on the grounds that they seemed to have expectations of her and her work which varied from her own views of the roles and responsibilities which she believed herself to be undertaking.

Her students constructed teachers in terms of their roles, their employment and their personalities.

Roles

Most frequently students referred to a teacher as one who teaches, within a transmission model (i.e. they do it *to* others) with little elaboration. But some expanded the role:

- they teach people to do things like maths, science etc. (Yr 7);
- a person who helps you learn what is needed to know in life (Yr 7);
- an adult who teaches you lifelong information (Yr 7);
- they show us how to do things (Yr 7);
- a person who teaches others about life, the world and anything (just about) (Yr 7);
- a person who teaches skills to a person no matter what age or social background (Yr 7);
- they teach students all that students need to know when they grow up and depend on themselves (Yr 7);
- a teacher is someone who helps students work to the best of their abilities and teaches them things that they will need to succeed in life (Yr 10);

- a person that helps you reach the best of your ability (Yr 10);
- a person which provides the knowledge to a group of people, improving their knowledge in that particular subject (Yr 10).

Employment:

- a person who is paid to teach us (Yr 7);
- a person who is paid to educate us (Yr 7);
- teaching is an occupation which teaches students what they know about a certain subject (Yr 10).

Personalities:

- it's a person who can change moods instantly and take it out on us (Yr 7);
- someone who's kooky (Yr 10);
- an old person who explains things and gives uniform detention and keeps the school in order (Yr 10).

She also asked her students why they thought someone would want to become a teacher. The responses were divided between income and conditions (such as holidays) and vocationally related reasons (liking and helping students to learn):

- maybe it's good money or maybe they like children and enjoy knowing that they're helping someone prepare for the future (Yr 7);
- to see their students become wealthy through a good job (Yr 7);
- because they enjoy teaching people new things and they want to help students the ways they were helped when they were at school (Yr 10);
- to help educate people for money and good holidays (Yr 10).

A number saw the teachers' motivation being related with power and control:

- because they want to boss kids around (Yr 7);
- to show they're smart and to meet new people (Yr 7);
- to feel power over someone else (Yr 10).

Finally, she asked 'What do teachers do when they make mistakes?'.

Strategies included covering up and defensiveness or correction, after being advised by students or noticing it themselves.

Cover up:

- they pretend they were just testing to see if we were watching or it's a typo (Yr 7);
- they deny that it is wrong or don't say anything (Yr 7);
- some teachers don't really care about it, if they make a mistake, but some send you outside if you prove them wrong (Yr 10);
- they get annoyed if you point it out or get embarrassed (Yr 10);
- cover it up (seven Yr 10 students used these words).

Correction:

- we put our hands up and tell them (Yr 7);
- they correct themselves or ask someone else if that is right, or if they know the answer (Yr 7);
- correct it and make sure everyone understands what is correct (Yr 7);
- sometimes they swear under their breath, but most of the time they just apologise (Yr 7);
- they go off at people or acknowledge their mistakes and congratulate the pupil who pointed it out (Yr 7);
- when teachers make mistakes they normally just stand corrected (Yr 10).

Clearly, from these responses, students have come across teachers who would appear to behave in varying ways and whose motivation to teach comes from a number of sources.

To write about teachers as if they are of one mind, with common beliefs about what they do and how they do it, is as foolish as suggesting that any professional group is homogeneous and culturally coherent. Indeed, as a professional group teachers 'constitute by far the largest population of professionals in industrialised nations' (Biddle, Good & Goodson 1997, p. 1). According to the Australian Bureau of Statistics (ABS 1996) in 1995 there were 255 600 full-time equivalent staff employed in Australian schools. Of these, most (71 per cent) were employed in government schools, 18 per cent in non-government Catholic schools and the remainder in various independents schools, either religious or secular.

Teachers come in different shapes and sizes; they have different social, academic and professional histories. They subscribe to political ideologies ranging from the far right to the far left. Some believe that the only way to teach is to tell; others subscribe to the view that if only the conditions are right then students can be fully self-directed and motivated. One group might think that their goal is to shape malleable young minds into a mirror of their own; others that their purpose is to perform a good public service and carry out the educational wishes of the government of the day; while yet another group may see their mission is to shape and change society itself through its future citizens.

Young (1998) argues that (p. 72):

> Today, the conversation of education is becoming a Babel. Teachers find it increasingly difficult to find a tongue in which to speak of themselves as educators. Some still stoutly defend the traditional vocabulary of 'student' and 'teacher' but have few defences against its various deconstructions. Others, perhaps recently a majority, speak the language of education as an equalitarian instrument of social justice, but in doing so have opened the gates to admit a 'Trojan horse' of great dimensions. Today, the Achaeans of the 'market' have begun pouring forth from it to ravage Education's fair city.

In this chapter we cannot hope to map the complex ideologies of the teaching profession, although we can say something about its demography, noting for instance that in 1995, 51 per cent of all teachers were aged 40 years and over and that female staff comprised over 67 per cent of the teaching force (ABS 1996). Instead we will aspire to look at the work of teachers, what it is and how it has changed. But we also acknowledge that teachers' belief systems, whatever they may be, are critical to the ways in which they go about their professional practice. It is important to note that this chapter will not examine the specifics of teachers' work, which is the aspiration of the remainder of this book, but rather sketch in the larger picture of the discourses within which that work is placed.

In order to place teachers' work not only in its professional context, but also its personal context it is important to first ask the question: What is it that motivates the individual to become a teacher? Why did you decide to become a teacher? Is it a vocation, a step to somewhere else, or just another job?

What is the teachers' vocation?

Originally, the term 'vocation' carried with it connotations of commitment and service. Derived from the Latin root, *vocare*, 'to call', it suggested selflessness and devotion to a particular form of work. Today the word 'vocation' has a narrower utilitarian ring to it, tied as it has become to vocational training. And yet, there are still many who would contend that teaching is more than a skilled occupation, it is one which is unavoidably moral, and is of inestimable social worth. Hansen (1994, pp. 4–5) claims:

> To regard teaching as vocational further presumes a sense of it (however inchoate) as an activity whose meaning is larger than the sum of its parts. It is larger than carrying out a finite number of pre-specified duties and responsibilities, with a preordained set of rewards as compensation. A person enacting a vocation has an active and creative relationship with the work. The work involves initiative, rather than carrying out passively a package of discrete tasks . . . This means supplementing and possibly extending the functional requirements of the job. It may mean questioning some of those requirements. This posture implies that the person with a sense of vocation will be his or her own final critic, a stance that may accompany any work perceived as more than routine.

During the years immediately following World War II teacher professionalism was closely associated with such a view of education as a public service. Nation building was seen as a collective enterprise with education as a central and critical enterprise. Many young men returning from active service sought out teaching as an honourable profession to be respected and appropriately rewarded (Lawn 1997).

To this day it is in the classroom that teachers have their greatest sense of agency — where their occupational commitment is most exercised. It is interesting to see that in two studies of teacher stress and work satisfaction (Tuettemann 1991; Smith & Bourke 1990), one undertaken in Western Australia and one in the Hunter region of New South Wales, similar results were obtained. It was clear that in their examination of the factors which secondary teachers rated as important to their job satisfaction, the researchers found that: appreciation from students; meeting success with difficult students; and, being acknowledged and appreciated by school administrators rated ahead of material rewards in the form of salaries for both male and female teachers. Results such as these suggest that there continues to be a strong service orientation to teaching, in spite of the ways in which teachers' work has been both intensified and 'extensified' (Woods, Jeffrey, Troman & Boyle 1997, pp. 121–5) — an issue to which we shall return later in this chapter.

However, the matter of teaching as a vocation is not one which is shared by all commentators. Is teaching, as Tedesco (1997) suggests, merely 'a transitory activity in the process of searching for more prestigious employment' (p. 28)? Certainly this could be said to be true in the late nineteenth and early twentieth centuries. A number of historians have pointed out that teaching was seen as the ladder out of the working and lower middle classes for intelligent youngsters (Coppock 1997).

Much of the negative media attention directed to teachers today suggests that their motivation is not an altruistic one, but rather that they adopt teaching as a career of last resort. Certainly, in submissions to the Senate Inquiry on the status of the teaching profession, *A Class Act* (Senate Employment, Education and Training References Committee 1998), concerns were expressed regarding the recruitment of teachers from university entrants in the lower ranks of achievement. For example, in a submission from the Department of Education Services, Western Australia it was reported (p. 170):

> Information from the Department of Education Services shows that the minimum tertiary entrance scores for students undertaking teacher education courses continues to decline. Tertiary entrance data obtained from the Tertiary Institutions Service Centre (TISC) shows that since 1990 the cutoff scores for entrance to Teacher Education Courses have dropped by around twenty to twenty-five points across all teaching areas and at all universities.

While most submissions to the Senate Inquiry indicated that sole reliance on tertiary entrance scores was an unsatisfactory predictor of success as a teacher, there was some agreement that, ideally, those seeking teacher education places at universities should be selected on a range of academic and personal criteria. Additional information derived by interview should be seen as important — information related to personal qualities, motivation, organisational ability and flexibility in thinking. Sadly, for reasons of cost, few institutions interview their teacher education candidates, except in the case of mature age students seeking entry by alternative means.

Of course, it needs to be remembered that in the case of those intending to become secondary teachers the majority proceed through post-graduate courses, rather than by way of undergraduate studies and many of these candidates are mature age students who have had experience in the work force and have chosen teaching as a second, or even third, career.

An indication of teacher status can be found in the salaries which the community is prepared to pay them. The 1996 median starting salary for education graduates was 83.3 per cent of average earnings. While education just falls within the ten best paid fields, it cannot be said to be a highly rewarded profession. It is also one which has no significant non-salary employment benefits (Senate Employment, Education and Training References Committee 1998, Appendix two, pp. xii–xiii). The majority of teachers reach the top of their salary scale within ten years.

So why become a teacher in the face of the perceived lack of status for the profession? For many of you, choosing to become teachers is a decision which you have made on the basis of your own school and classroom experiences; or, as parents, your children's experiences. These may have been positive ones which you wish to replicate or negative ones which you want to remedy. But there is a problem with this position in that, as students and/or parents you have only stood on what Lortie (1975) has nominated as one side of the teacher's desk, serving a kind of one-sided apprenticeship. This necessarily narrow perspective means that little is known of the teacher's intentions, planning and reflection. Teachers' work is far more than that which is visible to students and parents.

Lortie was prescient in discussing teachers' work in the 1960s and 1970s in relation to change. He saw change as inescapable, but that many teachers would become increasingly adroit at resisting change. He also argued that being dedicated would not be sufficient to attract what he named as 'ritual pity' (p. 221) from a public wishing to hold teachers accountable for perceived failings in school delivery of high performance standards.

Certainly, teacher resistance to change can be characterised as wilful and unhelpful; but, alternatively, it can be seen as a measured and reasoned voice, critical of change that may be regressive in character. After all, not all change is necessarily improvement. Aronowitz and Giroux (1991) claim that teachers have the capacity to be public intellectuals; an argument which closely accords with that of teaching as a vocation. They argue that if teachers are to take an active role in the debates about what they teach, how they teach and the purposes of schooling, it means that they need to take a critical political role in defining the nature of their work as well as shaping the conditions under which they work. They say (p. 109):

> We believe that teachers need to view themselves as public intellectuals who combine conception and implementation, thinking and practice, with a political project grounded in the struggle for a culture of liberation and justice.

The category of public intellectual is seen to provide for three things:

1. the development of a rigorous critique of knowledge as fixed and separate from what students already know, think, do and perform;
2. a basis for teachers to engage in a critical and activist dialogue among themselves; and
3. a possibility for teachers to redefine their role such that a more socially just critical discourse may emerge.

Again, we suggest that you spend some time asking yourself why you have chosen to become a teacher — profession, occupation, job, vocation? Whatever the reasons there can be no question that teachers' work is complex, demanding and difficult in this changing world of ours.

We shall argue that teachers' work falls into three broad categories:

1. intellectual work;
2. emotional work; and
3. work organisation.

Each of these areas of work has, paradoxically, changed and remained the same, in response to changing expectations arising from changing social, economic and technological conditions, as outlined in the two previous chapters. Furthermore, our discussion will take account of the industrial nature of teachers' work, the ways in which it is organised and the interaction between industrial and professional concerns.

The intellectual work of teachers

In secondary schools, as we demonstrated in the previous chapter, a great deal of what occurs in classrooms is related to specific content knowledge, or subject matter. Hence much of the intellectual work of the secondary teacher is tied to the organisation and communication of content and concepts relevant to the subject. This requires teachers not only to know and remain up to date with their subjects, but that they also know how that subject relates to other relevant bodies of knowledge. A maths teacher, for example, not only needs to know and understand the maths syllabus, but also needs to understand that maths is a form of human communication, which requires its own literacy and has its own aesthetic.

While subject matter knowledge may be the bedrock of the secondary teacher's intellectual work there is far more besides this aspect. The teacher needs to have a sound understanding of the many ways in which the learners in the classroom can engage with that knowledge, assimilate it into their own cognitive systems and use it effectively. This means that the teacher needs to be able to analyse the learning of students and make appropriate plans to support and enhance that learning. The teacher is both diagnostician and facilitator of learning. Simultaneously the teacher is also engaged with demonstrating a capacity to be flexible and resourceful in the face of that which the learners bring to the classroom and to manage learning for a range and diversity of students.

This kind of intellectual work is far more demanding than the notion of 'bricolage' critiqued by Hatton (1988). Bricolage is a kind of tinkering. French do-it-yourself stores are advertised as places of bricolage. It suggests that teaching is little more than loosely, and uncritically assembling, a scattering of ideas and strategies; a series of recipes of 'things that work'.

Of course these few paragraphs cannot hope to outline the depth, diversity and complexity of teachers' intellectual work; many chapters of this book are devoted to more fully describing, analysing and explaining such. What we do want to make clear is that as our knowledge of teaching and learning increases it renders the process more problematic and the task more complex. In past years it was perceived that instructing, or 'telling' students was sufficient for them to know and understand; and if that outcome was not achieved it was due to some inadequacy on the student's part, rather than a mutual responsibility forged between teachers and learners.

McWilliam (1996) in her provocative piece 'Admitting Impediments: or things to do with bodies in classrooms' makes the important assertion that she wishes to challenge three widespread assumptions which have become taken for granted in mainstream education (p. 368):

> The first is that teaching and learning is a binary formulation that can allow us to say all that we need to about the performance of formal or informal educational events, despite the very complex and contested cultural production of meaning and identities that is always going on in classrooms. The second is the assumption that pedagogical events are staged exclusively for the benefit of student learners. Teachers' work is understood to be precisely synonymous with facilitation of learning, life-long or otherwise, through 'design and delivery' and/or the provision of education as a sort of personal therapy . . . The third assumption I want to challenge is the classical idea that professional teaching is always dispassionate and unworldly in the sense that all should be given to students and nothing taken from them in terms of teachers' personal gratification.

McWilliam is reminding us that teachers' work is highly intellectually and physically interactive and is also of an intense emotional kind.

The emotional work of teachers

Earlier in this chapter we indicated that some research studies have suggested that a significant source of professional satisfaction for secondary teachers lay in positive relationships with students. In recent years a great deal has been written regarding the culture of care in primary schools — care as altruism, self-sacrifice and obedience and manifested as over-conscientiousness (Nias 1999). Studies, particularly those discussing the conditions of teachers' work in the United Kingdom, have represented primary school teachers as exhausted and depleted by the competing demands which are being increasingly made of them. Complex arguments have developed around primary teaching as a highly gendered occupation with caring seen as a necessary condition for the achievement of schooling's cognitive and social goals. Less attention has been paid to the emotional nature of teachers' work in secondary schools, in spite of the many social and emotional pressures experienced by today's adolescents and young adults; pressures which ultimately are played out in school classrooms. As well there are pressures which have come about as key stakeholders make greater and different demands of teachers.

Secondary school teachers are daily facing students who are coping with forms of alienation brought about by conditions which may be beyond the school's control. Youth policies in our various states and territories are coming to characterise young people as 'out of control' in need of legislation which governs their behaviour in public spaces, forbidding them to assemble in large numbers. Accounts on Sydney radio during 1999 cited instances of shopping centres playing bland 1950s music, while bathing their customers in pink lighting seen as unkind to adolescent skin. The purpose was to drive the unruly and unwanted youth away.

At the same time, youth unemployment has led to higher and higher retention rates beyond the compulsory years of schooling. In 1980 65 per sent of students failed to complete Year 12; 51 per sent in 1986 and 29 per sent in 1991 (Department of Employment, Education and Training 1993). By 1997, only 26 per sent of 19 year-olds had not completed Year 12 (Sweet 1998, p. 13). For many of these students who are staying on at school the competitive academic curriculum, which still dominates as the principal curriculum form, is not only irrelevant, but one which daily demonstrates their failures in achievement. At best they are in school as reluctant learners; at worst as angry, disruptive and subversive elements.

Concerns about identity, feelings of uncertainty and insecurity in a social context which is characterised by increasing instability in marriage, drug and alcohol abuse, and changes in conditions of employment produce great difficulties for students and their teachers alike. Poverty, hunger, violence and drugs enter classrooms with children, whereas in the not so distant past they were kept outside with the unschooled. Teachers are expected not only to cope with these problems and to help develop understanding of a whole range of social topics, from promoting tolerance to birth control, but also to succeed where parents and the religious or secular authorities tend to fail (Delors 1996, p. 143).

In some systems, such as in France, teachers see themselves to have a contractual obligation to deliver the curriculum, but not to ameliorate social conditions over which they have little control (Broadfoot & Osborn 1993). However, abdicating social responsibility has not been seen as an option by Australian teachers, nor their employers who have in recent years developed a plethora of policies designed to address such conditions.

The effect of this intensification and 'extensification' of teachers' work has been to require of teachers that they draw upon not only their intellectual but also their emotional resources. As Hargreaves (1998, p. 330) has observed:

> . . .teaching is an emotional practice that also involves heavy investments of emotional labour. It cannot be reduced to technical competencies of clinical standards alone. The emotions of teaching are, in this sense not just a sentimental adornment to the more fundamental parts of the work. They are fundamental in and of themselves. They are deeply intertwined with the purposes of teaching, the political dynamics of educational policy and school life, the relationships which make up teaching and the senses of self which teachers invest in their work.

For many teachers, they have exercised their profession, both intellectually and emotionally in isolated classrooms, fulfilling their responsibilities and obligations outside the gaze of their peers and their managers. Much of this is now changing. A third facet of teachers' work, its organisation, gives us a different trajectory on both its intellectual and emotional dimensions.

Teachers' work organisation — influences and patterns

Just as there are paradoxes and contradictions in relation to the changing nature of schools, so too are there anomalies in relation to teachers' work organisation. Writers such as Robertson (1996, 1997) have argued that the era of what has been known as 'Fordism'[1] has been characterised as one where there was a hierarchical ordering of authority, a specialisation of tasks and a separation of conception from execution. Mass schooling, with its objective being the provision of a work force able to fit a highly industrialised economic model concerned with high volume mass production, corresponded well with Fordist work practices. Robertson has gone on to examine teachers' work in the context of post-Fordism where economies move from high volume to high value in the ways in which we described the changing nature of the Australian economy in Chapter 1. She makes the case that teachers' professionalism has been significantly reconstituted as a 'new professionalism'.

Ironically, the new professional framework, as conceptualised by Robertson, is one where the teacher, as worker, still has little room for negotiation and therefore an even further reduced professional autonomy. Thus, at the same time that we are moving towards a post-Fordist regime, with its emphasis upon a knowledge-based economy, requiring flexibility and adaptability, we continue to persist with secondary schooling as an assembly line, managed by decision-makers sequestered in centralised bureaucracies remote from school classrooms. The little that has been devolved to schools is more to do with plumbing and the maintenance of playing fields and less to do with curriculum and assessment decision-making.

---

1 The term 'Fordism' derives from the endeavours of Henry Ford in the mass manufacture of motor cars. Whereas cars had been previously built by teams of skilled craftsmen with the division of labour a matter of local decision-making, under Ford's assembly line processes each worker now mass produced separate components, which were subsequently assembled piece by piece. The assembly line was itself subject to time and motion studies in order that output be maximised at minimum cost.

In this chapter we argue that it is imperative that we rethink teachers' work, but that change will be difficult in the face of the persistence of Fordist practices. On the one hand teachers are enjoined to attend to the needs of the market, to show greater initiative and creativity in their work practices, on the other they are now more subject than ever to centralised policies with respect to curriculum and assessment. Teachers, it would seem, are between a rock and a hard place. It is in this space that the relationship between the professional and industrial concerns of teachers most plays itself out.

It is worth considering here a specific case study which captures the tensions and contradictions of the 1990s in Australian education in relation to teachers' work organisation; that is, the National Project on the Quality of Teaching and Learning (NPQTL).

Teacher Award restructuring and the National Project on the Quality of Teaching and Learning (NPQTL)

As an outcome of an Australian mission to Europe, charged with examining among other things the role of education in national economic reconstruction, the report *Australia Reconstructed* (ACTU/TDC 1987) pointed to deficits in skill formation. It was argued that there should be a rationalisation of unions away from specific crafts and skills towards a more holistic industry orientation. Some 350 unions were reconfigured into less than 30 major industry unions (Burrow 1996). Unions were to be seen to be partners in the development of skill formation and career paths for all workers. This held true for the teachers' unions across the country. Teachers' wages and conditions were increasingly understood to be of both a professional and industrial nature. Items being considered by the teachers' unions and the Federal and state/territory governments included (Burrow 1996, p. 99):

- Standard teacher qualifications;
- Incremental salary scale and progression through the scale;
- Supervision of student teaching;
- Advanced Skills Teachers;
- Skills, responsibility and relativity issues for promotion positions;
- Length of the school year;
- Teacher duties and organisation of work;
- Performance appraisal;
- Tenure and transfers;
- Working conditions including leave and allowances.

As a result of protracted negotiations, a level of agreement was reached regarding national salary benchmarks, a common incremental scale and the new classification of Advanced Skills Teachers (ASTs). This classification was significant in that it was a recognition of the category of expert classroom practitioner and signified a professional and industrial valuing of classroom work as manifested both intellectually and emotionally.

Award restructuring in education was an important platform from which consideration could be given to the nature of teachers' work and the ways in which it was organised. It was perceived that by investigating the nature of teachers' work for the purposes of award restructuring it would also be possible to rethink its consequences in terms of learning outcomes for students. Thus the National Project on the Quality of Teaching and Learning (NPQTL) was born.

Although the industrial framework for NPQTL was award restructuring, the project quickly became one which engaged a number of stakeholders both directly and indirectly in a close investigation into aspects of teachers' work and teacher professional development. The Board of the NPQTL consisted of 24 senior representatives comprising: two Federal Government representatives; eight government school employer representatives; two National Catholic and Independent School peak organisation representatives; and 12 union representatives. (NPQTL 1994). Thus it may be seen that there was equal representation of union and employing bodies. A rare achievement in the context of states and territories who hold their autonomy as sacrosanct. However, there was no representation from the higher education sector and this was the cause of some concern. The difficulty was partly resolved by a series of consultations, throughout the project, with teacher educators and Deans of Education.

The project was organised into three working parties: National Professional Issues; Professional and Career Development; and Work Organisation and Related Pedagogical Issues (NPQTL 1994).

Arising from the work of the NPQTL three major initiatives were launched, these being: the National Schools Project (NSP, later to become the National Schools Network, NSN); the Australian Teaching Council designed to ultimately become responsible for national teacher registration; and, the development of a national set of standards for beginning teachers. Principally as a result of a change of government at the federal level, only the first of these reforms remains.[2] All the same, traces of the standards for beginning teachers are still to be found in a number of state documents which will be discussed in later chapters.

Responses to the restructuring initiatives and their implications for schooling have been mixed. Angus (1996), now a Professor of Education, but at the time of the reforms the Western Australian Ministry of Education representative, who was the chair of the working party which launched the National Schools Project, reflected that (pp. 147–50):

> For all the brouhaha of the new industrial relations it is unlikely that the work of teachers will be changed by award restructuring in any fundamental way. While the language may change, years after the 1988 National Wage Case there is little evidence to suggest that schools are more productive institutions as a consequence of structural efficiency reforms . . . Award restructuring has less cogency for workers in schools than workers in the clothing, food processing or some other industry subject to international competition and threatened with bankruptcy.

By way of contrast, Preston (1996), an independent researcher who has worked for

---

[2] It is, as yet, too early to comment upon the long-term impact of the federal coalition government, which represents conservative interests and came to power in 1996. However, it is already clear that the *Workplace Relations Act*, 1996, is one which returns labour relations to a confrontational and adversarial mode. Under such conditions it is unlikely that the impetus to reform teaching and teacher education through consensual agreement will continue at the pace experienced during the early 1990s.

various educational professional associations, unions and government authorities and spent six months in the secretariat of the NPQTL, argues (p. 177):

> The broad framework of award restructuring, developed in the context of the Accord and *Australia Reconstructed* continues to shape the cutting edge developments (in teacher professionalism) . . . developments which have the potential for a radical transformation of the teaching profession and teaching and learning in schools. It will take some time yet before the full impact of award restructuring can be assessed, but given a broad interpretation, that impact is likely to be profound.

It is not surprising that it was the Work Organisation and Related Pedagogical Issues working party of the NPQTL which gave rise to the National Schools Network. It became clear to the working party that the ways in which teachers' work was organised and regulated had impact upon pedagogy. The key reform questions which were to be addressed by the NSN were:

1. What is it about the way teachers work, in particular the way they teach and organise their work, that gets in the way of student learning?
2. How can educators support each other to make the changes that are good for both learners and teachers?

Agreements were developed between employing authorities and teachers' unions which enabled teachers to conduct workplace reform and reculturing in ways which stepped outside regulatory frameworks, on the understanding that practices were judged to be safe and socially equitable.

Member schools agreed to the following nationally negotiated set of principles (NSN web site 1998):

- to be responsible for improving learning outcomes for all students;
- to encourage greater student participation in the learning process;
- to establish equality of access, opportunity and outcomes for all students;
- to examine current work organisation to identify good practices and impediments to effective teaching and learning;
- to develop a model of participative workplace procedures and decision-making that includes the whole staff;
- to understand and accept the industrial rights and responsibilities of all parties;
- to encourage whole community involvement in decision-making about the reform process.

Schools within the ambit of the NSN began to experiment with innovative forms of team teaching, cooperative learning, timetable restructuring, assessment and reporting practices, parental and community involvement and sub-school development (Groundwater-Smith 1996).

For all the promise that we saw in the outcomes of the NPQTL, particularly the work of the National Schools Network, it would be fair to say that the settlement has not been a significant one. In the main, teachers' work continues to be organised and managed in recognisably Fordist ways. For most teachers they continue to work in isolation in their classrooms, with faculty boundaries clearly in place and the curriculum segmented by age and ability.

Thus far, in this chapter related to the changing nature of teachers' work, we have focused upon teaching as a vocation, with intellectual and emotional dimensions, occurring in an institutional context which organises it in particular ways. In this closing section we wish to turn to another aspect of teachers' work in terms of those who participate in it and the nature of the activist role which they may take. Teachers can be described, not only in terms of gender, but also in relation to race and ethnicity. We have already indicated that teaching is an aging profession, but it is also one where many of its mores and practices have arisen from the nature of its membership. Why is it that gender, race and ethnicity are so significant?

Who participates in teachers' work?

There can be no disputing that teaching is a profession which is dominated in numbers, if not in policy and power, by women (Spencer 1997). The notion of teachers' work as women's work has been seen to particularly apply to the primary school sector (Acker 1994). While this book is intended for those who propose to become teachers in the secondary sector it is important to consider the consequences of the feminisation of teaching overall. Women, as teachers of younger children, have been seen to be suited to the work on the basis of them being more nurturing and milder mannered than their male counterparts. It has also been suggested that teaching is commensurable with managing a household and parenting. Spencer quotes Webb who claimed that teaching was a good job for married women because it was manageable in the context of family life (Webb in Spencer 1997, p. 179):[3]

> First, teaching does not conflict strenuously with traditional demands family life puts on women. Second, it offers respectable employment during early adulthood, the time when women are likely to get married and begin family life. It brings in a second income, thus making it easier for the new family life. It brings in a secure financial start. Third a married woman can leave teaching without penalty if the couple decide to have children. If she decides to return to the classroom, it is likely that she will find a job and the school will not have changed much in her absence. Fourth many women find it possible to carry on the traditional duties of motherhood while carrying out their teaching obligations. Their hours at school coincide conveniently with their children's school day, and during vacations they can be at home to care for the young. Lastly, for a woman a teaching certificate can serve as a long-term insurance policy. In the unhappy event of a husband's death or illness or of divorce she is prepared to support herself and her family.

Such advice is not only deeply offensive, it also is based upon a series of premises which act to confirm in the public view teaching as, at best, a semi-profession (Etzioni 1969). Historically, work and family have been 'oppositionally' constructed for women teachers (Biklen 1995). Whereas for men there has been little suggestion that there is conflict between employment and parenting; indeed the one is seen as complementary to the other; for women it has long been seen that paid work outside the home takes second place to being mother and homemaker. In accepting such a view of teachers'

---

[3] It is worth noting that Webb was writing in the early 1980s, yet only a few decades before there were powerful sanctions which prevented married women having a career in teaching at all.

work there is an acceptance that teaching itself is not demanding and strenuous; that it is a source of a 'second income' and therefore undeserving of decent salaries and conditions; and, that it is relatively unchanging and does not require continuous professional development.

More insidiously the view also implies teaching as something which women can drop in and out of, leaving the career building to their male colleagues. It is clear, across the teaching profession, that there is an under-representation of women in senior administrative positions. At the time of writing this book there is not one Director General of Education, and only one Minister of Education, in Australia, who is a woman. Hence we have a hierarchical stratification in which decisions about teaching conditions are made by males and endured by females.

Gilbert and Gilbert (1998) have made a case that the very nature of the organisational management of a school acts to reinforce its gendered regime. Women are accorded pastoral roles, while males are expected to be the disciplinarians. Men are skilled in management and entrepreneurship; women are sound in public relations and the nurturing of staff. Men run science and maths departments, women manage the humanities. It is interesting to note that women in teaching have tended to find their niche at the levels of middle management. And yet, it is at this level that the greatest degree of teacher stress is experienced (Dinham & Scott 1996).

Of course gender is not the only varying factor in the matter of who participates in the teaching profession. Australia has become increasingly multicultural, particularly in recent decades. The number of people from language backgrounds other than English who undertake an Education course at university, leading to a teaching career, is disproportionately small (Senate Employment, Education and Training References Committee 1998, Appendix one, p. iv).

Teachers who are different can confront their mainstream colleagues and their students in ways which are unsettling and perceived to disturb the status quo. Lam (1996) in her discussion of a Chinese Canadian secondary school teacher suggests that teachers who are different are accorded the same status as 'stranger' (p. 19). She argues that difference can lead to relationships and treatments which are normally accorded to strangers who are often treated with suspicion and fear. Teachers who are different may be mistrusted, marginalised, used as scapegoats and discriminated against. Lam reports that Rose, as a Chinese teacher of French, felt like a 'displaced person' in the school. She was asked to recommend Chinese restaurants in town and expected to have specialised knowledge of Chinese food preparation. She was patronised for her 'good English' in spite of having been born in Canada (p. 23):

> When these people (the visitors) came to me at recess time and you know how they slowly mouth their English when they think you're either mentally deficient or Chinese, and then I said to them 'look I wasn't born in China!' I was too pissed off to be civil.

Teachers — old, young; male, female; Anglo, Aboriginal; language backgrounds other than English — participate in a profession which requires a great deal from them. Dedication, commitment, knowledge, compassion, to name but a few attributes, are important in the formation of a teacher's identity. However, there are other attributes which are more difficult to name and to sustain, among them courage and a capacity to challenge on issues of equity and social justice. Education is not just an individual benefit, but a social good which goes beyond a sum of the parts.

Teachers as activist professionals

As ones involved in a public enterprise, whether teaching in the government or non-government sector, teachers carry great social responsibility. In writing of teaching for the twenty-first century, Delors stated (1996, p. 141):

> . . . much will be expected, and much demanded of teachers. For it largely depends of them whether this vision (the pursuit of learning not only as a means to an end, but also as an end in itself) can come true. Teachers have crucial roles to play in preparing young people not only to face the future with confidence but to build it with purpose and responsibility. The new challenges facing education — to contribute to development, to help people understand and to some extent come to terms with the phenomenon of globalisation, and to foster social cohesion — must be met from primary and secondary school onwards. Teachers are instrumental in the development of attitudes — positive or negative — to learning. Teachers can awaken curiosity, stimulate independence, encourage intellectual rigour and create the conditions for success in formal and continuing education.

Sachs (1999) has argued that this social responsibility is best manifested as a form of activist professionalism within communities of practice which are collegial, negotiated and reformist. Acker (1999) reminds us that 'communities of teachers in schools are adult working groups. We are so obsessed with schools as places for (students) that we forget they are workplaces for adults' (p. 196); adults who are deeply professionally involved. The activist professional is not one who remains behind his or her classroom door, but is one who engages with colleagues in debates about not only pedagogy and practice, but the very role of the state in the policies and provisions which govern education in our schools.

It could be argued that the health of the education system in any state or territory is indicated by the capacity of its practitioners to be activist professionals, rather than mere functionaries. Indeed, one could argue that such an indicator is universal, and not exclusively a matter for Australia. Totalitarian regimes around the world seek to silence dissent with the starting point being schools and education.

A significant hallmark of professionalism is the capacity of its practitioners to organise and control their own work (Freidson 1994, pp. 172–3). In this sense teachers are in an ambivalent position. The organisation of their work is generally managed for them; they are not autonomous in the same ways as one who operates a medical or legal practice. At the same time they have no more constraint placed upon them, within the classroom itself, than do their colleagues in their surgeries or offices. For each is subject to the laws and regulations of that practice, but has degrees of freedom in interpreting them.

Professionalism is also seen by Freidson to be marked by selective recruitment, sufficient training, competence and ethical performance. Teaching, throughout Australia, is being recognised as having graduate status with a minimum of four years tertiary education. Specific teacher education components now extend well beyond the levels required in the past. Bachelor of Education courses are typically four years in duration; while post-graduate courses, building upon generalist first degrees, are moving towards a minimum of two years. While some attempts have been made towards Australia-wide teacher registration these have, as yet, not been successful. All the same beginning teacher competencies, as nominated state by state and territory, are so similar as to be almost identical.

A further view of professionalism cited by Freidson is the democratic notion that its practitioners 'are capable of controlling themselves by cooperative, collective means and that in the case of complex work, those who perform it are in the best position to make sure that it gets well done' (p. 176).

Conclusion

There can be no question that teaching is complex work. Unlike other professions teaching requires simultaneous interaction with large numbers of people. Decisions have to be made quickly and reasonably. No one day is quite like another. Also, as we have discussed earlier in this chapter, working in cooperative ways with colleagues is now a burgeoning practice in schools. However, the increasing insertion of performance appraisal practices in school management does leave open the question of who determines and monitors professional standards.

There can also be no question that teachers' work has altered and is continuing to alter in response to rapid social, economic and technological change. It is increasing in its complexity and level of demand as our society requires more and more of its schools. While Australian systems of education have not taken on the excesses of the British model, where teachers are seen as 'efficient and cost-effective employees' (Helsby 1999, p. 167) and where each is pitted one against the other in the public gaze as schools are placed in their order of achievement on a public league table, it is clear that regulatory frameworks are tightening and altering.

It is equally clear that in accepting the challenge to become a teacher, you have chosen not only an honourable and exciting profession, but one which makes great social and moral demands of you as a person and a citizen.

INQUIRY STRATEGIES

1. Following the example offered at the beginning of this chapter conduct a small focus group with school students asking them to define 'What is a Teacher?' and 'Why would someone want to be a teacher?' This might be something which you could do on your first practicum, with the agreement of the school of course. When undertaking focus groups it is a good idea to have students write their thoughts down first, in this way the quieter student is not subject to the influence of more assertive and dominant peers.

2. Brainstorm the number of roles you believe a teacher performs and the kinds of skills required to undertake those roles.

3. Imagine your state/territory government, for economic purposes, has decided to lower the school leaving age to 14. How would you professionally respond to the policy?

References

Acker, S. (1994). *Gendered Education.* Buckingham: Open University Press.

Acker, S. (1999). *The Realities of Teachers' Work: Never a Dull Moment.* London: Cassell.

ACTU/TDC (1987). *Australia Reconstructed.* ACTU/TDC Mission to Western Europe. Canberra: Australian Government Printing Service.

Angus, M. (1996). Award Restructuring in Schools: Educational Idealism vs Political Pragmatism. In T. Seddon (ed) *Pay, Professionalism & Politics: Reforming Teachers.* Australian Council of Educational Research (ACER), pp. 117–152.

Aronowitz, S. & Giroux, H. (1991). *Postmodern Education: Politics, Culture and Social Criticism.* Minneapolis: University of Minnesota Press.

Australian Bureau of Statistics (1996). *Education and Training in Australia.* Canberra: Australian Government Printing Service.

Biddle, B., Good, T., & Goodson, I. (1997). The changing world of teachers. In. B. Biddle, T. Good, & I. Goodson (eds), *International Handbook of Teachers and Teaching.* London: Kluwer Academic Publishers, pp. 1–10.

Biklen, S. (1995). *School Work: Gender and the Cultural Construction of Teaching.* New York: Teachers College Press.

Broadfoot, P. and Osborn, M. (1993). *Perceptions of Teaching: Primary School Teachers in England and France.* London: Cassell.

Burrow, S. (1996). Award Restructuring — The Teaching Profession. In T. Seddon (ed), *Pay, Professionalism & Politics: Reforming Teachers.* Australian Council of Educational Research (ACER), pp. 87–116.

Collins, C., Batten, M., Ainley, J. & Getty, C. (1996). *Gender and School Education.* Canberra: Australian Government Publishing Service.

Coppock, D. (1997). Respectability as a prerequisite of moral character: The social and occupational mobility of pupil teachers in the late 19th and early 20th centuries. In *History of Education,* 26 (2) pp. 165–186.

Delors, J. (1996). *Learning: The Treasure Within.* Paris: UNESCO Publishing.

Department of Employment, Education and Training (1993). *Retention and Participation in Australian Schools, 1967–1992.* Canberra: Australian Government Printing Service.

Dinham, S. & Scott, C. (1996). *The Teacher 2000 Project: A Study of Teacher Satisfaction, Motivation and Health.* Sydney: University of Western Sydney, Nepean.

Etzioni, A. (1969). *The Semi-professions and their Organisation: Teachers, Nurses, Social Workers.* New York: The Free Press.

Freidson, E. (1994). *Professionalism Reborn: Theory, Prophecy and Policy.* Chicago: University of Chicago Press.

Gilbert, R. & Gilbert, P. (1998). *Masculinity Goes to School.* Sydney: Allen & Unwin.

Groundwater-Smith, S. (1996). *Learning is When: Teachers help Teachers; Kids help Kids; Teachers help Kids; Kids help Teachers.* Ryde: National Schools Network.

Hansen, D. (1994). Revitalizing the Idea of Vocation in Teaching. At http://www.ed.uiuc.edu/EPS/PEs-Yearbook/94_docs/HANSEN.HTM

Hargreaves, A. (1998). The emotional politics of teaching and teacher development. In *International Journal of Leadership in Education: Theory and Practice*, 1 (4) pp. 315–336.

Hatton E. (1988). Teachers' work as bricolage: Implications for teacher education. In *British Journal Of Sociology Of Education*, 9 (3) pp. 337–357.

Helsby, G. (1999). *Changing Teachers' Work.* Buckingham: Open University Press.

Lam, C. (1996). The green teacher. In D. Thiessen, N. Bascia, & I. Goodson (eds), *Making a Difference About Difference: The Lives and Careers of Racial Minority Immigrant Teachers.* Ontario: Garamond Press, pp. 15–50.

Lawn, M. (1997). The puzzle of the public: (Re) constructing the teacher in the public service. In *Historical Studies in Education*, 9 (1) pp. 107–115.

Lortie, D. (1975). *School Teacher.* Chicago: University of Chicago Press.

McWilliam, E. (1996). Admitting impediments: or things to do with bodies in classrooms. In *Cambridge Journal of Education*, 26 (3), pp. 367–378.

National Project on the Quality of Teaching and Learning (NPQTL) (1994). *Report of the NPQTL, 1991–1993.* Canberra: Australian Government Publishing Service.

National Schools Network (1998). Web site: www.edunions.labor.net.au/nsn

Nias, J. (1999). Primary Teaching as a Culture of Care. In J. Prosser (ed), *School Culture*. London: Paul Chapman Publishing, pp. 66–81.

Robertson, S. (1996). Teachers' Work: Restructuring and Post-Fordism: Constructing the New 'Professionalism'. In I. Goodson & A. Hargreaves (eds), *Teachers' Professional Lives.* London: Falmer Press.

Robertson, S. (1997). Restructuring Teachers' Labor. In B. Biddle, T. Good, & I. Goodson (eds), *International Handbook of Teachers and Teaching.* London: Kluwer Academic Publishers, pp. 621–670.

Sachs, J. (1999). Teacher Professional Identity: Competing Discourses, Competing Outcomes. Paper presented to the Annual Conference of the Australian Association for Research in Education, Melbourne, November.

Senate Employment, Education and Training References Committee (1988). *A Class Act.* Canberra: Parliament House.

Smith, M. & Bourke, S. (1990). A Contextual Study of Teacher Stress, Satisfaction and Workload. Paper presented to the Annual Conference of the Australian Association for Research in Education, Sydney, November.

Spencer, D. (1997). Teaching as Women's Work. In B. Biddle, T. Good, & I. Goodson (eds), *International Handbook of Teachers and Teaching.* London: Kluwer Academic Publishers, pp. 153–198.

Sweet, R. (1998). Youth: The Rhetoric and the Reality of the 1990s. In Dusseldorp Skills Forum (ed), *Australia's Youth: Reality and Risk*. Sydney: Dusseldorp Skills Forum.

Tedesco, J. (1997). Enhancing the Role of Teachers. In C. Day, V. van Dolf, S. Wong-Kooi,. (eds), T*eachers and Teaching*. Leuven, Apeldoorn: Garant, pp. 23–35.

Tuettemann, E. (1991). Teaching: Stress and satisfaction. *Issues in Educational Research*, 1 (1) pp. 31–42.

Woods, P., Jeffrey, B., Troman, G. & Boyle, M. (1997). *Restructuring Schools, Reconstructing Teachers*. Buckingham: Open University Press.

Young, R. (1998). The teacher's vocation: Students, clients, customers. *Change: Transformations in Education*, 1 (1) pp. 72–83.

PART TWO

Changing Times, Changing Students

CHAPTER 4 From Adolescence to Young Adulthood

CHAPTER 5 Accepting and Rejecting Secondary Schooling

Students in our secondary schools and colleges span a period in life where the critical transition from childhood to adulthood is made. Depending upon the Australian state or territory, they leave their primary schools around 12 or 13 years of age and continue in their schooling for a further six or so years.

As the two chapters which follow demonstrate, adolescents cannot be thought to be a homogeneous or static group of young people. However, it is broadly indicated that this life stage is one where young people are establishing themselves as increasingly autonomous and independent. The first of the two chapters makes clear that varying theoretical perspectives on the construction of youth and of adolescence have had an impact upon the ways in which our educational provisions have been provided and are changing.

In Australia, contemporary understanding of adolescence requires that our schools develop more flexible and responsive policies towards all young people, at the same time as providing a learning environment which is stable and hospitable.

The second chapter in this section explores the nature of student engagement with their learning in secondary schools and colleges. It argues that variables such as race, ethnicity, gender, class and poverty act to influence the ways in which students will be able to participate in their education. Equally, the ways in which knowledge is organised, taught and assessed in the secondary context affects the extent to which students will comply or resist.

If secondary education is not to perpetuate cultural and social inequality, our schools and colleges need to be aware of and sensitive to the manner in which teachers can fully engage students in their own learning in ways which enrich and enhance their life chances.

CHAPTER

From Adolescence to Young Adulthood

Does it seem that long ago that the term 'adolescent' fitted you? More likely you remember being a 'teenager'. What did that mean for you? Chances are that time of your life was a time of change and transition for you. It was probably a time when you were sensing what sort of person you were and would become, a time of questioning established values and ways of doing things and a time of emotional ups and downs. Can you remember how you felt about your body, your looks, your friends, school, your parents and teachers? And now you are in the position of engaging with adolescents as the major part of your professional role. Your working day will be spent helping young people to make sense of and act in and on the world. You will be challenged to make your teaching relevant to their needs and aspirations.

But what does the category of 'adolescent' really mean? What does work in sociology, biology, psychology, psychiatry, even criminology, tell us about this time of life? And more particularly, how can this academic knowledge of adolescence help us be better teachers of the young people with whom we work? Perhaps the most important thing we can acknowledge about adolescence is that young people have a variety of life experiences in a variety of settings and come from many different social groups. Adolescents, therefore, cannot be thought of as making up a homogeneous or static group (White 1990, 1993; Wyn & White 1997).

This chapter is all about helping you to view adolescence historically and theoretically. It focuses especially on adolescence as a stage of transition from childhood to adulthood. Interestingly, there is also a focus on youth cultures and the variety of modes of dress, behaviour and style that such cultures engender. Most importantly, we will draw out implications for teachers and schools from this academic work.

So, what does 'adolescence' mean?

The term adolescence implies a certain limited age range. For this reason, the terms 'youth', 'young people' or 'young adults' are often preferable to describe a wider age range than is suggested by the term 'adolescent' (Griffin 1993). For instance, some writers differentiate between stages of adolescence by using the terms 'older adolescent' to refer to people 15–19 years of age, and 'young adults' to refer to people between the ages of 20–24. So, although chronological age can give us a broad indication of the adolescent stage, it cannot be 'a precise definition' of this stage of transition (Coleman 1992, p. 8). It is clear that some form of 'transitional stage' from childhood to adulthood is 'common to most societies' although there are large variations even in Western societies as to its operation (Hartley & Wolcott 1994, p. 9). This transitional period may begin as early as the age of 10 or 11 years with the onset of puberty, and for some, extend into their early or mid-twenties (Coleman 1992).

A brief history of youth and adolescence

Adolescence is often characterised in the media as a time of rebellion, crisis, pathology, and deviance, rather than as a time of evaluating, decision-making, commitment, and of carving out a place in the world. This pejorative view of adolescence is unfortunate and inaccurate. It is true, however, that adolescence necessarily requires adjustment in the self, in the family, and in the peer group and that all adolescents will experience certain pressures and stresses associated with these changes. Clearly, the challenges experienced can lead to personal and social growth or personal and social difficulties, including difficulties at school.

Historians refer to the period of 1890 to 1920 as the 'age of adolescence' as it was during this time that the concept of adolescence was introduced. Legislation that excluded young people from working and extended the years of compulsory schooling was introduced throughout Western industrialised societies (Santrock 1998). Throughout the twentieth century, adolescents became more visible, particularly politically during the 1960s and 1970s, in an increasingly complex society (Wallace & Cross 1990).

At present, young people and systems of education are actually experiencing two transitions: the traditional one from adolescence to adulthood and the very transition of society. The present social revolution is fundamentally a technological one (Greig 2000). This revolution is associated with changing economies (and an increasing reliance on market forces in the allocation and distribution of social services), changing labour markets characterised by growing part-time and declining full-time employment, declining demand for unskilled labour, and rising youth unemployment (Australian National Training Authority 1998). Changing patterns of family life are also part of today's scene. Over 54 per cent of two-parent families have both parents employed, while conversely, almost 8 per cent of two-parent families have neither parent employed (ABS 1997).

In Australia, the economic, social, political and cultural circumstances of young people have changed considerably over the past 15 to 20 years, and researchers have increasingly focused their attention on developing a comprehensive study of youth and their experiences. Youth-specific institutions, such as the Youth Research Centre at the University of Melbourne and the Federal Government's Department of Employment, Education, Training and Youth Affairs (DEETYA) — now DETYA with employment being separated out — have greatly contributed to the investigation of youth and their immense variety of social experiences. Youth studies have developed as a distinct field of inquiry, with writers who specialise in this particular area.

Adolescence — a time of storm and stress

Many of the developmental theories of youth base their analysis on the cornerstone concept of adolescence as a period of inherent biological and psychological processes. G. Stanley Hall, viewed as the father of the scientific study of adolescence, first published his ideas in a two-volume text, *Adolescence*, in 1916. Hall (1916) believed that development was controlled by genetically determined physiological factors, with the environment playing a role whereby heredity interacts with environmental influences to determine an individual's development.

According to Hall, the period from 12 to 23 years of age is characterised by much storm and stress with conflict and mood swings affecting the wider society. Hall borrowed the label 'storm and stress' from the German writers Goethe and Schiller, and saw a parallel between these themes and the psychological development of adolescents. He stated that the thoughts, feelings and actions of adolescents oscillate greatly between conceit and humility, good and temptation, happiness and sadness. Hall's views had implications for the social development (and education) of adolescents, as he conceived the biological processes during adolescence directed social development toward adulthood. Hall began the theorising and analysing of adolescence that has continued throughout this century (Santrock 1998).

Ironically, Hall's bio-psychological explanations of adolescent behaviour are somewhat resurging as we enter the new millennium. For example, Biddulph (1997) has argued that the physical changes that accompany puberty have a significant influence on the emotional and behavioural upheavals endured by adolescents, particularly males, during this life-stage. The sudden surge of testosterone in males and oestrogen in females is seen to drive physical and social growth, as adolescents have to learn how to live with their new bodies and emotions. They have to redefine who they are, relinquish their childhood roles, experiment and form adult identities, convince themselves, their peers and family of their new role, and then find a congruent role in adulthood. It is during this period that young people assert their independence from adults (such as parents, teachers or other authority figures) and test out their new personalities. It is, as Hall would argue, a period of storm, stress and turmoil for adolescents and anyone else in their sphere of social interaction, including teachers (Biddulph 1997).

Other theorists who have greatly influenced the bio-psychological approach to the study of adolescence have been Freud, Erikson and Piaget. Freud argued that, in order to examine adolescent development, we need to understand the unconscious forces behind trivial behaviours, such as the subconscious masculinity embedded in the character of adolescent males (Connell 1995). Erikson (1968) argued that adolescence is a period of identity confusion with adolescents faced with finding out who they really are, what they are all about and their life's aspirations. Piaget believed that adolescence was a period where individuals began to move beyond the word of actual experience and started to think in abstract, logical terms. Adolescents, he argued, developed images of ideal circumstances and entertained possibilities for the future. They were able to use systematic thinking and deductive reasoning to solve problems. Young people, he said, become more aware of the world around them, including all of its flaws and injustices. As they become aware of this, their behaviour and actions reflect their attitude toward society, be it positive or negative (Santrock 1998).

These bio-psychological approaches were criticised for not paying enough attention to how the social world influences the fundamental identity and social role processes described above (Connell 1987, 1995).

Learning how to be adults

Social learning theorists like Bandura, ecological theorists like Bronfenbrenner and anthropologists like Margaret Mead stressed the influence of society on adolescent development. Bandura (1997) argued that adolescents learn how to be male (or masculine) and female (or feminine) adults by observing the behaviour of other adults. For example, an adolescent male may observe his father behaving in an aggressive and hostile manner with other people, and consequently will adopt this behaviour in his own interchanges with others (Webb 1998).

Bronfenbrenner (1984), in his ecological theory of adolescent development, stated the behaviour of an adolescent is influenced by a great variety of interactions with social agents and institutions, such as family and peers, schools and neighbourhoods, as well as the law, the mass media, the political system, and so on (Evans & Poole 1991).

Mead's (1961) work in Samoa emphasised the sociocultural nature of adolescent development. Although criticised, her work is still very influential in analyses of youth and youth culture as it moved debates about adolescent development away from 'storm and stress' biology towards the importance of social process. Importantly, Mead's work showed that the transition from childhood through adolescence to adulthood could be relatively stress-free but that this depended on the way in which social attitudes to such matters as sex, birth and death were constructed and communicated.

Towards a sociology of youth and adolescence

There have been major sociological approaches that have influenced the study of young people over the years. Central to these have been functionalist and Marxist or conflict approaches. More recently, critical theorists and proponents of Foucault have advanced their own ideas about adolescence and the study of youth issues.

Functionalist approaches

Proponents of functionalism saw adolescence as a period of 'continuous socialisation', where young people were gradually distanced from their parents and relations, and were also taught the emotional and social skills essential for building adult gender and sexual identities, and that this fostered social harmony. Interestingly, functionalists explained defiance or rebellion in adolescents as having conservative rather than traumatic consequences. Researchers found that close relationships were the norm for young people, who also respected their parents' opinions on education, employment, politics and choice of friends. Functionalist research also highlighted the tendency of adults to stereotype adolescents on the basis of widespread generalisations based on information relating to a limited, but highly visible, group of 'deviant' or 'turbulent' youth. Youth extremists were found to be the exception to the rule as they were actually still learning adult skills and identities through their rebellion (Roberts 1983, pp. 14–15).

Functionalist proponents of the idea of 'continuous socialisation' see the period of adolescence as essential for the preparation of individuals for conventional adulthood.

Youth cultures are not seen to be the basis of rebellion, but are important facilitators for consolidating the attitudes, identities and hopes of youth, and also impart the skills and knowledge necessary for an individual to fulfil their adult roles within the family, the economy and society as a whole. Like the proponents of the bio-psychological interpretation of youth, youth cultures should be accepted and not opposed by adult society. The 'continuous socialisation' theorists believe adults should be less suspicious and hostile toward mechanisms of adolescent socialisation, as they are an essential part of society as a whole (Roberts 1983; Santrock 1998).

Conflict approaches

Conflict theorists, including Marxists, criticised functionalists for being too conservative in their approach to youth and their relations with adults. Proponents of the disturbed and turbulent view of adolescence replaced bio-psychological explanations of adolescent development with social-psychological ones. The result was a theory of adolescence that highlighted intergenerational conflict (Wyn & White 1997).

Conflict theorists believe that a conflict exists in all societies, between the young seeking freedom, power and wealth, and the adults/elders who do not wish to concede to them (Roberts 1983). The 'conflict of generations' perspective views the period of adolescence as one characterised by identity crisis, role confusion and contradictory socialisation, which results in pronounced conflict with the older members of society and increased susceptibility of influence (often undesirable) of peer groups and youth cultures (Davis 1990).

Youth subcultures and style

In the 1970s, a driving theoretical force in the study of young people became known as the Birmingham School. The seminal work from this group was Hall and Jefferson's (1976) *Resistance Through Rituals*. Here, it was argued, that young people are alienated from society because they lack control over their lives economically and politically. Society is controlled by a relatively small group of people (the dominant group) who make decisions affecting young people (the subordinate group) not on the basis of what is best for the them, but for capitalistic reasons. Youth subcultures — such as Mods, Skinheads, Rockers and latterly Goths — were said to form as a reaction to the lack of control that young people experienced over their own lives.

Members of the Birmingham School used a neo-Marxist framework to explain the relationship between the dominant and subordinate classes, and to convey how popular youth culture and working-class youth challenged the dominant ideology through their political struggles. Youth subcultures were seen to be the manifestation of the conflict between working-class youth and the ruling class. 'Youth' was identified as being a new and sociologically important area of study (Wallace & Cross 1990).

But this kind of theorising about youth was criticised for being over-reliant and over-fascinated with atypical aspects of youth culture. It was clear that most boys and girls did not belong to clearly defined subcultures. Indeed, the work of researchers like Willis (1977) and Corrigan (1979) presented the unspectacular picture that most adolescents were rather 'normal'. These studies presented young people as not suffering from a great deal of emotional turmoil and stress during adolescence, and who were not in constant conflict with adult members of society and the institutions they represented.

Sercombe (1993) states that youth subcultures are an interesting but still marginal youth phenomenon that involves only a minority of young people. Consequently, he argued that youth subculture should not be allocated too much importance in relation to the study of youth as a whole.

Young people and power

Another view about why young people develop and respond to society in the ways they do is that put forward by Foucault. He believed every member of society, including adolescents, is caught in the constantly shifting mesh of power relations that exist at every social level. Young people, he argued, have their own power, but still engage in power plays with adults and other groups in society. According to Foucault, the more techniques of power exercised upon a group, the more powerful they became. In the case of adolescents, adults subjected them to many power processes that were directed at disciplining, training and subjecting the individual (and the body) through extended schooling and other institutional projects. This disciplining and training was aimed at making them into useful adults. However, at the same time, adolescents may use this same discipline and training for purposes for which it was not designed, such as resistance within the schools and within society generally to the ideas and objectives of adults (Connell 1995; Sercombe 1993).

Adolescents and identity

As well as sociological theories influencing the way we view adolescence, psychological approaches are important in attempting to understand how young adults respond to their world. Integral to psychological understandings of adolescence is the issue of identity development. Personal identity is the sum of an adolescent's self-definitions or self-concepts. These multiple self-concepts form an individual's global identity. An individual's self-concept is his/her conscious, cognitive perception of personal strengths, weaknesses, abilities, attitudes, roles and social statuses, physical appearance, personality traits, and values that begin at birth and are continually shaped through different experiences. How an individual evaluates and understands his/her self-concept, determines their self-esteem or self-worth (Slavin 1997).

The concept of self can, according to Rice (1996), be further broken down into:

- actual self (overall basic self-concept);
- ideal self (the kind of person the adolescent would like to be);
- temporary or transitive self (influenced by situation, context or even mood); and
- social self (the self the individual thinks other people see).

Various writers (Peterson 1990, Rice 1996) have researched factors that contribute to healthy self-esteem in adolescents. The following are said to be predictors of solid self-esteem:

- harmonious friendships;
- good performance in school, in extracurricular activities, and in chosen interests;

- already determined career goals;
- healthy body image;
- lack of alcohol or substance abuse;
- lack of depression, suicidal thoughts, anxiety, promiscuity or eating disturbances;
- few stressful events such as a difficult school transition, serious illness, or rejection (through death or family breakdown) of a parent, or relative early entry to puberty;
- engagement in non-violent inter-generational conflict with parents for a variety of reasons (but recognising that their parents love and respect them); and
- relatively harmonious home lives.

By late adolescence, most adolescents' self-concept has stabilised and they begin to feel they have developed an integrated sense of self especially in relation to their ideal selves (Rice 1996; Slavin 1997).

The role of peers in identity formation

The importance of peer interaction, and the need for adolescents to 'fit in' and 'belong' cannot be underestimated in relation to the formation of identity (McFadden 1996). Peer acceptance is a very important part of identity formation. Adolescents spend more than 50 per cent of their waking hours with their peers at school or in recreational pursuits, as opposed to only 15 per cent with adults, including their parents (Steinberg 1993). Although the perceived importance of peer acceptance for adolescents is greater than those of parents, or indeed any other adult, friends' opinions usually only influence small, day-to-day decisions, particularly in relation to fashion and relationships. It may surprise you that researchers have found parents have a greater influence on adolescents in relation to more important decisions and general values and morals, than friends (Santrock 1998; Steinberg 1993). Be that as it may, peer relationships and opinions have a very significant influence on adolescents' self-esteem, self-concept and consequent identity development.

The process of identity development

Identity development is a complex and multifaceted process that continues throughout an individual's lifetime. Identity development in adolescents involves changes and investigations into their self-concept, is affected by how they evaluate their self-concept (that is, their self-esteem or self-image), and results in a change in their general sense of identity — who they are, where they come from and where they are directed. Identity is comprised of many components — physical, sexual, vocational, social, ideological, moral and psychological characteristics — that the individual has to attempt to synthesise in order to develop a coherent self-identity. According to Rice (1996, p. 36), an individual's identity is made up of the following:

- their physical appearance and personality traits;
- their gender as well as their sex roles;
- their social relationships and group membership;

- their chosen vocations and employment;
- their religious and political affiliations;
- their moral and value ideologies; and
- their psychological adjustment, self-esteem and body-image.

Through their role experimentation and interactions with different people within their community and wider society, it is argued that adolescents should be able to establish a stable sense of identity (Crossen 1997). This successful identity development, according to Erikson (1968), will allow young people to cope with situations that require them to redefine their identity later in life, such as in marriage, when becoming parents, in gaining employment and in leaving home.

The role of schools and teachers in adolescent development

The work of schools and teachers at the beginning of the twenty-first century will involve the provision of stability and growth for adolescents in the midst of social and cultural transition, in a time of enormous social, political, economic, technological and cultural change. Adolescents faced with many contradictory social values reflected in the print media, radio, TV and video games, and through differing parental expectations and other social interactions, may well respond by commencing sexual activity earlier and engaging in drug, substance or alcohol abuse. They may suffer from eating disorders or engage in other dangerous behaviours, or reject and leave school altogether.

As teachers, however, we need to be proactive and ensure that despite social inequalities and disadvantage, students are provided with the opportunity to successfully gain the credentials that education has to offer. These credentials are essential for effective competition in the labour market and the attainment of a legitimate livelihood (Wyn & White, 1997; Qld Board of Teacher Registration 1996).

Consequently, as teachers we must be able to assist students to address these transition issues as well as provide students with opportunities to learn, to integrate technology into their lives, and to become adequately prepared for participation in the adult world. This is especially relevant for groups most subject to marginalisation such as Aboriginal people and Torres Strait Islanders, students from non-English speaking backgrounds (NESBs), students with disabilities, and students who are socially and economically disadvantaged (Qld Board of Teacher Registration 1996).

This process of support must all take place in a social climate whereby adolescents now have to be educated to a higher level than ever before; a level previously reserved for a select few of the academic elite (King 1999).

Conclusion

As Santrock (1998) cogently argues, contrary to the popular stereotype that anchors much writing on youth, the majority of today's adolescents, despite facing more numerous and complex demands, expectations, risks and temptations, successfully negotiate the path from child to adult, without immense turmoil. The youth of today complete high school at a higher rate than previous generations, have better relationships and more open communication with others, and quite successfully negotiate the physical, cognitive, and social challenge of adolescence (Klingman 1998). While it is true that a significant minority of young people do have serious difficulties dealing with the problems presented by adolescence (take, for example, the disturbing youth suicide rate), other factors such as ethnicity, culture, gender, socioeconomic status, geographical location and personal characteristics (such as learning difficulties) should not be ignored (Eckersley 1998). The age of human development of an individual cannot, on its own, explain disturbed or delinquent behaviour, or emotional or psychological problems. The different experiences of a heterogeneous group called 'youth' are very difficult to explain in an all-encompassing way.

However we term the 'transitional' stage under discussion in this chapter, the category of youth or adolescent has been shaped historically and affected by social and technological change and resultant changes in patterns of education and employment. As a teacher it is important for you to realise the crucial role that education plays in the construction of the category of youth and/or adolescent. Historically, differing forms of education, and related requirements, have provided the link between school and work, often defining the status of the individual: without work, or in education, as more helpless, dependent and therefore childlike; in work, as more independent and like an adult.

Young people all experience the transition from childhood to adulthood and during the journey they need respect — an issue very much bound up with status — information and support (particularly from trusted adults), protection (particularly for the vulnerable like homeless young people), and gradually increasing independence. The majority of young people also experience the transition from school to work in either late adolescence or young adulthood and require contexts that deliver both a sense of control and opportunity for growth. Above all, young people need the constructive social and emotional support of trusted adults, either in the family or in school, during this crucial, challenging and formative period of their lives.

The Queensland Board of Teacher Registration (1996, p. 3) summarised the needs of most adolescents in the following way. Adolescents, it said, need:

- acceptance and belonging;
- security;
- independence and self-assertion;
- recognition and significance;
- challenge through new experience; and
- achievement through mastery.

As we enter classrooms to teach adolescents this is an extremely useful list to remember.

INQUIRY STRATEGIES

1. How different do you think things are for today's adolescents compared with the period in which you went through this stage of growth?

2. What can you remember about teachers who were effective with you at this stage of your life? How did they treat you? What lessons did you learn from your experiences of good teachers you had at that stage of your life and how could those lessons be applied by you in a teaching context?

3. What is your view about the relative importance of biology, psychology and the environment in adolescent development? What experiences do you bring to this debate that convince you that perhaps society is more influential than biology or vice versa?

4. Can you remember particular youth subcultures that were held up as broadly representative of young people's experiences when you were growing up? What was your view about how representative such subcultures were of the lifestyle of the average young person?

5. What do you think might be the interplay between psychological and sociological factors in the development of adolescents? Try to relate identity formation with a sense of 'fitting in' and 'belonging'.

6. What differences are there between the ways that males and females cope with adolescence? Do you see these differences as largely biological or sociological or a combination of both?

7. Scarcely a day goes by for young people where there is not some image or reference in the media about what it is to be an adolescent. Advertising images are especially powerful and prevalent for today's young people. Collect some print and/or digital examples of the ways in which adolescence is portrayed in the media and consider how they might influence the identity formation of young people.

References

Australian Bureau of Statistics (1997). *Social Trends.* Cat. No. 4102.0. Canberra: AGPS.

Australian National Training Authority (1998). *Australian Vocational Education and Training. Young People 1997 — an overview.* Leabrook: National Centre for Vocational Education Research.

Bandura, A. (1997). *Self-efficacy: The Exercise of Control.* New York: W H Freeman.

Biddulph, S. (1997). *Raising Boys: Why Boys are Different and How to Help them Become Happy and Well-balanced Men.* Sydney: Finch.

Bronfenbrenner, U. (1984). Ecology of the family as a context for human development. In *Developmental Psychology*, 22, pp. 723–742.

Coleman, J.C. (1992). The nature of adolescence. In J.C. Coleman & C. Warren-Adamson (eds), *Youth Policy in the 1990s: the way forward.* London: Routledge.

Connell, R.W. (1987). *Gender and Power: Society, the Person and Sexual Politics.* St Leonards: Allen & Unwin.

Connell, R.W. (1995). *Masculinities.* St Leonards: Allen & Unwin.

Corrigan, P. (1979). *Schooling the Smash Street Kids.* London: Macmillan.

Crossen, C. (1997). Growing up goes on and on and on. In K.L. Freiberg (ed), *Human Development Annual Edition 98–99* (26th edition). Guilford: Dushkin/McGraw Hill.

Davis, J. (1990). Social changes and images of youth. In *Youth and the Condition of Britain: Images of Adolescent Conflict.* London: Athlone.

Eckersley, R. (1998). It's all news. Making and remaking the myths of youth. *Youth Studies Australia*, March, pp. 25–27.

Erikson, E. (1968). *Identity, Youth and Crisis.* New York: Norton.

Evans, G. & Poole, M. (1991). *Young Adults: Self-perception and Life Contexts.* London: Falmer Press.

Greig, A. (2000). Globalisation. In R. Jureidini and M. Poole (eds), *Sociology — Australian Connections* (2nd edition). St Leonards: Allen & Unwin.

Griffin, C. (1993). *Representations of Youth: the Study of Youth and Adolescence in Britain and America.* Cambridge: Polity Press.

Hall, G.S. (1916). *Adolescence.* New York: Appelton.

Hall, S. & Jefferson T. (1976). *Resistance Through Rituals: Youth Subculture in Postwar Britain.* London: Hutchinson.

Hartley, R. & Wolcott, I. (1994). *The Position of Young People in Relation to the Family.* Hobart: National Clearing House for Youth Studies.

King, S.P. (1999). Leadership in the 21st century: using feedback to maintain focus and direction. In D.D. Marsh (ed), *ASCD Year Book 1999 — Preparing our schools for the 21st century.* Alexandria: Association for Supervision and Curriculum Development.

Klingman, A. (1998). Psychological education: studying adolescents' interests from their own perspective. *Adolescence*, 33, pp. 435–446.

McFadden, M.G. (1996). 'Second chance' education: accessing opportunity or recycling disadvantage? *International Studies in Sociology of Education*, 6, pp. 87–112.

Mead, M. (1961). *Coming of Age in Samoa: a Psychological Study of Primitive Youth for Western Civilisation.* New York: Morrow.

Peterson, C.C. (1990). Disagreement, negotiation and conflict resolution in families with adolescents. In P.C.L. Heaven & V.J. Callan (eds), *Adolescence: An Australian perspective.* Sydney: Harcourt Brace Jovanovich.

Poole, M. (ed) (1992). *Education and Work.* Hawthorn: Australian Council for Educational Research.

Queensland Board of Teacher Registration (1996). *Report of the working party on the preparation of teachers for the education of young adolescents.* Toowong: Qld Board of Teacher Registration.

Rice, F.R. (1996). *The Adolescent: Development, Relationships and Culture* (8th edition). Sydney: Allyn & Bacon.

Roberts, K. (1983). *Youth and Leisure.* London: Allen & Unwin.

Santrock, J.W. (1998). *Adolescence* (7th edition). New York: McGraw Hill.

Sercombe, H. (1993). Youth theory: Marx or Foucault? In: R. White (ed), *Youth Subcultures: Theory, History and the Australian Experience.* Hobart: National Clearing House for Youth Studies.

Slavin, R.E. (1997). *Educational Psychology: Theory and Practice* (5th edition). Sydney: Allyn & Bacon.

Steinberg, L. (1993). *Adolescence* (3rd edition). New York: McGraw-Hill.

Wallace, C. & Cross, M. (1990). *Youth in Transition: The sociology of Youth and Youth Policy.* Hampshire: Falmer Press.

Webb, J. (1998). *Junk Male.* Sydney: Harper Collins.

White, R. (1990). *No Space of their Own: Young People and Social Control in Australia.* Sydney: Cambridge University Press.

White, R. (ed) (1993). *Youth Subcultures: Theory, History and the Australian Experience.* Hobart: National Clearing House for Youth Studies.

Willis, P.E. (1977). *Learning to Labour: How Working Class Kids Get Working Class Jobs.* Farnborough: Saxon House.

Wyn, J. & White, R. (1997). *Rethinking Youth.* St Leonards: Allen & Unwin.

CHAPTER

Accepting and Rejecting Secondary Schooling

We hope that this chapter affects your thinking about the institution of school in quite radical ways. It will certainly challenge the way you have probably thought about schools and schooling since you were in school yourself. It is one thing to understand that in today's society many minority groups are educationally disadvantaged due to their race, ethnicity, geographical location, socioeconomic status, and gender. It is quite another thing to think about schools as cementing rather than disrupting this disadvantage; but in this chapter that is what we will be suggesting to you.

This is not to argue that schools are organised towards or that teachers intend to keep certain kinds of people in disadvantaged positions. It is patently clear that systems of education and policies are established to achieve the very opposite. In recent years, however, we have witnessed a proliferation of research that reveals how the education system perpetuates and legitimises social inequality, due to the economic, political and ideological practices that permeate schools. The area of Aboriginal education is a good example of this. No-one would argue that current national and state education policy is aimed at continuing to keep Aboriginal and Torres Strait Islander people in disadvantaged positions. Clearly though the indicators all point to the persistent social and educational disadvantage of Australia's original inhabitants (Adams 1998).

Many students respond to a form of schooling which says to them that they are not suitable for, or indeed capable of, education by rejecting or opposing it; a response that is entirely understandable. Ironically, however, there are other disadvantaged students who accept schooling and succeed 'against the odds'. We have been slow to learn about the stories of these students and what they have to say about continued engagement with schooling and processes of cultural support (Munns & McFadden 2000). The various educational processes we will be discussing in this chapter are indeed complex but crucial for you to understand as a teacher, for it is through your actions that students can actualise pathways to opportunity and success.

Making sense of education and disadvantage

To make sense of this chapter it will be important for you to think in terms of certain school practices having unintended social and educational consequences that operate to entrench disadvantage. It is just as important for you to realise as well that you as a teacher have a crucial role to play in making the education for students in your class relevant, productive and positive. Research is showing time and again that it is the concrete actions and decisions of teachers that have the most significant impact on students (American Council on Education 1999; Ailwood et al. 2000). This chapter will reinforce that the most important factor in success for disadvantaged students is the influence of the teacher.

The chapter will also explore the way in which oppositional student response to education is dependent upon context, that is, the subject being taught, the teacher, and their particular teaching style. For many students, the education experienced is disempowering rather than empowering. Both the curriculum of schooling and the pedagogical approach taken by teachers is clearly implicated in processes of educational disablement. In this sense, curriculum and teaching style is central to the continued production of social inequality.

Indeed, what teachers teach, how they teach it, and the way that student learning is assessed, all convey powerful messages to students about what knowledge, skills and attitudes the teacher (and ultimately society, through a publicly accountable school curriculum) considers both important and valid.

Schooling and life chances

Students do not learn in a vacuum. School is a place where much complex interaction takes place that has a significant impact on the identity formation of young people and their consequent success in adult life (Evans 1994). Fitzgerald's (1978) work *Outcomes of schooling: aspects of success and failure*, a report to the Commission of Inquiry into Poverty in the late 1970s, reported on the impact of educational and cultural disadvantage on people who were poor. His findings echo over the years, and the themes and threads of his work still speak to us with insight and continued relevance. He argued that (pp. 5–6):

> Children and teenagers of . . . poor families have restricted opportunities to benefit from educational services . . . Poor students are much more likely to be found among the 'early leavers' who, . . . face a common prospect of long periods of unemployment or a succession of dead-end jobs. Hence failure at school is often a prelude to a lifetime experience of defeat or limited chances for success.
>
> It is evident that a lot of disadvantage suffered by poor people is embedded in the structures and processes of the education system itself . . .
>
> Unresponsive and discriminatory practices followed in education find their counterparts within the economic systems and the industrial work force.

He also said that all parents, regardless of socioeconomic background, desire success for their children and that the concrete practices of teachers in schools intersect with the needs of students, particularly young people striving to find their personal identity, to produce either satisfaction or opposition. It is worth quoting at length from his report about the relationship between young people and schooling (p. 6):

> In expressing their needs young people state an overwhelming preference for useful experiences linked with 'personal and social development' and 'preparation for life in society and work' rather than for 'academic qualifications'. But they often feel compelled to continue with 'unreal' or irrelevant curricula in a vague quest for formal credentials. This arbitrary order of things serves to reinforce the status of teenagers as children at a time when the development and emotional forces within them demand experiences which help towards establishing their own autonomy, practical and social competence, vocational clarification and personal adult identity . . . Learning has become an abstract 'academic' thing . . . [student] interest wanes — particularly during grades nine and ten in studying 'subjects for the sake of something else' as one [student] expressed it. 'I just lost interest' was a recurrent theme, and the resultant 'stirring' was universally reported. Hence teachers find strong undercurrents of resistance that undermine discipline, authority, relationships and academic performance. This almost forces teachers into an authoritarian — even police — role which makes authentic teacher-pupil relationships very difficult.

Finally, Fitzgerald pointed to the way in which education, though not necessarily school, was seen by most young people as the way to get on in life and as a pathway to relative success (pp. 6–7):

> . . . young people clearly indicated desired attributes in teachers. Teenagers wanted competence and control, but predominantly wanted teachers with a capacity to relate to students, to help, to care, to be human; the sort of role that teachers themselves sincerely desire . . .
>
> Our research has indicated that young people who have been classified as failures at school frequently prove to be keen learners in the world of work and often demonstrate on the job a marked capacity for complex intellectual thought and for problem solving. The great majority of our respondents report that their levels of self-confidence have risen strongly since they started work. Once this has occurred, many of them show interest in further training and education to increase their competence on the job. Their confidence as learners can be regained, provided of course that the job is well-designed for satisfaction. Herein lies the hope and the challenge for new learning structures . . . There is evidence that [education] can widen horizons and reawaken motivation for learning.

Fitzgerald's (1978) work helps us to keep the prospect of school as a place where human potential is realised rather than thwarted at the forefront of our thinking.

The school as an institution of social and cultural reproduction

Connell (1994, p. 129) states that evidence of 'socially unequal outcomes' is 'one of the most firmly established facts about Western-style educational systems in all parts of the world'. He continues:

> Children from working class, poor, and minority ethnic families continue to do worse than children from rich and middle-class families on tests and examinations, [are] more likely to be held back in grade, to drop out of school earlier, and [are] much less likely to enter college or university.

The dilemma for working class parents, according to Connell (1994, p. 134), is that the school system — and its link to broader systems of education — 'has become the main bearer of working-class hopes for a better future'. Connell concludes that education is a universal benefit containing powerful mechanisms of exclusion and privilege. We need to tease out the mechanisms of privilege and exclusion to which Connell refers.

Students 'at risk' of educational alienation

According to Evans (1994), approximately 15–30 per cent of students in many OECD countries are at risk of educational alienation or withdrawal and must be provided with support to prevent their rejection of schooling and consequent social, economic, political and cultural marginalisation. Those students deemed to be most 'at risk' of educational disadvantage and subsequent poor school retention and achievement include students:

- in poverty — the age young people leave school increases with family income, that is, youth from low income families tend to leave school earlier than those from high income families (Driessen & Dekkers 1997; Wyn & White 1997);
- from minority racial and ethnic groups, including those of indigenous heritage — the most oppressed group in Australian society (Hinkley & McInerney 1998; McFadden, Munns & Simpson 1999);
- who live in low socioeconomic status single-parent families (Roscigno 1998);
- who have experienced or are experiencing homelessness, have suffered physical, sexual and emotional or drug and alcohol abuse (McFadden 1996);
- who have participated in juvenile crime (Juvenile Justice Advisory Council of NSW 1993);
- who have families or parents (especially single-parent or step-families) engaging in frequent geographical mobility (Astone & McLanahan 1994);
- who lack supportive social, emotional and technical structures that emphasise the importance of education (Rosenfeld, Richman & Bowen 1998); and
- who recognise or are conscious of their own powerless status within society (Connell 1994).

Towards an explanation of student resistance to education

In the mid- to late-1970s and into the 1980s, many Marxist writers on education said that schools simply mirrored the inequity of capitalist society and that there was nothing that students or teachers could do about that (Bowles & Gintis 1976). This was a very pessimistic view of the role of education in social change.

Researchers like Willis (1977) (see also Willis 1981, 1983) did not agree with this pessimistic view of education. Willis set out to study the processes of social reproduction by studying the cultural relations of working-class males in an inner city English school in Birmingham. He argued that the students he studied, 'the lads', resisted the dominant social values and meanings of society by resisting the form of education that school offered. Willis believed that the resistance of students to what it was that schools were teaching, and to the educational practices in school, was a creative cultural response to a teaching paradigm whose social relations and cultural form embodied the oppressive essence of capitalist society.

Using working-class culture as a resource and appropriating elements of popular culture, Willis argued the lads constructed a 'counter culture' in opposition to the culture of schooling that mirrored the shop floor culture of the workplace, valorising manual work and manualist forms of action and despising intellectual work as feminine. Ironically, in choosing to oppose school, the working-class boys in Willis' study rejected the promise of upward mobility through education, and of their own volition, cemented their existing class position.

McRobbie (1991) carried out similar work with working-class girls. She found that the girls in her study rejected the female school ethos of passivity and domesticity for sexuality. They too resisted school, but again, as with the boys, their rejection of school operated to cement their own domestic oppression.

In the early 1980s, Connell et al. (1982) in Australia, like Willis in the UK, also reacted against the negativity of social reproductive positions and wanted to find out what the relationship between schooling and inequality really was. His research team was interested in how schools and teachers could 'make a difference' to students' lives. The outcomes of the research pointed to a positive role for education in social change. They found that the economy certainly did have effects on opportunities provided for individuals but that to say schools were simply servants of the capitalist order was simplistic and misleading. The work also highlighted the importance of the following factors in any analysis of the relationship between education and social disadvantage:

- cultural background of teachers;
- curriculum on offer to students;
- mismatch between curriculum offered and student interests and culture;
- mismatch between teacher culture and student interests and culture; and
- influence of home background on student success.

Research in this area and at this time clarified the crucial role of curriculum and teaching practice in the reproduction of social disadvantage. Connell et al. (1982) highlighted the way that the classroom is a site where there is a dramatic interplay of systems, policy and personality. Both teacher and taught bring to the classroom exchange experiences and cultural backgrounds. The teaching of curriculum clearly occurred in a defined social setting within a cultural context.

The 'hidden curriculum'

As well as arguing that schools mirrored the social and economic structures of society some theorists argued that the language and symbols of school worked against certain cultural groups who both lacked the cultural capital to succeed in school and who were left behind in trying to achieve it (Bourdeiu & Passeron 1977). In this sense, the classic work of writers like Giroux (1983) and Apple (1982) alerted educators to a 'hidden curriculum' of schooling that influences students' learning of the roles, norms, attitudes and structures of the classroom (which reflect those in society), and thus which effectively prepare them for the fulfilment of socially and culturally reproductive roles as adults.

The 'hidden curriculum' refers to the values and patterns of behaviour, including language use, that are often not formally taught, but are integral parts of the education system, such as:

- the teaching method;
- type of assessments used;
- the tone, language and behaviour of the teacher; and
- the attitudes and behaviour of classmates.

Within this hidden curriculum exists 'high status knowledge' that is considered by society to be important, providing access to high-status, high-power occupations within the economy. However, the school system, according to other influential writers like Willis (1983), does not encourage nor allow disadvantaged students to attain this knowledge. Schools thereby act as a mechanism of social reproduction because they are seen to close off rather than open up opportunities for disadvantaged people.

Put simply, the administrative environment of the high school is said to be characterised by independent, masculine learning environments, more suited to the autonomous, ambitious and competitive learning styles of Anglo-Saxon, middle-class males (Connell 1994). Female students, those of different ethnic origins and the economically and geographically disadvantaged, consequently learn that to succeed in society they must adopt certain middle-class behaviours. For example, school systems value and reward such things as independence, individualism, academic achievement and competitiveness. If students do not realise this and respond appropriately they may resign themselves to being less successful in modern Western society (Askew & Ross 1989).

The role of language was seen as crucial to the operation of the hidden curriculum of schooling. As Willis said (1977, p. 124), 'for the working class the cultural is in a battle with language'. He also said that language was central to 'the lads' eventual self-imposed exile to the shop floor. Language, he said, was the mediator between student and teacher culture and an extremely effective and reliable political tool, regulating and reifying boundaries of race, class and gender. In language we have our most effective 'symbolic resource' — the 'primary instrument that we use to communicate. It is the highest ordering of our sensuous impressions of the world and the ultimate basis of our hope and capacity to control it' (Willis 1990, p. 11).

Resistance to teachers and teaching

Students, regardless of their class, race or gender, express a belief in the utility of education for pursuing their goals in life. However, this belief does not necessarily coincide with acceptance of the form schooling takes. What students are constantly rejecting or sometimes, at best, merely complying with regardless of class, gender, race and ethnicity is schooling that disempowers them (McFadden 1995). For example, Wehlage, Smith and Lipman (1992) state that students placed in low ability classes tend to endure reductivist teaching characterised by (pp. 85–6):

> . . . repetition of drill and practice and the accumulation of fragmented bits of information with no apparent relevance to either real world problems or the kinds of thinking tasks productive adults perform.

This limits students' access to knowledge and therefore their power to determine the options in their lives. This form of teaching has been referred to as the pedagogy of poverty, a teaching style consisting of routine and repetitive tasks and surveillance. As Hatton notes (1998, p. 15), as a form of teaching it:

> . . . ironically gives more power to students than its practitioners realise . . . [and] is a form

of pedagogy which students might have an interest in maintaining since it allows them to abdicate responsibility for their own learning.

Research consistently shows that students, regardless of gender, race, ethnicity or class, react against what they perceive as poor teaching methods. For example, Foley (1991), detailing the results of an ethnographic study of South Texas society and schools conducted over a 15-year period, saw student opposition to teachers as dependent upon the context, the subject being taught, the teacher, and the teacher's particular teaching style. The most common criticism made by students of schooling was that work was not challenging and was seen as boring (p. 545).

> In this study, schoolwork did not challenge academic workers to be creative and develop their potential. Pupils therefore enjoyed outwitting teachers and slowing down the boring routines of pedagogical formalism.

As Connell notes (1994, p. 137), particularly for students in disadvantaged schools:

> Conventional subject matter and texts and traditional teaching methods and assessment techniques turn out to be sources of systematic difficulty. They persistently produce boredom. Enforcing them heightens the problem of discipline, and so far as they are successfully enforced, they divide pupils between an academically successful minority and an academically discredited majority.

What many students often find themselves faced with are pedagogical contexts that they find inappropriate to their needs. For many students, education is experienced as disempowering rather than empowering. Both the curriculum of schooling as well as the pedagogical approaches taken by teachers are clearly implicated in this process of educational disablement. Students from certain kinds of backgrounds have experiences of schooling that restrict their opportunity to extend their knowledge and that place them in powerless and subordinate positions as learners (McFadden 1995).

This occurs because of the educational practices of schools (Connell 1994). For example, streaming on perceived ability, and practices such as setting rote learning tasks for those perceived as unable to learn, all affect the process of learning. Perceptions about student capabilities are often made by teachers on the basis of race, ethnicity, class and gender and operate to restrict opportunity to learn in the first place (Mac an Ghaill 1994; Muncey & McQuillan 1996; O'Connor 1997). As Cooper (1993, p. 15) points out:

> There is a compelling body of school-based research which can be seen to relate to various aspects of attribution theory. A number of important studies have shown that the particular identity that comes to be held by a school pupil can owe a great deal to the preconceptions and assumptions that teachers have about their pupils . . . What seems to have been regularly demonstrated over the last thirty years . . . is that school pupils are often keen to embrace the identities which schools and teachers ascribe to them. The attribution process sets in motion the self-fulfilling prophecy whereby behaviour (by teacher and pupil) begins to conform to the initial attribution.

In other words, students carry with them the identities that the practices and procedures of schooling help to construct and it is this identity that they have available as a resource to deploy in future educational encounters. Many students respond to a particular form of schooling which says to them that they are not suitable for, or are indeed incapable of, education by rejecting or opposing it. This is a response that is entirely understandable (McFadden & Walker 1997).

Emile Durkheim, who lived from 1858–1917, was a key sociologist whose central interest was how social order was preserved. For Durkheim, social order was a moral issue (Furlong 1991). Furlong notes that educational sociologists working in the area of student resistance are all 'Durkheim's children' in that their focus is on the exploration of 'social circumstances', which lead to unacceptable student actions rather than on student pathology (p. 295). In his analysis of Durkheim's legacy, Varenne (1995) argues that Durkheim, if faced with the oppositional behaviour so common in schools today, would probably have responded as follows (p. 383):

> He would probably talk of people cursing teachers, disrupting classrooms, and dropping out, as symptoms of something pathological at work. The pathology would however be a social pathology, not an individual one. It would be the sign of the need to investigate how particular instances of institutions were not operating in such a fashion as to require the kind of disordering resistance that someone like Willis (1977) documents.

Following this line of argument, it may be that the key factor in students' response to schooling, and in determining educational outcomes, is the capacity of teachers to understand the students, their backgrounds, social and economic circumstances, needs for knowledge, and intellectual capacities; and to build on that understanding with pedagogical and curriculum practices that challenge and engage students, expand their options and assist them to solve their problems and achieve their goals (Walker 1988). As McFadden and Walker (1997) note, such an approach recognises the existence of cultural constraints, but also recognises the potential of education to enable change rather than be socially and culturally reproductive.

The impact of curriculum, pedagogy, assessment and school organisation

Basil Bernstein's work (see Bernstein 1996 for an overview) has helped educators to deconstruct the relays of power and control at work in schools that operate to keep people in disadvantaged positions and limit their access to knowledge. Bernstein sees curriculum, pedagogy and assessment practices essentially as semiotic message systems. He argues that what is taught, the way it is taught and the way the success of learning is assessed communicates powerful messages to students about:

- what is important to the teacher;
- the world and their place and potential in it;
- appropriate social relationships; and
- what is considered valid and worthwhile knowledge.

Cumming's (1994) and Cormack's (1996) work utilises Bernstein's framework in suggesting appropriate curriculum and teaching practice for secondary school students. Cumming points to the role 'outmoded' curriculum, pedagogical and assessment practices play in the alienation from schooling of many young people (p. 7). Their work has also been informed by notions of student empowerment (Boomer et al. 1992). Cormack's (1996) work on student alienation in the middle years of schooling, a Commonwealth of Australia Project of National Significance, specifically targets curriculum and pedagogy:

Curriculum: There is evidence to suggest that the curriculum can be a factor in the alienation of students in the middle years of schooling. The term 'boring' is frequently cited in reports from student surveys and focus group discussions conducted as part of this study (and in other research) in the context of learning programs . . .

Pedagogy: The learning environments that are created by teachers, together with methods that they employ can contribute to student alienation in the middle years. Relying on a set of conventional teaching strategies (e.g. teacher talk, notes, structured question and answer exercises), can stifle student motivation, interest and achievement . . .

Organisation: Timetabling arrangements, staffing schedules and student grouping procedures can have an impact with regard to student alienation in the middle years. For many young people, daily routines associated with a large number of teachers, short periods of time, and frequent locational changes, are reducing their capacity to learn effectively (Australian Curriculum Studies Association 1995: unpaginated).

Structuring student opportunity — some illustrations

Schooling, and education more broadly, structures student opportunity in both subtle and direct ways. This kind of structuring occurs in relation to categories of disadvantage including gender, race, socioeconomic status and ethnicity. In essence, students' educational experiences are structured through the interplay of teacher assumptions and expectations and play out in classroom practice and interaction.

Girls and technology

In a fascinating application of Bernstein's ideas, Singh (1995) demonstrated how a primary school technology studies classroom in Queensland structured opportunity for valid realisation of knowledge differently for boys and girls. Some girls in the class, who in fact had greater computer expertise and access than many of the boys, were positioned by the discourse of the teacher as powerless to represent their knowledge as valid. When a problem came up with the computers it was the boys who were called on by the male teacher to do the fixing. The girls, on the other hand, were often called to run errands as classroom messengers. When the girls related their experience of the classroom to the researcher they discussed their frustration with their role. They were having their interest in and enthusiasm for computers and technology eroded by the expectations, language and behaviour of the teacher. The boys were thought more able to handle the technology and he behaved accordingly. The classroom then played a role in the girls making a seemingly free choice to eventually opt out of computers — confirming the expectations of the teacher. This 'free' choice would obviously affect the girls in the future.

Street Kids Access Tertiary Education (SKATE)

The SKATE research examined the effects of a tertiary education bridging program on the lives of students educationally and socially disadvantaged by episodes of homelessness (McFadden 1996, 1998). Amongst other things, the study explored what students in this 'second chance' education program thought about their first chance at education (Munns & McFadden 2000). Most of these students had been considered 'drop-outs' (Rumberger 1995). When interviewed about their experience of the first chance, the average age of these students was 21.

Most of the SKATE students had negative memories of schooling. But for some these memories were described as 'painful' or 'horrible'. Being 'left behind' academically led to pain, and 'being different' — whether it be physically, racially or academically — led to 'horrible' or 'awful' consequences. For Birk, her memories of the Quota system of spelling, still used in many primary schools today, best illustrates how getting behind leads to being academically different and inevitably to pain and embarrassment:

Birk: I remember in 6th grade when I finally worked out what had happened to me, like how left behind I was, um, we had this thing, it was a special spelling, and what you did was, everybody started off with twelve spelling words . . .
MMcF: Quota!
Birk: Yeah, that's right, the Quota system, right. I remember they started me off on six spelling words, and that's in 6th grade, and I couldn't do that, so then they took me back to the Year 5 spelling words, and this is when I was in 6th grade, and I couldn't even do that. I went back to Year 3, in 6th grade. I was still on six words, and like all the others they're on like 24, in Year 6. Like it was just really bad . . . it was awful I remember 'cause you had to like read out your score in front of the whole class, and it was like, oh shit, 'cause everybody knew I was doing like 3rd grade work . . . it was awful.

For Birk, the easiest way out of not suffering the ignominy of ritual embarrassment was to find as many ways of not attending school as she could, or when there, to absent herself from class.

School was also seen in retrospect by many students as a 'waste of time' because for them it had proved 'frustrating' and been full of 'problems', particularly with teachers. There is a direct link, however, from school to home in the chain of frustration, the medium being the emotionality of the child. What was happening at home, whether the teachers knew it or not, was affecting the students' responses to school. And students remembered being absolutely frustrated in their attempts to reach out and express this emotionality:

Jeremy: School was a waste of time for me, like a real frustrating time that I was trying so hard to get someone's attention to say look my dad's doing these things to all of us . . .
MMcF: Can you remember all of that?
Jeremy: Oh, shit yeah!

The way schools treated the emotional fragility of these students is perhaps best captured by Eleanor in this powerful indictment of her schooling:

Eleanor: School was a waste of time for me.
MMcF: What was a waste of time about it?
Eleanor: Well, instead of being encouraged to do well, and to use it to my benefit, I think I was destroyed as a person through school. (. . .) For instance through my behaviour, like being raped and what not, and all this anger, instead of dealing with it, I was sort of broken more, in a sense, you know, but I was expressing emotions which were not accepted.
MMcF: So are you saying that the sort of anxiety you were feeling there wasn't supported?
Eleanor: No, it was, um, how can I put this . . . it was punishable!

'Conventional' schools are seen as places of 'control' and 'conformity', places where there are 'no compromises'. They are also seen as places where the problems students frame in response to the constraints under which they live are not addressed. While this may seem harsh, it is a perception shared by the students. This perception of 'control' coupled with those of lack of responsiveness and support leaves many students seemingly no option but to 'opt out'. For a small number of students school was seen as a good place to be, but this was primarily because it gave some respite or escape from home.

Successful schools and classrooms

Recent research suggests that a pedagogical framework that is sensitive to cultural issues and difference, and which recognises the capacity of students to engage in decisions about their own learning can enable students to mediate disempowering educational experiences and construct a positive self-image as a learner. As Cooper says (1993, p. 30) in relation to the education of disaffected students:

. . . the process of knowledge creation is opened up to the pupils who, as a result, come to develop confidence in their abilities to explore and manipulate knowledge. They come to develop a sense of ownership of the knowledge they create, and a faculty for asking pertinent and critical questions . . .

Implied here is a sense of power over the process of education. Cooper's (1993) framework emphasises activity, responsibility, personalising knowledge, flexibility, choice and ownership as opposed to passivity, distance, regulation, and control. His work has been mirrored by others.

Family and community

The research indicates that successful schools and classrooms do not just happen. They are successful because they recognise and cater for the involvement of family and community and construct relevant and meaningful programs. In addition, the teachers of successful schools translate relevant programs into productive and achievement-oriented classroom practice sensitive to individual needs.

Wang, Haertel and Walberg (1996) suggest that classroom, home and community, and school contexts play a key role in fostering development and educational achievement for all students. Active engagement of family members (such as participating in school management teams, involvement in parent-developed workshops, provision of tutoring, and assisting teachers in classroom or after-school activities) also associated with improved student achievement; increased school attendance; and decreased student drop-out, delinquency, and pregnancy rates. Most notable is the acknowledgment that the love, interest, and support of a single family member can mitigate against adversities and promote students' educational engagement.

Teachers and classroom practices

Wang, Haertel and Walberg (1996) argue a teacher's concern, high expectations, and role-modelling are key protective factors that mitigate against the likelihood of academic failure, particularly for students in difficult life circumstances. Sustained, close relationships between the teacher and the student can reduce stress and provide positive supports, as well as help students to develop the values and attitudes needed to persevere in their schoolwork and achieve a high level of academic performance. Teachers are also viewed as promoting educational resilience by encouraging students to master new experiences, believe in their own efficacy, and take responsibility for their own learning.

Importantly, classroom practices that consistently produce achievement advantages in 'at risk' youth, include:

- maximising learning time;
- setting high expectations for all students;
- providing ample opportunities for student–teacher interaction;
- maintaining a high degree of classroom engagement;
- tailoring instruction to meet the needs of individual students;
- engaging students in setting goals and making learning decisions; and
- participating in group learning activities.

Peart and Campbell (1999) found that four characteristics consistently emerged as critical for effective teachers of disadvantaged young people:

1. good interpersonal skills;
2. the ability to communicate subject matter well through good instructional methods;
3. the ability to motivate students; and
4. not allowing ethnicity to affect their treatment or expectations of students.

Peart and Campbell (1999) also found that the teachers most effective in encouraging disadvantaged students in their schoolwork were those who made a connection with these students that communicated respect and caring on a personal level. Interaction on this level was viewed as validating the personal culture of the student. Yet this approach, they said, has to be balanced with appropriate self-disclosure as the teacher shares his or her feelings. They also found teacher enthusiasm to be important in fostering interest and attentiveness in the student. Those teachers who are able to set standards and maintain strong control in the classroom must also be listeners who allow students to take responsibility for learning. Also integral to this teacher characteristic is the frequent and suitable use of encouragement and compliments regarding student behaviour that is appropriate for the teaching context.

Further, they found a teacher's high expectations and belief in students' abilities to be key factors influencing students' academic achievement and may lead students to internalise these high expectations. Teachers who have high expectations of students while clearly conveying a belief in their capabilities are more likely to develop positive emotional connections with students. The key seems to be conveying a belief in student capabilities along with holding high expectations. This can be and is achieved by teachers maintaining high academic standards for all of their students, regardless of ethnicity, race, gender, or social class, and communicating a belief that all students can meet these high standards.

Schools

School-wide practices associated with student achievement and psychosocial benefits include:

- a school-wide culture that reinforced students' academic accomplishments;
- public recognition, awards and incentives associated with school-level achievement;
- smaller organisational units (mini-schools, charter schools, and houses);
- an emphasis on student involvement and belonging that reduced feelings of alienation and disengagement;
- attachment to teachers, classmates and the school;
- effective and responsive instructional programs that shield against adverse circumstances;
- student engagement in school life; and
- positive social interactions among peers and with adults.

The 'resilient' student

The notion of the 'resilient' student is becoming prevalent in discussions of 'at-risk' students who succeed in education against the odds. The resilience construct has provided the conceptual base for a series of studies on the capacity of adolescents from minority backgrounds to maintain a positive self-concept and constructive attitudes toward school and education despite exposure to adverse social circumstances. For example, Jackson and Martin (1998) have described the way individuals develop protective factors that enhance resilience.

Rosenfeld, Richman and Bowen (1998) have identified social support provided by the family, the peer group, the school, and the community as an important characteristic of resilient students. Because of its association with resilience, they argue that social support is likely to promote academic resilience and positive educational outcomes for students. In general, they found that higher-achieving at-risk students appear to receive more social support from their parents, teachers, and friends than do low-achieving students from the same at-risk categories.

Key factors: family, school and community

The research cited above, that certain characteristics of family, school and community environments may alter or even reverse expected negative outcomes and enable students to manifest resilience despite risk, points to certain key factors. These can be grouped into three major categories:

1. caring and supportive family, peer and student/teacher relationships;
2. positive and high teacher expectations; and
3. opportunities for meaningful family, community and individual participation at school.

Key factors: programs

It is unrealistic to think that any program or effort will eliminate all at-risk conditions. Programs are, however, being put into place that address the needs of disadvantaged students at risk of educational failure or withdrawal and also prepare adults to work with learners at risk. Such programs according to MacDonald, Manning and Leary (1999):

- address more than one at-risk condition or behaviour;
- involve teachers, administrators, parents, and community organisations in collaborative efforts;
- teach learners to accept responsibility for academic achievement, behaviours, and long-term educational plans;
- provide opportunities that address both academic and non-academic needs (such as programs that increase self-esteem and provide opportunities for students to discover useful ways to spend their leisure time);
- prepare students who are at risk for instructional and advisory experiences in advance, so that they will understand what teachers expect of them and what the learning outcomes are intended to be;
- ensure that all programs and experiences have real-world perspectives, so that students see how instructional and advisory experiences relate to their own lives;
- provide students with supplemental educational opportunities by using mentors to serve as positive role models;
- ensure that teachers understand what puts a student at risk, what behaviour the student might show as a result, and what school programs are appropriate for them;
- teach teachers to be able to identify students who are at risk and to plan, implement, and evaluate educational and advisory experiences for them; and
- ensure that teachers have opportunities to work as team members with other teachers and parents in collaborative settings.

Clearly, addressing the needs of disadvantaged students is a collaborative activity involving teachers, family, the community and students themselves. The involvement is not merely around the academic but also the non-academic concerns and needs of students and relating these to community, family and teacher expectations. When there is a better mutual understanding of teacher expectations and student needs there is obviously more chance of educational success.

Productive pedagogy

The most recent research (Ailwood et al. 2000) on the relationship between education and disadvantage focuses on productive pedagogy. Compared to students at risk of school failure, students influenced by productive pedagogy involving the concepts in the following list have higher aspirations, more achievement motivation, and better social and academic self-concepts:

- students spending more time working independently;
- motivated and enthusiastic teachers spending more time interacting with students;
- students being more satisfied with their schoolwork and peer relationships;
- classroom rules made clear to students;
- teachers being supportive and holding high expectations of students;
- student-centred and highly responsive classroom learning environments with well-structured classroom management systems;
- teachers engaging in ongoing professional development programs based on implementation needs identified by teachers and administrators;
- shared decision-making (within the classroom and school);
- actively constructing and imparting knowledge from a standpoint that is relevant to and recognises the lived realities of disadvantaged minority groups (directed at enhancing students' critical understanding of how certain groups in society are marginalised through the complex processes of social interaction within institutional settings, that also act to perpetuate inequalities that other groups benefit from);
- teachers providing well-managed classrooms and encouraging parental involvement;
- challenging instruction that encourages higher order thinking; and
- encouraging student choice in selecting instructional activities.

Productive pedagogies, such as the abovementioned, ensure that four basic dimensions are satisfied in order to cater to the needs of all students from a variety of sociocultural groups. According to Ailwood et al. (2000), these dimensions must include:

1. *intellectual quality* — comprising deep knowledge, deep understanding, higher order thinking, substantive conversation, meta-language, and an approach to knowledge as problematic;
2. *relevance* — including background knowledge, problem-based curriculum, knowledge integration;
3. *a supportive classroom environment* — involving student self-regulation, engagement, social support, explicit criteria, student direction; and
4. *recognition of difference* — ensuring inclusivity, narrative, cultural knowledge, citizenship and group identity.

Recent research has also shown that effective teaching must address not only the cognitive but also the affective (that is, feelings, attitudes and values) dimensions of a student's life (Peart & Campbell 1999). The ability or inability to establish a positive student–teacher relationship clearly influences the learning climate and the teacher's impact in the life of the student. The participants in Peart's and Campbell's study highlighted the role of the teacher's interpersonal skills as a determinant of the teacher's effectiveness. According to their research, students also view effective teachers as being noted for their knowledge of subject matter, their ability to communicate material, and their evident enthusiasm for their subject. Related to interpersonal style and teaching ability was the ability of the teacher to motivate the student. Many of the participants in the research viewed an active intervention in their lives as an indication that teachers really cared and wanted them to do well.

Conclusion

At the beginning of this chapter we said that we hoped its contents would challenge you to think differently about the institution called school. Hopefully, what the chapter has done is help you to start posing some critical questions about your practice as a teacher. Your questions will no doubt broadly revolve around:

- social relations and power;
- the division of labour in the knowledge production process; and
- the images of identity that students develop through education.

We believe the more questions you have at this stage the better. Some questions you may find yourself asking follow. What are the social relations at work in my classroom; between me as teacher and students, and between students? Does my framing of pedagogy allow for sharing, collaboration and participation in knowledge production? And what of the products of this knowledge production process? Who owns the knowledge? What are the products? Are they authentic and meaningful to the students? How culturally relevant are they? Do they have only me (as teacher) as audience or do they speak to wider social realities and concerns?

Further, what is the division of labour in the knowledge production process in my classroom? Who selects content? Who decides pacing and sequencing of lessons? Who judges success? Are my students alienated from the knowledge production process I want them to control by their very lack of control of the process? These are searching and challenging questions.

And finally, how will the students in my class see themselves as learners? This chapter has suggested that schooling is more likely to meet the needs of students in a rapidly changing society by addressing how they can actively participate and be included in the processes of their own learning. By exercising some control over (that is, determining and negotiating) the direction of their own learning, students may indeed feel more in control of their lives.

Education has a social, economic and institutional context. Each has to be taken into account to produce valid readings of the effect of schooling on students' lives. In the classroom, the economic, personal and the social meet and it is here that students and teachers must negotiate their lives. The result helps to define the sort of individuals students become and the choices they see as being available in their lives as they unfold after school. It is clear that schooling experiences help to construct students' personal and social identities. Students experience these identities as either a resource to draw on, gain strength from, and deploy in other learning contexts or as a constraint.

INQUIRY STRATEGIES

1. Think about school as a social institution. Go back to basics and discuss in a group why you think public schools were established. Now think about why you believe we have mandated public education today. What then are the links in purpose between the schools of the past and of today and what are the major differences?

2. For what reasons do you think secondary school students sometimes choose to reject school? Can you put these reasons into any particular categories and do you think that such choices about schooling are more prevalent for certain students? What kinds of students might they be?

3. What would be your interests and concerns if you were in your middle to final years of secondary schooling at present? What might be the problems in your life that would occupy you and that you would like to find solutions to? What messages might you be getting from other youth and mainstream media about your potential role in the world?

4. You are patently and demonstrably an educational success story. Well, you've made it this far! What factors do you think have contributed to your success as a student? Think particularly about your life as a secondary student. And if you were not a great success story in secondary school, then what made the difference for you?

References

Adams, I. (1998). The educational plight of Indigenous Australian students in the early years of schooling. *Unicorn*, 24, pp. 5–15.

Ailwood, J., Chant, D., Gore, J., Hayes D., Ladwig, J., Lingard, B., Luke, A., Mills, M. and Warry, M. (2000). The four dimensions of productive pedagogy: Narratives and findings from the school reform longitudinal study field. Work Paper presented to the Change in Education Research Group Symposium, University of Technology, Sydney, 4–5 February.

American Council on Education (1999). *To Touch the Future: Transforming the Way Teachers are Taught. An action agenda for college and university presidents*. Washington: American Council on Education.

Apple, M. (1982). *Education and Power*. London: Routledge & Kegan Paul.

Askew, S. & Ross, C. (1989). *Boys Don't Cry: Boys and Sexism in Education*. Philadelphia: Open University Press.

Astone, N.M & McLanahan, S.S. (1994). Family structure, residential mobility, and school dropout: A research note. *Demography*, 31, pp. 575–584.

Australian Curriculum Studies Association (ACSA) (1995). The middle years of schooling and alienation. News sheet included with *Curriculum Perspectives*, 15 (unpaginated).

Bernstein, B. (1996). *Pedagogy, Symbolic Control and Identity: Theory, Research, Critique*. London: Taylor & Francis.

Boomer, G., Lester, N., Onore, C. & Cook, J. (eds) (1992). *Negotiating the Curriculum: Educating for the 21st Century*. London: The Falmer Press.

Bourdieu, P. & Passeron, J.C. (1977). *Reproduction in Education Society and Culture*. London: Sage.

Bowles, S. & Gintis, H. (1976). *Schooling in Capitalist America*. London: Routledge & Kegan Paul.

Connell, R.W. (1994). Poverty and education, *Harvard Educational Review*, 64, pp. 125–149.

Connell, R.W., Ashenden, D.W., Kessler, S. & Dowsett, G.W. (1982). *Making the Difference: Schools, Families and Social Division*. St Leonards: Allen and Unwin.

Cooper, P. (1993). *Effective Schools for Disaffected Students: Integration and Segregation*. London: Routledge.

Cormack, P. (1996). *From Alienation to Engagement: Opportunities for Reform in the Middle Years of Schooling*. Canberra: Australian Curriculum Studies Association.

Cumming, J. (1994). *Schooling, Futures and Learning: Report of a forum on shaping school futures*. A report for the Incorporated Association of Registered Teachers of Victoria.

Driessen, G. & Dekkers, J. (1997). Educational opportunities in the Netherlands: Policy, students' performance and issues. *International Review of Education*, 43, pp. 299–315.

Evans, P. (1994). Tackling educational disadvantage. *OECD Observer*, 186, pp. 20–22.

Fitzgerald, R. (1978). *Outcomes of Schooling: Aspects of Success and Failure*. Report of the Commission of Inquiry into Poverty. Canberra: Australian Government Printing Service.

Foley, D.E. (1991). Rethinking school ethnographies of colonial settings: a performance perspective of reproduction and resistance. *Comparative Education Review*, 35, pp. 532–551.

Furlong, V.J. (1991). Disaffected pupils: reconstructing the sociological perspective. *British Journal of Sociology of Education*, 12, pp. 293–307.

Giroux, H.A. (1983). *Theory and Resistance in Education: a Pedagogy for the Opposition*. South Hadley: Bergin Press.

Hatton, E. (1998). *Understanding Teaching: Curriculum and the Social Context of Schooling* (2nd edition). Sydney: Harcourt Brace.

Hinkley, J. & McInerny, D. (1988). Facilitating conditions and academic achievement in a cultural context. Paper presented at the Annual Meeting of the American Educational Research Association San Diego, 13–17 April.

Jackson, S. & Martin, P.Y. (1998). Surviving the care system: education and resilience. *Journal of Adolescence*, 21, pp. 569–583.

Juvenile Justice Advisory Council of NSW (1993). *Future Directions for Juvenile Justice in NSW*. Sydney: Juvenile Justice Advisory Council of NSW.

Mac an Ghaill, M. (1994). *The Making of Men: Masculine Sexualities and Schooling*. Buckingham: Open University Press.

MacDonald, R.H., Manning, M.L. & Leary, S.L. (1999). Working with young adolescents at-risk: lessons learned from Project Enable. *Clearing House*, 73, pp. 25–28.

McFadden, M.G. (1995). Resistance to schooling and educational outcomes: questions of structure and agency. *British Journal of Sociology of Education*, 16, pp. 293–308.

McFadden, M.G. (1996). 'Second chance' education: accessing opportunity or recycling disadvantage? *International Studies in Sociology of Education*, 6, pp. 87–111.

McFadden, M.G. (1998). Boys and 'second chance' education: Same jeans different consequences. *Change: Transformations in Education*, 1, pp. 51–67.

McFadden, M., Munns, G. and Simpson, L. (1999). The battle to remain on higher ground: school curriculum and pedagogy versus culturally supported school resistance. Paper presented at AERA Annual Meeting (Montreal, Canada), 19–23 April.

McFadden, M.G. & Walker, J.C. (1997). Resistance theory. In L.Saha (ed), *International Encyclopedia of Sociology of Education*. London: Pergamon Press.

McRobbie, A. (1991). *Feminism and Youth Culture: From 'Jackie' to 'Just Seventeen'*. London: Macmillan.

Muncey, D.E. & McQuillan, P.J. (1996). *Reform and Resistance in Schools and Classrooms: An ethnographic view of the coalition of essential schools*. New Haven:Yale University Press.

Munns, G. & McFadden, M.G. (2000). First chance, second chance or last chance? Resistance and response to education. *British Journal of Sociology of Education*, 21 (1), pp. 59–75.

O'Connor, C. (1997). Dispositions toward (collective) struggle and educational resilience in the inner city: a case analysis of six African-American high school students. *American Educational Research Journal*, 34, pp. 593–629.

Peart, N.A. & Campbell, F.A. (1999). At-risk students' perceptions of teacher effectiveness. *Journal for a Just & Caring Education*, 5, pp. 269–284.

Roscigno, V.J. (1998). Race, institutional linkages and the reproduction of educational disadvantage. *Social Forces*, 76, pp. 1033–61.

Rosenfeld, L.B., Richman, J.M. and Bowen, G.L (1998). Supportive communication and school outcomes for academically 'at-risk' and other low income middle school students. *Communication Education*, 47, pp. 309–325.

Rumberger, R.W. (1995). Dropping out of middle school: a multilevel analysis of students and schools. *American Educational Research Journal*, 32, pp. 583–625.

Singh, P. (1995). Discourses of computing competence, evaluation and gender: the case of computer use in the primary classroom. *Discourse: studies in the cultural politics of education*, 16, pp. 81–110.

Varenne, H. (1995). The social facting of education: Durkheim's legacy. *Journal of Curriculum Studies*, 27, pp. 373–389.

Walker, J.C. (1988). *Louts and Legends: Male Youth Culture in an Inner City School*. St Leonards: Allen and Unwin.

Wang, M.C., Haertel, G.D. & Walberg, H.J. (1996). *Fostering educational resilience in inner-city schools*. Publication Series No. 4. Accessed online via Journals @ Ovid (Accession No. ED419856). Also available via: http://www.temple.edu.LSS. (retrieved 12 March 2000).

Wehlage, G., Smith, G. & Lipman, P. (1992). Restructuring urban schools: the New Futures experience. *American Educational Research Journal*, 29, pp. 51–93.

Willis, P. (1977). *Learning To Labour*. Farnborough: Saxon House.

Willis, P. (1981). Cultural Production is Different from Cultural Reproduction is Different from Social Reproduction is Different from Reproduction. *Interchange*, 12, pp. 48–67.

Willis, P. (1983). Cultural Production and Theories of Reproduction. In L. Barton and S. Walker (eds), *Race, Class and Education*. London: Croon Helm.

Willis, P.E. (1990). *Common Culture: Symbolic Work at Play in the Everyday Cultures of the Young*. Buckingham: Open University Press.

Wyn, J. & White, R. (1997). *Rethinking Youth*. St Leonards: Allen & Unwin.

PART THREE

Learning to Teach in Contemporary Australian Secondary Schools

CHAPTER **6** Communication and Relationships

CHAPTER **7** A Context for Learning

CHAPTER **8** Negotiating the Practicum

CHAPTER **9** Learning, Teaching and Technology

aving considered the rapidly changing social, economic and technological landscape in which today's schools operate, and the nature of today's secondary school students, the four chapters which follow develop practical strategies for the ways in which new teachers may become effective classroom practitioners.

Our first concern is to take account of teaching as a communicative activity and the centrality of communication and human relationships in educational processes. We develop a discussion of communication which takes account of not only that which occurs in classrooms between teachers and students, but also professional communication within the school and communication between the school and its parents and caregivers.

The chapter which follows examines more closely the actual classroom environment as a context for learning. It examines ways of thinking about both the 'what' and 'how' of learning and teaching in Australia's secondary schools. The chapter suggests that generative learning occurs when teachers and students work together to create a community of enquiry.

The penultimate chapter addresses the particular concerns and tensions which face pre-service teachers as they engage in the practicum. The rites of passage associated with the times when student teachers increasingly take on the responsibilities of classroom management and negotiate not only with their students, but also the teacher of the class, are not always smooth sailing. Competing expectations of the school students, the cooperating teacher and the university adviser need to be accommodated as you, the neophyte teacher, are developing your own personal theories of practice.

Finally, this part considers the ways in which technology may be used in teaching and learning such that school students become more active agents in transforming their own learning. This requires teachers to build different and more interactive learning environments and become more responsive to their students, whose knowledge of technology may far surpass their own.

6
CHAPTER

Communication and Relationships

If you get the chance, ask any high school teacher to talk about the number of people that they communicate with on any given day and the range of topics that they communicate about. One thing is certain, there will be lots of communicating!

Teaching is at heart a communicative activity. Working in a school means negotiating a myriad of relationships with students, colleagues, parents and other members of the school community. This chapter will take a broad look at the social relations between those within a school community. The following two chapters will connect ideas pertaining to communication and relationships more specifically to classroom learning and to the practicum. Our intent in this chapter is to examine some of the personal, social and ethical dimensions of relationships between teachers and others within a school community. The range of issues associated with communication and relationships in high schools is vast and in this chapter we will only consider some of these issues. The chapter is structured into three sections:

1. communication between teachers and students;
2. communication and relationships with other members of staff;
3. communication with parents, caregivers and others in the community.

We will use a set of relationship 'dilemmas' as a starting point for understanding processes of communication, learning how to participate in the communicative practices within a school and developing principles for those practices. Following each dilemma we suggest some possible courses of action and raise some issues and questions for further inquiry. Because of the wide range of issues and questions we have embedded the suggestions for further inquiry into the body of the chapter.

Communication is seemingly simple — we just do it. At the same time, each communicative act is incredibly complex — it requires a facility with language and knowledge of how to use that language in a range of social settings and for various purposes. How we communicate is also an expression of our identity and the social context in which that identity is created. The words and gestures we use, the clothes we wear and the tools we have access to are central to our identity and are an integral part of the ways in which we communicate. The ways we express ourselves can also be linked to our social circumstances. Thus patterns for communication and social relations can both shape and reflect our social backgrounds (gender, class, ethnicity, race, sexual orientation) and our location within particular institutions (Gee 1999; Poynton 2000). As a teacher working in a school some knowledge of the complexity of communication is vital both as part of learning to engage in the communicative practices that are part of a school culture and understanding how these practices relate to the educational and ethical responsibilities that teachers have.

Communication and relationships are good umbrella terms for bringing together ideas developed in educational psychology, educational sociology and related fields such as linguistics and philosophy. This chapter will attempt to weave some of these ideas together through an analysis of various communication and relationship dilemmas that teachers might face and by considering some practical ways of dealing with these dilemmas.

Communication between teachers and students

The intellectual, emotional and physical dimensions of teachers' work are clearly manifest in the relationships and patterns for communication that develop between students and teachers both in and outside classrooms. Think of a teacher moving around a classroom while students are working. In stopping and talking with particular students the teacher may be engaging intellectually with the task at hand and responding at an emotional level to the quality of work. At the same time the movement around the class and the physical distance between teacher and students communicate certain messages about a teacher's social role in the classroom. The intensity, the diversity, and the complexity of classroom communication and relationships can be both exciting in terms of educational possibilities and daunting in terms of managing the various webs of communication in a classroom. In this section of the chapter we consider, in the first instance, some of the conventions of classroom communication. We then go on to examine some communication dilemmas, the social, emotional and ethical issues underpinning these dilemmas, and some practical ways in which they can be addressed. The issues we have chosen are ones of common concern for beginning teachers — establishing relationships and persistent problems in relation to managing communication in the classroom.

In the introduction we alluded to the way in which communication and social relations both create and reflect particular institutional contexts. Think of the following examples of a teacher's communication with students: explaining a concept, admonishing a student for being late, writing an evaluative comment on a student's assignment, getting a class to pay attention, chatting with a group of students while on playground duty. Each of these communicative acts presupposes a relationship between a teacher and students that is predicated on their roles and positions within the institutional setting of the school. Teachers are invested with certain authority and responsibility within a school because of their knowledge and qualifications. Each time a teacher communicates with a student they are establishing and re-establishing their position in the classroom and the communicative conventions attached to this position. Some conventions may be formalised through policy such as school rules or departmental codes of conduct for teachers. Other conventions may be localised to the classroom, such as class rules or the degrees of formality in student/teacher relationships. Some patterns for communication will reflect the personalities of the individuals involved; other patterns and conventions may reflect broader social dynamics based on, for example, gender, class, ethnicity and age. When looking at the personal and social politics of teacher–student interactions it is possible to ask questions about the ways in which power and emotions are played out in these relationships and how this might enable and/or constrain participation in classroom practices (Boler 1999). The politics have educational and ethical consequences.

There are ethical and moral standards that underpin the communication and relationships that exist in classrooms. It is these standards that enable judgments to be made about whether particular sets of classroom communication are good or bad, effective or ineffective, ethical or unethical. In other words the communicative practices and relationships that are part of any classroom are based on sets of values. The standards can vary according to individual and societal values. Nick Burbules (1993), an educational philosopher, talks about trust, respect, tolerance, patience, willingness to listen, honesty and concern as communicative standards or moral concepts that are central to classroom communication. While these concepts are broad, they do provide a language for talking about the ethical dimensions of the communications and relationships between teachers and students in high schools.

In this section we present four dilemmas as a starting point for exploring some of the issues that teachers face establishing and maintaining good working relationships with students. Each of the dilemmas invites you to think about the role that you might adopt as a teacher, the principles that could be drawn on to guide practice in these contexts and practical activities that can foster forms of communication that are guided by these principles. Central to each of the dilemmas are questions relating to the principles and practices associated with defining, establishing, redefining and re-establishing social roles and relationships in the classroom.

The first two dilemmas are concerned with establishing patterns for communication and social roles in the classroom. The second two dilemmas are concerned with class situations in which there is tension or conflict between teachers and students. Each dilemma is intended as a starting point for discussion.

Starting up — dilemmas 1 and 2

One of the key aspects of teaching is to set up class relationships in which you and the students can work together to achieve various educational goals. This raises the questions: How do you start up a relationship with a class? How do you establish constructive patterns for communication and appropriate boundaries for relationships between teacher and students? We present two dilemmas relating to this issue. The first concerns the initial lessons with a class and the actions that can be taken to start up relationships in a productive way. The second dilemma explores the issue of friendship between teachers and students and raises questions about where lines should be drawn in student/teacher relationships.

Advice about establishing patterns for communication and relationships often revolves around classroom management. You may have heard the saying 'Don't smile until Christmas' or had it suggested to you that you get classroom management 'sorted out' first. These pieces of advice may serve a purpose, but they do not address the broader educational and ethical issues associated with classroom relationships, in particular how members of the class should treat each other and the ways in which a communication ethic can be established. In light of this consider dilemma one below.

Day One — dilemma 1

Carole Nishi was beginning her job at a school halfway through term 1. She had been doing casual work prior to this and was excited to finally pick up a long-term position. She was replacing a teacher who was on medical leave for three months. Carole did not have much time for preparation — the department head spent a few minutes with her in the morning briefing her on what each class was doing, and giving her an outline of the teacher's unit plans. Carole had Year 8 first period. The department head suggested that she start with a worksheet that he was giving his class and that they could talk in more detail after the class.

When Carole told the Year 8 class that she would be there for the next three months there were groans all round. The teacher that she was replacing was well liked by the students and Carole knew instantly that it would be hard work to replace him. Even in her first lesson with the class there were constant rejoinders — 'Mr Mac did not do things like this', 'Mr Mac let us talk', 'Mr Mac wasn't boring'. Carole also knew that the students were testing her out and pushing her, primarily because they were resentful of losing a teacher they liked and respected, and because their classroom routine for social studies had been changed.

The issues

For Carole, the dilemma is not simply starting up with a class, but starting up with a class that has established routines. This dilemma is not dissimilar to the situation that student teachers find themselves in during the practicum; that is, stepping into someone else's classroom and trying to find a position within pre-existing patterns of classroom communication. One of the issues in this case concerns the actions that can be taken by a teacher to define their own role in a class and articulate and establish patterns for classroom communication. In this case the teacher also has to step into someone else's shoes with little time for preparation and for a limited period of time.

Possible actions

Some teachers have a start-up plan that they put in place when beginning work with a new class. Obviously such a plan may vary according to the year level and the subject area. It should involve establishing expectations for classroom interactions that are consistent with teaching and learning objectives. It is also important to note that a start-up plan may take some time to implement. Establishing levels of trust and respect among members of a class can take time. The length of time that one has with a class is therefore an important factor to take into account when planning what can be done to establish class relationships. Here are some related points that are worth thinking about as part of a start-up period. Some of these points are broad and may need to be adapted according to the context.

- Identify factors that contribute to the development of positive relationships between teachers and students. This is very broad but can include the following: patience and respect; interest and concern for all students; avoidance of demeaning or embarrassing comments.

■ Set expectations for classroom communication. This could include an articulation of the ground rules guiding participation in class activities such as turn-taking, speaking and listening, respect for others, terms of address. Rules can be set by the teacher or through negotiation with a class.

■ Specify ideas and methods for establishing patterns for communication. This may include: how you introduce yourself to the class; what you say to the class about yourself and your background; how you find out the names, abilities and interests of students in the class.

■ Link communication practices to educational purposes. Each teacher will have their own styles and methods for communicating with the individuals in their class, yet it is of value to be able to justify the communication practices that you wish to promote in your classroom. This is important by way of showing the ways in which the patterns for communication in a classroom link to the educational purposes underpinning your practice and your professional and ethical responsibilities.

■ Connect your start-up plans to existing practices for communication that may exist in the school or classroom as a way of making the transition from one teacher to another.

Questions for discussion

1. What action would you take if you were Carole in her second lesson with this class?

2. In what ways might the issues be different if this was the start of the year and Carole was the designated teacher for the class; if Carole was a student teacher on practicum; or if she was a relief teacher for the day?

3. What start-up activities would be appropriate with students in the senior years of high school?

4. In what ways might start-up activities need to be adapted and modified to suit the needs of particular subject specialties; for example, working in a gym or a lab?

Degrees of friendship — dilemma 2

The first dilemma was concerned with some broad issues that teachers face when establishing relationships with a class. In the following dilemma a more specific set of questions are raised about friendship between teachers and students and the professional boundaries and limits that pertain to relationships between students and teachers.

Jeff was in his first year of teaching maths at a public high school in a rural town. He was 23 and was teaching Years 11 and 12. Jeff was extremely affable and easygoing. The students were not that much younger than he was and in many ways Jeff wanted them to like him, to see him as a friend. The males in the class regarded Jeff as one of their 'mates'. Talk of maths was typically interspersed with talk about various sporting activities, local and national. Many of the females in the class also liked Jeff, but they generally did not join in the discussions about sport. Jeff felt a little more awkward in the way in which he related to the female students in the class. He was flattered because he knew that many of them liked him, but he also felt some degree of discomfort in knowing where to draw the line in his relationship with them.

The issues

The issues in this dilemma pertain to the degrees to which 'friendship' can or should be part of the relationships that develop between teachers and students. To tease out the issues we will examine and ask some questions about Jeff's relationships with both males and females in the class.

It is not uncommon to assume or hope that certain levels of friendship will develop between students and teachers. Yet what might be considered an appropriate form of friendship between a teacher and students? Or further, is friendship an appropriate form of relationship between students and teachers? To respond to these questions it is of value to examine friendships in light of the professional obligations and responsibilities held by teachers and the degree to which the friendships might effect and, more seriously, compromise a teacher's ability to fulfil their professional obligations. In the above dilemma expressions of friendship are underpinned by assumptions and emotions pertaining to gender and sexuality. This perhaps brings into sharper relief some of the ethical questions relevant to relationships between students and teachers.

You might wish to consider in the first instance the influence that Jeff's 'friendly' relations with the male students might have on the teaching and learning practices in the classroom. For example, how might this influence the participation of female students or the processes associated with evaluation? Secondly, you might want to think about Jeff's uncertainty regarding how to relate to the female students in the class. There are strict codes of professional conduct that regulate and render illegal relations between teachers and students that are of a sexual nature. Each school and school system will have documents relating to this. The issue in this case does not concern any such relations, but what it does do is raise some questions regarding how Jeff can articulate and set limits in response to his own and the female students' emotions and feelings, and in light of professional codes of conduct.

Possible actions

- Know and apply ethical regulations governing student/teacher relations.
- Set social boundaries for relationships with students that do not compromise professional practice and that are not underpinned by stereotypical or prejudicial assumptions about students based on, for example, gender, culture or sexual orientation.

Questions for discussion

1. Do you think that friendship between teachers and students is an acceptable part of professional practice? In thinking about your response to this question do you see any differences between friendliness and friendship in the ways that

relations between students and teachers are expressed?

2.   What specific action would you take if you were in Jeff's shoes?

3.   In what ways might the issues in this case be different if the teacher was female?

Re-establishing communication — dilemmas 3 and 4

'Classroom management' is understandably one of the big concerns for many beginning teachers as well as experienced teachers. In this section of the chapter we will examine communication and relationship issues related to 'classroom management' or the behaviour of students in a class. The notion of 'management' sometimes has negative overtones and is sometimes used synonymously with 'control'. In broad terms classroom management can refer to the overall organisation of the classroom environment. In more specific terms it can refer to the strategies that teachers use to 'manage' behaviour. In the next two dilemmas we consider students' behaviour in light of various processes of communication, types of relationships and some of the complex social factors that can underpin behaviour. Two related points that we want to stress are, first, there is not a generic set of 'management' techniques that can be used by a diverse range of teachers working in diverse school settings with diverse groups of students. Second, behaviour is often talked about as a purely individual matter, for instance if a student has been diagnosed with Attention Deficit Disorder it is perceived as an individual psychological problem. However it is also of value to consider the group processes in a class by way of understanding such student behaviour.

Confronting language — dilemma 3

In this dilemma we focus on a confrontation between a student and a teacher. This instance provides an opportunity to think about the ways emotions and power are expressed through the language and body language of the participants.

> One minute the Year 7 class were getting on with their work, the next there was a pretty violent scuffle in the back of the room. Raman, the teacher, yelled across the room and ordered Rick, one of the students, to stand outside. Rick folded his arms defiantly and said 'You can't make me'. Raman repeated that she wanted Rick to stand outside. Rick then tipped over a chair and sat down at his own desk. The class went quiet as they waited to see how Raman would respond.

The issues

There are two layers of confrontation in this dilemma — that between a group of students and that between a student and teacher. Within both layers there are dynamics of power and emotion that may reflect a complex set of personal assumptions and social circumstances (Boler 1999). The question for Raman is what action does she take — does she let the situation lie and let the class just get on with their work, does she insist that Rick stand outside, does she question the others involved in the scuffle and find out what caused the fight in the first place? The consequences and efficacy of various courses of action need to be carefully considered. Is the conflict between student and teacher defused or exacerbated? Does the teacher act fairly to deal with the situation?

Raman, in this case, has the difficult task of dealing with the conflict in the 'heat of the moment'. This can include not only the emotional response of the students but also her own emotional reaction to the conflict — anger, stress, frustration, loss of control and so on. Furthermore there is the task of building up a stock of knowledge that might help her understand the circumstances producing conflict and a set of resources and strategies that might be valuable in resolving some of these communication issues over the long term. In the above case there is not a lot of contextual detail. Yet let's assume that there is something serious about this scuffle, that it is not a one-off incident over a minor issue and that there is persistent tension between some of the students and/or between the teacher and students. The problem in this respect may have its roots, not just in an individual's psyche or behaviour, but also in the various social and institutional processes that surround individuals' actions and assumptions (Popkewitz 1998). For example, teachers and students could come from backgrounds which don't share the same values about, amongst other things, education; and teachers and students may hold assumptions about others in the class that are discriminatory or stereotypical. The difficult task for teachers is to both examine their own assumptions and consider how and why their actions and response might vary according to, for example, the social or ethnic background of particular students.

Possible actions

- Defuse tension. This can be done in a number of ways: providing choices is one, and other ways include judicious use of humour, avoiding public conflict, providing a 'cooling down' period, and avoiding destructive and demeaning comments.
- Develop an awareness of how language (including body language) functions to create and reflect particular relationships, interactions and emotions. What might be the effect, for example, of Raman moving to Rick's desk? Draw on this to understand the operations of power within an interaction. This is especially important in terms of how teachers use their institutional power to control, regulate, discipline, negotiate, mediate and so on.
- Have a set of follow-up actions in relation to longer-term behaviour. This might involve discussion with students and speaking to others on staff to see if there are any patterns of behaviour and social relations or any circumstances that might explain the behaviours in question and inform future teaching strategies. It might also mean devising plans that are specific to the social circumstances.

Questions for discussion

1. What action would you take if you were in Raman's shoes?

2. What might be some issues related to the ways in which teachers express their emotions in class; for example, anger, frustration, stress, disappointment, sarcasm?

3. Teachers have certain power in a classroom by virtue of their institutional position. This power need not be oppressive. In what class management

situations might teachers' power be legitimately expressed and in what situations might its expression be unreasonable?

The wrong foot — dilemma 4

In this dilemma there are recurring problems associated with communication in the classroom.

Steve dreaded going to the Year 9 English class. Things had not started off on the right foot and he was constantly frustrated in his efforts to just get the class to pay attention, let alone do the set work. Steve would often have to wait for ten minutes for all students in the class to stop talking. In every class there seemed to be some incident — conflict between students, aggressive behaviour directed by a couple of students toward him, complaints that the class was boring, sullen and uncooperative responses. Steve's remonstrations seemed to have little effect. He tried to reason with the students, but on occasions he would find herself yelling at the students or sending students to the department head. While not all members of the class were a problem, there seemed to be a sizeable group that had no interest in being there and no qualms about being disruptive and disrespectful. The pattern of communication in the class seemed to be based on little cooperation at best, and confrontation at worst. Steve felt forced into adopting teaching practices such as writing notes on the board and handing out worksheets as a means of management, yet he knew this exacerbated the level of boredom. He did not know what to do to change the pattern.

The issues

The issue for Steve, in this case, is to try and turn a bad situation around, to re-establish classroom relations that are both respectful and consistent with his teaching and learning goals. A further challenge is to turn this situation around in a way that is sustained over the long term. This may take concerted action both inside and outside the classroom. You may hear some say that it is the teacher's responsibility to 'control' a class. This view implies that teachers are responsible for dealing with whatever attitudes and problems come their way. While teachers do obviously have considerable responsibility for the conduct within their classes, it may be more productive to view responsibility for dealing with recurring problems as a shared one. If responsibility is shared there may be a greater chance of developing a systematic and coherent response that builds on management and support structures within the school. Extending the responsibility for recurring problems to include parents, other teachers and administrators is an acknowledgment that some issues cannot be dealt with in an isolated fashion in one class by one teacher. Seen in this way teachers may be less likely to close the door and hope that no-one knows there are problems.

Possible actions

- Identify reasons and causes — at the moment the problem is a fairly general one. Are there some specific aspects of the classroom communication that could be specified as a starting point for tackling the problem? For example, are there recurring patterns related to the type of tasks, are there key people involved? Ask a colleague to observe lessons in order to get another perspective and to discuss possible action. Are there reasons that have their roots outside the classroom?

■ Class-based actions — renegotiate or renew agreements for acceptable forms of classroom communication and relationships as well as the consequences for unacceptable classroom communication. Apply consequences promptly, fairly and consistently. Assist students to take responsibility for their own actions.

■ Enlist the support of school-based support services; for example, year adviser, department head, other teachers. Consider initiating contact with parents/caregivers.

■ Address communication problems through attention to both management strategies and teaching strategies. Addressing the problem of communication only through attention to management strategies and without attention to the ways in which students can engage with the subject material can be ineffective or even counterproductive.

Questions for discussion

1. One of the problems here concerns the extent to which teachers are expected to, or assume that they should, cope or manage on their own. Is admitting to a problem a sign of weakness or a sign of strength?

2. Continual concerns with classroom management can be emotionally draining for teachers. What might be some effective ways of acknowledging and dealing with this sort of stress?

3. If students continue to treat others with disrespect and demonstrate little by way of social responsibility, what options are available for a teacher and the school? As you develop a list of options consider how effective they might be in changing attitudes or behaviours.

Communication and relationships with other members of staff

When one begins to teach, the focus is understandably and rightly on working with students, yet it is of crucial importance to recognise that working in a school involves developing relationships with colleagues, other teachers, school administrators and school support staff (Mitchell & Dobbins 1998). Working with colleagues provides a mechanism for, amongst other things, support, teamwork, sharing ideas and resources, professional development, research and friendship. At the same time, it is not uncommon within a high school workplace for some tension and conflict to exist between members of staff. Different personal and social politics may underpin this tension. Collaboration, friendships, politics, criticism and conflict are all part of the communication and relationships among staff in a school. In this section some of the issues relating to staff communication will be explored.

Andy Hargreaves (1994) has written extensively about the culture of high schools. Central to Hargreaves' conception of a school culture are the patterns for communication that exist between members of a school staff. He talks about four patterns or forms of relationships between those in a school staff. We will discuss these very briefly by way of providing some background for thinking about programs, practices and issues in staff communication. The forms that Hargreaves identifies are individualism, collaboration, 'contrived collegiality' and 'Balkanisation'.[1]

In discussing these forms Hargreaves makes some interesting observations that challenge some of the conventional wisdom about staff relationships. For example he portrays individualism as both a necessary and positive part of a school's ecology. He notes that individualism is portrayed by some as a problem because it is perceived as being isolationist and serving to fragment and militate against sharing and collective action. However Hargreaves also suggests that individualism enables teachers to express their autonomy and individuality. He is critical of those school cultures that work to suppress individualism through processes that emphasise consensus and conformity.

It is worth noting that much of the prescriptive and descriptive literature in teacher education over the last couple of decades has emphasised the value of collaborative and collegial principles and practices (Darling-Hammond 1994; Goodlad 1994). Yet there is much debate about what these terms mean, and how they get played out in practice. (For a recent debate on these matters see Fielding 1999; Hargreaves 1999; Warren Little 1999.) In fact Hargreaves (1994) wonders whether collegiality and collaboration are 'cups of comfort' or 'poisoned chalices'. He praises those forms of staff collaboration that develop with some degree of spontaneity and that underpin collective and critical reflection. He is trenchant in his criticism of collaboration that is contrived as part of a 'managerialist' strategy or collaboration that means little more than a 'cosy' and 'complacent' workplace (p. 195). In talking about high school cultures as 'Balkanised' Hargreaves is referring to the pattern of organisation in which small groups of people work together, the common manifestation being subject departments. He suggests that this form of organisation is in some ways inevitable but it often has the effect of creating rigid hierarchies of power and divisions along subject lines that promote conflict between departments and render the curriculum as both inflexible and resistant to change.

Hargreaves' ideas provide a useful way of interpreting and understanding some of the practices and politics associated with communication amongst staff in a high school. For those new in schools, particularly as a student teacher or beginning teacher, the patterns, politics and complexity of a school culture can take some working out. The patterns and politics can be minor — who uses what coffee cups in the staff room? They can also be substantive — who makes decisions about school policy, curriculum initiatives, staffing and so on. Lave and Wenger's (1993) notion of legitimate peripheral participation also has relevance to how teachers learn the patterns and politics of a school culture. A new person in a workplace starts out on the periphery and as he or she becomes more knowledgeable about the customs of the workplace and adept in the workplace practices, they move from the peripheral to full participation in the culture of that workplace.

There are many issues relevant to staff relationships that could be discussed, but we will focus on one issue that is pertinent to beginning teachers located on the periphery

---

[1] Hargreaves' use of the term 'Balkanisation' has been discussed in Chapter 2 (see footnote 1).

of a school culture. The analysis of this dilemma will provide a backdrop to an examination of some innovative practices associated with developing staff communication and collective workplace practices. This analysis will also link back to questions of shared responsibility raised in the previous section of this chapter.

Feeling isolated — dilemma 5

As you read the following case think about the level of personal and institutional responsibility for both the problem and for actions that could be taken to solve the problem.

> *Maria's first teaching appointment was as the only art teacher in a rural school some 12 hours drive from the major city she had lived in all her life. For Maria there was a lot that was new — new town, new job and new colleagues. Maria was excited about the job, but also nervous about the adjustments she would need to make.*
>
> *The first few months were exhausting. Maria spent a lot of time planning. She taught each grade level including Year 12, which brought with it the extra pressure of ensuring that the class were prepared for their final exam and the submission of their major work. Maria also just felt generally insecure about the adequacy of her teaching and management strategies and whether she was doing a reasonable job. As the only art teacher Maria also had a lot of administrative responsibilities — ordering supplies and equipment for the art room, keeping track of materials, accessing print resources and information about exhibits and galleries and so on. In fact Maria had total responsibility for pretty well everything to do with how art was taught in the school.*
>
> *Maria had no choice but to work independently. There was no separate art department; art was part of the Design and Technology Department. The head of this department was a nice person but he had little interest in art or in providing any systematic support for Maria. The department head's attitude toward art was in many ways a reflection of a school climate that did not really value art. As a new teacher and as an art teacher Maria felt out on the margins. While Maria got on reasonably well with the staff, she did not have anyone she felt she could talk to about some of the stresses of the job.*

The issues

Issues related to isolation loom large in this case, both because Maria is a new teacher in a new town, and because of her position as the only art teacher in a school in which art is on the margin. Problems associated with isolation are not uncommon among beginning teachers. Given our previous comments, a comprehensive approach to this problem requires consideration of the courses of action that can be taken by Maria *and* the institutions that have some interest in and responsibility for the conditions and workplace practices in which beginning teachers are placed.

Questions for discussion

1. What actions could Maria take to address the problems of isolation that she is experiencing? In responding to this question think about actions that might be useful as a means of establishing relationships within the school and community that provide both friendship and support and advice on teaching matters.

2. What actions could or should the relevant institutions (e.g. school, district or state/territory authorities, union) take to deal with the issues faced by beginning teachers such as Maria? Think here of the sorts of practices and structures that could be set up both within and across schools that could provide a source of support, teaching ideas and sense of community. In responding to this question keep in mind the distances that may exist between schools in rural locations. Do you think that telecommunication technology could be used to provide support structures across distance?

Joint practices

To augment the ideas that you have developed in response to the questions we are going to briefly consider some models for workplace relations that have been set up in some schools as a means of constituting teaching and professional development as collective or collaborative activity. The premise of these models is that the exchange of ideas between teachers, through both formal and informal means, is central to teachers' learning and classroom practice. It is of value to keep Hargreaves' critique of 'contrived collegiality' in mind when making judgments about how these programs operate in practice.

Model 1: Mentoring

The notion of mentoring has become commonplace in much professional development literature in schools and other organisations (Arthur, Davison & Moss 1997; Furlong & Maynard 1995). A mentor, typically a skilled and experienced person in a work setting, provides guidance and support to someone new or inexperienced in that setting. Some schools and districts have established mentoring programs for beginning teachers. An experienced teacher meets regularly with a beginning teacher to discuss issues, plan teaching activities and team teach. Perhaps more common are less formal mentoring relationships. For example, a beginning teacher might have a desk in the staffroom next to an experienced teacher and through the course of their conversations the new teacher learns from and seeks the advice of the more experienced teacher. Mentoring can also take place through contacts outside of a school through, for example, support programs established for beginning teachers at a district or regional level. Groups of beginning teachers get together on a semi-regular basis with, say, subject specialists to talk about their experiences and exchange ideas. This sort of institutional support can be invaluable for beginning teachers who are adjusting to the demands of being a full-time teacher.

It is also worthwhile to think about some of the interpersonal dynamics of a mentoring relationship, particularly in relation to the degree to which those in the relationship are open and willing to build criticism into their conversations. The challenge for mentors can be how to frame remarks that not only support and encourage, but also thoughtfully criticise and evaluate a beginning teacher's practice. For a beginning teacher this raises questions about how one receives criticism and the extent to which one is prepared to reveal weaknesses and vulnerabilities in seeking to improve practice.

Model 2: Learning communities/school-based professional development

As mentioned earlier, the notion of collaboration is now pervasive in both the

101

prescriptive and descriptive literature concerned with professional development and staff relationships in schools. In a similar vein you may also hear many people talking about 'community' — schools as 'learning communities' (Retallick 1999) or schools as 'communities of inquiry' (Sachs 1997). The concepts of community and collaboration are, in many ways, complementary ideals that define the means and ends of particular forms of communication and staff relationships in schools. Much of the literature in this area is oriented toward teachers jointly investigating or organising aspects of their own workplace practice in order to understand, change and improve that practice. Key assumptions of these programs are that learning about teaching, justifying one's practice and sustaining curricula change and improvement require some form of collective action (Carr & Kemmis 1986; Fenstermacher 1994).

Communication structures within schools that enable teachers to work together can be particularly valuable for beginning teachers as a mechanism for support and learning about the school and about teaching. Groundwater-Smith's (1999) study of teachers' work at an inner city Sydney school documents the ways in which a team of Year 7 and 8 teachers work together across departments. Through regular meetings these teachers are able to develop approaches that are consistent and coherent. Everyone is cognisant of problems and there is a sense of shared responsibility for the ways in which these problems are dealt with. It is worth thinking about the value of these sorts of communication structures in schools in light of the problems of isolation that can be experienced by beginning teachers.

Communicating with parents, caregivers and the community

It is sometimes easy to think of high schools as islands with the business of teaching and learning existing in isolation from the world outside the school grounds. However there is increasing attention being paid to the relationships between schools and the community. In part this is a mechanism for accountability and the need to make curricula practices public and transparent. Developing lines of communication between high school teachers and the community — parents, caregivers, educators in primary schools, TAFE colleges and universities, as well as other community groups — is also essential for a coherent and integrated program of education. In this section of the chapter we will examine some of the current practices and issues associated with communication between teachers and parents/caregivers and between schools and the community. We will also consider some current initiatives that are aimed at enhancing connections between schools and the community.

Communication with parents and caregivers

Ros Brennan, the former president of the New South Wales Parents and Citizens Association, made the following observation: 'Time for communicating with parents is never factored into the allocation of subject loads. We make allowances for playground duty but not parental consultation' (2000, personal communication). On that note we want to take a look at some of the ways and means by which teachers communicate with parents. Communication usually falls around two issues — assessment and the sending home of report cards or problems involving students that require a meeting with parents/caregivers. There are other occasions for communication such as parents and citizens meetings, school board meetings, concerts, speech nights and the like. We would argue that these occasions serve an important purpose yet typically involve only a small number of parents and teachers (e.g. board meetings) or are special events, whose prime purpose is to showcase achievements. In teasing out some of the issues associated with communicating with parents and caregivers we will elaborate on two aspects — writing reports and the factors that constrain communication.

Report writing — dilemma 6

Report card writing provides a way of examining some of these issues. Report card writing is the prime means by which teachers communicate with parents/caregivers about students' educational achievements and progress. Writing report cards is often an intense time for teachers. It means that processes of evaluation have been sufficiently completed to enable grades and comments to be recorded. For a teacher with five or six classes, this requires time and an understanding and knowledge of the individuals in the class. The actual structure of report cards will vary from school to school and may also vary depending on the assessment purpose. A mid-year progress report may be different from a 'final' end of year report. Some reports may have space for grades only; others may be more oriented toward written commentary. Notwithstanding these variations, a question needs to be raised regarding the adequacy of report cards to capture a sense of students' educational progress in ways that are useful and informative for those reading the report. With this question in mind consider the following dilemma.

> *Tom was writing his first set of reports. Others in his department had warned him to be well prepared for this process by getting work marked and grades finalised with plenty of time to spare to actually draft the reports. Tom found that writing reports for the students who were doing well was relatively straightforward. However he really struggled to know how to word comments for those who were not doing well in class. There seemed to be so much that could or should be said, but in the space provided for comments and given that he had no real sense of who the individual parents were, it was hard to draft comments in ways that were meaningful or that might lead to a change in attitude, behaviour or results. To say that a student 'needs to work harder' coupled with a 'D' grade just did not seem to be all that informative.*

The issues

Tom is working under a set of constraints that make it hard to know what to write — he is writing to an audience he does not know, there is little space on the report card for detailed comments and he wants his comments to be informative and unambiguous. This is a significant challenge, as the report card can carry considerable import as an official school document and a marker of a student's performance. How the report is read and interpreted by parents/caregivers is a crucial part of the communication between school and home.

Possible actions

In many ways it is difficult, particularly for a new member of staff, to do anything other than work within some of these constraints. The actual structure for report cards and methods for reporting is a matter of ongoing debate — how best to communicate information about a student and what information is of most importance (refer to Chapter 12 for further details on this debate as well as an examination of innovations in this area). Depending upon the amount of space for comments it is of value to think about how they can be written in ways that are not simply gratuitous or recipe-like and that reflect a thoughtful, honest and informed assessment of a student's achievements. Similarly, consider other less formal means of reporting to parents/caregivers that might augment a final report card. These might include phone calls to parents/caregivers, form letters outlining what is being done in class and the expectations that are set for students and web pages which publish information and student work.

We suggested that most communication between teachers and parents takes place during critical times. This begs the questions: What opportunities exist in high schools to establish communication between teachers and parents during non-critical times? What factors might constrain this communication? There are numerous reasons why communication between teachers and parents tends to be a peripheral part of high school practice. Time is a crucial factor, many teachers simply do not have the time to pursue this line of communication given their existing workloads. The age of students and the independence that can be associated with adolescence can also be a factor explaining the degree of parental involvement in school activities. At the same time, the culture of some high schools and the taken-for-granted practices within some schools are simply not open to or welcoming of communication with parents.

Questions for discussion

1. In your high school experience — as a student, parent of a student or teacher — what avenues existed or exist for communication between parents and teachers?

2. What level of communication do you think would be useful in a high school context?

Communication with the community

The final section of this chapter is concerned with some general questions about the communication and connections that exist between high schools and other educational and community organisations. We are thinking here of the communication that high school teachers might have with teachers in the local primary schools, the nearest TAFE college or university, or with community organisations such as drop-in centres, welfare groups, libraries, sports and recreation associations and so on. Links with these groups and organisations can be important as a way of developing coherence between the various educational sectors and for giving the curriculum a community context. Without these connections and lines of communication, broad educational programs can be segmented, transitions between educational sectors can be difficult and the practices of schools can lack relevance to their social and/or local context.

Efforts to extend the range of ways in which high schools communicate with other groups typically involve concerted group action by teachers and others in the community. Over the last few years there have been a number of innovative programs in Australia and overseas that have been oriented toward connecting high schools with related institutions. These innovations have taken place at a broad policy level as well as at the local school level. Examples include:

- partnerships between high schools and TAFE colleges for the delivery of vocational education courses;
- links between high school and primary school teachers to develop transition programs for students coming into high schools (the case of Stromlo High School reported in Chapter 2 is an example);
- service school initiatives whereby students provide various forms of community service as part of their course work (Willinsky 1998);
- partnerships between schools and education faculties to develop school-based professional development programs at pre-service and/or in-service levels and as part of curriculum development; for example, the New South Wales Higher School Certificate On-line (2000), a partnership between the New South Wales Department of Education and Charles Sturt University.

While these projects are to be applauded, perhaps one of the most pressing issues that needs to be communicated by schools to parents and others in the community is the changing and complex role that high schools play in the education of young people. A key and necessary part of this is ensuring that both beginning and experienced teachers are prepared for this challenge.

Conclusion

No one chapter could adequately capture the range of communicative practices that are part of a school culture. Nevertheless what we have set out to do in this chapter is to frame some of the communicative practices central to teachers' work and also pose some dilemmas that occur as part of these practices. The dilemmas in many ways demonstrate clearly how the communications and relationships that teachers develop within a school, be it with students, other members of staff or members of the community, are incredibly complex and demanding. It is within these relationships and through the communication that the intellectual, emotional and physical dimensions of teaching are clearly represented. In addition, taking account of the personal and social dimensions of communication are important both for understanding various relationships that are part of the work of a teacher, as well as developing practical strategies and courses of action that sustain a clear ethical and educational agenda.

References

Arthur, J., Davison, J. & Moss, J. (1997). *Subject Mentoring in the Secondary School.* London: Routledge.

Boler, M. (1999). *Feeling, Power, Emotions and Education.* New York: Routledge.

Brennan, R. (2000). Personal communication.

Burbules, N. (1993). *Dialogue in Teaching.* New York: Teachers College Press.

Carr, W. & Kemmis, S. (1986). *Becoming Critical: Education, Knowledge and Action Research.* Victoria, Australia: Deakin University.

Darling-Hammond, L. (ed) (1994). *Professional Development Schools.* New York: Teachers College Press.

Fenstermacher, G. (1994). *The Knower and the Known: the Nature of Knowledge in Research on Teaching.* Washington, DC: American Educational Research Association.

Fielding, M. (1999). Radical collegiality: affirming teaching as an inclusive professional practice. *The Australian Educational Researcher,* 26(2), pp. 1–34.

Furlong, J. & Maynard, T. (1995). *Mentoring Student Teachers: The Growth of Professional Knowledge.* London: Routledge.

Gee, J.P. (1999). *An Introduction to Discourse Analysis: Theory and Method.* New York: Routledge.

Goodlad, J. (1994). *Educational Renewal: Better Teachers, Better Schools.* San Francisco: Jossey-Bass.

Groundwater-Smith, S. (1999), Participative learning: The school as a learning community and as a member of a National Reform Organisation. In J. Retallick, B. Cocklin & K. Coombe (eds), *Learning Communities in Education.* London: Routledge, pp. 211–229.

Hargreaves, A. (1994). *Changing Teachers, Changing Times: Teachers' Work and Culture in the Postmodern Age.* Toronto, Canada: OISE Press.

Hargreaves, A. (1999). Fielding errors? Deepening the debate about teacher collaboration and collegiality: response to Fielding. *The Australian Educational Researcher,* 26(2), pp. 45–53.

Lave, J. & Wenger, E. (1993). *Situated Learning: Legitimate and Peripheral Participation.* Cambridge, USA: Cambridge University Press.

Mitchell, J. & Dobbins, R. (1998). Charles Sturt University extended practicum program: Deliberate and serendipitous learning. *Mentoring and Tutoring,* 4(2), pp. 32–40.

New South Wales Higher School Certificate On-line. (2000). *HSC On-line.* Charles Sturt University and NSW Department of Education and Training. Available at: http://hsc.csu.edu.au/

Popkewitz, T. (1998). *Struggling for the Soul: The Politics of Schooling and the Construction of the Teacher.* New York and London: Teachers College Press.

Poynton, C. (2000). Linguistics and Discourse Analysis. In A. Lee & C. Poynton (eds), *Culture and Text: Discourse and Methodology in Social Research and Cultural Studies.* St Leonards, Sydney: Allen & Unwin.

Retallick, J. (1999) Transforming schools into learning communities. In J. Retallick, B. Cocklin & K. Coombe (eds), *Learning Communities in Education.* London: Routledge, pp. 107–130.

Sachs, J. (1997). Revisioning teacher education. *Unicorn*, 23(2), pp. 45–56.

Warren Little, J. (1999). Colleagues of choice, colleagues of circumstances: Response to M. Fielding. *The Australian Educational Researcher*, 26(2), pp. 35–43.

Willinsky, J. (1988). Learning to do: Students develop information technology projects. Located at http:www.blarg.net/~building/tech_willinsky.html.

7

A Context for Learning

Consider the following:

- It is the start of the year in your first year of teaching. You know that you will be teaching one of the Year 7 classes. These classes are 'unstreamed' and the semester-long course that you are teaching serves as an introduction to the study of this subject (your teaching area) in high school. You are familiar with the relevant curriculum guidelines, you also have certain goals that you want to achieve. What sort of classroom environment do you want to establish? What ideas about the subject do you want students to develop? How are you going to do this? What might you need to think about?

- In thinking about the time you have, the curriculum goals and your own goals, you decide to begin with a four-week unit of work. You have a sense of what it is you want the class to learn. How are you going to set up the activities that will support students' learning? What might you need to think about?

- As you get into the unit, you notice that most students are interested and engaged, but there are four or five students who just seem really switched off — you want to plan a lesson that encourages these students to participate. How are you going to do this? What might you need to think about?

These questions and challenges link together to highlight the intention of this chapter, which is to encourage you to think about the connections between educational activities, the physical and social context in which those activities take place, and what is being learnt. To do this we believe it is helpful to explore some of the assumptions and theories about teaching, learning and knowledge that are associated with these connections. We will draw on these connections to develop some practical strategies for establishing teaching practices that support and extend student learning.

There are many debates regarding what we learn and how we learn in both school settings and outside of school. There are also many debates regarding what students *should* learn and how they *should* learn in school. This chapter can only touch the surface of these debates. We offer some ideas that attempt to set the 'what' and 'how' of learning into a social, school and classroom context, and to use an understanding of the context as the basis for planning teaching and learning activities. In line with this we want to build on some of the 'learning principles for the future' discussed in Chapter 2. We also want to stress the need to adapt, modify and challenge the ideas that we present so that they are relevant to your workplace or practicum context or to the problems posed at the beginning of the chapter.

Teaching and learning — social means and social ends

It is sometimes easy to think of teaching and learning as processes without any reference points; that is, to focus on 'the how' as a set of general principles, without taking account of the 'who', 'what', 'where' and 'why', and the ways in which these factors interact with 'the how'. In this chapter we argue that it is useful to think of learning as a *social* process. We also argue that it is valuable to tie teaching and learning to a social context; that is, to think about the processes with respect to the purpose, the objects, the people involved and the resources they have access to. *We therefore want to conceptualise teaching and learning as activities made up of both individual and collective actions directed toward particular ends and located in particular social and cultural contexts.* The diagram below shows how these ideas and features of context are interconnected in a high school setting. These ideas have been adapted from theories of learning that focus not only on individual psychology but also on the ways that other people influence what and how an individual learns (see for example Engestrom 1999; Wells 1999; Wertsch 1995). We will refer to 'social practices' or 'social activities' as all that goes on in a social context that involves a particular group of people and is directed toward a particular set of ends.

Teaching and learning prism

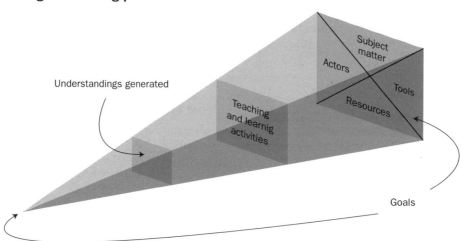

Teaching and learning activities are underpinned by an interaction between the people involved (actors), the subject matter, the tools for thinking about particular subjects and the available resources within an educational context. The shape of the prism in this diagram represents the ways in which understandings can be generated through this interaction. These concepts will be developed in the remaining parts of the chapter.

Some ways of thinking about educational ends

An enduring feature of the lesson plans that student teachers are often asked to produce during their teacher education is the 'aim', 'objective' or 'outcome' stated at the beginning of the plan. While the planning of a lesson does not necessarily begin with a clear objective — often planning begins with strategies or resources in mind that lead back to, or inform, the learning objectives — having some sense of the ends toward which the class activities are directed is very important. It provides a purpose for what you are doing and some standards or measures for assessing student work and your own teaching. Some important things to think about in relation to educational goals are listed below.

- First, question for yourself where educational goals come from and what sort of societal and cultural values they might reflect. If we think for a minute of broad educational goals, they might be focussed on, for example, individual development and personal growth, and/or social justice and equity, and/or preparation for the workplace. These goals are often the subject of public and political debate primarily because there are different, and sometimes competing, sets of values underpinning them.
- Second, each school and school system (e.g. state or territory Department of Education, Catholic Education Office, independent school) has its own set of curriculum documents and guidelines that articulate educational goals. The goals are often described in terms of *knowledge* (subject-based), *skills* (intellectual, social, technical and physical) and *attitudes* (in relation to the subject and to others, e.g. empathy, curiosity). Whether system-wide goals and associated curriculum documents are prescriptions or only guidelines varies both across the systems and year levels.
- Third, teachers have responsibility for interpreting curriculum documents and guidelines and developing goals for units and individual lessons. Making learning goals explicit is crucial by way of assisting students to know what they are trying to achieve and for developing the means to achieve those goals. This is not to say that goals always exist in advance of the means; new goals can always be developed through the activities taking place in a classroom and students can be involved in negotiating goals.
- Fourth, the degree of alignment between educational means and ends is important to consider. Insufficient attention to one or the other and/or the relationship between them can make it difficult to achieve goals that are substantive and worthwhile. For example, focussing only on the process of critical thinking does not consider what it is that students may be thinking critically about. Likewise, a student may have a 'correct' answer to a problem or question without necessarily knowing or understanding the process of reasoning needed to develop that answer.

With these comments about goals in mind, the next challenge is to think about the ways in which they can be achieved.

Some ways of thinking about the means

In 1938 John Dewey, an influential American educational philosopher, made the comment that one learns by doing. This seems simple in the saying, but it is worth teasing out what 'doing' involves — think of how you learn to play a sport, drive a car, read a map, design a web page, speak a language, solve quadratic equations or critically respond to a poem. Generally you would not learn to do these things simply or only by watching from the sidelines or reading about it in a book. So what is it that people are doing when they are learning to engage in activities such as the ones mentioned above, or any others that you care to think of? To respond to this question we want to take a closer look at the context in which this 'doing' is taking place. Note at this point that 'doing' is taken to include thinking, feeling and talking as well as physical action. The reason why we want to look at the context for learning is because we are arguing that learning is a process of making meaning, not in isolation from but in association with a particular set of people, resources, ideas and purposes.

Think of the above examples again. There is a social component or social motive underpinning participation in these activities. One is joining with others who also engage in these practices, and the practice has a social purpose; for example, to communicate an idea or to get from A to B. Furthermore, it would be difficult if not impossible to learn to do any of these activities on your own, without someone to demonstrate or offer advice or without reference to existing ideas and bodies of knowledge. Similarly it would be difficult, if not impossible, to learn to do any of these activities without a set of appropriate resources and a set of tools for thinking about what is being done. Finally, it would be difficult, if not impossible, to get better at the 'doing' without ongoing participation; for example, the opportunity to try something, think about it, apply ideas, revise ideas, talk about it, try new ideas and so on.

From this perspective learning is not just the accumulation of knowledge through rote memorisation, nor is it simply a series of cognitive or psychological processes. Rather, learning is a social process; it develops through participation in a social practice or activity (Lave & Wenger 1993; Wells 1999). In order to participate in the practice one needs to know certain things and have some sense or understanding of the purpose of the practice. Participation is also dependent upon an increasing mastery of the resources and tools associated with the practice or activity. Making sense of that practice develops through the opportunity to construct, apply and revise ideas with others. What this means for the teaching and learning activities that you might establish in a high school context will be explored in the remaining parts of this chapter.

A context for educational means and ends

Three features of a school context that we think have particular salience to a discussion of educational means and ends are (refer back to diagram):

1. subject matter;
2. the actors — teachers, students and their social milieu;
3. available resources.

The relationship between these factors influences the nature and type of teaching and learning activities. Below we tease out in some detail the connections between these contextual factors and teaching and learning in classrooms. As you read each section keep in the back of your mind the problems raised in the beginning of the chapter; that is, to think about the 'what' and the 'how' of the learning in your teaching area, in units and individual lessons.

Subject matter

We will briefly discuss three aspects of subject matter:

1. ways of thinking about 'school knowledge';
2. ways of thinking and doing particular subjects;
3. reasons and motivations for learning about a 'school subject'.

Ways of thinking about 'school knowledge'

Disciplinary or subject-based knowledge is one of the key organising features of high schools. The structure of subject departments, the timetable, curriculum documents, staffing and, most importantly for our purposes, teaching and learning practices, are all intimately tied to concepts of knowledge and what is deemed important for students to know. Not surprisingly, there is considerable debate regarding what this knowledge is and why it is worth knowing. In Chapter 2 we talked about the ways 'school knowledge' is bound by disciplines with little opportunity for integration across disciplinary divides or for questioning the disciplinary boundaries. Furthermore, there is an unfortunate tendency to simplify and polarise conceptions of 'school knowledge' and associated teaching and learning practices. On the one hand, 'school knowledge' is often represented as inert information, or something that exists in books, that is transmitted to and received by students, memorised and reproduced in tests and exams. On the other hand, 'school knowledge' is considered to be something that is 'constructed' or 'discovered' through 'student-centred activities'. These views of knowledge are related to other dichotomies — traditional/progressive approaches to teaching, teacher-centred/student-centred practices and product/process debates. The conception of learning that we have presented in this chapter renders such dichotomies as problematic. Understanding a subject requires more than memorising facts and figures. At the same time, to focus only on process and student constructions does not necessarily pay sufficient attention to the mastery of existing knowledge within a subject area or to whether the ideas constructed by students have any basis in fact (Alexander 2000; Barrow 1990; Phillips 1995).

Gordon Wells uses the term 'knowledge building' as a way around such dichotomies. Knowledge building is intended to 'capture the need for firm foundations and a design that is oriented toward purpose and use, as well as the constructive and transformative effort needed in any major building project' (1999, p. 90). This is consistent with the view of learning that we discussed in the previous section — *knowing and learning develop through participating in a social practice or activity in ways that take account of and build on existing ideas, resources and tools.*

You may be wondering how this relates to the particular subject or subjects that you will be teaching in high school. One way is to think about subjects that you are teaching as having a 'knowing how' and 'knowing that' component and to think about how the 'knowing how' and 'knowing that' might be linked. For instance, we might know that when liquid is frozen it expands. We might use particular methods of scientific investigation and reasoning to prove this or to explain this. These methods are the 'know how' in science. Likewise, we might know that the 1930s was a time of great economic hardship for many in Australia. We might come to know this through checking newspaper accounts of the time, interviewing people, examining government documents and making an assessment based on the evidence. This is the 'know how' in history. Furthermore, we might claim to know that sport and recreation are important to our physical and emotional health. There are various ways in which we could gather evidence to support this claim (surveys, personal experience, physiological tests), but ultimately this knowledge depends on people knowing how to play sports or participate in recreational activities. This knowledge also provides a rationale for learning the 'know how' associated with various sports and recreation. It is the links between the 'knowing how' and 'knowing that' within different subject areas that are useful to think about by way of developing learning activities in which students can build and apply knowledge. We develop these ideas in the next section by expanding on what it is that people are 'doing' when they come to know something.

Ways of thinking and doing particular subjects

Think about the sort of things that people 'do' to develop, understand, and apply knowledge in your subject area — this includes both in school and in the 'real' world. Remember that 'doing' includes ways of thinking, feeling, acting and expressing ideas. As an example, consider what people might be doing in the following maths-related activities:

- a Year 7 maths student calculating the size and area of various shapes;
- a maths teacher explaining the relationship between the formula for the area of a triangle and the area of a square or rectangle;
- a mathematician writing a section of a textbook that explains the theories and uses of pi as a means of calculating the area of a circle;
- a Year 12 art student working out the dimensions of his/her major work;
- an architect drawing a scale plan of a building;
- a real estate agent making a quick estimate of the size of an apartment;
- a farmer deciding on the area of land to be used for crops;
- a curtain maker working out the amount of material required for a set of curtains.

Performing these tasks requires some ways of thinking about size and/or area. The ways of thinking might involve measuring, calculating, applying formulas, estimating, using a scale, drawing shapes, linking knowledge of size and area to specific problems and explaining or communicating ideas. Thinking about and representing ideas in each of these cases involves the use of language (spoken and written), symbols (mathematical symbols) and/or pictures and diagrams. The language, symbols and pictures can be thought of as both the cultural and conceptual tools drawn on to do the tasks; to think about, develop, apply and communicate ideas. The ideas developed by the Russian psychologist Lev Vygotsky (1978, 1997) in the 1920s and 1930s, which gained popularity in English-speaking countries in the 1970s and 1980s, have been influential in this respect.

According to Vygotsky, language and other signs, such as pictures and symbols, can be thought of as 'tools' that mediate both our social action and our thinking, remembering and reasoning. To participate in a practice one needs to learn to use these conceptual tools. A set of physical tools may exist alongside the conceptual tools. In the present examples, physical tools might include tape measures, calculators, pens, architectural software and so on. Thus, doing any of the above tasks and understanding the maths associated with the tasks (or doing any other complex task and understanding it) requires being able to use a range of intellectual and physical tools.

There are often particular ways of thinking and doing associated with certain subject areas and it is worthwhile to specify the tools, especially the language, needed to think and act in your subject areas. For example, in order to describe a geographical feature of the landscape, you might draw on a set of geographical vocabulary and symbols, as well as an understanding of what it means to describe something.

Our key argument is that making explicit the tools associated with 'doing' a particular subject is a crucial step in devising activities to help students not only learn the subject matter but also participate in the practices associated with that subject.

Here are some examples of the general ways of thinking, doing and communicating in some of the subject areas studied in high schools:

- science — hypothesising, predicting, conducting experiments, observing, recording, interpreting data, explaining connections between phenomena, writing lab reports;
- history — collecting, sorting and interpreting evidence, sequencing events, explaining causes, making judgments, developing arguments;
- technology — designing artefacts, constructing artefacts using different materials, categorising objects, evaluating tools and artefacts;
- visual art — creating artefacts, interpreting and responding to works of art, expressing ideas using different media;
- English — creating texts, interpreting and responding to literature, explaining responses by referring to specific features of a text, developing arguments, using different media.

You might want to think about what actions and tools are associated with your subject areas. One way of doing this is to look at relevant curriculum documents, particularly the ways in which learning outcomes are specified. It is here that you can often locate the actions that are part of the doing in your subject area. Think how this might help you articulate goals relevant to the problems posed at the beginning of the chapter.

Learning to participate in a practice and learning how to use the tools associated with a practice does not happen overnight; one builds up competence and expertise over time. What can you do as part of your teaching practice to create opportunities that will enable students to develop competence in the practices that are part of your teaching area/s? How can you structure and sequence activities that will enable students to use the relevant tools?

Developing competence typically requires more than meaningless drills and mindless repetitions. Learning to participate might require the opportunity to investigate, try, apply, revise, go back, reapply, and revise ideas and skills. For example, with respect to learning maths, Pirie and Kieren (1994) advocate 'folding back' as a means of returning to earlier actions throughout the process of developing mathematical understanding. Thus, when learning an abstract concept, a student might 'fold back' at various points to concrete representations of that concept. What is interesting is that Pirie and Kieren argue that despite the highly structured nature of mathematical knowledge, and despite the structured and linear sequencing of many maths programs, learning maths does not necessarily follow a linear pathway.

Further means of developing competence in the practices associated with your teaching area might include the provision of: a range of experiences and opportunities to use the language that is part of your subject; a range of media through which students can express their ideas; and feedback and opportunities to sound out ideas with others and reflect on learning. We will return to some of these ideas later in the chapter; at this point it is sufficient to note that the crucial task for teachers is to think about how different sets of class activities can be structured and sequenced in order to support student participation and 'knowledge building'.

Reasons and motivations for learning about a 'school subject'

That school is 'boring' is a common refrain among students in high schools. This is hardly surprising if school knowledge is seen as bits of information which are 'learnt' through sitting at a desk copying notes from the board, being talked at, 'filling in the blank' worksheets and various other tasks that have little purpose and do little to spark interest. A key question for teachers is: What is it about the subject matter that is important, engaging and of interest to students? This is not to suggest that only the immediate needs and interests of students should determine the curriculum. Rather, it is to suggest that what is interesting, engaging or important about a subject needs to be made explicit and that ways of developing new interests among students need to be explored.

Kieran Egan (1997), who has written extensively on matters relating to school curricula and student learning, argues that it is vital to identify in the subjects that are being taught something that appeals to the imagination and the emotions. One of his ideas is to ask of a topic for a lesson or unit 'What is the story on this?'. Egan suggests asking this question in the way that newspaper editors do — locating a dramatic incident, idea, character, problem or event that will engage a reader. The lesson or the unit then involves 'telling the story' (p. 248):

> If the teacher thinks of the lesson or unit as more like telling a good story than conveying a body of information, then the need to focus on how to tell the story as crisply and vividly as possible comes to the fore rather than the attempt to meet sets of knowledge, skills and attitudes, objectives. If the story is told well, such objectives will be met in a more meaningful context.

Egan goes on to say that by 'story' he is not suggesting that teachers talk for long periods of time, rather that lessons and units have a structured storyline. Various class activities, such as excursions, discussions, library research, debates, films, video, presentations, experiments, readings, creative work and so on can be part of the storyline. The storyline can be maintained through a lesson or unit by keeping in mind a key problem, concept or theory, and by making connections between the topic and human interests and emotions.

In a complementary way, Wells suggests (1999, p. 91) 'starting with "real" questions that are generated by students' first-hand engagement with topics and problems that have become of genuine interest to them'. The key ideas here are to start with an experience that serves to generate questions. The experience might include the presentation of a problem, a controversial video, a current event, a story, a song, an excursion — in fact, almost anything other than writing notes from the board, opening the textbook to 'page x' or handing out a blackline stencil worksheet. The second part of the process is using this experience to generate questions. This part of the process is not simple, but it is critical to establishing a focus for research or inquiry. Generating questions that are challenging and achievable, as well as consistent with curriculum guidelines and expectations, requires a comprehensive understanding of the subject and curriculum documents as well as considerable negotiation skills.

What both Egan and Wells and many other educational writers are saying is that a topic needs to be engaging. Engaging is a good word because it captures the idea of 'doing' subjects that are interesting and important, that appeal to the intellect and the emotions. The unstated part of this assertion is that the subjects are interesting and important to a particular group of people. It is to a more detailed examination of the people in a class that we will now turn.

The actors — teachers, students and their social milieu

We have argued that learning is a social process and that learning comes through 'doing', through participating in the activities that are part of a practice. The key question is: How can teaching and learning activities be established that enable students to engage in the practices associated with the subject area? In other words how can teachers and students work together in ways that support 'knowledge building' and extend learning? Responding to this question requires paying particular attention to the people in a class and the social relations and the patterns for communicating that can exist between those people. Three areas for consideration are:

1. teachers' and students' backgrounds;
2. scaffolding and collaboration;
3. communicating ideas — how and with whom?

Teachers' and students' backgrounds — a context for participation

There are many factors that can account for the ways in which teachers and students participate in classrooms. The social, economic, cultural and linguistic background of both teachers and students, their age, gender, values, attitudes, interests, motivations, knowledge and assumptions about teaching and learning can influence how they participate in classroom activities. Ways in which background can serve to advantage some and disadvantage others in the educational system has been documented in other chapters. Our concern in this part of the chapter is to consider ways in which you can establish classroom relations that enable those in the class to both participate and work together to build, apply and communicate ideas about a topic or subject. This assumes that activities are inclusive and that they make provision for individual differences and learning styles. Taking account of differences between individuals and across groups through teaching practices is certainly an issue for all teachers. Within any class there will be a range of abilities, interests and backgrounds. There is often a tendency to teach somewhere to the 'middle' or to the dominant group. Those who can easily complete tasks, those who have problems completing tasks or those who are not part of the dominant group can be left out.

The following suggestions may assist in establishing a class climate that supports participation and joint action.

- Build relationships and patterns for communication that are based on respect, honesty and trust (refer to Chapter 6 for more detail).

- Think about the ways in which teachers' assumptions about students and how they learn can influence expectations regarding what students are able to achieve. Consider the degree to which particular stereotypical assumptions — for instance, about gender or ethnicity — can limit expectations.

- Provide a range of opportunities for the ways in which students can participate in class. The range of opportunities is endless and will vary from subject to subject, but here are some ideas:

  – use various forms of individual, group and whole class activities, with attention to groupings of students (e.g. ability, gender);

  – vary tasks and topics within a unit; have a range of reading and other resource materials that accommodate different levels of literacy within a class;

  – negotiate and provide choice regarding topics for study, methods of investigation and means of assessment;

  – use school support services to provide additional assistance for students with particular needs such as non-English speaking background (NESB) or learning assistance;

  – use a variety of means for communicating ideas — spoken, written, graphic, multimedia, video and so on; encourage students to communicate their ideas in a variety of ways as well;

  – provide different types of guidance through demonstration and modeling, feedback, positive encouragement and so forth.

Scaffolding and collaboration

'Scaffolding' is a term commonly used in education circles to describe the supports that teachers can set up that will enable students to participate in class activities (Bruner 1983; Cazden 1988). Most of the ideas mentioned above represent forms of scaffolding. In recent years the use of the term scaffolding has been applied to the ideas related to social learning developed by Vygotsky (1997, p. 54; 1978, p. 55). It is worth taking time to consider some aspects of Vygotsky's ideas and how they can be linked to scaffolding. Vygotsky saw the only 'good' learning as 'that which is in advance of development' (1978, p. 89); that which *extends* a student's current understanding. Vygotsky also developed the idea of the 'zone of proximal development'. The zone of proximal development is the potential for a student's development that is created through interaction with experts and peers. The zone represents what a student can do on their own and what they can do with guidance from someone with expertise, or in collaboration with others. A teacher, then, can provide 'scaffolding' or the supports that students need to do a task that they could not do on their own *and* that will enable students to develop the competence to do the task independently. In other words the scaffolding, like the supports provided to construct a building, is only temporary. What the scaffolding implies is that students and teachers are jointly involved in the construction of ideas and understandings.

Collaboration is also a term often used to describe the sort of work practices in which students are working with each other to construct ideas. Collaboration used in this way implies more than group work, rather an opportunity to develop and negotiate understandings by talking ideas through with others. This might be through whole class activities, structured group work or the chance for students to discuss ideas with those around them in the class. To link collaborative work back to the idea of 'knowledge building', what is crucial is the opportunity for students to inquire into a particular issue or topic, to check ideas with peers and to change ideas in light of better arguments, further evidence and so on.

Communicating ideas — how and with whom?

Think for a minute of your own high school experiences and the main ways in which you communicated your ideas. In most of your subjects these were probably through speaking and writing. In most subjects, and more so in senior years, it was probably your written work, in particular, that was used for assessment purposes. We want to examine these modes of communicating in a little more detail by way of thinking about their learning purpose and their part in the activities associated with school subjects. Again we want to examine who is actually involved in these speaking and writing activities and how they can influence participation and learning.

Firstly, in relation to spoken discourse in a classroom, the pattern of a teacher asking a question (initiating), a student answering (response) and a teacher providing feedback (follow-up) is recognised as being the predominant means of teacher–student communication. There are estimates that 70 per cent of all communicating in secondary classrooms is based on this initiating, response, follow-up (IRF) sequence (Wells 1999). Of course an IRF sequence and its purpose may vary considerably depending upon the teacher and the context, and there is much disagreement in the literature regarding its value. As Wells notes, if it is just an opportunity for teachers to ask questions of the 'known answer' variety then its value may be questionable.

Secondly, there is considerable criticism regarding much of the writing that takes place in schools. These criticisms include the following: there is a narrow purpose for much school writing — to display what is known for assessment or to help memorise information; the audience for much school writing is either 'unknown' and/or the teacher; for many students writing is a laborious task and there is little interest in redrafting; and ways in which written tasks (often completed alone) could be coherently linked to spoken tasks are underdeveloped (Wells 1999).

Our concern is that class communication, if predominantly conceived in the above ways, does little to assist students to learn to participate in a practice in any sort of critical or purposeful way. This takes us back to thinking about the action and activities associated with particular subject areas that we have discussed previously and the ways in which speaking and writing might be part of that action and important to learning. What we want to do is further the discussion of action by thinking about ways in which changes to the mode of communicating and the audience or social relations can extend learning opportunities.

Consider the following example. As you read through this example think about how the mode of communication and the type of social relations or audience in each activity might affect the nature of student participation and the opportunity to build ideas collaboratively with others. Think too about a possible sequence between any of the written and spoken activities.

The following activity could take place in a range of subject areas and with students of varying age. Note this lesson may also be part of a series of lessons related to the topics concerned with advertising, school-business alliances, health, etc.

> **Lesson objective** — Students to develop a point of view on the question 'Should large individual soft drink companies be allowed exclusive rights to sell their products in schools?'
>
> As you read through the range of activities listed here (noting that there are many other possibilities) think about how the mode — spoken or written — and the audience — peers, teacher or others — might affect student participation and learning.
>
> - Students discuss the question in small groups — students develop reasons for and against exclusive selling rights in schools.
> - Students discuss the question with the whole class — students present reasons for and against exclusive selling rights and the teacher records these on the board.
> - Students discuss the question in writing. Response to be marked by the teacher.
> - Students discuss the question in writing. Response to be considered for publication in the school newsletter.
> - Students discuss the question in writing. Response to be read and evaluated by peers.
> - Students discuss the question in pairs, through joint writing at a computer. Response to be posted on the class web page.
> - Students discuss the question in writing and present drafts to the teacher before rewriting.

In each of these activities the purpose — to discuss and develop a point of view on exclusive selling rights in schools — is the same. However the activities differ in relation to who is involved and what mode is employed (spoken/written). The question is how does this affect what gets said or written. Let's think, first of all, about speaking and writing and their different functions. Speech enables us to develop meaning through action, whereas writing enables us to preserve meaning and develop meaning through reflection. Each serves a crucial function in education in terms of generating ideas and reviewing and revising ideas. Yet how can they be used to complement each other in class activities? Talking first can be a useful way of building vocabulary, ideas and interest. It is also of value to think about how spoken discussion can be brought into the process of writing, so that it is less of an individualistic experience. Joint writing, and reading and commenting on drafts, are two ways of doing this.

The audience and the social relations between those engaged in both written and spoken communication are also important, for a number of reasons. What you communicate and how you communicate is very much dependent upon the people with whom you are interacting. Think of the nature and type of participation that is possible in large group discussions compared with small group discussions. Each have their pros and cons because they enable different types of participation and different ways of talking about an issue or idea. In the case of writing, a sense of audience is critical for a number of reasons. In the first instance having a real audience can make the writing task more meaningful; it has a communicative purpose beyond being assigned a grade. It also opens up the possibility for response and further dialogue. Having a sense of audience is also fundamental to how ideas might be 'pitched'. Writing a letter to a friend about a problem at work might be very different from writing a letter to the boss complaining about the problem. The problem is more difficult when it comes to essay writing, particularly at the senior level, where the focus is typically on demonstrating an understanding of an idea through a structured line of argument. We would argue that essay writing is often difficult precisely because there is no sense of audience. However, if writing an essay is also seen as a chance to build ideas in order to become a member of a particular practice (of geographers, historians, scientists, sociologists and so forth) then the people with an interest in the practice would be a potential audience. This might include peers, teachers and other experts in the field. To extend the idea of audience, think too about where student writing can be published. Possibilities include the school web site, the local newspaper, a school or class journal.

While the above discussion has focussed on participation and social relations associated with speaking and writing, the ideas we have presented also have application to communication using other media such as video, drama, music, graphic art, dance and so forth. At this point it is also worth making special mention of the changing communications and education landscape associated with multimedia technology and the Internet (Kress 1998; Lemke 1998). Three points are worth thinking about in light of the discussion on social relations and learning in classrooms. First, the Internet opens up the potential for a wide public audience through web page publications, email list-serves, online discussions and so forth. Second, multimedia technology enables students to express ideas using a combination of sound, graphics, text and links. Third, there can be dramatic variation in levels of computer competence within any given class and it is not necessarily the teacher who has the technological expertise. How these factors influence social relations and learning among groups of students and teachers is currently the subject of considerable research and exploration by educators. There is much potential for teachers to investigate and document ways of integrating communications technology into their teaching practice and to consider how it can be used to serve worthwhile educational ends.

Resources and physical space

The final aspect of the context that we wish to consider in this chapter, and that is closely tied to the people and subject matter, are the available resources. We will talk particularly about the resources that teachers and students may or may not have access to in classrooms and the physical 'space' in which teaching and learning takes place. We are considering the teaching space to be a resource. We will also consider human resources and the role of those people closely connected with classrooms that we did not mention in the 'actors' section of this chapter. Our intention is to think about the interrelationship between resources and space and teaching and learning practices. As you can imagine, the resources vary enormously from school to school and from classroom to classroom in terms of both access and use. This raises questions related to both equity and efficacy of learning.

We list below some types of resources that may exist in high schools. As you read through the resources think about the following: What access do students and teachers have to resources and how can they be utilised to support and extend teaching and learning in the various subject areas? A related question, particularly for some resources such as computers, concerns what teachers and students need to know in order to use the resource in the first place.

- Teaching 'space' and its physical arrangement: think of, for example, regular classrooms with desks and chairs; specialty rooms, such as labs, workshops, kitchens and gymnasia, with benches, equipment, tools, etc.; outdoors areas such as the oval for PE and the agriculture plot. How does the space affect movement, social relations and a teacher's actions? Think about the ways that desks in rows or desks in clusters might affect the patterns for communication in a classroom and more specifically the teaching and learning practices. For many subjects, particularly those using specialised equipment, there is little flexibility regarding the organisation of the work space. Benches and equipment are in fixed places in ways that affect movement and social interaction. There is often a need, both to adapt teaching and learning practices to suit the environment, and to modify the environment, if possible, to suit the teaching and learning practices you wish to establish.

- Equipment resources, of two kinds: equipment that teachers use as part of their teaching practice, such as videos, computers, pens, paper, photocopy machines and so on; and equipment associated with the practices in subject areas, such as pens, paper, computers, sports gear, sewing machines, lathes, musical instruments, paint, maps, bunsen burners, etc.

- Information resources: the resources that students and teachers might draw on for information and ideas — library, Internet, teaching materials and resources such as kits, videos, textbooks.

- Human resources: these include support staff, technicians, specialist supports, ESL (English as a Second Language), Learning Assistance, ATSI (Aboriginal and Torres Strait Islander), counsellors and librarians. Parents, experts in the field and people in the local community might also be part of the human resources that are part of class activities.

- Time: while not a tangible resource, the time allocated to certain subjects influences the ways in which content is presented. For example, a school timetable structured around 40 minute periods can lend itself to very different forms of teaching practice than those structured around 80 minute periods. Likewise, the length of a course influences the depth to which a subject can be taken.

One of the most critical resource issues in schools at the moment is related to computer technology. In part this is a question of the number of computers in a school and the type of access to the Internet. Yet other resource issues related to computer use include: the level of technical support; where computers are located in the school (in labs or classrooms); the time that teachers need to learn how to use them as a teaching tool; the degree of student access; and the level of parental support and funding for equipment. As we mentioned previously, the use of this tool will inevitably change the teaching and learning relations and the ways in which ideas are represented. Of course underpinning this are questions related to the distribution of these resources and the funding allocated to computer technology in comparison with other teaching resources.

Conclusion

The key concept underpinning this chapter is that learning is a social process, and that we come to know certain things through participating in various social practices. In order to understand social practice we have argued that it is important to take account of the context in which that practice is located. The features of the context that we have focussed on in this chapter are the subject or topic, the actors involved and the resources that they have access to. Each of these factors is in a dynamic relationship with the processes of teaching and learning taking place in any classroom context. The task for teachers is to develop activities, and goals for those activities, that are purposeful, interesting and engaging. Keep in mind that this is not easy, learning to do this does not happen overnight. It is something that teachers keep working at during their careers. Yet what it does require is skill, creativity, knowledge and an interest in the task at hand.

The approach to learning that we have developed in this chapter is primarily concerned with establishing class activities that enable students to work together, to participate in the practices associated with various subject areas in order to 'build knowledge'. Such an approach to learning can set up a tension with one of the insistent demands of high school teaching — to cover the curriculum. In particular, the pressure to prepare students for external exams at the end of Year 12 often flows down to what is to be covered in Year 7 or 8. It is this pressure to 'cover' material that can lead teachers to adopt an approach based on transmitting information, as other approaches can be seen to take too much time or might not ensure adequate coverage of the content. How you will resolve this tension in your own teaching practice is a subject worthy of much discussion. We hope that the ideas presented below help you to think about this (Wells 1999, p. 263):

> Although suggestions or recommendations may be made by administrators at various removes from the classroom, it is the teacher who, in the last resort, decides whether to have students working collaboratively in groups or to 'teach' them from the front of the class; whether to value conjectures, supported by argument, or to 'correct answers' as defined by the textbook; whether to attempt to get all students to achieve the same outcomes at the same time, or to recognise the various forms of diversity in the student community and to take account of these differences, by negotiating appropriate challenges for each individual and providing the assistance that each needs in order to meet them.

INQUIRY STRATEGIES

1. One of the problems posed at the start of the chapter concerned starting up with a class; establishing an environment for learning in a particular subject area. Specify a subject and year level, consult relevant curriculum documents and develop a plan for establishing a learning environment. What are four main things that you might do in this start-up period?

2. (a) Think of a subject or topic that bored you when you were at school, mainly because of the way in which it was taught. You will be an unusual student if you were never bored! Think about how you, as a teacher, might approach the topic or subject to make it more interesting and engaging. Write a list of possible activities that you might build into a unit of work.

(b) Think of a writing task that you did at school that really engaged you. Specify what it was about the task that motivated you. How could you draw on this knowledge to develop writing tasks in your own classroom?

3. You are teaching a unit on the impact of immigration on Australian society. You decide that you will try to make the material more immediate and fresh by exploring the effects of immigration on the local community. Try to make explicit the following:

- the various knowledge areas and conceptual tools needed to investigate this topic;

- the range of activities that would help students investigate this topic;

- the possible range of people involved, both as subjects of the study (e.g. local immigrant families) and participants/helpers in the study (e.g. local community organisations and historians);

- personal background factors that might influence how you and the students approach the topic.

If you prefer you could devise your own topic for this exercise. For example a biology teacher might choose the topic of the role of amphibious life in the local ecology.

References

Alexander, P. (2000). Toward a model of academic development: Schooling and the acquisition of knowledge. *Educational Researcher*, 29(2), pp. 28–38.

Barrow, R. (1990). *Understanding Skills: Thinking, Feeling and Caring*. London, Ontario: The Althouse Press.

Bruner, J.S. (1983). *Child's Talk*. New York: Norton.

Cazden, C.B. (1988). *Classroom discourse: The language of teaching and learning*. Portsmouth, NH: Heinemann.

Dewey, J. (1938). *Education and Experience*. New York: Collier Macmillan.

Egan, K. (1997). *The Educated Mind: How Cognitive Tools Shape Our Understanding*. Chicago: University of Chicago Press.

Engestrom, Y. (1999). Activity theory and individual and social transformation. In Y. Engestrom, R. Miettinen & R.L. Punamaki (eds), *Perspectives on activity theory*. New York: Cambridge University Press.

Kress, G. (1998). Visual and verbal modes of representation in electronically mediated communication: the potentials of new forms of text. In I. Snyder (ed), *Page to Screen — Taking Literacy into the Electronic Era*. London and New York: Routledge.

Lave, J. & Wenger, E. (1993). *Situated Learning: Legitimate and Peripheral Participation*. Cambridge, USA: Cambridge University Press.

Lemke, J.L. (1998). Metamedia Literacy: Transforming Meanings and Media. In D. Reinking, M. McKenna, L. Labbo & R. Kieffer, D. (eds), *Handbook of Literacy and Technology: Transformations in a Post-Typographical World*. Mahwah, NJ: Lawrence Erlbaum Associates.

Phillips, D.C. (1995). The good, the bad, and the ugly: The many faces of constructivism. *Educational Researcher*, 24(7), pp. 5–12.

Pirie, S. & Kieren, T. (1994). Growth in mathematical understanding: How can we characterise it and how can we represent it? *Educational Studies in Mathematics*, 26, pp. 165–190.

Vygotsky, L. (1978). *Mind in Society*. Cambridge, Ma. and London, England: Harvard University Press.

Vygotsky, L. (1997). *Thought and Language* (Kozulin, Alex, trans.). Cambridge, Ma. and London, England: MIT Press.

Wells, G. (1999). *Dialogic Inquiry: Toward a Sociocultural Practice and Theory of Education*. New York: Cambridge University Press.

Wertsch, J. (1995). The need for action in sociocultural research. In J. Wertsch, P. Del Rio & A. Avarez (eds), *Sociocultural Studies of Mind*. New York: Cambridge University Press.

CHAPTER

Negotiating the Practicum

> Learning to teach is a social process of negotiation rather than an individual problem of behaviour. This dynamic is essential to any humanising explanation of the work of teachers.
>
> (Britzman 1991, p. 8)

The practicum, or prac as it is often called, is a time to learn about teaching by being on-the-job, by experiencing what life is like in a school. Your own experience as a student, irrespective of how long ago this was, no doubt provides you with a set of 'scripts' for the roles that teachers and students play in these institutions. However, when you enter a school as a student teacher you are on the other side of the desk, so to speak. This brings with it a set of uncertainties and complexities that need to be negotiated. The 'real world' of the practicum includes, amongst other things, learning about teaching, teachers' work and schools; learning about being a student teacher and the various expectations and relationships that this entails; and learning about yourself as a beginning teacher.

The practicum is an intense time. The learning curve is steep and there are bound to be highs and lows. While each practicum situation is different, the purpose of this chapter is to provide you with some ways of thinking about how you can prepare for and navigate your way through some of the things that might happen during your practicum experience.

The following points will provide a framework for the chapter:

- what is the practicum;
- the practicum setting and practicum relationships;
- expectations of you as a student teacher; and
- uni and school, theory and practice — what are the connections.

We hope that the material in the chapter will provide a useful starting point for negotiating your practicum experience. By this we mean:

- navigating your way through the various parts of the practicum experience;
- questioning the assumptions and expectations that you and others bring to the practicum; and
- working with others involved in the practicum to understand and evaluate your professional learning and to develop your own theories of practice.

What is the practicum?

The practicum can be conceptualised in many ways. Consider these:

- 'The practicum is a time to apply theories learnt on campus.'
- 'The practicum is a time to learn about teaching through experience and through critically reflecting on experience.'
- 'The practicum is a time to learn about the real world of teaching.'
- 'The practicum is a time in which student teachers are socialised into the culture of a school.'
- 'The practicum is a time to assess the qualities of a beginning teacher.'
- 'The practicum is a time to find out whether you really want to be a teacher.'

These statements all say something a little different about the practicum and its purpose. Those involved in the practicum — student teachers, school teachers and university advisers — may have different ideas about the purpose of the practicum and where it fits into your teacher education program. Your thoughts on the practicum may include one, none, or a combination of the above ideas.

It is worth saying at the outset that there are ongoing debates about the practicum — about what should be learnt in the practicum, about how that learning should take place and about the purpose and value of this learning (Calderhead & Shorrock 1997; Gore 1995; Zeichner 1996). Much of the debate revolves around the question: Is learning to teach a matter of training or a matter of education? When conceived as training, the practicum can be seen as a time in which one acquires a set of skills by being apprenticed to an expert teacher. Others argue that this concept of the practicum is problematic because a focus on skills and training does not take into account the complex nature of teaching. Thus when conceived as education, a process of systematic and critical reflection is seen as an appropriate means to learn about teaching (see for example, Grimmett & Erickson 1988; Schon 1987).

A related part of this debate concerns the amount of time that the practicum should have in a teacher preparation program. Here the issues are a little more complex. One argument is that more time should be spent in schools because learning to teach is a matter of training and best done in schools. Another argument is that more time should be spent in schools because one learns about the complexity of teachers' work by being in a practice setting. Still others argue that the issue is about the quality of the experience, not the quantity, and that more time in school does not necessarily mean a better quality of experience and learning.

These debates have been hard fought in the United Kingdom over the last decade. In 1988 a conservative government mandated that 80 per cent of teacher education should take place in schools. The purpose of this mandate was to impose a training model. Many critics have argued that the measures taken in the United Kingdom undercut the campus-based coursework. While in Australia the debates have not been as heated as the United Kingdom, the same issues exist and we will return to some of these later in the chapter. At this stage it is sufficient to note that there are many concepts of the practicum, and that underpinning these are assumptions about the nature of teachers' work and the appropriate means to learn this.

We seek below to articulate some of our own assumptions about the practicum, so that you know where we stand on some of these issues and why the ideas in this chapter have been framed in a particular way. We hope that through your experiences on campus and in schools you will debate and challenge these ideas and assumptions so that you can develop your own point of view on these matters.

Here are our ideas:

- First, on a number of occasions in the book we talk about the intellectual, emotional and physical dimensions of teachers' work. One critical part of learning how to do this type of work comes through experience, and critical reflection on that experience, in the practice (Featherstone, Munby & Russell 1997; Goodlad 1994; Schon 1987; Fish 1989). The practicum, as the name suggests, is a time for learning about a practice by being in a practice. It is impossible to learn to teach without engaging in the practice of teaching, in the same way that it is impossible to learn to drive a car without actually getting in a car and going out onto the road. Likewise, learning to teach does not happen overnight. The practicum provides an initial experience; it is the first part of workplace learning.

- Second, the experience of being a student teacher in a school has its own dynamic, its own set of relationships, rules, intellectual and emotional responses, tough judgments and unpredictability (Britzman 1991; Knowles & Cole 1993). One criticism of practicum experiences is that the actual practicum curriculum is not explicit; that is, there is not necessarily clarity surrounding the what and the how of student teacher learning and the teaching associated with that learning. Furthermore there is not necessarily an examination of the values held by the institutions and people involved in the practicum experience (Calderhead & James 1992; Zeichner 1990). Many reforms in practicum programs over the last decade have sought to make the practicum curriculum explicit; to ask questions about the 'what' and 'how' of practicum pedagogy by way of assisting student teachers and their advisers to understand and design the practicum dynamic in ways that enhance learning.

- Third, there is more to the practicum than just learning a set of teaching techniques. This chapter does not contain any sure-fire recipes or list of tips that will make you a good teacher and that will get you through the practicum. Rather the practicum is a time for *learning* about yourself, about teaching and about being a student teacher. To this end it is important to be able question your values, to articulate and evaluate your learning and to be able to frame learning goals.

- A fourth and related assumption is that learning to teach is a very public affair. You are required to demonstrate particular skills, dispositions and knowledge to your advisers and to students in your classes in a regular and ongoing way. This is a very difficult thing to do. It involves taking risks and being prepared for criticism. However it is not a solo affair; being able to talk with peers and advisers about your ideas and your work is central to learning about teaching and being able to justify your professional practice.

- Finally, there may be a range of views about teaching, education and the practicum held by teacher educators, be they working in schools or on campus. Different views are inevitable and important to recognise and discuss.

Based on this concept of the practicum and learning to teach, the remainder of the chapter discusses some of the specific parts of the practicum that we believe are important to negotiate. However, before moving on we do want to note that there will be variations in the ways in which each teacher education institution organises and conceptualises the practicum. Perhaps one of the most common areas of difference and one that does cause confusion is the nomenclature used for the particular positions that people have in the practicum. You might hear terms such as 'student teacher', 'pre-service teacher', 'associate teacher', 'supervising teacher', 'sponsor teacher', 'school adviser', 'mentor', 'university supervisor', and 'university associate'. For the purposes of this chapter we will use the terms *student teacher*, *school adviser* and *university adviser*.

Practicum settings and practicum relationships

This section of the chapter will focus on ways of understanding your practicum school, especially the professional relationships that are central to working in a school. Particular attention will be paid to the relationships with staff members who you are likely to encounter as a student teacher and how these relationships can be negotiated.

Practicum settings — getting the lie of the land

When you enter your practicum school you will become part of the fabric of life in that school. Your practicum may be only a few weeks in duration, but even in that short time you will become part of the broader pattern of social practices that make up the culture of the high school in which you have been placed. Central to the culture are those people with an interest in what happens in the school — teachers, students, support staff, administrators, parents, caregivers and other members of a school community. The culture is also determined by, amongst other things, the architecture, the timetable, the location and administrative structures, as well as the school's history, traditions and guiding principles. While there are many common features of high school culture, you will find that each school has its own dynamic, its own patterns for communication, its own structures, its own politics and rules.

Take, for example, a school staff meeting. This is a distinctive part of high school life. Most schools have a regular time after school to hold a meeting for the staff. How these meetings are run and what is on the agenda both shape and reflect the school culture. In some schools staff meetings are run along egalitarian lines — teachers take responsibility for chairing meetings and establishing the agenda. In other schools the meetings are run in a more authoritarian manner with the principal directing the proceedings. In some schools the staff meeting is a time to discuss key issues pertaining to the curriculum; in others it is a part of school life that is endured rather than enjoyed. Certain members of staff may talk more than others at these meetings. The staff meetings therefore say something about the patterns for communication and participation among staff in a school.

In this section of the book we want to concentrate on the part of the school culture that involves the work you will be doing with teachers and other members of a school staff. Our premise is that the relationships and interactions between members of staff, including your relationships with teachers as a student teacher, is a critically important part of a school culture. As a member of staff during the practicum, you will need to work with a number of people within the school as part of both your teaching practice and your general involvement in the activities taking place in the school. Your school adviser is the person you will work most closely with and we will discuss this relationship in more detail in the next section of the chapter. At the same time, you may need to work with the school librarian to design a unit that involves the resources in the library. You may need to talk to a school administrator to find out about an aspect of school policy. You may need to consult an ESL teacher in order to take account of the English language abilities of those in your classroom. Outside the classroom, staff meetings, departmental and committee meetings and the staffroom at morning tea and lunch are all occasions in which teachers communicate with other members of a school staff. These interactions are a part of the culture of a school. As a student teacher you have a particular position in the culture. This position has its own special set of professional relationships and interactions.

Practicum relationships

One of the most important professional relationships you will develop during the practicum is with your school adviser. Indeed, there are many who argue that the relationship that develops between a student teacher and the school adviser can often be a key to the success of the practicum (Calderhead & James 1992; Graham 1999; McIntyre 1992).

In most practicum schools student teachers are allocated to work with one or two teachers who take on an advisory role. These teachers have responsibility for both supporting and evaluating your teaching practice. They are the people with whom you work on a day-to-day basis. Typically a person from your university is also appointed to your school and they too play a role in supporting and evaluating your teaching practice.

The first stage in the practicum is placement in a school. It is worth thinking for a minute about the placement procedures and institutional arrangements associated with placements. Each teacher education institution will have its own procedures for organising practicum placements. This may be in relation to the ways in which connections are made with schools, placements determined and school advisers appointed. At the same time, in all states and territories, there are various awards and agreements between teacher education institutions, employing authorities and teacher unions that underpin the work that teachers do as school advisers. In some cases there is financial remuneration provided to teachers, in others being an adviser is built into a teacher's duty statement or it is linked to a program of in-service professional development. Given this, you will find that different teachers have different reasons and motivations for being school advisers — these may be associated with their interest in the process of teacher education, as well as other benefits associated with the responsibility. So too, depending upon the institution, teachers will have different degrees of responsibility for the evaluation of student teachers; in some cases they will have prime responsibility, in others it will be shared with the university adviser. Furthermore, each teacher will bring to the role a personal set of experiences and values in relation to the practicum.

The actual placement of student teachers in a school and with an adviser in the appropriate subject is often a large administrative task. Not only that, the process is not unlike a blind date — you are matched with an adviser, the date being the length of the practicum. Not surprisingly, it is important and desirable that the relationship that develops between student teachers and advisers be a positive one.

Each person comes to the relationship with a different institutional position as well as with their own set of expectations, values and experiences. As the relationship unfolds it will have its own dynamic, its own politics and emotions. This can be extremely important in terms of the processes of teaching and learning that are central to this relationship. It can be important to how values about educational practices are discussed, learning goals are established, joint tasks and demonstration are undertaken, and feedback and evaluation are provided. It is therefore of value to think about how you can develop a productive professional relationship with your adviser. So too, the university adviser can play an important role in the conduct of the practicum and their relationship with both you and your school adviser can be of significance, especially in cases where there are problems in the practicum context. In light of this, consider the following scenario. As you read the case, think in particular of how the relationship between the teacher and student teacher is structured and its impact on teaching and learning processes.

> After spending the first couple of days at the school observing classes, Haleema and her adviser Pam had a brief discussion about Haleema's teaching load. Pam told her that she wanted her to experiment and try new things. She also told Haleema that given her responsibilities as head of department, she was extremely busy and that she hoped that Haleema would be able to work independently. Haleema was going to teach Year 10 science and Year 7 science. Year 10 were doing a physics unit and Year 7 a unit on biology. Pam gave Haleema a few resources, they had a quick look at the curriculum guidelines and then agreed that Haleema would start teaching in two days time. Haleema was glad on one level to have the freedom to do what she wanted, but on another level she was a little nervous. She wasn't quite sure what was expected of her in terms of lesson plans and directions for the content. This was especially so with the Year 10 class because she did not have a background in physics and the class seemed to be lacking in motivation.
>
> As the prac got going Haleema felt really happy with the Year 7 class; they were keen and interested. The Year 10 were another kettle of fish — they were bored, listless and made it clear that they did not want to be in class. Haleema didn't get much feedback from Pam about her teaching — the odd comment, but nothing in writing and nothing to give her some direction with planning. Haleema spoke to the university adviser about this. The university adviser said that she would speak to Pam, however Haleema said that she would rather she not do that; she didn't want to do anything that might be deemed to be critical of Pam.

One of the problems in this case may be that there are no clear protocols for this relationship, no procedures for teaching and learning within this relationship such as time for meetings and types of feedback. The other dilemma is that Haleema is in a vulnerable position because she is being evaluated by Pam and therefore she does not want to do anything that might jeopardise the relationship or Pam's perception of her teaching abilities.

The above case is one illustration of what might be called the micro-politics of practicum relationships. There are various rules, both implicit and explicit, for what might be said or not said. There are various ways in which power and authority, as they exist in any relationship, are played out in the practicum context. These rules and degrees of authority serve to both create and reflect student teachers' and teachers' institutional positions and responsibilities (Mitchell 1996). A common manifestation of these 'rules' amongst practicum students is to do what needs to be done in order to pass the practicum. We say this not to imply that you should slavishly follow the rules, rather to consider the degree to which the circumstances surrounding the rule can be opened for discussion and relationships created that enable this level of discussion to take place.

Some of the 'rules' regarding the practicum can sometimes seem contradictory or at least can create certain tensions. In the above instance, doing whatever needs to be done in order to pass sits oddly against the often more explicit message that the practicum is a learning experience. Similarly, an expectation to experiment and try new things during the practicum can sometimes be coupled with an expectation to conform to existing practices (Bullough & Gitlin 1996). Likewise there is much rhetoric surrounding the collaborative nature of teachers' work yet, as a student teacher, there is sometimes an expectation that you succeed on your own (Furlong & Maynard 1995). So too, as Britzman (1991) notes, the name 'student teacher' carries its own set of contradictions and tensions — not quite a student, but not a 'real' teacher. Consider the following case study as a means of examining this tension.

Colleague and student
After 30 minutes of disrespectful behaviour Paul had to take action. He asked two students to leave the room. As they were leaving, they mouthed a couple of obscenities. Paul, without thinking, responded with a few of his own. These were not directed specifically at the students, but certainly said out of frustration. Paul's school adviser was not in the room when this incident happened. At lunchtime the deputy principal came to speak to Paul. The students had told the deputy principal that Paul had sworn at them. The deputy read the allegations to Paul and told him that he had been completely out of line in saying this to the students. Without hearing Paul's side of the story the deputy said that he did not think it appropriate for Paul to return to class and that he would be contacting the university to terminate the practicum.

As Paul walked out of the room he felt humiliated. He was stunned that the deputy principal did not even ask him for his version of the events. Within the space of five minutes their relationship had changed completely. Prior to this incident Paul had been treated like a colleague, now he felt like a student, yet with less rights than the students in his class. A meeting was held between the deputy principal, the school adviser and the university adviser. Paul was not invited to attend this meeting.

This case again illustrates some of the vulnerabilities associated with being a student teacher. Britzman describes the tension in the following way (p. 14):

> Marginally situated in two worlds, the student teacher as part student and part teacher has the dual struggle of educating others while being educated. Consequently, student teachers appropriate different voices in the attempt to speak for themselves yet all the while act in a largely inherited and constraining context. This struggle characterises the tensions between being and becoming a teacher as student teachers draw from their past and present in the process of coming to know.

Juggling these competing and contradictory demands is not easy. It requires a careful reading of the situation as well as clear and open communication skills. How you deal with these demands will depend both on your principles as well as the pragmatics of the situation. As Britzman (1991) says, these are matters for social negotiation.

As a student teacher the important question is: What rules and resources do you have access to that will enable you to negotiate aspects of your practicum experience?

In the following section we will consider ways in which expectations regarding the practicum can be made explicit and how this can be used to negotiate your practicum experience. Knowing these expectations provides a resource useful for this negotiation.

Expectations of you as a student teacher

Clarifying expectations about the practicum is crucial to being able to negotiate various aspects of your practicum experience. You will no doubt have certain expectations and assumptions about schools, teaching, students and the practicum. Others will have expectations about you as a student teacher. These expectations include those formally set by the university as well as those established by the school and by your advisers. In this section of the chapter we will examine the various sets of expectations and ways in which these expectations can be related to each other.

What do others expect of me?

A variety of sources can be used to begin to define what is expected of you during the practicum. On a broad scale, various professional and governing bodies have attempted to define the competencies expected of beginning teachers. These have served to set some state and national standards that can be used to frame a practicum curriculum. In addition, each university will have guidelines for the conduct of the practicum and the roles and responsibilities of the practicum participants. A practicum handbook is usually the place in which this information is found. The guidelines may specify such things as your teaching load, procedures for supervision and evaluation and your responsibilities while in the school.

There are also statutory regulations for professional and ethical conduct. These regulations will cover occupational health and safety, child protection, relationships between teachers and students and so on. Over the last decade, and in response to a wide variety of social issues pertaining to the physical and emotional safety of young people, regulations governing the responsibilities of teachers have been defined and refined. Being familiar with these specific codes of ethical conduct is an essential part of professional practice (refer to Chapter 16 for more detail). In addition, having a broad sense of what is expected in terms of teaching competencies can be useful in developing your own learning goals.

Some of the institutional guidelines for the practicum need to be rigidly followed and others can be interpreted with some degree of flexibility. Depending upon the people you are working with and the school you are located in for the practicum, it is likely that there will be degrees of variation in the way in which the practicum is conducted. You may be in a practicum setting where the key players — your school and university advisers and you — have very fixed ideas about the conduct of the practicum, or you may be in a setting where there is considerable flexibility in the way that the guidelines are interpreted. Perhaps what is of greatest importance is making the guidelines explicit, so that there is some consensus among the key players regarding the goals and purpose of the practicum, and so that you have a sense of what is important for the conduct of your practicum experience.

Setting learning goals and developing standards of practice

Having a clear sense of what it is that teachers do and are expected to do, and having a sense of the actions and activities that constitute good teaching practice, can help to provide direction and goals for your learning during the practicum. In this section of the chapter we will examine some ways in which learning goals can be established and negotiated. We will do this by considering practicum reports, system-wide guidelines, two case studies and a cycle of reflection and action.

There are two key assumptions underpinning the ideas here. First, if you know what is expected of you in the practicum, you can begin to articulate and direct your own learning. Writing an essay for an assignment provides a useful analogy. If you know the criteria used to assess the essay then these can be used as a guide when writing the essay and as a means of ensuring that the criteria have been met. If you do not know the criteria, writing an essay can be difficult because the goals toward which your writing is directed may be less clearly defined.

The second assumption is that making goals explicit and clarifying the means by which goals can be met can be an important topic for discussion between student teachers and their advisers.

Practicum report forms

The practicum report form that has been developed by your institution, and that is completed by advisers at the conclusion of the practicum, will provide one way of framing the teaching competencies expected of you during the practicum. A sample of one institution's report form is presented below. Rather than seeing the report form as an end point, it can be used as a starting point for articulating and discussing goals for your own learning about teaching and some of the actions that can be taken to help achieve those goals. This is not to suggest that the report form simply be a checklist, rather to think about how the ideas contained within it can be used to inform a design for what it is that you want to learn and how you can go about doing this. In this respect the report form can be a useful document to review and discuss with your school adviser at the *outset* of the practicum.

Competency standards for beginning teachers

Various government and professional organisations have sponsored projects that have sought to define the competencies expected of beginning teachers; for example, NSW Ministerial Advisory Council on the Quality of Teaching and Learning, Queensland Board of Registration, National Project on the Quality of Teaching and Learning (NPQTL), the Australian Teaching Council (ATC). These competencies are one way of setting standards of practice appropriate for beginning teachers. Being familiar with these or similar documents used by a school system or employing authority can also provide a starting point for describing expectations and developing your own learning goals for the practicum.

The competencies expected of beginning teachers developed by the National Project on the Quality of Teaching and Learning, for example, were developed through a process of research and consultation with teachers across Australia. The following headings provide the outline for conceptualising the areas of teachers' work within which a beginning teacher would have some knowledge and skills:

- planning;
- teaching practice;
- relationships with students;
- assessment and reporting;
- self-evaluation and reflection; and
- professional responsibilities.

Practice Teaching Competencies

Note: Practicum report form used by Charles Sturt University, Wagga Wagga, NSW. The teaching competencies used in this report form have been based on the ideas developed by the National Project on the Quality of Teaching and Learning (see below for more details). Student teachers and their advisers use this report form to develop learning goals and as a tool for formative and summative evaluation during the practicum.

- Please comment on and rate the student's work in each of the following categories (written comments should be made in the boxes on the right-hand side of the page).
- Please add additional pointers if required.

Note the rating scale:

1	2	3	4	*
Not demonstrated	Demonstrated with a lot of support	Demonstrated with minimum support	Demonstrated effectively and independently	No opportunity to demonstrate

Areas of competence	Outcomes	Pointers	Rating	Comments
1. Planning	■ plans comprehensive lessons ■ reviews effectiveness of lessons and units to inform future planning	■ considers content, context, purpose and strategies ■ asks questions, seeks advice, takes note of what has happened, reteaches after reflecting	1 2 3 4 * 1 2 3 4 *	
2. Teaching practice	■ knows content relevant to activities	■ clearly explains ideas ■ adapts content to suit the students and the strategies	1 2 3 4 *	

Areas of competence	Outcomes	Pointers	Rating	Comments
	demonstrates flexibility and responsiveness	can make changes to plans if necessary	1 2 3 4 *	
	displays repertoire of teaching strategies	uses, for example, questioning, demonstrating, group work, modelling, discussion, problem solving	1 2 3 4 *	
	structures learning tasks effectively	makes linkages between parts of lessons introduces and concludes lessons	1 2 3 4 *	
	actively reflects on all aspects	nominates aspects that need improvement reviews own learning thinks of alternatives identifies strengths	1 2 3 4 *	
3. Managing student behaviour	sets and maintains clear expectations	develops routine procedures responds to responsible student behaviour introduces lessons	1 2 3 4 *	
	takes appropriate action if students disrupt teaching and learning	sets consequences for inappropriate behaviour applies consequences fairly and consistently	1 2 3 4 *	

Areas of competence	Outcomes	Pointers	Rating	Comments
	■ reflects on quality of learning	■ identifies elements which facilitate learning and barriers which constrain learning	1 2 3 4 *	
4. Relationships with students and staff	■ develops positive relationships	■ displays interest and concern for students ■ displays patience ■ avoids destructive criticism	1 2 3 4 *	
	■ contributes positively to working environment of the class ■ contributes to regular meetings ■ reflects on extent to which he/she contributes to positive interactions with supervising teacher	■ co-operates with class teacher ■ brings in extra resources ■ accepts and responds to advice ■ willingly discusses issues ■ negotiates future directions	1 2 3 4 *	
5. Reporting	■ uses formative and summative assessment and evaluation procedures	■ talks about and understands classroom events	1 2 3 4 *	
	■ monitors student progress during lesson	■ shows awareness of individuals ■ assesses 'over the shoulder' ■ observes and takes action ■ gives feedback	1 2 3 4 *	

Areas of competence	Outcomes	Pointers	Rating	Comments
6. Professional responsibility	▪ understands rights and responsibilities of teachers and students	▪ respects individuals	1 2 3 4 *	
	▪ exhibits enthusiasm and commitment	▪ volunteers for extra-curricular activities, attends meetings, is punctual, well-prepared, etc.	1 2 3 4 *	

Below we consider some of the detail associated with these broad areas and investigate ways in which they can be used to plan for and negotiate your own learning. We also want to reiterate that these are ways of conceptualising what might be expected of a beginning teacher, not someone at the start of their practicum. In this respect they can be used to provide some directions for learning.

Below are some examples from the NPQTL document that outline competencies expected of a beginning teacher. The following is an example related to teaching practice. Two aspects of teaching practice are listed with accompanying examples of actions.

Competencies expected of a beginning teacher

Aspects of teaching practice	Examples
▪ Uses a wide repertoire of teaching strategies.	▪ Selects appropriate teaching and learning processes. ▪ Balances the content and process goals of teaching and learning. ▪ Adapts the content that is being taught to suit the students and context of teaching.
▪ Demonstrates flexibility and responsiveness.	▪ Explains and modifies tasks when necessary. ▪ Recognises learning opportunities in issues raised by students.

In essence, what documents such as these competency frameworks do is provide one way of identifying or describing aspects of teaching as well as examples of action that are constitutive of good teaching. Our argument is that it is of value to consider such documents or ones used in your state or territory or by the school system in which your practicum school is located because they provide a platform for thinking about teaching, directing learning and discussing ideas with advisers. Ideas can be adapted and modified to suit the local context *and* ideas developed in the local context can be calibrated with those developed at a system or state level.

Negotiating learning goals with advisers — two case studies

The following case studies demonstrate various ways in which student teachers and their school advisers work together to clarify and negotiate expectations.

Planning for students' learning/Planning for learning about teaching

Tan was teaching Year 11 legal studies during the practicum. She and her school adviser, Simon, met regularly to discuss the day-to-day planning required for a series of lessons on the institution of marriage as part of a Family Law unit. As part of their discussions Tan and Simon considered the curriculum documents and requirements, the amount of time available, the textbook and other resources from the library and Internet. They also considered the ways in which students responded to the ideas and to the activities in class. Through the discussion Tan began to get a sense of the range of factors that underpinned planning for students' learning.

A key question for Tan became: What action could she take that would ensure that material was covered in three weeks and that would enable her to draw on strategies beyond using the textbook and 'talk and chalk' as a means of encouraging student interest and participation? From this a focus for Tan's own learning and self-evaluation, as well as Simon's evaluation, was developed. This would include demonstrating the means by which curriculum material and requirements could be used to underpin and develop teaching strategies, activities and methods that encouraged student participation.

In this case study it is possible to see two levels of planning take place. One level concerns planning material and activities to teach the class, the other concerns planning for learning about teaching. It is this second level that can often be forgotten or dropped off in the general business and 'busyness' of a school day. Yet it is this aspect of the practicum that is crucial to a process of systematic reflection of, and inquiry into, one's own teaching practice. This process of reflection and inquiry is central to developing, making explicit and justifying actions and understandings associated with teaching. Making time for this type of reflection and discussion is therefore crucial. It is also important to document this as the following case illustrates.

Responsibility, evidence and evaluation

Tony was completing an extended practicum as part of a two year Master of Teaching program. He had completed two practicums prior to this and there was an expectation that he would assume a considerable range of teaching responsibilities during this final practicum. Tony's school adviser, Ros, was expected to take on a mentoring role rather than the more direct supervisory role expected of teachers in initial practicums. A specific part of this role was to assist student teachers to develop their own learning goals and begin to take responsibility for systematically evaluating their own practice.

At the outset of the practicum Tony and Ros talked about expectations, teaching competencies and goals. They drew on the practicum report form, Tony's previous experiences and their knowledge of particular classes he would be teaching to develop a set of expectations and learning goals. They decided to meet once a week for a semi-formal discussion to report on what had happened during the week and to set directions for the following week that would focus specifically on aspects of Tony's teaching practice and what he was learning. They also agreed that Tony would take responsibility for leading the discussions, for documenting and providing evidence of what it was he was learning.

In the first instance Tony was concerned about management, so this became something that he concentrated on in planning and evaluating his own practice. At the end of the week Tony and Ros discussed and documented the action that Tony had taken to develop his practice in this area. In the course of the discussion Tony admitted that some students in the Year 9 class were really unpredictable and he was not sure what other steps he could take to work with these students. As the conversation progressed Tony and Ros began to talk in more specific detail about the reasons for certain students' behaviour and some of the teaching strategies that could be drawn on in light of this. This provided a focus for Tony's teaching and learning for the following week.

At the conclusion of the practicum both Tony and Ros had sets of papers documenting their discussions and the evidence used to illustrate Tony's teaching and learning. This material was drawn on both to write the final report and to develop a professional portfolio.

Thinking about your learning — a cycle of reflection and action

One of the key ideas developed in this part of the chapter, one of the key competencies generally expected of teachers and, no doubt, a key theme in your teacher education program is 'reflection'. This refers specifically to the systematic investigation into and evaluation of your own teacher practice. It is a means of developing theories about teaching practice. It is vital as a mechanism for articulating and justifying professional practice. Yet what are some practical ways of making this more than gratuitous navel gazing or yet one more thing to fit into an already busy schedule? In other words, how can reflection be carried out in meaningful and purposeful ways that assist you to better understand and improve your teaching practice? Below are a couple of questions and strategies that might be useful in devising a plan for reflection and investigation that have been adapted from the ideas developed as part of an action research cycle (Carr & Kemmis 1986; Grundy 1995).

- What is it you are going to inquire into or reflect on? It is useful to have some aspect of the class practice to reflect on that presents itself as problematic and important. For example, in the above case Tony was reflecting on student responses to his classroom management strategies. The focus for reflection can be developed before, during or after a particular lesson, series of lessons or incident.
- What is happening or happened in the class in relation to your focus for reflection and inquiry? In the above case Tony might describe particular actions that he took and the ways that students responded. Or he might note patterns for behaviour at different times of day or between different groups of students.
- Explain why something happened in the way it did. What evidence do you have to support this explanation? For example, Tony might find that it is two students who are continually disruptive during the week. In talking to them Tony may find reasons for their behaviour in class.
- Develop and sound out ideas with peers and advisers. This process of collaborative reflection can be of significance in terms of justifying actions and designing new courses of action. Tony discusses his 'theory' with his adviser. She adds a bit more background to the problem in ways that help flesh out Tony's ideas.
- Draw on this to inform future practice.

What do I expect of my practicum experience?

Thus far we have considered a range of expectations that others may have of you during the practicum and how important it is to know what these are. These expectations need to be considered alongside your own expectations and your own assumptions and values in relation to the practicum experience. Articulating your own expectations and assumptions can be useful in preparing for the practicum and understanding the experience while you are in it. Your expectations and assumptions about schools, students, teachers, the practicum and your own teaching may well be challenged in both positive and negative ways during your experience in a school. In this section of the chapter we will consider some ways in which you can examine your own assumptions and expectations.

In a fascinating study of two people undertaking their practicum in a secondary school, Deborah Britzman (1991, p. 8) makes the following observation:

> Learning to teach is not a mere matter of applying decontextualised skills or mirroring predetermined images; it is a time when one's past, present, and future are set in dynamic tension.

> Learning to teach — like teaching itself — is always a process of becoming: a time of formation and transformation, of scrutiny into what one is doing, and who one can become.

Britzman's point is to weave together the social context and personal values to account for the ways in which student teachers learn about teaching. Prior to entering the practicum you already have a range of experiences that shape your values and expectations. These might include your own educational experience, your teacher education coursework, your experiences as a parent, youth group leader, sports coach and so on. More broadly it might include those experiences central to your identity in terms of, for example, your social and cultural background, gender and sexuality. This set of experiences means that you enter the practicum with a rich stock of knowledge, resources and values. Articulating these can be a useful starting point for negotiating the practicum experience. What can be interesting, exciting, painful and problematic is how these values, assumptions and expectations are confirmed or challenged in the practicum context.

The practicum provides an opportunity to consider your expectations and assumptions in light of the day-to-day realities of a school context. Sometimes the reality is better than expected, sometimes it matches your expectations, sometimes it is simply different and in some cases it is worse. The most difficult circumstances are those in which your assumptions and expectations about a particular aspect of the school workplace are not met and your values are challenged as a consequence. Below are some hypothetical situations that demonstrate some ways in which this might be the case.

- I loved PE at school and I have a real passion for sport and exercise. I assumed the students in my Year 9 PE class would share this enthusiasm. They don't.
- I went to small all-girls private school. For my practicum I am in a large, public, co-ed high school. The experiences are very different and are challenging my assumptions about single-sex and co-ed schools and my assumptions about public and private education.
- I expected that the students would have more respect for me and for others in the class. Their reactions have forced me to take on a different role than I thought I would. It is not a role that squares with what I assumed to be good teaching practice.
- I expected my school adviser to be an enthusiastic role model. He has been teaching for 20 years and seems to be really cynical in his attitude toward kids and how the school works.

There are no easy ways of resolving these contradictory assumptions and expectations. Reconciling these can be a process of adjusting your own assumptions and expectations and/or seeking to challenge or effect change in the practice. Some expectations may be unrealistic, while others may be perfectly reasonable. Some adjustments may be minor, others more significant; and some practices may be easy to change, while other changes may be impossible in the circumstances. In part, this gets back to the tensions related to being a student teacher in a school and the micro-politics of the practicum. This requires a careful reading of the politics and your own institutional position within those politics, to work out ways of articulating your own values especially if they are different from or contradict those held by other teachers in your practicum school. As you negotiate the practicum, be prepared to have your expectations and assumptions challenged. While this can be difficult, it can also be positive in that it requires you to examine your assumptions and develop a perspective on the type of teaching and educational practices that you want to work toward.

Juggling emotions

Earlier in the chapter we indicated that teaching and being a student teacher has an emotional dimension. We would argue that a component of the practicum that evokes considerable emotional response is meeting your own and others' expectations of your teaching practice. This relates to the very public nature of what you are doing and to the judgments associated with this — judgments that advisers and students in your classes make of you and judgments that you make of yourself. So too, the joy of a successful class and the disappointment associated with a class that 'flopped' are emotional responses. When things do not go as well as expected they can be difficult to talk about because they represent a challenge to your sense of self as a teacher. In discussing some of his own experiences as a student teacher, Featherstone (1997) makes a telling comment. He says that it is important to realise that you are not the only one experiencing these concerns and emotions. One of the problems he identifies is that student teachers can be isolated (p. 16):

> One reason that I enjoyed the first weeks of my education courses [after the practicum] so much was the validation and relief I felt when I discovered that I was not the only one experiencing problems and having success in the classroom. I know that I was not physically isolated during my first teaching experience, but at times I felt mentally and emotionally isolated. I needed to hear other pre-service teachers' stories of what they had gone through . . . Hearing others' stories and offering my own helped to remove the sometimes sharp pain of feeling inadequate as a teacher. It helped me feel normal.

This statement highlights the value of talking to others about the practicum experience. Featherstone identifies the importance of talking to peers because of the similar range of experiences that they will be encountering. There are various informal and formal means of establishing and sustaining communication with peers during the practicum. In some settings there may be many student teachers located in one school and so it is possible to meet up with peers on a regular basis. In other settings student teachers can be more isolated from peers. The use of email and online discussions is now used in some teacher education programs as a means of promoting contact between student teachers during the practicum period (Lafferriere 1998; Schlagal, Trathen & Blanton 1996).

We have argued in this section of the chapter that framing and reframing your own and others' expectations of the practicum is an important part of learning to teach and learning about being a teacher. Making these expectations explicit is an important part of negotiating the practicum. It is also important by way of examining and questioning the values and assumptions that underpin these expectations.

Uni and school, theory and practice — what are the connections?

Thus far we have argued that the practicum is a crucial part of a teacher education program in terms of learning about teaching and learning about the work of teachers. However it is only one part of a teacher education program. What about the other parts of teacher education programs and what relationship do they have to the practicum? A common criticism of teacher education programs is that the campus and school-based parts are fragmented and lack a common purpose (Goodlad 1994; Gore 1995; Sachs 1997; Tom 1997). Depending upon your point of view the criticism can cut both ways. The campus-based components can be seen as 'too theoretical', bearing little relation or application to the real world of schools. Or the practicum component can be seen as having only a technical or skills orientation, with the consequence that student teachers get caught up in the busy world of schools and have little opportunity to critically reflect on their practice or understand the relevance of theory to their work. Evaluating the relevance of these criticisms to the schools and university in which you are located requires asking some questions about the purpose of the campus-based part of the program in relation to the practicum *and* the purpose of the practicum in relation to the campus-based coursework.

It is perhaps useful to assume that you will encounter diverse and differing points of view both across campus and school-based parts of the program as well as within the different program parts. McIntyre (1990) and Fish (1989) argue that taking account of diverse points of view is a necessary and productive aspect of learning to be a teacher. They argue that it is important to be able to evaluate the various ideas that you come across in order to develop your own point of view about good teaching. A key question is: What makes one point of view more authoritative than another? How you make judgments about the worth of the ideas in each program part depends upon the criteria that you use for making those judgments. This can mean bringing theoretical and practical criteria to making judgments about the ideas presented in each part of the program. It is then possible to ask about the practical adequacy of the ideas presented on campus and the theoretical adequacy of the ideas presented during the practicum. For example, you may talk about taking account of difference and diversity in your teaching practice in a campus-based subject. This might include acknowledging differences based on gender, cultural background and so on. These pedagogical theories may be underpinned by more general social theories related to, for instance, feminism, anti-racism or social justice. When teaching in the practicum you might begin to realise that certain aspects of the context enable and/or constrain taking practical action on these matters. These practical considerations can then be used to review the adequacy of, and fine-tune, the pedagogical theories.

Theory and practice

The fragmentation between campus and practicum work stems, in part, from a lack of clarity regarding what is meant by 'theory' and its relation to 'practice'. Chambers (1992) presents some different ways in which you might hear theory talked about:

- 'There is too much theory and not enough practice.' This implies a distinction between talk (theory) and action (practice).
- 'The theory on campus should be relevant to the practical context.' Here theory is taken to be a set of instructions or principles that can be applied in a practice setting.
- Theory is developed through empirical research. A psychological theory of learning developed through observation and analysis of children's work is an example.
- Theories about what should happen in education and schooling. These can be called normative theories; theories of educational democracy and feminist theories of education are examples.

Theories of practice develop through reflection on practice and function to inform practice. They can include combinations of the above types of theory.

These are just some ways of conceptualising 'theory' and it is important to note that these are not mutually exclusive categories; there is often overlap between categories. Seen in this light it is probably simplistic to say that the campus work is concerned only with theory and the school-based work is concerned only with practice. One of the key directions underpinning the reform of teacher education programs over the last decade has been to provide opportunities and structures for teachers and student teachers to develop and make explicit their own theories of practice.

A view that has become popular in the teacher education literature revolves around the notion of theories of practice (for example see Carr & Kemmis 1986; Cochran-Smith & Lytle 1993; Schon 1987). This concept presupposes that we all have theories for why things are as they are, and as teachers or beginning teachers we are constantly developing and invoking particular theories to account for particular actions, behaviours and standards. Articulating these theories is considered a necessary part of justifying one's professional practice. A theory of practice can be developed through systematic inquiry into, or reflection on, a practice. It provides a means of understanding a practice and taking action based on that understanding. If teaching is to be seen as intellectual and moral work then developing such theories is essential.

During the practicum you will no doubt hear as well as develop many of your own theories of practice. Some of these may be based on conventional wisdom — 'Don't smile until Christmas' is an example. These may be theories about teaching and learning — about ways of organising a classroom, or presenting ideas, of evaluating student work and so on. Some of these theories may also be specific to the context — that is, to this particular class, or to this particular subject area. Theories of practice may also be informed by broader social theories concerned with say curriculum, sociology or psychology. In addition, theories of practice may be informed by particular values and beliefs concerned with the purpose of schooling, the moral responsibilities of teachers, theories of justice and equity and so on. It is bringing these various theories to bear on and through practice that is useful for justifying teaching practices.

The following case study outlines some ways in which student teachers develop their own theories of practice.

Adele was placed in a school that had a reputation for a lot of 'mucking up'. She was aware of this prior to the practicum and had thought hard about how to deal with such behaviour. Her 'theory', which was based partly on her own experiences as a school student and partly on some ideas discussed in one of her campus classes, was that this behaviour was attention-seeking and calculated to provoke a reaction; remonstrations by teachers therefore only added fuel to the fire. She vividly remembered one teacher who was frequently 'wound up' by provocative students. This had always caused great hilarity and only seemed to encourage the students to devise yet more innovative ways of getting a reaction. Adele therefore decided that the best approach was to ignore disruptive behaviour as much as possible and to concentrate her energies on those students who were serious about learning.

Shortly into the practicum, however, Adele realised that her strategy was both unrealistic and inappropriate. For one thing, the noise level in the classroom was such that it was difficult to conduct any constructive lesson. Adele had also learnt from her teacher adviser that some of the disruptive students came from quite troubled backgrounds. These students were in need of attention of a positive nature, and Adele could not ethically ignore their educational and social needs.

Classroom management continued to be a problem for Adele throughout the placement. However, with the help of her school adviser she managed to develop strategies to minimise disruptive behaviour. One was to intervene early in disruptive situations, in as calm and no-nonsense a manner as she was able to achieve. Another was to avoid long sessions of 'chalk and talk' and to incorporate regular activities that involved active participation by as many students as possible.

At the end of the practicum, Adele's beliefs about the motivations for 'mucking up' had changed to some degree. She felt that she had a better understanding of the underlying cause of some of this behaviour, and a richer and more realistic approach to minimising disruption in the classroom. Some of the ideas that had been covered in the campus-based class on adolescent behaviour did have some relevance here. Her 'theory' had been modified by her first experience as a teacher, and she hoped that she would be a better professional for it.

In the above case the student teacher was articulating particular theories of practice based on her experiences and values. What is crucial to consider in developing a theory of practice is the evidence that you have to support the theory and the reasons you develop to justify the practices associated with the theory. This can be seen to link to the importance of documenting practices and subjecting those practices to public and critical examination. Documenting and examining those practices with advisers and peers is therefore of critical importance to learning during the practicum.

Conclusion

The intent of this chapter has been to provide you with an understanding of the practicum and how it can be negotiated. The social negotiation that takes place in the practicum is critical to learning to teach. It is also a complex process. The complexity is reflected in the following themes that have been developed in this chapter:

- There are a range of views and policies concerning the nature and purpose of the practicum, and you may well encounter a variety of these views among the people you work with during your practicum experience. Identifying and clarifying the expectations that you and others have of schools, students, teachers and the practicum is crucial to the process of negotiation in the practicum as well as being crucial to understanding the culture of a school. It is also important to set the practicum into the context of an entire teacher education program and consider its purpose alongside the campus-based coursework.
- There is an understandable concern associated with 'getting through' and passing the practicum. However we have suggested that the complexity of learning to teach is more than just a series of hoops to be jumped.
- Learning to teach is a public activity. This is both in the doing of teaching and the talking about it with advisers, colleagues and peers. As part of this, the relationship that develops between a student teacher and their advisers is of central importance to the practicum experience and how it can be negotiated.
- Bear in mind that the practicum can be a test of your physical, emotional and intellectual resources. Keeping contact with other student teachers and seeking the support of your advisers is useful in sustaining these resources.

INQUIRY STRATEGIES

1. (a) This chapter has considered a number of dilemmas that student teachers face during the practicum. Consider one or more of these dilemmas from the perspective of the various people involved. Think about what you would do if you were in the shoes of the student teacher, or if you were in the shoes of one of the other people. What actions would you suggest to work through some of the problems?

(b) If you have already had some time working in schools as a student teacher, what has been one dilemma you have faced? Discuss with fellow students the circumstances surrounding the dilemma — who was involved, what was the context, what actions did people take? What was helpful and what hindered working through the dilemma? With the benefit of hindsight, what other actions might have helped to resolve the dilemma?

A useful way to consider dilemmas, the perspectives of participants and some ways of resolving problems is through role-play. In small groups or pairs role-play a practicum situation that is problematic and that requires some action. Debrief by considering how the actions helped to deal with the dilemma.

2. One of the concepts developed in this chapter relates to directing your own learning during the practicum. To support this it helps to have a sense of what you expect of yourself as a learner, what others expect of you and what sort of goals you have for your own learning. One way of bringing some of these things together is to review the practicum report form used by your institution. Discuss with fellow students the institutional expectations and how you might meet them and then use this as a starting point for developing your personal set of learning goals. These might include and also go beyond some of the criteria developed in the report form.

3. Developing a positive working relationship with your school and university adviser is an important part of the practicum. The following areas for investigation are designed to help you clarify roles, expectations and the things that you can do to develop a productive professional relationship with your advisers.

(a) Define for yourself the kind of support, critique and help you want during the practicum. Calibrate your ideas with those established by the institution in which you are located. (Check practicum handbooks, speak to people working in the practicum area in your faculty.)

(b) What actions could you draw on to initiate and negotiate a productive relationship with an adviser? Think for example of introducing yourself, preparing some questions, establishing meeting procedures, keeping records, etc.

References

Britzman, D.P. (1991). *Practice Makes Practice: A Critical Study of Learning to Teach.* New York: State University of New York Press.

Bullough, R. & Gitlin, A. (1996). *Becoming a Student of Teaching: Methodologies for Exploring Self and School Context.* New York: Garland Publications.

Calderhead, C. & James, C. (1992). Recording student teachers' learning experience. *Journal of Further and Higher Education*, 16(1), pp. 3–12.

Calderhead, J. & Shorrock, S. (1997). *Understanding Teacher Education.* London: Falmer Press.

Carr, W. & Kemmis, S. (1986). *Becoming Critical: Education, Knowledge and Action Research.* Victoria, Australia: Deakin University.

Chambers, J.H. (1992). *Empiricist Research on Teaching: A Philosophical and Practical Critique of its Scientific Pretensions.* Dordrecht, Netherlands: Kluwer Academic Publishers.

Cochran-Smith, M. & Lytle, S. (1993). *Inside/Outside: Teacher Research and Knowledge.* New York: Teachers College Press.

Featherstone, D. (1997). Common themes in learning to teach. In D. Featherstone, H. Munby & T. Russel (eds), *Finding a Voice While Learning to Teach.* London: Falmer Press.

Fish, D. (1989). *Learning Through Practice in Initial Teacher Training: a Challenge for the Partners.* London: Kogan Page.

Furlong, J. & Maynard, T. (1995). *Mentoring Student Teachers: The Growth of Professional Knowledge.* London: Routledge.

Goodlad, J. (1994). *Educational Renewal: Better Teachers, Better Schools.* San Francisco: Jossey-Bass.

Gore, J. (1995). *Emerging Issues in Teacher Education.* Perth, Australia: NPDP Project.

Graham, P. (1999). Powerful influences: a case study of one student teacher renegotiating his perception of power relations. *Teaching and Teacher Education*, 15(5), pp. 523–540.

Grimmett, P. & Erickson, G. (eds) (1988). *Reflection in Teacher Education.* Vancouver, Canada: Pacific Educational Press.

Grundy, S. (1995). *Action Research as Professional Development.* Perth, Western Australia: Innovative Links Project.

Knowles, G. & Cole, A. (1993). *Through Preservice Teachers' Eyes: Exploring Field Experience Through Narrative and Inquiry.* New York: Maxwell Macmillan International.

Lafferriere, T. (1998). *A six-phase tentative model for professional development in telelearning.* Available: http://www.tact.fse.ulaval.ca/model/ang/model.html

McIntyre, D. (1990). The Oxford internship scheme and the Cambridge analytical framework: models of partnership in initial teacher education. In M. Booth, J. Furlong & M. Wilkin (eds), *Partnerships in Initial Teacher Training.* London: Cassell.

McIntyre, D. (1992). Initial teacher education and the work of teachers. Paper presented at the British Educational Research Association, Stirling, UK.

Mitchell, J.M. (1996). Developing reflective teaching: negotiation in the practicum. *Asia-Pacific Journal of Teacher Education*, 24(1), pp. 47–62.

Sachs, J. (1997). Revisioning teacher education. *Unicorn*, 23(2), pp. 45–56.

Schlagal, B., Trathen, W. & Blanton, W. (1996). Structuring telecommunications to create instructional conversations about student teaching. *Journal of Teacher Education*, 46(3), pp. 175–183.

Schon, D. (1987). *Educating the Reflective Practitioner: Toward a New Design for Teaching and Learning in the Professions.* San Francisco: Jossey-Bass.

Tom, A. (1997). *Redesigning Teacher Education.* New York: State University of New York Press.

Zeichner, K. (1990). Changing directions in the practicum: looking ahead to the 1990s. *Journal of Education for Teaching*, 16(2), pp. 105–131.

Zeichner, K. (1996). Designing educative practicum experiences for prospective teachers. In K. Zeichner, S. Melnick & M. Gomez (eds), *Currents of Reform in Preservice Teacher Education.* New York: Teachers College Press.

9

CHAPTER

Learning, Teaching and Technology

Technology is both buzz word to be marvelled at and a fear-inducing metaphor for change. It is both exciting and threatening, on the one hand with the power to unlock knowledge and yet on the other presenting the possibility of knowledge exclusion. Technology can be an object or artefact, a set of particular skills and knowledge and both a process and/or a practice. For example, the computer is clearly a piece of technology, but there is also a technology associated with wine production. Even the wheel is still a technological object.

It is clear, however we view technology, that changing technology is part and parcel of the rapidly changing social, cultural, political and economic times in which we live. It is also clear that changing technology is a key driver of these changes. At present, university lecturers, teacher education students like you, and teachers in schools are, however, ill-equipped to deal with the enormity and complexity of the technological changes going on around us.

In relative terms, our programs of study and schools as sites of learning are still largely low-tech learning environments in a high-tech world. If this does not change, they will rapidly become redundant. This issue has been highlighted in the recent review of teacher education in New South Wales.

As the generation of students we teach grow up with and adapt easily to change, the majority of teachers and teacher educators feel locked out by technology rather than excited by and included in its potential to change knowledge production and delivery strategies.

We hope this chapter will help you and the teacher educators who teach you, as well as classroom teachers who read this text, feel more comfortable about the pedagogical potential of available and emerging technology. We also hope the chapter will help you to see technology as an integrated element of your practice rather than a marginalised classroom possibility.

In the midst of a 'revolution'

It is becoming somewhat of a cliché to say that our society is in the midst of a dramatic technological revolution. But in truth, rapid advances in technology have indeed changed everything from the way we do our daily work, to how we communicate with each other, to how we engage in leisure pursuits. This so-called 'revolution' centers on information technology and is linked to the notion of a 'knowledge society' within which education is ascribed a central role in every aspect of life. As educational practitioners, we are being challenged to rethink basic tenets of teaching and learning and implement new classroom technologies in creative and productive ways (Kellner 1998, p. 103).

New technologies such as online communication mean that, as teachers, we need to begin to think differently about learning and teaching. For example, the web has enabled new forms of communication and information delivery, as well as fostered new associations and collaborations among people within a 'cybersociety' (Kumari 1998, p. 364). The web transcends time and space constraints, alters power and control relationships, makes new expressive styles possible, and creates new relationships among people and information (Sparrow, Davies & McFadden 1998).

Just a cursory analysis of some recent statistics indicates the magnitude of the impact technology is having on our lives. In 1996, almost 20 per cent of Australians aged 16 years and over had used the Internet and 10 per cent of households had an Internet connection. According to the Australian Bureau of Statistics (ABS), since 1996 there has been a 280 per cent increase in the number of households that have Internet access (ABS 1999, cited in Dixon 1999). The ABS further states that in 1998 more than eight million adult Australians had used a computer at any site (such as work) and four million adults had accessed the Internet. It is estimated that there are over 70 000 000 Internet users worldwide, with this number expected to reach 250 000 000 by the end of 2000 (Dixon 1999).

The changes are so prevalent that writers like Russell and Russell (1997) refer to a 'cyberspace curriculum', involving an integrated approach to teaching and learning that uses computers across primary and secondary schools. This cyberspace curriculum covers, among other things, communication, interaction, informational retrieval and knowledge construction. Some schools even seek to provide an information technology-oriented curriculum across the preschool, primary school and high school levels, by requiring all students to own a laptop computer.

Transforming teaching and learning with technology — some principles for effectiveness

Anderson and Alagumalai (1997) believe that to effectively teach using technology we as teachers need to transform how we think about learning and knowledge. Accordingly, they believe, this will necessarily affect how we as teachers should deal with:

■ assisting or facilitating students to actively construct knowledge instead of objectively learning it;

- altering their classroom role by conducting learning activities, mediating information processing and guiding problem-solving activities to engage students in learning activities rather than merely 'teaching' knowledge;

- using available information technology so students may access and explore the abundance of resources available by working individually (but not competitively) and collaboratively, while taking a more active role in the educational process (Holmes & Russell 1999);

- providing students with the necessary academic, social, political, cultural and economic skills that allows them to effectively participate in a knowledge-based society (Kumari 1998);

- actively engaging students in their learning by providing stimulating, enthusiastic and relevant instruction;

- competently provide instruction and enhance understanding of pertinent information, while effectively and efficiently using technologically mediated processes of communication and learning.

Achieving transformations such as those listed above and reorienting how we think about teaching and learning to change our pedagogical practices is no easy matter, particularly for teachers who may not be comfortable with either the pace or direction of technological change. There are, however, some key principles that can help us effectively transform our practices (Wild 1996).

Implementing an active learning model

Much present discussion of the relationship between technology, learning and teaching revolves around the application of online learning models and the convergence of communication and information technology (CIT) tools. The Maricopa Roundtable, a consortium of community colleges interested in flexible delivery in the United States, identified that a new active learning model should be implemented when engaging in online teaching and learning. This active learning model involves:

- a broad model moving beyond the classroom and bringing the virtual world into the classroom;

- learning being both a product and a process;

- the curriculum being more flexible;

- students and teachers learning from and supporting each other in a positive learning environment;

- student-centred and guided learning, which may be guided until responsibility and autonomy increases, using a greater variety of high quality material selected by the student, thereby involving the learner in a qualitatively different learning experience (Holmes & Russell 1999);

- a diverse model of lifelong learning responsibility that involves collaboration between the student and educational institutions;

- a shared learning model with greater involvement from the larger community;

- an open learning model that meets the diverse needs of students by accessing appropriate technology;

■ providing students and teachers with problems and challenges to overcome, which assists in promoting 'deep learning' (Anderson & Alagumalai 1997).

Wild (1996) says that we should view teaching and learning online using a conversational framework, within which discursive, adaptive, interactive and reflective components exist. For this to take place there must be facilities that emphasise dialogue between the learner and the object of learning (that is, the different types of knowledge, such as academic knowledge). As such, certain pedagogical characteristics must be present, which include:

■ facilities for dialogue between learner and materials (information);
■ facilities for dialogue between learner and content (author/instructor);
■ learners need to take action on information;
■ learners must negotiate task goals;
■ learners need to reflect and interact with descriptions of the world;
■ materials may need to be extended or adapted;
■ feedback, especially intrinsic feedback, on learners' actions must be provided.

Benefits of technology in teaching and learning

Stating the benefits of teaching and learning using communications and information technologies is a predictable theme in current educational literature. These benefits are said to include: learning that is more interactive and collaborative; flexibility; more time and attention given to students' ideas and concerns; enhancement of students' technological skills; the creation of new and expanded knowledge bases and networks; increased student motivation and interest; and inclusion of students with physical and geographical restrictions (Anderson & Alagumalai 1997; Russell & Russell 1997).

Risks and drawbacks of technology in teaching and learning

It is important as well to be aware of the perceived drawbacks, risks and limitations of technology in teaching and learning. These drawbacks and risks include: technical issues such as breakdown of equipment and inadequate software; the challenge of attaining appropriate skill levels, including information literacy; the limits of learner appeal; alienation of students; demands on teacher time; difficulty (in some cases fear) of teacher adjustment to different modes of teaching; institutional and structural blockages like rigid timetabling and inadequate budget allocations; and loss of social 'connectedness' (Rowntree 1995; Bigum 1997; Holmes 1997; Kellner 1998).

Learning, teaching and technology — some useful frameworks

Green and Gilbert (1995) believe that technologies such as online communication may transform teaching and learning from passive reception by learners to active engagement. They state that using technology offers the possibility of connecting teaching and learning more authentically to the real world therefore allowing for more relevant learning to occur.

As teachers we must be clear, however, about why we believe technology will enhance learning and, indeed, lead to a qualitatively different learning experience for our students. We need to understand both the 'why' of using technology in the classroom and the 'how' to integrate technology effectively in our programs.

First, the 'why' of using technology. When he was Chair of the Commonwealth Schools Commission, Garth Boomer wrote (1987, cited in DEETYA 1997, vol. 1, p. 50):

> With any technology past, present, or future, we can conceive of three ways of dealing with it in the curriculum: 1. Learning the technology (e.g. learning the techniques of video filming); 2. Learning *about* the technology (e.g. study the video industry and art forms); 3. Learning *through* the technology (e.g. learning about biological interdependence by making a film on pond life).

So, to understand why we use technology in the classroom the framework of:

- learning technology (i.e. how to use technological tools);
- learning *through* technology (i.e. technology as a medium of learning); and
- learning *about* technology (i.e. learning about technological systems, uses and functions)

provides a powerful conceptual frame (DEETYA 1997, vol. 1, p. 50). This framework has learning at its centre. Importantly, as you integrate technology into your lessons and programs, your students will learn about technology per se but also be learning explicitly about how technological systems work. Not only that, they will be learning your particular discipline content through the medium of technology. This interplay of learning is crucial for you to understand as a teacher.

Now to the 'how' of technology use in the classroom. We argued in the previous section that technology, particularly communications and online facilities, should be integrated into the classroom in a conversational or discursive way. In this sense, interaction and conversation is at the heart of how we might use technology in the classroom. Essentially, there is wide support that computer networks can enhance three basic types of interaction:

1. **learner–content interaction** (in the development of multimedia literacy attained through research projects using a greater variety quality information accessed through new information and communications technologies that promote interactive and self-guided learning, discovery and construction of knowledge);
2. **learner–teacher interaction** (in the development of different learner–teacher interactions, wherein the learner is more in control of his/her own learning and the teacher, within a flexible learning environment, acts as a guide or facilitator assisting students to maximise the benefits associated with use of information and communications technologies);
3. **learner–learner interaction** (through more collaborative work on research projects in a flexible learning environment that encourages communication, peer tutoring, and motivated use of new information technologies).

In implementing learning activities that effectively integrate information technologies, we as teachers should keep this interactional framework in mind to help us with the 'how' of using technology in the classroom. The types of interactions made explicit here facilitate constructivist learning as students cooperate and collaborate with each other within a learning environment that encourages personal autonomy (i.e. having control over one's learning). As teachers then, we need to consider the learner's learning state, the learning environment, the resources available, and the flexible interface between learner and teacher (Anderson & Alagumalai 1997).

In this sense, Bigum (1997) advocates the use of a 'reflexive model' of teaching, related to this interactive learning approach, in which computer technology is seen as acting as a resource (or tool). Linking back to our learning framework, each use contributes to how the technology is understood and the changed context shapes how computers are used. What really matters is the learning setting within which computers are used and what effect this use has on the people who use it: their thoughts, opinions and accumulated knowledge.

Clearly, the integration of technology (particularly CIT — communication and information technology) into the regular classroom represents a significant change to teachers' work and to pedagogical practices. If, however, we can effectively alter our modes of thinking and acting to adjust to the challenges presented to us, we will assist our students to maximise the benefits that technology can contribute to students' learning.

Your role in effectively using technology in the classroom

Kumari (1998) argues that it is important that you view yourself as a learning facilitator when integrating information technologies into your classroom. In this role, you can use such technologies as the Internet and other software programs (including CD-ROMs) to facilitate students' learning, enhance their comprehension and provide rich contextual learning environments in a dynamic way. By recognising that students may be more familiar and competent than you in using these technologies, you can actually contribute to the construction of collaborative teacher–student relationships. By taking a constructivist approach, you can re-visualise your role as being the director of student learning, in that you provide guidelines and pathways for students to actively construct their knowledge and to take responsibility for learning in a more student-centred process (Jonasson, Peck & Wilson 1999).

To enhance the learning of your students, you must be willing to rethink your orientation toward traditional resources, such as textbooks, and become willing to use a variety of information sources and technologies in creative and productive ways when developing your teaching program (American Council on Education 1999). You will need to be able to guide and assist students to generate rich, complex, and meaningful understandings of information relevant to their current and future needs, and also develop in your students problem-solving and cognitive reasoning skills that encourage engagement in self-directed and collaborative learning (Simpson, Payne, Munro, & Hughes 1999).

In a very practical way, to effectively enhance students' learning experiences using different information technologies, you will need to engage in appropriate professional development that provides you with the skills to:

- use particular software applications, including specific aspects such as using HTML (hyper text markup language), graphic manipulation, maintenance and use of web spaces;
- integrate information technology into existing curricula by researching different Internet sites in advance of teaching and linking them to a lesson plan related to a specific topic within the curriculum. This allows you to ensure that students are guided in their exploration of the Internet and attain productive and relevant information that is conducive to their effective learning about a specific topic;
- deal with information technology related changes in the curricula;
- establish new ways of teaching and learning that are purposeful and make implementing information technologies more 'routine' and less 'occasional';
- develop curricula units that allow students to extend their everyday educational experiences and engage in learning activities that include:
  - exploration and critical analysis of the Internet, different resources and different means of producing data;
  - foster the exchange of Internet resources with students within their classrooms and with students who may be located in other cities, regions or countries;
  - data collection and production of material by individual students and students working in collaborative groups;
  - students working collaboratively and communicating with students within their physical classroom and with students located in other cities, regions or countries;
  - peer review processes, whereby students evaluate their own and each others knowledge products (Kumari 1998).

In addition, Todd (1999) argues that teachers need to ask important questions prior to setting learning activities that integrate information technologies, if students are to gain optimal learning benefits. These questions include:

- Is the task meaningful?
- Is the task clearly linked to current learning?
- What information and critical skills are required for the task and do the students possess them?
- How do I know students have the skills to complete the task?
- Does the task encourage students to plagiarise or construct their own knowledge?
- Does the task encourage use of multiple sources?
- Does the task require students to use analytical skills or merely cut and paste?
- Do the product outcomes send them off to one of the 'cybercheat' houses?
- How do I know if they 'cybercheated'?
- Do I have the appropriate skills to manage this task and facilitate the students' learning?
- Do the students have the appropriate intellectual scaffolding necessary for confidently managing the large amounts and varieties of information they are likely to find?

Technology in action

Now let us see technology in action in real settings. From each of the following case studies of practice there are valuable lessons to be learned about the role of technology in teaching and learning. In the specific classroom ideas that are included note carefully the way in which the frameworks about why and how we use technology in the classroom are applicable to the lesson content and the learning activities in which students are engaged. Each of the classroom ideas here have been tried and proven.

Palmerston North Girls' High School in New Zealand — lessons learned about integrating technology into the curriculum

Boyd, Kelliher, Scott and Pech (1998) studied the experiences of teachers and students at Palmerston North Girls' High School during and after the introduction of information technologies in three subject areas. They observed that some of the negative implications for teachers of integrating information technologies into these subjects included:

- high initial workload that decreased over time;
- belief by teachers that they needed more computer training but difficulty in accessing such training as available money was spent on purchasing hardware and software;
- a high students-to-computer ratio;
- computers and information technologies integrated into some subjects more easily than others;
- additional, unplanned expenses arose after the initial expense of the hardware (such as paper, overhead projectors, software packages);
- students needed to be provided with basic keyboard skills prior to using more complex information technologies.

Despite the negative implications for teachers, however, they still managed through effective teaching practices to enhance the learning of the students. Students reported that the positive implications of the integration of information technologies into their classrooms included:

- increased knowledge of computer skills considered useful for further studies or employment;
- positive changes in attitudes towards using computers and information technology;
- expansion of possible learning styles to include, for example, visual learning;
- use of computers instigated a change towards student-centred and informal and flexible lessons — students felt their roles as students had changed from mere receivers of knowledge to creators of knowledge and also to providers of knowledge;
- students were able to develop group work, peer tutoring, problem-solving, communication, interaction and presentation skills;
- students felt more motivated in the classes that used computers.

Clearly, if teachers modify their teaching practices and meet the challenges presented to them by the negative implications of integrating information technologies into their classroom, they can provide students with experiences that significantly improve their learning. The teachers at the school were described as motivated and dedicated to their students' education and able to enhance their students learning despite the initial problems that technology presented.

From their study, Boyd et al. (1998) recommended that schools wanting to effectively integrate information technologies into teaching to enhance the learning experiences of the students should:

- introduce professional development in information technologies prior to implementation;
- provide sufficient resources and support for teachers so they may effectively integrate information technologies into their planned learning experiences;
- develop links with other schools or educational institutions in order to share resources and minimise costs as well as provide collaborative learning experiences for students;
- ensure students develop and apply keyboard skills in primary school to facilitate their use of these technologies;
- Develop learning goals for students and evaluation/assessment methods, so students may attain specific skills (see also Cusack, Gurr & Schiller 1999).

It is evident that many of the negative implications of integrating communication and learning technologies into the curriculum may be overcome by effective teaching practices and pedagogy.

River Oaks Public School, Ontario, Canada — lessons about school curriculum

Smith (1999) has documented his experiences as Principal of River Oaks Public School in Ontario, Canada, over eight years, in implementing a school-wide integrated approach to technology in learning and teaching. Smith poses the question whether our present modes of utilising technology in the classroom are trying to 'fit twenty-first century tools into a curriculum of the 1960s and 1970s' (p. 26). He picks up the issue of local learning contexts as information-poor environments that will becoming increasingly redundant in an information-rich world. This is a significant issue.

Further, he argues that curriculum restructuring and integration is essential if we as teachers are to utilise information technology in classrooms. At his school, the focus was on restructuring curriculum to ready students for their life in the global economy, where individuals 'have access to information anytime and anywhere, where information technology is used to help us be more productive, efficient and creative in our work and where information technology provides the opportunity for us to collaborate with others and share our knowledge' (p. 27). At River Oaks, information and technology skills were not seen as a curriculum add-on but were an integral element of the regular teaching and learning process. The ultimate curriculum goal for the school, Smith states, was to have a curriculum synchronised with the real world.

At River Oaks, this meant structuring opportunities for students to collaborate digitally and face-to-face with peers and 'experts' in a student-centred rather than teacher-centred classroom. It also meant providing opportunities for students to explore and create using technology as a tool where students were often in the role of instructor and peer mentor.

Clearly, school organisation and resource allocation have to be in step with policy to ensure an integrated approach to using technology in the classroom. At River Oaks, computers were relatively distributed to Year groups according to perceived curriculum need (balanced towards the older students). Relatively few pieces of software were needed for all students but this software was judiciously chosen for its utility and functionality and was broken down into: integrated applications; multimedia and publishing; specialised applications like photoshop; and the web. A continuum of software applications was developed from K through to 12 across these categories both to facilitate and indicate staff and student training needs.

The Outback Satellite Education Trial — lessons learned about the application of technology

Boylan and Wallace (1999) were involved in the evaluation of a fascinating application of technology for students in NSW studying in extremely remote locations. The 12 students involved were scattered across the western border of New South Wales and from the Queensland to the Victorian border — representing about one-sixth of the landmass of New South Wales. These Year 3/4 students had previously come together as a class using unreliable airwave technology. The trial applied satellite technology and the Internet to establish a one-way video and two-way audio link between teacher and students (essentially a computer-mediated conferencing system).

Boylan and Wallace (1999) argue that access to the web provided a gateway to an array of resources and experiences not previously dreamt of by these students. They visited 'virtual' zoos, the Louvre, and explored space through the Hubble telescope. They could see the faces of their teachers. They could have their work displayed for other students to see and comment on. They could interact with each other, sing songs, and even watch a video together. For the first time, these students reported they felt part of a classroom.

The pedagogy utilised in the satellite trial tended to remain teacher-centred rather than student-centred, although Boylan and Wallace point out that student-to-student interaction increased as the teacher explored the teaching tools available in the software and became more comfortable with their application. As the trial developed, the students also evidenced more independence in their approach to learning. A crucial finding from the research was that the technology could be applied usefully to students studying in remote and rural school contexts and to students in urban areas who were isolated by sickness and/or physical disability. In essence, the technology was seen to provide access to resources not previously available.

NSW HSC On-Line — lessons learned about technology as a resource

The NSW HSC On-Line project was set up by Charles Sturt University and the NSW Department of Education and Training (NSW DET) to construct a web site for teachers and their students working towards the NSW Higher School Certificate (HSC). The HSC is the credential awarded to students who have satisfied requirements set out by the NSW Board of Studies. The site has won numerous awards including a NSW Premier's award for public sector service delivery.

The site includes:

- a variety of tutorial and web links relevant to a broad range of HSC subjects, including English and mathematics;
- an area providing hints on study methods and examination techniques;
- an area designed to explore issues associated with the use of technology in teaching and learning;
- links to Australian school home pages on the web;
- links to the home pages of teacher professional associations;
- an area in which users can explore post-school options.

The NSW HSC On-Line web site has been constructed to make it accessible to a majority of users. As technology advances users will obviously come to expect more sophisticated features such as video and sound on the site, and the project will be challenged to provide such features whilst maintaining the capacity to deliver to those receiving via narrow bandwidth. Users in remote and isolated areas, one of the main target audiences of the site, are most likely to be in this category.

The HSC On-Line site is at: http://www.hsc.csu.edu.au and a new site is currently being developed for the implementation of the new HSC in late 2000.

An extensive evaluation of the site, which included survey and case study work in schools, indicated that student users believed the site provided quality learning material (Sparrow, Davies & McFadden 1998). Users believed the information was focused, filtered, innovative and easily accessible to students, teachers and the community. Students and teachers said the concept of NSW HSC On-Line was exciting and a worthwhile innovation.

The most significant challenge, however, to emerge from the evaluation was that the site was comparatively under-utilised and that teachers and students had difficulty enunciating effective teaching and learning practices relating to its use. Interestingly, teachers said little about how they used the site with class groups. There was little use of the site for small-group teaching. Tellingly, students saw teachers as wholly responsible for encouraging their use of the Internet for educational purposes. Students in all case-study schools expected their teachers to lead the way towards online learning. Significantly, students believed that many of their teachers were reluctant to use the Internet for teaching and that this led to their own experiences and technological expertise being marginalised in the classroom.

Clearly, the shift from traditional classroom interaction to more collaborative learning using the resources of the Internet requires the support of focussed training and development to help teachers assimilate the use of technology into good teaching practice. Respondents in the evaluation of NSW HSC On-Line liked what they saw. Both teachers and students indicated that they would like more material, more quality assured links and more subjects up online (Davies, Jeffries & McFadden 1998).

Technology and project work

As teachers we need to be aware that the Internet community provide both a ready resource for our students but can also help to stimulate engagement by providing appropriate audiences, purposes and presentation points for the products of student work. Project-centred, small-group activities are seen to be an efficient way for students to:

> . . . use and explore the resources available on the Internet, while, at the same time, facilitating collaborative learning . . . Projects can involve students in communication, collaboration, self-directed learning, problem-solving, researching and publishing findings . . . Projects are effective motivators in every key learning area and [can be] designed for students at all stages of schooling.

> (NSW DET Curriculum Support Directorate 2000, p. 3.)

Below are some student Internet project sites recently published by the Curriculum Support Directorate of the NSW DET. Also provided below are links to student project sites that involve students across Australia and overseas in project work. The NSW DET advises that you can expect the current projects at these sites to end and be replaced by new ones throughout the year.

The *Network for Education* site: http://www.dse.nsw.edu.au/stand.cgi/staff/F1.0/F1.5/index.htm includes projects that target NSW syllabus areas.

Other useful project sites include:

Education Network Australia (Edna) http://www.edna.edu.au/EDNA/, *OZprojects* http://www.ozprojects.net.au and the British Council site, *Montage*, which is devoted to the running and presentation of school project work http://www.bc.org.au/montage/.

The sites below are examples of existing project sites or competition sites that provide national entry opportunities for students. The *Australian Schools Web Challenge* is at http://www.learning21.org/. Some recent winning web sites are from Sefton High School in NSW at: http://www.ar.com.au/~unistar/celebration/multiday/default.htm and Norfolk Island Central School at: http://www.school.edu.nf/bounty/.

Another award winning site is *Murder Under the Microscope*, an environmental who-dun-it that combines CD-ROM and web technology to provide students with an interactive group opportunity to solve an environmental mystery. The site is at: http://www.microscope.aone.net.au/.

Explore these project sites and you will get a sense of what is possible and see the results of student work. We are sure you will be pleasantly surprised and hopefully motivated to get your future students involved in similar work.

Technology and mathematics

Year 7 might be studying a thematic unit on sport and exploring the concept of 'averages' with their teacher in maths. Analysis of data in sport can enhance children's understanding of the link between rates, ratios, percentages and averages which are used extensively, especially in cricket. The students have calculated and discussed many sporting averages. 'economy rate' and 'strike rate' for bowling are also discussed in relation to other 'rates' the class knows about like water rates, interest rates and land rates. The teacher wants them to explore the difference between rates and averages.

The students find, or are asked to find, a web site with bowlers' strike rates like: http://mullara.met.unimelb.edu.au:8080/home/chris/cricket.dir/genpages/rec_tesstk.html or http://www.khel.com/cricket/tests/AUS/players/index.html where you can click on a player and then on 'Graphical Analysis' to see a graph in colour.

From the information available, the teacher works with the students to set up a table that transforms the information into:

Bowler	Balls Bowled	Overs Bowled	Wickets Taken	Runs Conceded

For example:

Shane	19 794	3299	313	7752

Then the students can work out, using a calculator, the 'economy rate' — how many runs off each ball, as an average, and 'strike rate' — how many wickets taken per balls bowled.

Here, the students have to be able to use the Internet and learn to eliminate superfluous data from the web site, set up a modified table and use their calculators to estimate and predict while dividing.

Another Year 7 class has been working on a thematic unit involving reference to the Australian conventions for naming large numbers. The Federal Budget has just been presented with extensive reference to 'billions', the class becomes interested in the different naming systems and, in particular, the difference between an American and an Australian (or imperial) billion.

The class connects to the Internet site:
http://gwinfo.gwc.maricopa.edu/div/mat/berisha/InstructionalMaterialMAT122/names_of_large_numbers.htm

The students then discuss the different conventions of using mathematical notation to represent numbers more compactly and how numbers might be named in each country's system. They ponder which version of 'billions' the Federal Treasurer referred to. What version do most Australians use when they think of billions? Which system is better? Are some Australian Lotto millionaires actually billionaires?

Here, the students are learning to appreciate that alternative naming systems exist for large numbers and to devise reasons for the selection of consistent systematic number naming. As well, they are developing an awareness of the use and appreciation of large numbers in society. (See Bobis, J., Mulligan, J., Lowrie, T. & Taplin, M. (1999) for an in-depth treatment of technology and mathematics in the classroom.)

Technology and legal studies

A Year 10 class is studying the *Crimes Act 1900* (NSW) and the criminal justice system. They are asked to form groups of four to five people. Using the Internet sites the teacher provides (including access to the Crimes Act — see below for the complete list), they must find and document one example of an actual crime or alleged crime for each of the following five categories of crime:

1. offences against persons (*Crimes Act 1900*, Part 3, sections 17–93);
2. offences relating to property — stealing and like offences (*Crimes Act 1900*, Part 4, Div. 1, sections 93J–193);
3. offences relating to property — criminal destruction and damage (*Crimes Act 1900*, Part 4, Div. 2, sections 194–203);
4. preliminary crimes (attempts, conspiracy) (*Crimes Act 1900*, Part 8a, section 344A);
5. public order offences (*Crimes Act 1900*, Part 3a, sections 93A–93E).

Each group is asked to present their findings in a table that asks the groups to report on:

- the actual crime;
- the source of the (alleged) crime (such as *The Age* newspaper);
- which court processed the alleged or actual offender (such as local, district, supreme);
- what penalty was (or might be) applied to the (alleged) offender.

The Internet sites provided are all reliable government maintained sites that provide up-to-date information. They include:

- Window on the law (the Commonwealth Attorney General's Department):
  http://www.law.gov.au/wotl
- ABC Radio National law report site:
  http://www.abc.net.au/rn/talks/8.30/lawrpt/
- *Sydney Morning Herald* newspaper site:
  http://www.smh.com/
- *The Age* newspaper site:
  http://www.theage.com.au/
- Australasian Legal Information Institute site:
  http://www.austlii.edu.au/
- Scaleplus — an Australian Government law site:
  http://law.agps.gov.au/

Here the students not only learn about classes of crime and systems of criminal justice but they learn about methods of reporting crime and the way in which computers are being used to store and retrieve information about crime and justice.

Technology and history

Year 11 are studying the new HSC course in history. They are focusing on the Ayatollah Khomeini and Muslim Fundamentalism. The teacher makes Internet inquiry a feature of the unit to enhance students' electronic research and source analysis ability while helping them gain knowledge about the Ayatollah Khomeini.

The class are given a number of links to web pages that deal with the history of the Ayatollah Khomeini. Some are biased and some are just straight narratives. The students are given the task to read through the sources and answer specific questions about each piece. Some of the texts are quite lengthy so the questions help the students to establish what information they are looking for before they set out on their Internet journey. They are encouraged to read through the questions first.

When they have finished answering the questions they must use their answers to write an obituary of the Ayatollah Khomeini. The teacher encourages the students to share their work with other students and the teacher. They are also encouraged to seek some feedback via email on their answers to source-specific questions and to submit their obituary via email.

Below are examples of these source-specific questions and the related obituary activity.

Source 1

http://www.fordham.edu/halsall/mod/1979khom1.html — From the Ayatollah Khomeini

1. What does the word Ayatollah mean?

2. The Ayatollah says 'if you have chosen a course other than Islam — you do nothing for humanity — all you do is write and speak in an effort to divert our movement from its course'. What does he mean by this?

3. Why was the Ayatollah so fearful of Western influences?

Source 2

http://www.bbc.co.uk/persian/revolution/ — Events as they happened
Activity

1. Construct a chronology of events during the Iranian Revolution, which features the main people involved.

2. Review your answers to all the questions and use them to construct an obituary.

3. Read over your obituary. If possible ask someone else to read it.

A Year 8 history class is studying medieval times. The students are asked to produce three pages on medieval medicine for a web site. Each page has to be a summary of material from two textbooks that are used in class and they are also expected to include an image chosen from library materials that supports their written material. In addition they have to provide at least one URL from the web that expands on their own summaries. Students use a word processing package, such as Word 98, to complete the assignment.

By engaging in this assignment, students learn a range of technology-related skills:

- word processing (something many are not too familiar with);
- the use of the facilities in a package like Word to create hyperlinks from their index page to their contents pages;
- the use of tables to place graphics in a web page;
- the use of a scanner to scan two or three images and save them as jpeg files;
- the use of a search engine to find appropriate URLs for links for their medieval material;
- the use of bookmarks to record their URLs and how to copy and paste these into their web documents.

This assignment will prove a challenge but will be rewarding as students look for URLs and use a scanner for their images. The final reward for them will be that their material will be placed on the school's web site and they can demonstrate their skills to their parents.

New roles, new texts, new demands

While use of information technology and multimedia resources requires students (and teachers) to develop, implement and enhance traditional skills associated with print literacy, visual literacy, and aural literacy, writers in this area have highlighted the importance of developing critical multimedia literacy in students (DEETYA 1997; Downes & Zammit 2000). Critical multimedia literacy involves harnessing and development of student' skills relating to:

- framing questions that allow for productive and challenging investigation of a concept, problem, issue or phenomenon that may be based in real-world contexts;

- discovering, gathering and interpreting information from a variety of sources that are relevant to the goals of the learning experience;

- judging the quality of information or images and critically analysing its relevance or applicability or bias in presentation;

- understanding that information technology allows the individual to access various texts (from TV news and educational text presentations, to rock music videos or even advertising) that all produce meaning in a multiplicity of ways that must all be critically analysed;

- presenting the findings of this search for information in an effective and understandable manner, including applying the concepts that have been explored and investigated;

- interacting with the information and making knowledge one's own and thus being empowered by this knowledge. This involves students taking responsibility for their learning and not just gathering information from electronic sources and simply rewriting the facts (Kellner 1998; Kumari 1998; Todd 1999).

Literacies, including critical multimedia literacy, 'always come in association with practical purposes and are always embedded within larger practices: for example, running a home, completing an assignment, organising an event, giving orders, exchanging information, being at leisure' (DEETYA 1997, vol. 1, p. 15). In addition, teachers need to recognise that literacy has three interlocking dimensions: the operational (focusing on competency and usage), the cultural (focusing on meaning and context) and the critical (focusing on social practices of interpretation and classification) (DEETYA 1997). This sociocultural understanding of literacy has led to a 'growing understanding of how and why various social groups have different and unequal access to literacy (and knowledge)' (Downes & Zammit 2000, p. 1). But to understand technological literacy we need to connect this sociocultural view of literacy with technology as both artefact and process (DEETYA 1997, vol. 1, p. 20):

> Bigum and Green (1993 p. 5) identify four ways in which literacy and technology might be associated: 'technology *for* literacy'; 'literacy *for* technology'; 'literacy *as* technology'; and 'technology *as* literacy'. 'Technology for literacy' means applying various information technologies to literacy pedagogy. 'Literacy for technology' refers to text-mediated practices that enable people to operate particular technologies, such as reading a manual to tune a television set . . . To speak of 'literacy as technology' is to recognise that the various socially constructed and maintained practices and conceptions of reading and writing that exist comprise so many social technologies: ways of applying means to ends, tools/techniques to purposes . . . The notion of 'technology as literacy' is involved in talk of people being computer literate, information literate . . .

The new literacy demands of the information age mean that students need opportunities to find and use information provided by various information technologies, and to go through the process of meaningfully and authentically applying and continuing to develop critical literacy skills (Downes & Zammit 2000). Teachers must enhance students' development and application of these skills through devising learning activities that involve students:

- efficiently accessing and locating specific information from a variety of sources;
- critically evaluating different kinds of information (such as visual, aural, textual images) in terms of content, purpose, audience and the techniques of ideological positioning;
- discerning the quality and authority of information being located;
- interpreting the information and understanding its meaning from a variety of viewpoints;
- ethically applying this information in a variety of ways, such as engaging in democratic decision-making, problem-solving or even becoming involved in political action designed to contribute to social transformation.

In this sense, students should be provided with purposeful, meaningful opportunities to develop and enhance their information literacy skills as well as skills related to other literacies through the integration of information technologies into the curricula. By providing support and guidance during this process, teachers help to effectively prepare students to continue to engage in lifelong, independent learning, involving higher order thinking, and critical and creative investigation, when they leave the school environment (Roschelle & Pea 1999).

Equity, access and technology

All students within the education system regardless of gender, race, age, ethnicity or disability should have equitable access to new technologies. While many schools and systems are attempting to achieve this, certain students are still not being provided with sufficient access to these resources.

There is a clear challenge for education to provide access to new technologies and to the literacies needed to overcome the divisions and inequalities that have been a persistent problem for contemporary societies (Kellner 1998).

However, this may not be easily achieved due to the following factors:

- access to these technologies is easier for the privileged elite;
- powerful 'in-groups' may dominate virtual classrooms;
- specific and online language, which is often ethnocentric, male-oriented and centred on middle-class values, is not accessible to everyone (particularly students from non-English speaking backgrounds [NESB] and indigenous students) especially the large amounts of written text which alienates those with reading difficulties or visual impairments;
- some geographically isolated and poor communities have limited access to learning technologies (Roschelle & Pea 1999).

Kirkup (1995) believes that some females are disadvantaged by online learning. Some girls are less comfortable with aspects of science and technology and have different learning styles that lead to different patterns of use of technology in learning (especially within the classroom context, where males may dominate technological resources or direct the females as they use the resources — see also Singh 1995).

Cusack, Gurr and Schiller (1999) observed that schools in economically poorer districts of New Zealand have attempted to redress the inequalities of access to information and communications technology, by developing school information and communications technology networks through investment with community partnerships. These networks are seen as being more effective than implementation efforts in economically advantaged districts. The New Zealand government is also aiming to have an Internet connection in every school so students who may have been previously disadvantaged by their lack of access to information technologies will have this situation addressed.

It is evident that teachers, educational administrators and policy-makers all have a significant role to play if existing inequalities relating to the effective access and application of communication and information technologies are to be redressed.

Conclusion

We have highlighted in this chapter the many benefits of using technology in teaching and learning. These benefits include: the construction of collaborative, supportive and interactive learning environments; more time and attention for students' ideas and problems; the potential of electronic networks to enable the connection of multiple information sources and databanks, and the creation of new epistemological and communication potential.

Technologically mediated teaching and learning will, however, need to be situated in a conversational framework to include discursive, adaptive, interactive and reflective components. Such a framework emphasises dialogue and transformation of teaching and learning: from passive reception to active engagement; from the classroom to the real world; from text to multiple representation; from isolation to interconnection; and from products to processes. We have referred to this framework as an interactional approach to learning and teaching.

It is important for you to recognise that this interactional approach is made up of three basic types of interactions:

1. learner–content interaction;
2. learner–instructor interaction; and
3. learner–learner interaction.

We argued that it is also important for you to recognise why technology is used in the classroom to enhance learning and that our technology curriculum agenda should be about:

- learning technology;
- learning *through* technology; and
- learning *about* technology.

The research we referred to in this chapter underscores that learning environments built on interaction can allow students to maintain personal autonomy (through control over their own learning) and relatedness (through being given tasks and tools for cooperating with each other), while at the same time engaging productively in their own learning.

We have also explored implications for teacher professional development and student information literacy and hopefully demonstrated that we as teachers in a technologically mediated world need to go beyond limited definitions of literacy to recognise the social and cultural elements of technological literacy alongside traditional literacies.

Importantly, we have also cautioned that technology can exclude as well as include and that such exclusion can be a product of race, class, gender, geographical location or physical capacity. As teachers we have a clear duty to be aware of both the exclusive as well as the inclusive potential of technology.

INQUIRY STRATEGIES

1. How has technology changed the world from the one you remember growing up in? List some of the major technological advances in the last 25 years and tease out, in groups, the impact of those changes on society (think about the labour market, the media, communications, the economy, households and relationships).

2. The media has picked up on the way in which technology, particularly online technology, can help deliver its message in new and creative ways. From your reading of the media (including the visual and aural) what are the various ways that young people are being invited to participate in and engage technology? Include here, for example, competitions and reader polls like radio stations' 'Hottest 100'.

3. Conduct your own Internet search on technology in learning and teaching and share sites of relevance with your peers.

4. Make it a task when you are on field experience in schools to conduct your own mini-evaluation of your school's approach to technology in teaching and learning. Share your findings with your peers. Find out whether your school has a stated technology policy. Examine the school's curriculum and make your own judgments about the integrated or add-on nature of technology in teaching and learning. Explore the allocation of resources and the distribution of computers in particular. Ask teachers about their classroom practices in relation to technology and ask if you can observe classes where technology is being used to enhance learning.

References

American Council on Education (1999). *To Touch the Future: Transforming the Way Teachers are Taught. An Action Agenda for College and University Presidents.* Washington: American Council on Education.

Anderson, J. & Alagumalai, S. (1997). HTML: the next language of communication for information technology in open learning, *Unicorn*, 23, pp. 11–20.

Bigum, C. (1997). Teacher and computers: In control or being controlled? *Australian Journal of Education*, 41, pp. 247–261.

Bigum, C. & Green, B. (1993). Technologizing Literacy; or Interrupting the Dream of Reason. In P. Gilbert & A. Luke (eds), *Literacy in Contexts: Australian Perspectives and Issues.* Sydney: Allen & Unwin.

Bobis, J., Mulligan, J., Lowrie, T. & Taplin, M. (1999). *Mathematics for Children: Teaching Children to Think Mathematically.* Sydney: Prentice Hall.

Boyd, S., Kelliher, A., Scott, J. & Pech, D. (1998). Taking the first byte: Lessons from a classroom-based IT initiative. SET — *Research Information for Teachers*, 1, pp. 1–4.

Boylan, C. & Wallace, A. (1999). *Distance Teaching and Learning Using Satellite Technology Systems: A report on the evaluation of the New South Wales Outback Satellite Education Trial.* Wagga Wagga: Centre for Rural Social Research, Charles Sturt University.

Churchill, R., Williamson, J. & Grady, N. (1997). Educational change and the new realities of teachers' work lives. *Asia-Pacific Journal of Teacher Education*, 25, pp. 141–157.

Cusack, B., Gurr, D. & Schiller, J. (1999). The impact of technology on the work of educational leaders. *Hot Topics (Australian Council for Educational Administration)*, 3, July, pp. 1–2.

Davies, O., Jeffries, D. & McFadden, M. (1998). NSW HSC On-Line: Successes and challenges in on-line education. *Australian Education Network Newsletter*, 10, (2), pp. 1–2.

Department of Employment, Education, Training and Youth Affairs (DEETYA) (1997). *Digital Rhetorics: Literacies and technologies in education — current practices and future directions* (3 vols). Canberra: Commonwealth of Australia.

Dixon, J. (1999). @ UNIONS — the Internet is union business. *NSW Teachers' Federation.* 1998. Eric Pearson Study Grant Report.

Downes, T. & Zammit, K. (2000). New literacies for connected learning in global classrooms: A framework for the future. In P. Hogenbirk & H. Taylor (eds), *The Bookmark of the School of the Future.* Kluwer, Boston.

Green, K.C. & Gilbert, S.W. (1995). Great expectation: content, communication, productivity and the role of information technology in higher education. *Change*, 27, (2) pp. 8–19. March–April.

Holmes, D. & Russell, G. (1999). Adolescent CIT use: Paradigm shifts for educational and cultural practices? *British Journal of Sociology of Education*, 20, pp. 69–78.

Holmes, P. (1997). Learning to teach with new technology: classroom management of a laptop computer program does have its frustrations. *Unicorn*, 23, pp. 21–30.

Jonasson, D.H., Peck, K. & Wilson, B.G. (1999). *Learning with Technology: A constructivist perspective.* New York: Prentice-Hall.

Kellner, D. (1998). Multiple literacies and critical pedagogy in a multicultural society. *Educational Theory*, 48, pp. 103–122.

Kirkup, G. (1995). Gender issues and learning technologies. *British Journal of Educational Technology*, 26, pp. 218–219.

Kumari, S. (1998). Teaching with the Internet. *Journal of Information Technology for Teacher Education*, 7, pp. 363–377.

NSW Department of Education and Training (DET) Curriculum Support Directorate (2000). *Curriculum Support for Teaching in English 7–12.* 5, pp. 1–16.

Roschelle, J. & Pea, R. (1999). Trajectories from today's WWW to a powerful educational infrastructure. *Educational Researcher*, 28, pp. 22–25.

Rowntree, D. (1995). Teaching and learning online: A correspondence education for the 21st century. *British Journal of Educational Technology*, 26, pp. 205–215.

Russell, G. & Russell, N. (1997). Imperative or dissonance? Implications of student computer use for a cyberspace curriculum. *Unicorn*, 23, pp. 2–9.

Simpson, M., Payne, F., Munro, R. & Hughes, S. (1999). Using information and communications technology as a pedagogical tool: who educates the educators? *Journal of Education for Teaching*, 25, pp. 247–262.

Singh, P. (1995). Discourses of computing competence, evaluation and gender: the case of computer use in the primary classroom. *Discourse: studies in the cultural politics of education*, 16, pp. 81–110.

Smith, G. (1999). Teaching, learning, technology and effectiveness. *Information Transfer*, 19 (4), pp. 24–39.

Sparrow, B., Davies, O. & McFadden, M. (1998). *Teaching and Learning on the World Wide Web: An evaluation of NSW HSC On-Line.* Sydney: Access Australia.

Todd, R.J. (1999). Transformational leadership and transformational learning: information literacy and the World Wide Web. *Bulletin (National Association of Secondary School Principals NASSP)*, 83, pp. 4–12.

Wild, M. (1996). Building knowledge networks: The scope of the World Wide Web. *Australian Educational Researcher*, 23, pp. 45–54.

PART FOUR

New Ways of Understanding Curriculum and Assessment

CHAPTER *10* Literacy Teaching Across the Curriculum

CHAPTER *11* Changing Trends in Curriculum Design

CHAPTER *12* New Ways of Thinking About Assessment and Reporting

This section embodies three chapters. The first of these examines literacy teaching across the curriculum. It is argued that adequate literacy skills are seminal to the kinds of learning valued in the secondary school curriculum. Further, the chapter develops understandings of 'critical literacy' whereby the reader is not a mere decoder of text, but a critical interpreter.

The chapter which follows discusses changing trends in curriculum design. The specific focus is upon the notion of outcomes-based education which has required of teachers, and the systems which employ them, that they are explicit about what they expect their students to be able to make, do and perform within a framework of agreed criteria. Such a curriculum regime believes that all students can be successful learners, although some may require more time and assistance than others.

The section concludes with a chapter which focuses upon new ways of thinking about assessment and reporting. It is argued that authentic formative assessment is the key to improving student learning outcomes and that students need to be participative in the assessment processes. The chapter emphasises that the purposes of assessment should influence the specific practices and that a distinction needs to be made between those assessment processes designed to enhance learning and those designed to make a summative statement about what has been learned.

10

CHAPTER

Literacy Teaching Across the Curriculum

Teachers in secondary schools who are not English teachers often feel that 'Language and Literacy' issues properly belong to the English department; sometimes they even blame the English department for not doing their job if the students have trouble with reading and writing tasks. This chapter starts from the premise that all teachers are teachers of literacy. It considers the ways in which 'literacy' is used as something of a political football in discussions of schools, suggesting this is a constructed 'crisis' that gives rise to many reform efforts. The chapter includes a summary of some key research and results of tests, and shows how these can be interpreted in different ways and lead to different school-level activities. Literacy is an expanding and developing field, meaning more than mere decoding of written texts. It is an orientation to the world of symbols and representation around which our kind of society is organised. As such it is a crucial aspect of all fields of teaching, and one in which there are no clear 'recipes' for success, although much continues to be learned about how literacy and knowledge are intertwined.

Constructing a 'crisis' of literacy

Before going into more specific details about literacy and literacy debates, it is important to recognise that 'literacy' is used as a 'code word' (Green, Hodgens & Luke 1994) which signals that something more is going on when governments, educators or the media engage in discussions on literacy. This is a necessary precursor to being able to understand what is at stake when people talk about literacy, especially in some of the wilder media coverage of the topic. This is also why educators other than English teachers need to pay attention to issues of literacy in the secondary school.

The term 'literacy' only came into prominence in the 1970s (Green, Hodgens & Luke 1994). Before that, public discussion and research discussion was mainly framed in terms of reading and writing, often with spelling and grammar thrown in for good measure. There have been consistent 'campaigns' around the improvement of literacy levels throughout the last century, usually organised as a way to control the work of teachers. The 'back to basics' movements usually express some dissatisfaction with schooling, and hark back to some presumed 'golden age' when students were all well drilled in spelling and grammar, taught to read through a particular phonics method, and teachers knew their place and did their job. Of course, there is no 'golden age' when all students learned to read — otherwise adult illiteracy rates would not exist, even among native born English speakers. It is also important to recognise that what counts as 'literacy' has also changed over the years and that, contrary to much of what is discussed in the press and public forums, literacy standards have actually increased in the past 50 years or more.

In their study of the debates on literacy in Australia from 1946–90, Green, Hodgens and Luke (1994) show that there are many dimensions of life and school over time that are associated with discussions of literacy and its changes. For example, they discuss how different values about young people and schools are embedded in debates at different times. These are summarised in the following table (also cited in a more accessible source by Cormack 1998).

Dimensions associated with literacy

Negative values	Positive values
■ Delinquency ■ Revolutionary or subversive ideologies ■ Sexual immorality and moral decay ■ Barbarity ■ Technological incompetence ■ American cultural influence ■ Mental and physical handicap ■ Republicanism ■ Socioeconomic 'disadvantage' ■ Inadequate assimilation into Anglo/Australian culture ■ Poor initial education	■ Allegiance to the Crown and Commonwealth ■ Protestant religious virtues ■ Discipline and obedience to authority ■ Mastery of British 'proper speech' ■ Innate intellectual gifts ■ Mono-cultural Anglo/Australian nationalism ■ Scientific and technological competitiveness ■ Mental and physical health ■ Employability and job competence

The different kinds of values represented in such a listing provide the context for understanding something of what is at stake in discussions about 'literacy'. Rarely are they straightforward discussions about students and what they can (or cannot) do. By mobilising certain key words of the time, or dominant values, it is possible to infuse the literacy issue with a sense of crisis. You might be able to find a range of other associations for the term 'literacy' in current newspapers or policy documents illustrating the point further.

Throughout the Australian history of mass education, literacy has been associated with citizenship. Literacy used in this context can be a 'code word' for anxiety about the nation state. In the nineteenth century, for example, the introduction of compulsory schooling was seen as a means of guaranteeing the pre-condition of an informed citizenry, taken up by various 'sides' in the debates as variously promoting democracy, independence from Mother England or moral salvation of the individual. In the last decade, literacy has similarly been connected to debates over whether the future voters of Australia know enough about their political institutions, history and processes to be good citizens of the Australian nation in a time of globalisation. Thus, whenever there is a discussion of literacy and standards, there is a need for caution in interpretation: what else is at stake in the discussion? What are the interests being served by such a discussion? What else is being loaded into the debate?

For the most part, discussions of 'standards' in literacy are largely derailed by this overloading of the term. Literacy is constantly produced as being 'in crisis' (Green, Hodgens & Luke 1994) whereas there has not been a constant set of skills or competencies being measured. Indeed, many researchers would argue that skills have increased both in scope and in the percentage of the population with access to them over the last century. As Jo-Anne Reid has noted (1999, p. 197):

> In spite of the media rhetoric about national literacy failure, it is certainly not 'normal' to find illiterate children in Australia, or in any of the countries of the First World (United Nations Children's Emergency Fund (UNICEF) 1990).

When discussing literacy problems, it is important to keep this warning in mind: what we in Australia will find unacceptable as a level of workable literacy is far higher than in those countries where access even to teaching or literacy tools for most young people is out of the question. Yet it is also important not to dismiss all concern with literacy and standards as mere rhetoric or political ideology. There are, as we will show later in the chapter, serious issues for the teaching of literacy and many ways that teachers can intervene in these debates and with the young people they teach.

What is meant by 'literacy'?

Since there is a great deal of debate about the term literacy, it is not merely a matter of putting down one definition and then proceeding. Not only does literacy carry the 'baggage' of other issues, as noted above, but also literacy, even in its most limited definitions, is complex and being constantly investigated, producing new ways of understanding it. Hence new definitions abound. For our purposes, however, it is useful to point out some of the key issues for discussion of literacy. First, literacy does mean an orientation to texts of various kinds. To talk of literacy is to consider an orientation to the world of print — what is called the Gutenberg version of literacy, after the 'inventor' of the printing press — but also to the world of representation more generally. In recent years, the appearance of different kinds of texts other than books leads many to include in discussions of literacy those texts that are more available, such as computer-generated multimedia, web pages, email, and a wider range of visual texts, including photography, graphics, and performances. The plural term 'multi-literacies' (New London Group 1996) has been developed to take account of this variety of text and representation that students are now expected to 'read'. The term emphasises the wide range of changing kinds of text and new settings for texts that schools and other places in society need to consider.

If we include these multiple kinds of literacies, then it follows that all teachers have to pay attention to literacies and the teaching of literacies. Teachers who have specifically taught language or book literacy have long understood that literacy is not merely a matter of decoding written texts. There is certainly a need to integrate reading, writing, listening and speaking: many factors come into the processes of 'reading' a text. To be literate in an area requires a complex set of orientations to the world, understanding context as well as the specific linguistic features of a text. For teachers of all discipline areas and all age levels, attention to the relationship of the text to its context is a crucial dimension of teaching.

Different kinds of literacies are demanded in different settings and different media. Technological literacy includes but is not only restricted to being able to use a keyboard and applications. This is a developing field. We do not yet know a great deal about how literacy, learning and technology are related (Snyder 1999) and the kinds of technology-related pedagogies in schools are yet to move much beyond using the computer and Internet as a substitute for the fordigraph machine or the library. The emerging new kinds of teaching and learning that might be possible are only just beginning to emerge — and new generations of teachers in all subject areas will be part of inventing new kinds of pedagogy associated with the new technologies. Students in schools, who may be more literate in the technologies than their teachers, are likely to be partners in the inventions of new forms of 'digital' literacies, although we need to be wary of assuming that all technology is likely to lead to improved literacy for all students (Lankshear et al. 1997).

Literacy is a social practice or set of practices, not just a matter of skills in coding and decoding. It requires the capacity to judge the nature of the social setting so that the reader or writer can recognise the literacy demands that are appropriate. Literacy enhances people's capacities to move around in their world and develop a sense of agency in relating to it. In a workplace, for example, people will need various forms of literacy to follow instructions, make records, solve problems, to do things, to learn information for later use and to assess the usefulness of information (Mikulecky, Ehlinger & Meenan 1987, p. 2):

> Literacy in the workplace relies heavily on extralinguistic cues and makes use of social systems. For example, workers often move back and forth from print to equipment and then perhaps back to a different piece of print. Workers read, look, do, and ask others. The social aspect of asking and discussing is important.

The authors of this last statement about on-the-job literacy compare workplace literacy demands to literacy experiences in schools which are primarily internally focussed, not social or connected to 'real jobs'. One of the issues facing teachers in schools is the ways in which learning — especially various forms of literacy attached to different subject matters — can be made relevant to the lives of the students in our schools. Many students can learn literacy if they are given a context.

The capacity to read 'context' is what many literacy workers call 'critical literacy'. In this, they emphasise the role that understanding context has on even the ability to marshal the most basic skills such as word recognition in a given situation. Lankshear (1997) suggests that there are three different 'versions' of critical literacy, which might involve any or all of (p. 44):

- *having a critical perspective on literacy* or literacies per se, *where literacy itself is the object of critique*;
- *having a critical perspective on particular texts*, where the critique of texts and their world views is the object;
- *having a critical perspective on* — i.e. being able to analyse and critique — *wider social practices* . . . which are mediated by, made possible and partially sustained through reading, writing, viewing, transmitting, etc., texts. Here social practices, their histories, their normative work, and their associated literacy practices and artefacts, etc., are the target of analysis and critique.

Approaches to critical literacies may seem easier in the humanities areas where teachers have some experience of dealing with texts as texts. Yet in all subject areas there are ways of helping students to understand where the text came from, what is at stake in it, exploring how the text works to persuade the readers of its 'truth', the history of this kind of text, and so on. Further ideas of how this might be built into specific classroom strategies will be developed below. Here, we want mainly to explore the range of dimensions that come into discussions of 'literacy'.

Standard Australian English

In Australia, Standard Australian English is the recognised and dominant form of English for public purposes, including school purposes. This is seen as an important focus for school literacy teaching: providing all children with access to the linguistic features which dominate in public life and written texts. The Australian Language and Literacy Policy (DEET 1991a, b) makes clear that all languages written and spoken in Australia, including the various Aboriginal and immigrant languages and dialects, are to be treated with respect and equality. Yet most of schooling does not really support or bridge between other languages or forms of language and Standard Australian English (SAE). What this does, effectively, is to privilege those students who come to school already familiar with the forms of SAE, orally and in writing, without providing enough avenues for others to continue their own language development or make the transition to familiarity with SAE. Students who are not literate in their own language are less likely to become literate in SAE, and many feel that their language, dialect or creole is not valued in the school (Heath 1982). Schools ought to be able to value students' existing language forms and provide access to standard forms of English.

Indeed, there has been a history of bilingual education in Australia, using Aboriginal and community languages as the medium of teaching, for periods which might range from total immersion in early years of schooling to regular instruction in a community language other than English at least once a day. In recent years, however, there has been a lessening of government support for such programs, which are often staff-intensive. There remains a problem in being able to offer either continuity in a language instruction, or significant enough time for the study of other languages, including for native SAE speakers. This may be seen, for example, in a secondary school where Japanese may be offered for Years 7 and 8 but not continued through the secondary school — especially if a teacher leaves and is replaced by a teacher expert in another language altogether. Currently there are problems in providing adequate language teaching in languages other than English in most secondary schools. Bilingual education, especially in Aboriginal schools, is also available only to a small minority of students. If the Northern Territory proceeds with its espoused policy of removing bilingual education for Aboriginal Communities, then there will be almost no seriously bilingual education in Australia. Yet bilingual education is important for cultural identity and continuity. It also adds to the diversity of Australia's linguistic heritages, and specifically contributes to the capacity of students who are not native in SAE to have access to the concepts, knowledge banks and ways of working in a range of disciplinary areas. There is a direct relation between literacy in a first language and capacity to perform literacy tasks in other languages. Thus bilingual education, access to instruction through a community language and specific attention to the transfer of skills to SAE are all important strategies to equalise students' chances for successful transition to adult life and work through access to literacy.

Who is 'at risk' of not being adequately literate?

Being literate is a marker of an educated person and is the means by which many are given access not only to further education but also employment and other life chances. 'Basic' literacy in the early twenty-first century requires more than knowing letters and words, some spelling and handwriting. These are no longer enough to be able to function as a worker or an informed citizen. Literacy is not an issue for all students but there are significant populations for whom poor levels of literacy are an indicator of key problems, linked to future life chances, including health, employment options and further education and training. If we consider not only school-level data but also issues surrounding adult literacy, we can see how the consequences of school practices around literacy have implications for longer term life chances. In this section, we outline the results of some tests of literacy levels, including middle years, Year 9, Year 3 and adults, to show how these have implications for secondary teachers.

A major study into Year 9 literacy levels in schools (ACER 1997a) showed not only that there was a problem with literacy levels of achievement, but that there was a significant difference between the achievements of different groups. As with other tests, boys and girls had significantly different outcomes. Thirty four per cent of Year 9 boys and 26 per cent of girls were seen to be 'without basic literacy skills', according to this study. This is a similar percentage of students seen as having difficulty in primary school Year 3. The results of a 1996 national survey into school English (ACER 1997b) also showed girls and boys performing at different levels, and at similar percentages under what might be expected for Year 3. Thirty four per cent of boys did not meet national standards for Year 3 in reading and 35 per cent in writing, compared to 23 per cent of under-performing girls in Year 3 reading and 19 per cent in writing. A staggering 81 per cent of the special Indigenous student sample were unable to perform adequately at their year level. Socioeconomic status is also a crucial divider of literacy achievement: 53 per cent of students from low socioeconomic backgrounds could not meet the Year 5 reading standard compared to 13 per cent from high socioeconomic backgrounds.

It is important to recognise in the previous paragraph that the percentage of students who can be seen as under-performing for their age level is not just a consistent 'average' across year levels. In the middle years a number of studies have shown that for a significant proportion of students, results actually decline in the middle years of schooling (roughly Years 5 to 8 or 9). In a keynote to a 1999 national conference on middle schooling, Peter Hill and Jean Russell (1999) give an overview of research on literacy findings relevant to the middle years (http://www.sofweb.vic.edu.au/mys/other.htm). In summarising the findings of the study of the Victorian Quality Schools Project, they argue:

> The mapping of student learning progress across the compulsory years of schooling revealed that there was virtually no growth during the middle years in reading, writing, speaking and listening . . . [R]eading progress can be seen to plateau in Years 5 to 8 for most students, while for the lowest 25 per cent there is an actual decline in achievement, particularly in the first year of high school (Year 7). It is also evident that underachievement is greater among boys than girls and that that underachievement persists for longer.

Even more interestingly, they parallel this with a declining interest in students' enjoyment of school across the compulsory years, lowest in the middle years and increasing only marginally towards the end of the compulsory years (ten).

The low levels of achievement in literacy are not easily made up. Rather, those who are failed by schools in terms of provision of literacy often have few options for further access to literacy. Australia has recently participated in an adult literacy survey where a wide sample of Australians were surveyed in their homes (ABS 1997) on their literacy levels and practices. Although there are limits to this kind of survey (for example, no test of writing ability), the results are worrying when extrapolated to the community as a whole. The Australian Council for Adult Literacy (ACAL 1999) suggests that the levels of literacy skills of Australians aged 15 to 74 years old were in the order of:

- Level 1: 2.6 million
  (a person with poor literacy skills)
- Level 2: 3.6 million
  (a person who can read but only deal with simple, basic materials with non-complex tasks)
- Level 3: 4.8 million
  (people able to integrate information from several sources and solve more complex problems, usually seen as minimum required to deal with the demands of everyday life and work)
- Level 4: 2.3 million
  (people who demonstrate the ability to use higher order thinking and information processing skills)

Almost half of Australian adults are expected therefore to have difficulty coping with the literacy demands of everyday life. Unemployed people had much greater difficulty than those in the work force. People who had another language as their first language were at the lowest end of the scale, although 14 per cent of native English speakers were also at Level 1. Such results suggest a need for ongoing provision of systematic adult education and training in literacy (and numeracy). Yet they also have important implications for what happens in schools, especially for students for whom school is largely an experience of failure.

Those students who leave school early are, unfortunately, relatively easy to predict even in primary school. They are overwhelmingly from groups with low socioeconomic status: Aboriginal, rural and isolated students, and those from a background of poverty. In a 1999 report for the Dusseldorp Skills Forum, Richard Curtain notes major consequences of leaving school early. Fifteen per cent of 15–19 year olds are 'at risk' of not making a successful transition from education to work, a risk increased if the young person is female, or in the Northern Territory, Western Australia, South Australia, Queensland, or Tasmania. Twenty four per cent of 20–24 year olds were at risk of not making the transition to long-term work, 23 per cent of them not having completed year 12 at school. Thus, completion of school makes a crucial contribution to life chances. Nine per cent of the total youth population is locked into marginal activities (part time work in dead-end or casual activities) for up to three years (Curtain 1999).

The Human Rights and Equal Opportunity Commission (HREOC) conducted an inquiry into provision of education in rural and remote areas, following a series of consultations in rural areas (1999, *Bush Talks*, http://www.hreoc.gov.au). They cited a key problem of retention of rural students in all areas of Australia where there are problems of gaining access both to school-level education and to further education and training. In Western Australia, for example, the 1996 *National Report on Schooling in Australia* figures of Years 11 and 12 drop-outs showed 25 per cent for Perth metropolitan schools compared to between 50 and 75 per cent in country areas (MCEETYA 1996, p. 63). The factors contributing to such poor participation in schools are varied and complex (HREOC 1999):

> Family factors, previous educational experience, inadequate access to secondary schools, the high turnover in teachers, lack of subject choices, poor skills in the use of technology, poor facilities, poor future employment prospects, and disincentives created by government assistance schemes are amongst the causal factors.

Race, gender, socioeconomic status and location are all important markers to watch in terms of literacy. If we do not understand that lower levels of literacy achievement are skewed systematically towards particular groups and away from other groups, then we are unable to work through what might be done in particular circumstances. Not only is it important to note the gender, class, race and location differences at different levels on tests but also the large proportion of the age cohort. If significant numbers of students and adults are not performing at the expected or wanted level, what does that mean about the kinds of teaching that has occurred? If between a fifth and a third of students are missing out, what does that imply about the success of schooling? What does it imply about the sorting and selecting functions of schools? What might the findings imply about the need to change school organisation? How do students who missed out at primary school ever get access to secondary subjects? If we are to avoid the levels of adult illiteracy, what else might be possible?

Who's to 'blame'?

For many people, the answers to the questions raised in the last section are relatively straightforward. Introduce a new test, change the curriculum with a new program, or change the teachers are the common responses in terms of government reforms and funded projects. The issue of testing and how much notice to take of them is hotly contested. The range of arguments is varied, with some blaming teachers for their inadequate performance, some blaming students and the inadequate home backgrounds they bring to school, while others point to the problem of teaching to the test and a narrowed curriculum. Blaming teachers' competencies is a favoured response to test results that show less than desired levels of achievement of literacy. There have been many versions of this 'blaming' that are resurrected when the 'crisis' of literacy levels is high. In the 1990s and early years of 2000, there have been projects to improve literacy in the early years, through changing teacher education, through providing special projects federally or in employer and professional associations, and through the introduction of national and state/territory tests that allow comparison over time. The development of national curriculum profiles and statements has also been at least in part a way of controlling the work of teachers so they alter their practice to demonstrate student achievement levels in standardised bands.

There are also debates that point to the problem that the complexity of literacy is not being adequately captured in measurement techniques. Tests only measure what can be measured and literacy is more complex than the measures it is taken to represent. We can point to what many teachers suggest, that tests only capture a small part of what students can do in 'ordinary' circumstances. For them, literacy can't only be defined in terms of what is tested on a certain day under certain test conditions but is more properly looked at as a range of capacities demonstrated over time, in appropriate conditions of use rather than in tests. Still others will point to the problem that tests tend to divide literacy into separate parts — for example, reading, writing, listening and speaking and their subsets — whereas literacy in context is not a separate set of skills.

Then there is the problem of how people interpret the test results. They may generalise them to the whole population when this is not the aim of the test. Or they may read 'averages' wrongly. For example, if an *average* group of students is expected to perform at a particular level (a benchmark, for example), then it follows that the *average* is made up of some students above the average, and some below it; that is, the *average* is constructed from the full range of students. Some are therefore expected to be above and below by the nature of the construction of the scale. No student actually looks like the *average*.

One pernicious side-effect of testing is that the results can be interpreted as finding a 'natural' or 'normal' difference in the achievement levels of students. 'Blaming the victim' or 'deficit' views of students are ways of suggesting that tests merely measure 'natural' or 'genetic' differences among the cohort. What follows from this position is that there is no point in educating students: they are biologically or environmentally incapable of learning from school. The paradox of such a position is that it undercuts any justification for teaching or for schooling. If differences in students are already fixed, then education is not worth pursuing.

The absence in any of these debates which blame teachers, school curriculum or students is that there is no attention to student background and how this might affect systematic variations in student performance. Schools are not totally responsible for the outcomes of schooling: there is too strong a correlation between socioeconomic background and location with achievement in schools. Students with the worst achievement levels are Aboriginal, come from rural and remote areas, or are poor. While girls might outperform boys generally within each of these groups, Aboriginal students and those from rural or low socioeconomic backgrounds as a whole are outperformed by middle-class, metropolitan and Anglo-Celtic background students. There has been a consistent mismatch of some students' home backgrounds with the approaches used by schools for middle-class, white students. It seems to be assumed and built into many current (and past) school practices that students who do not come to schools accustomed to literacy are too stupid to learn rather than being given opportunities to learn in ways that are too speedy or culturally inappropriate.

By failing to develop a wider range of teaching strategies, many schools fail significant numbers of students. In doing so, schools contribute to the creation of gaps among different groups of students in terms of their achievements, especially in terms of real access to literacy. It is a tough issue to explore without falling into some of the traps which were outlined above. Nor are there easy answers: if there were, many teachers with good will and school systems with project money available to spend would already have found them. However, there are some significant projects that have already demonstrated a better way.

We do know that single-issue projects that focus on only one dimension of the issue of literacy are usually not successful. If Aboriginal literacy programs do not take account of the specific colonial history of 'white man's literacy', and the current context for the specific group/s to be taught, particularly the link between Aboriginality, poverty, rurality and unemployment, then such literacy programs will fail. Similarly, a 'boys and literacy' campaign that does not take into account the different class, race and locations of students is not going to help redress the lower levels of literacy amongst the Aboriginal, rural and poor populations. Indeed, it might exacerbate the problems it was established to address. Gilbert (1998) argues that we need to understand how masculinity is constructed at school and how for many boys, their masculinity is partly a reaction to what they perceive to be women-oriented specialities in literacy and therefore they do not engage in English, in literacy or often in schools generally. She argues that (p. 30):

> The boys and literacy issue is not just about more books for boys, more men teachers, more remedial reading instruction or more self-esteem work for young men. It is about a complete reworking of the complex interplay of literacy, masculinity and schooling.

It is relatively easy to pontificate about literacy problems and their solutions, and much harder to do something about it in classrooms every day. The next section demonstrates a number of ways of teaching different dimensions of literacy that teachers in secondary schools have found effective.

Teaching towards a greater spread of literacy

To teach literacy related to any field of representation does mean paying attention to the specific features of the text. In secondary schools, this has often been reduced to vocabulary tests for specialist words, but there is a lot more than that involved. This often requires the teacher to marshall new ways to understand the specific features of their discipline areas and specialisms. These include technical dimensions such as specialist vocabulary but also more complex issues of the tone, sentence structures, genres of reports or other texts generated as part of the work of the field. A science report is quite different from a history book project, for example, and not only in the different vocabulary used. Sometimes, students merely need to have the differences in the different areas underscored for them. At other times, there might need to be explicit teaching about a form, often through comparisons with spoken or other forms.

Quite often, students need to be oriented to the ideas and their relation to their current levels of understanding before they can participate in reading or producing particular forms of text. Some important, practical steps can be taken to promote literacy in the planning of units and the conduct of lessons. The first is to provide a climate of talking about the ideas, finding ways to use the vocabulary, and exploring the range of texts used. Britton (1972) emphasised how 'the movement in words from what might *describe* a particular event to a generalization that might *explain* that event is a journey that each must be capable of taking for himself (sic) — *and that it is by means of taking it in speech that we learn to take it in thought*' (p. 114, original emphases). Talking is not the same as dealing with written text — there are different conventions operating — but talking helps orient to the issues and ideas that are under consideration. The importance of 'getting the ideas' as a way into the formal literacy demands of a subject cannot be overestimated. If students are already working with key concepts when they are introduced to a text, they are more likely to be able to deal with the particular forms of representing the ideas in a text — that is, they are more able to learn from the text.

The second important feature of a classroom devoted to building literacy is to help students make connections among the knowledge and issues under consideration with what else they know and understand, including making cultural connections. If students begin to understand the connections between one area and another, they are more likely to be able to take on board the new area of knowledge. A third emphasis is to ensure that students can explicitly dissect the range of texts available, as well as their own texts, and relate them to others. In particular, it is important for students to understand links and boundaries among different disciplines.

A 'discipline' is a human construction. It is a way of dividing up how to know the world. Often this is obvious to people who have plenty of life experience, but for many students the division of the world's ways of knowing is strange and needs some basic explanation. This is one of the significant differences from most of the students' previous experiences in primary school, where much of the knowledge is encapsulated in narrative form, or stories. Only some students successfully make the transition to understanding the organisation of the secondary school and its various subjects. This is one of the reasons behind the development of attention to 'middle schooling' in the 1990s: people began to recognise why many students' achievement levels either stayed static or become lower than their Year 6 levels. Many attempts to address this have worked to integrate curricula across discipline areas, so students can understand that real-life problems draw upon different kinds of knowledge. It makes an easier transition for students who can then explore the similarities and differences among what are usually kept as separate disciplines.

One of the ways that a discipline area such as Biology or Visual Art works is by exposure to a range of texts that are used in the discipline. That is, we cannot teach students to write, think or work within a discipline unless they are able to be immersed in and work with texts that characterise the community which produces the texts. Kress (1985) in his study of educational texts, for example, shows how each subject area really has its own specialist *genre*, or systematic way of writing, thinking and representing its work. There is no generic skill of 'interpreting text'. Rather, each subject area has a specific range of ways which need to be understood before a student can, for example, identify a key argument or even key terms on a topic. Often what is thought of as students' problems in decoding is actually a problem of understanding the ideas. If written text is the only method of gaining access to an idea, then both the idea and the literacy will not be experienced successfully. Access to people who really work in a discipline may also help students to understand its social conventions. Conventions occur in all social situations, from a family dinner table, to a political speech to a committee meeting. People who are accustomed to the setting learn how to 'read' and produce texts appropriate for that setting. Students can learn about the conventions of the disciplines involved in secondary school curricula. They can also be part of building new conventions that reflect the changing society we live in, such as building new ways for producing knowledge through the use of new technologies. (Refer to Chapter 9 for a discussion regarding the impact of technology upon learning and teaching.)

In secondary schools, the area where many subject teachers experience problems is with explanations and expository texts. These are texts which concentrate on giving explanations and reasons why an argument or thesis is given. In a study of school writing, Martin (1985) found the following kinds of factual writing:

- procedure — 'how something is done';
- description — 'what some particular thing is like';
- report — 'what an entire class of things is like';
- explanation — 'a reason why a judgment has been made'; and
- exposition — 'arguments why a thesis has been proposed'.

Many students emerge from primary schools with a familiarity with personal writing, narrative and some with reports. However, few have been supported to read and write, or understand the differences among different kinds of factual writing. In one example, Martin shows the different ways that various kinds of writing, or genres, use prepositions, conjunctions, nouns and verbs. Consider the differences between the following statements (p. 19):

Firearms cause fatalities.

Using a preposition this would come out as:

Fatalities occur because of firearms.

And with a conjunction as:

A lot of people die because too many people have firearms.

Note that as we translate the original sentence back towards the typical spoken form, we have to be more explicit about what we mean. Firearms turns into 'too many people have firearms' and fatalities becomes 'a lot of people die'. These additional details do help to clarify the argument. But in writing we do not normally express reasoning in this way.

Students need to be taught explicitly the differences between spoken and written forms of reasoning and explanation. This kind of basic attention to the literacy demands of texts, different in different subjects, can help many students to become versatile in understanding the social construction of their world. Students who can read and produce the different kinds of texts are demonstrating their induction into the disciplinary world that the adult teachers expect. The above set of explanations presented by Martin might well be connected to studies of society and environment (SOSE) discussions of contemporary issues, or to a study of history or to a study in science of how firearms work. The differences in the final form of acceptable explanation will be quite strong in the different subjects. In SOSE, a more personal or persuasive argument might be developed, while in history a different focus again might emphasise the changing role of war in relation to how it is fought. Yet all subjects would need to discuss the ideas, make connections and show how the forms of the explanations vary according to purposes and setting.

However, it is necessary to remind ourselves that disciplines are also changing, and that many of the conventions taught in schools are never used in 'real-life' exercise of the disciplines. Perhaps as teachers we can assist students to engage in more 'real-life' versions of the subjects they study. Perhaps, also, we can recognise the importance of inter-disciplinary research and writing that is becoming more common in universities and workplace research. Most major problems of the world cannot be addressed only from within the confines of a single subject discipline.

Conclusion

Literacy is not merely a set of skills and competencies for dealing with texts. It is used as a symbolic marker of an educated individual and for the distribution of rewards in societies like ours. It is also a means of accessing significant further education, formally and informally. Thus, the urgency with which many policies and reform initiatives focus on literacy is not misplaced. However, as we argued above, much of the reform attention is not necessarily effective in promoting access to literacy for those most in need of it. As a teacher, it is important to recognise both the symbolic and political dimensions of the literacy debates and also the practical ways in which each teacher can provide students access to their subject matter and 'big ideas' through a range of ways of dealing with texts in context.

It is too easy to have a knee-jerk reaction to accusations about the role of schools in producing literacy, by defending schools, and rejecting the basis of all the accusations. However, all teachers need to develop some level of understanding of these complex issues that can then be built on further through experience in schools. There are serious problems in many secondary schools, and some of them include problems with literacy. Secondary schools are too often organised on the assumption that either all students come provided with skills and the teachers should just teach their subject matter, or that those who do not already perform should just be shunted into remedial 'holding' classes until they are able to leave. It appears that suspension and expulsion policies are also used as a means of ensuring that certain students will not be taught in schools.

These may seem like harsh words — and they are. Words like these are also used as the basis for many reform efforts directed at schools, so there is a need to examine what is at stake in discussions of student achievement. Too often literacy is cited as the problem when there are many, interlocked problems. Yet if schools can work better across the curriculum to provide a range of access points and achievement in literacies for students, some of these problems will be at least partially addressed. The numbers of schools who currently do this is small but growing.

To engage in the support of literacy is a whole-school issue. This does not mean that it is not worth trying to address literacy in single classroom lessons, but it does suggest that more systematic efforts to make a difference need whole-school support. While English teachers may be in the forefront of certain pedagogical knowledge about the teaching of literacy, they do not know the dimensions of the literacies required in other areas of knowledge such as science or health. Nor can they teach them: this is properly the province of the teachers from those areas. The different kinds of literacy work required in different subject areas and problem-solving situations need to be taken into account when planning, teaching and assessing. The development of a range of 'literacies' can thus be seen as a whole-school responsibility, requiring action on the part of every secondary teacher. Teachers need support to access a level of informed professional opinion and further opportunities to invent new teaching strategies. The regular results of national and state/territory tests, similar to those summarised above, will continue to provide a source of input to these debates. As well, there are many professional associations which provide up-to-date support for the development of new approaches to teaching and learning.

INQUIRY STRATEGIES

1. Examine some current policy documents, ministers' press releases, union newsletters, professional association journals or newspaper coverage of issues about literacy. How is literacy being used as a 'code word' in the different sources? How is this similar or different to the values identified by Green et al. (1994)?

2. Examine some lesson plans from different areas of the curriculum and consider the literacy demands required of students to complete the work satisfactorily. What is the range of literacy work required? How else might literacy of different subjects be addressed in the classes?

3. What are some teaching and learning strategies for ensuring that students with poorer access to literacy might gain access to the 'big ideas' in a subject?

References

Alloway, N. & Gilbert, P. (eds) (1997). *Boys and Literacy: Teaching Units.* Carlton: Curriculum Corporation.

Australian Bureau of Statistics (ABS) (1997). *Aspects of Literacy: Assessed Skill levels Australia 1996.* Canberra: Australian Government Publishing Service.

Australian Council for Adult Literacy (ACAL) (1999). *Surveys and Beyond: The case for adult literacy.* Canberra: ACAL.

Australian Council for Educational Research (ACER) (1997a). *Literacy Standards in Australia.* Canberra: J.S. McMillan for DEETYA.

Australian Council for Educational Research (ACER) (1997b). *Mapping Literacy Achievements: Results of the 1996 National School English Literacy Survey.* Canberra: J.S.McMillan for DEETYA.

Bigum, C., Durrant, C., Green, B., Honan, E., Lankshear, C., Morgan, W., Murray, J., Snyder, I. & Wild, M. (1997). *Digital Rhetoric, Literacies and Technologies in Education: Current practices and future directions.* Canberra: Department of Employment, Education, Training and Youth Affairs.

Britton, J. (1972). *Language and Learning.* Hamondsworth: Puffin Books.

Cormack, P. (1998). Literacy research and the uses of history: Studying literacy, schooling and young people in new times. *Australian Educational Researcher*, 25, 3, December, pp. 23–36.

Curtain, R. (1999). Young people's transition from education to work performance indicators. Report to Dusseldorp Skills Forum at http://www.dsf.org.au

Department of Employment, Education and Training (DEET) (1991a). *Australia's Language: The Australian Language and Literacy Policy.* Canberra: Australian Government Publishing Service.

Department of Employment, Education and Training (DEET) (1991b). *Australia's Language: The Australian Language and Literacy Policy — A Companion Volume to the Policy Paper.* Canberra: Australian Government Publishing Service.

Gilbert, P. (1998). Gender and schooling in New Times: The challenge of boys and literacy. *Australian Educational Researcher*, 25,1, April, pp. 15–37.

Green, B., Hodgens, J. & Luke, A. (1994). *Debating Literacy in Australia: A Documentary history.* NSW: Australian Literacy Federation.

Heath, S.B. (1982). *Ways with Words: Language, Life and Work in Communities and Classrooms.* New York: Cambridge University Press.

Hill, P.W. & Russell, V.J. (1999). Systemic, whole-school reform of the middle years of schooling. Keynote to the National Conference on Middle Schooling at http://www.sofweb.vic.edu.au/mys/other.htm

Human Rights and Equal Opportunity Commission (HREOC), (1999). *Bush Talks* at http://www.hreoc.gov.au

Knobel, M. & Healy, A. (eds) (1998). *Critical literacies in the primary classroom.* Newtown, NSW: Primary English Teachers' Association (PETA).

Kress, G. (1985). *Linguistic Processes in Sociocultural Practice.* Geelong: Deakin University.

Lankshear, C. with J.P. Gee, M. Knobel & C. Searle (1997). *Changing Literacies.* Buckingham: Open University Press.

Martin, J.R. (1985). *Factual Writing: Exploring and Challenging Social Reality.* Geelong: Deakin University.

Mikulecky, L., Ehlinger, J. & Meenan, A.L. (1987). *Training for job literacy demands: What research applies to practice.* The Institute of the Study of Adult Literacy, Pennsylvania State University, Pa. pp. 1–13. Reprinted in (1993). *Out of School Literacies Reader.* Geelong: Deakin University.

Ministerial Council for Employment, Education, Training and Youth Affairs (MCEETYA) (1996). *National Report on Schooling in Australia.* Canberra: Australian Government Publishing Service.

New London Group, (1996). A Pedagogy of multiliteracies: designing social futures. *Harvard Education Review*, 66, pp. 60–92.

Reid, J. (1999). Holding firm to the bonds of convention: Primary English, Child Study and the 'Competent teacher'. *Changing English*, 6, 2, pp. 197–218.

Snyder, I. (1999). Literacy and technology studies: past, present, future. Paper presented at the ACER Research Conference October 1999: *Improving Literacy Learning* at http://www.acer.edu.au

11

CHAPTER

Changing Trends in Curriculum Design

In May 1998, the Ministerial Council on Education, Employment, Training and Youth Affairs (MCEETYA — formerly the Australian Education Council) released a discussion paper, *Australia's Common and Agreed Goals for Schooling in the Twenty First Century*, a review of the 1989 Common and Agreed Goals for Schooling in Australia (The Hobart Declaration).[1]

The paper conveyed a national commitment to the preparation of students through schooling for their effective contribution to wider society. MCEETYA published the document to provide a framework for cooperation between schools, states, territories and the Commonwealth. The goals are intended to assist schools and school systems to develop specific objectives and strategies, particularly in the areas of achieving specific curriculum outcomes and assessment. The goals include:

1. To provide an excellent education which develops the talents and capacities for all young people to their full potential, and is relevant to the social, cultural and economic needs of the nation.

2. To enable all students to achieve high standards of learning and to develop self-confidence, optimism, high self-esteem, respect for others and achievement of personal excellence.

3. To promote equality of education opportunities, and to provide for groups with special learning requirements.

4. To respond to the current and emerging economic and social needs of the nation, and to provide those skills which will allow students maximum flexibility and adaptability in their future employment and other aspects of life.

5. To provide a foundation for further education and training, in terms of knowledge and skills, respect for learning and positive attitudes for lifelong education.

---

[1] MCEETYA is chaired by the Federal Minister of Education, Training and Youth Affairs and its members are the Ministers for Education and Training of each of the Australian states and territories.

6. To develop in students:

a) the skills of English literacy, including skills in listening, speaking, reading and writing;

b) skills of numeracy, and other mathematical skills;

c) skills of analysis and problem-solving;

d) skills of information processing and computing;

e) an understanding of the role of science and technology in society, together with scientific and technological skills;

f) a knowledge and appreciation of Australia's historical and geographic context;

g) a knowledge of languages other than English;

h) an appreciation and understanding of, and confidence to participate in, the creative arts;

i) an understanding of, and concern for, balanced development and the global environment;

j) a capacity to exercise judgment in matters of morality, ethics and social justice.

7. To develop knowledge, skills, attitudes and values which will enable students to participate as active and informed citizens in our democratic Australian society within an international context.

8. To provide students with an understanding and respect for our cultural heritage including the particular cultural background of Aboriginal and ethnic groups.

9. To provide for the physical development and personal health and fitness of students, and for the creative use of leisure time.

10. To provide appropriate career education and knowledge of the world of work, including an understanding of the nature and place of work in our society.

In many ways this statement reflects a significant shift from what have been termed input-driven programs of education toward outcome-based education (OBE) (Griffin 1997). As society attempts to meet the challenges of rapid technological and social change governments have become increasingly interested in the outcomes of, and accountability for, the education systems they fund.

At a time of rapid social change, increasing globalisation, and continual technological innovation, education has had to be modified in order to address these changes and prepare young people for adult participation in a society and a global economy that is very different from the one their parents entered. Students must now possess critical thinking skills, be aware and tolerant of cultural pluralism, understand the notion of global citizenship and the responsibilities associated with it, and be able to effectively use the technology that is present throughout modern industrial societies (Eastin 1999, p. 20; Hill & Crevola 1999, p. 117).

Federal and state/territory governments are now substantially reshaping the funding, accountability and support arrangements of schools so curriculum reform can be achieved and all students can be provided with the maximum opportunity to achieving various learning outcomes to the best of their abilities (Hill & Crevola 1999, p. 120).

This shift to outcome-based education needs, however, to be understood within the context of other shifts and changes in curriculum over the last 15 years. But first, to understand changing trends in curriculum and recent curriculum reform we must clarify what we mean by the term *curriculum*.

Curriculum as object and action

Grundy (1998) differentiates between curriculum as object and action. She uses the metaphor of *football* to explain this differentiation. Football, she says, can be both object, that is, the physical thing with which a variety of games are played, and action, that is, the actual game that is played where the physical object, the football, is only one element of the game. The first thing to note here is that the football, depending on the game to be played, can look very different, from a rugby ball, for example, to a soccer ball. The next thing to note is that the actual game develops according to the strategies used by, and the capacities of, those who are engaged in it and the way they follow, or don't, the codes and rules of the game.

Most importantly, Grundy argues that we do not find out a lot about football by just reading the rule book or looking at the football as object. We have to see the game in action to make sense of it (p. 29):

> . . . the game of football gains its meaning through being played. So, with the curriculum, the important thing, according to this view, is the way in which it is 'played out' in the teaching/learning situation.

In terms of schooling, the object view of curriculum equates to syllabuses, curriculum documents, and statements and guidelines about teaching intent such as programs and units of work. Similarly, the action view of curriculum equates to what actually happens in the classroom between teachers and students in relation to the teaching of a syllabus and an intended program of learning activities. This view of curriculum obviously focuses more on outcomes than intent but, clearly, intent is an important part of the action. The action is also affected by the social and cultural background of teachers and students and the institutional setting in which they find themselves; what is often called the 'milieu' of teaching (Schwab 1969, cited in Grundy 1998).

And so, the two views of curriculum — as object and action — are crucial to keep in mind as we discuss shifts and trends in curriculum more broadly. As Stenhouse (1975, pp. 2–3) noted:

> . . . curriculum study is concerned with the relationship between the two views of curriculum - as intention and as reality. . . . The central problem of curriculum study is the gap between our ideas and aspirations and our attempts to operationalise them.

We can then re-read the opening statement of this chapter from MCEETYA as a clear statement of intent. The central curriculum problem in relation to this statement of intent being how these intentions are actualised in schools and classrooms. The documents and syllabuses, or curriculum objects, that result from shifts and changes in curriculum policy can therefore be viewed as the basis on which teachers construct and operationalise their students' learning experiences, but they do not necessarily represent the curriculum per se. For the remainder of this chapter it will be crucial for you to keep in mind the two views of curriculum: as object or intent; and action or reality. It is important for you to realise that in using the term *curriculum*, educators, politicians and the general public can attach significantly different meanings, often conflating curriculum as object with curriculum as enacted in schools, the assumption being that what is written down is what actually happens.

Curriculum as contested

There is a great deal of debate in society about what curriculum should be taught to whom and why. Hopefully without stretching the football metaphor too far, people in Australia argue about the relative merits of the different football codes like Rugby Union, Rugby League, AFL and soccer, and also within each code about preferences of style. This is also true of arguments about education (Kemmis, Cole & Suggett 1983). People argue about what kind of education is best. Some prefer a rigid and structured approach. Others prefer a more negotiated approach. Regardless of approach, the preference indicates a valuing of one kind or style of education over another and it is to this valuing we now turn.

Kemmis, Cole and Suggett (1983) identified three broad orientations towards curriculum that reflect certain values and orientations to education and the roles of students and teachers:

1. vocational/neo-classical;
2. liberal/progressive; and
3. socially critical.

The vocational/neo-classical orientation values education as a preparation for the world of work. In this framework the needs of society are privileged over the needs of the individual. The liberal/progressive orientation values education as a preparation for life with the emphasis on the development of the full potential of the individual. In this framework the needs of the individual are paramount because it is through the individual that society will be reconstructed and improved. The socially critical orientation values the centrality of education to both life and work. This framework privileges the construction of a more just society through individuals' educational engagement in social issues where students are involved in 'critical reflection, social negotiation' and action on these critical social issues (Kemmis, Cole & Suggett 1983, p. 9).

Importantly, in relation to our two views of curriculum — that is, to curriculum as object and action — each of the above orientations suggests different views of knowledge and desired student outcomes. The vocational/neo-classical orientation views knowledge as objective and public. Through schooling, students find their place in society and develop the skills to fulfil their allotted role. The liberal/progressive orientation views knowledge as subjective and private and expressed in the practical capacities of individuals. Students learn how to learn at school and pursue truth and good throughout their life. The socially critical orientation views knowledge as constructed through social interaction. Students develop as critical thinkers able to transform and be transformed by their interactions in a given social and cultural context.

In addition, each orientation suggests markedly different approaches to learning and teaching (including assessment), school organisation (including allocation and use of resources and teaching spaces) and links with the community (Kemmis, Cole & Suggett 1983).

Recent trends in curriculum reform

Three kinds of major curriculum reform have been witnessed in Australia over the past 15 years. First, there has been an attempt to implement a national core curriculum for the compulsory years of schooling. Second, there has been an attempt to broaden senior secondary education to include more vocationally oriented subjects in order to cater for the wider range of students remaining at school during their post-compulsory years. In addition, there has been an explicit attempt to blur the boundaries between vocational and general education at both national and state/territory system levels. Finally, national and state/territory governments have made their intention clear through K-12 syllabus reform that all students should possess, by the time they leave school, certain 'generic competencies' or exit outcomes. These exit outcomes include: communication skills, literacy skills, technology, numeracy and problem-solving skills, abilities to work cooperatively, and knowledge and appreciation of our multicultural, democratic and capitalist society (Lokan et al. 1995; Lokan 1997).

As stated in the introduction to this chapter, Australian and overseas systems of education (such as the United States) are shifting significantly from input-driven curriculum models to outcome-focused ones. Input-oriented models generally expose students to a segment of the curriculum over a specified time then assess the students and normatively assign grades, regardless of whether all students have achieved mastery of the material and the associated skills (Lokan et al. 1995, p. 8; McNeir 1993, p. 1). Outcome-based educational programs may refer to the students' achievements arising from instruction, or may be more system-level indicators of achievement such as retention rates, completion rates, scores on state/territory examinations (such as the HSC or ELLA tests), or the post-school destination of students (Griffin 1997, p. 6). An overview of how this shift towards outcome-based education affects different elements of curriculum is provided by Griffin (1997, p. 8).

From input-driven to outcome-based programs

Components and change criteria	Typical of input-driven programs	Typical of outcome-based programs
1. Desired outcomes	1. non-specific, not necessarily observable; typically global statements or lists of decontextualised objectives; transmission of context	1. Specific and observable, representing levels of progress on a continuum; changes in the student
2. Instructional content	2. Subject-matter based	2. Outcome-based
3. Time for instruction	3. Fixed time units	3. Learner continues until outcome can be demonstrated
4. Mode of instruction	4. Emphasis on teacher as a transmitter of specialised information	4. Teacher as a facilitator of learning, using a variety of instructional techniques and groups

5. Focus of instruction	5. What the teacher is able to and likes to teach	5. What the learner needs to learn to demonstrate outcomes
6. Instructional materials	6. Narrow source of materials (text or work books)	6. Variety of text, media and real life materials based on various learning styles
7. Feedback on learner performance	7. Delayed feedback	7. Results reported immediately after performance in understandable terms
8. Assessment	8. Norm-referenced assessments based on relative performance of others	8. Criterion (outcomes) referenced interpretation of assessments indicates progress in terms of outcomes on learning continuum
9. Exit criteria	9. Final assessment in grades or percentages	9. Learner demonstrates the specified outcomes and outcomes at pre-specified levels on a continuum
10. Learning emphases	10. Learner is encouraged to acquire a fixed body of knowledge transmitted under the control of the teacher	10. Learners need to develop communication, inquiry, conceptualising, reasoning and problem-solving learning skills
11. Learner responsibility	11. Learner is responsible for following a predetermined course of learning	11. Learner needs to develop independence and responsibility for self-monitoring
12. Context of instruction and assessment	12. Teaching, learning and assessment are contextualised to the extent where no prediction of learning is possible	12. A mix of content and abstract together with application in new and generalised contexts is used to assist in generalising the student's performance

This focus on outcomes has drawn heavily on the work of Dr William Spady. Spady argues that outcome-based education (OBE) is a total school and/or system approach where the organisation of the school and/or system and all its programs and instructional efforts are structured around and directed to achieving clearly defined outcomes that society wants all students to demonstrate when they leave school (Spady 1993).

Spady and Marshall (1991, pp. 18–22) identify three different types of outcome-based curriculum:

1. **traditional approach** — which entails the descriptions of learning outcomes within an existing curriculum framework;

2. **transitional approach** — which lists the outcomes required by students when they complete schooling (that is, exit outcomes); and

3. **transformational approach** — which exemplifies and describes the nature of life performances to be undertaken once the student enters the 'real' world as an adult.

This latter approach is held to be the most effective to OBE. This framework becomes instructive and useful when we examine the emergence of outcome-based approaches to education and curriculum in Australia.

Baron and Boschee (1996) report that in the United States, many schools that have been implementing OBE over the past 20 years have witnessed student achievement significantly improve. The Johnson City Central School District in New York has been implementing OBE since 1977 and has seen their students score above the national norm on the California Achievement Tests by steadily increasing margins. Students at the Frederick County (Maryland) School District, which adopted an OBE approach in 1986, have been sitting Advanced Placement exams at twice the prior level, while the drop-out rate has more than halved.

The underlying premise of OBE is that each learner's needs should and must be accommodated through multiple learner-centred instructional strategies and assessment strategies that are appropriate to the student's and the school's local, cultural and social context. As there are no proscribed instructional strategies associated with OBE (except that they should be primarily student-centred), students are provided with opportunities to be challenged and develop original approaches to problem-solving. Teachers then, may use multiple learner-centred assessment techniques to quickly and conveniently measure student achievement, and identify and enhance strengths while remedying weaknesses, using techniques that may have previously not been accepted as conventional assessment techniques (Hill & Crevola 1999). OBE assessment techniques, such as student portfolios, reflective journals, oral interviews and student self-appraisal, all effectively involve the learner in monitoring and assessing his/her own learning achievements (Baron & Boschee 1996; Hill & Crevola 1999).

Previous educational practice has focused on the sole use of norm-referenced interpretation of assessments, competitive assessments and the ranking of students. This assessment usually uses a narrow range of instruments, such as written tests, for measuring essential knowledge and skills, and tends to separate assessment from the actual learning process. Such forms of assessment are viewed as being inappropriate for use in OBE and are effectively replaced by the use of 'authentic assessment' devices such as student portfolios that are made and changed by the students themselves. Devices such as these are said to provide high quality, regular and accessible information to students, parents and the community about how the student is demonstrating levels of knowledge, skills and understandings (Griffin & Smith 1997).

Towards outcome-based education (OBE)

Frameworks for OBE emphasise systems-level change, observable measurable outcomes, and the belief that all students can learn (McNeir 1993, p. 1). And while defining student outcomes or standards has become a major feature of educational policy intent in many countries, educators still find the task of focusing on what students should learn and not on what teachers should teach extremely challenging (Hargreaves & Moore 1999, p.1). Also, in keeping with the notion of curriculum as a contested arena of educational policy, even though clearly stated outcomes are widely viewed as being desirable, there is much disagreement and debate about:

- whether such specified outcomes should be regarded as mandates or guidelines;
- whether outcomes should be specifically or generally defined;
- how outcomes should be measured and assessed;
- whether outcomes should apply to all students equally or exclude those suffering educational disadvantage;
- whether there should be sanctions applied to teachers and students who fail to meet specified outcomes (Zlatos 1993, pp. 12–16).

For the classroom teacher, outcomes are defined by student acquisition of specifically defined skills, knowledge, and understandings that demonstrate learning has occurred. According to Spady (1993, 1994) this is best achieved by focusing on how the student has changed as a result of learning, as opposed to focusing on the tasks that they perform to demonstrate learning. Therefore, effective OBE involves the teacher, the school and the system publicly specifying what students are expected to learn and collecting the necessary evidence to demonstrate that this learning has occurred. The focus is clearly on what has been achieved rather than what has been provided.

Student assessment is viewed as being the most important element of OBE. Identifying outcomes requires the teacher, the student and the system to demonstrate that they have been achieved. Linking achievement, assessment and outcomes in a developmental model lends itself to criterion-referenced or standards-referenced assessment. Increasingly, criterion-reference interpretation is being used in conjunction with performance/standards assessment (Griffin 1997). OBE certainly requires a rethink of assessment strategies to recognise outcomes, and a change in teaching to emphasise students' performances in observable and measurable terms. This then also involves a change in resourcing and curriculum emphasis.

Outcome-based education in Australia

School education in Australia is constitutionally a state/territory responsibility, with the general pattern of curriculum decision-making being that state/territory education departments specify broad guidelines and schools decide the details of what to include in their programs (Lokan 1997, p. 1). From 1989 through to the present, however, state/territory education systems throughout Australia have been affected significantly by successive national governments' attempts to coordinate statements about curriculum content in the major areas of learning in schools.

Sets of learning outcomes known as National Profiles (that is, expected student learning outcomes) and Curriculum Statements (curriculum content descriptions), were developed after several years of consultation, development and validation. This is the closest approach to a national curriculum seen in recent Australian history. These documents set out eight key learning areas (KLAs) and state specific outcomes to be achieved by every student. The profiles are organised within KLAs into a number of content strands. Within each strand there are eight levels, and within each level, there is a series of outcome statements which lead to an overall situation where thousands of outcome statements are listed to be achieved by students (Griffin 1997, p. 6; Lokan 1997, p. 1).

Schools now produce curriculum documents that describe a series of learning outcomes to be achieved by students. In Victoria, for example, the curriculum is planned in accordance with the Curriculum and Standards Framework (CSF). This framework clearly encourages teachers to view themselves as learning facilitators. Teachers must devise learning programs that allow students, with different learning styles and abilities, the opportunities to demonstrate that they have achieved the specified, sequential learning outcomes within and across each of eight KLAs (McNeir 1993 p. 1; Perry 1996, pp. 1–3). This is considered one of the most confronting tasks for teachers when implementing effective OBE.

The use of national profiles in Australia represents an example of the traditional approach to OBE as identified by Spady and Marshall (1991). The outcome statements and pointers (or indicators) in the curriculum statements are grounded in existing practices and curricula and implemented by curriculum and discipline specialists. The existing, rigid subject discipline basis has been retained (Griffin 1997; Spady & Marshall 1991). The Australian education system does, however, exhibit signs of a transitional approach to OBE as 'exit outcomes' have also been implemented into various syllabus documents and government educational policies. To be considered transformational education systems themselves would have to undergo reform (Spady & Marshall 1991).

The benefits of OBE

The implementation of OBE is said to require a shift from the transmission mode of instruction to a process and facilitation model that focuses on outcomes rather than relative performance. Proponents argue it requires that students take more responsibility for performance and learning and places less emphasis on the teacher as being the main holder of expertise and being more focused on the learning needs of the student (Hill & Crevola 1999, p. 123). OBE is said to provide teachers with the opportunity to involve students in the devising and application of evaluation criteria to be used to measure their achievement of learning outcomes, or in peer and self-evaluation (Hargreaves & Moore 1999). In opposition to input-based education, OBE is said not to rigidly proscribe how students should be assessed by their teachers, and consequently to provide more room for student involvement and collaboration in development, assessment and implementation (Hargreaves & Moore 1999, pp. 5–6).

OBE is also thought to lend itself to several types of learning outcomes that require changes to traditional teaching and learning methods as well as assessment. These teaching and learning methods include inquiry, problem-solving, creative reasoning, conceptualising, and learner responsibility. Each of these methods involves the student determining the pace and content of learning. This is viewed as beneficial if it assists students to feel more in control of their own learning and encourages them to be more motivated and involved in the learning process (Battistini 1995).

Researchers argue OBE provides teachers with the opportunity to invest their own energy and imagination into planning activities for their students targeted at them achieving certain learning outcomes within and across subject disciplines. Outcomes are said to provide a structure that helps teachers to clarify and sharpen their curriculum intentions, assisting teachers both to think about what their students need to learn and to devise learning activities to help students achieve these outcomes (Hargreaves & Moore 1999).

It is also claimed that OBE provides students and teachers with opportunities to develop programs that encourage continual self-evaluation and critical reflection as they work towards achieving learning outcomes. The trend in OBE is to provide a framework that can assist both students and teachers to focus on the results of learning, not the actual act of learning. Teachers may also use the performance of these outcomes to review the effectiveness of these learning activities, and may engage in more immediate self-evaluation that will enhance their teaching skills and practice (Griffin & Smith 1997).

Griffin and Smith (1997) and Battistini (1995) also stated that working in teams, creating networks and accessing resources effectively assists teachers and schools to translate the theory of OBE into practice within their local cultural and social context.

Some teachers interviewed by Hargreaves and Moore (1999, p. 6) reported that adjusting outcomes to different student abilities enriched the learning in their classrooms and helped them to develop higher expectations of low achievers. They stated that modified learning programs enhanced students' achievement, self-esteem and motivation as they achieved and were challenged by specific and modified learning outcomes. Teachers, as a result of OBE, may develop more detailed understanding of how students learn according to their different needs and abilities, as well as what classroom routines, structures, organisation and management motivate and engage students in a way that assists them to maximise their learning opportunities (Hill & Crevola 1999).

OBE is also thought to help teachers, by providing a standards framework, to immediately evaluate students' achievements and demonstration of outcomes, while also providing a guide to assist teachers select appropriate content, methods, resources and organisational procedures. As teachers know where students' learning is heading, they may be more focused in their methods of helping their students to maximise their learning potential through informed, well-thought-through teaching practices (Hargreaves & Moore 1999).

OBE seeks to transform the whole ecology of schooling to enhance the learning of students. As Spady (1994) and (Hill & Crevola 1999, p. 121) make clear, OBE is not about incremental improvements to classrooms, schools and school systems, but is about improving education by:

1. clearly focusing and wholeheartedly committing to ensuring that all students achieve defined and challenging standards of performance;
2. underpinning the implementation of OBE with coherent and deep beliefs and understandings;
3. rigorously and thoroughly examining, redesigning and managing every aspect of schools and school systems so high standards are achieved.

While there are clearly thought to be many positive implications related to the implementation of effective OBE, there are still many who believe that the negative implications of OBE are too great to warrant its implementation.

Criticisms of OBE

Critics of OBE believe there has been a shift in education policy towards cultural conservatism and vocationalism and away from educational progressivism. This is especially true of outcomes reporting and the development of standards and benchmarks for assessment. In addition, critics argue that school organisation and curriculum have been subject to a degree of government and political intervention and control not witnessed since the 1950s. Teachers now have to ensure they meet nationally based competency standards while ensuring students achieve nationally developed, state/territory-implemented learning outcomes.

Many teachers believe that the current approach towards OBE is a disguised version of Bloom's 'mastery learning' and represents a move to restore a behaviourist version of education (Alford 1998; Hargreaves & Moore 1999).

The locus of curriculum planning and decision-making has been viewed as shifting away from schools and individual teachers and towards more centralised educational, bureaucratic political institutions. Schools and teachers who previously had a significant influence over the curriculum may feel unenthusiastic about implementing OBE if they believe they have been disempowered by government and industry through a curriculum that is politically determined and accountable to government (Hargreaves & Moore 1999; Lokan 1997).

State/territory-based curriculum frameworks, which are based on a nationally agreed framework, were introduced by the mid-1990s and their use is mandatory in all public schools (with private schools accountable to strict government requirements relating to curriculum). The sequential series of learning outcomes are monitored yearly by the government through criterion-referenced LAP tests in Victorian primary schools and Basic Skills testing in NSW primary schools. Consequently, teachers' power to create, adapt or select their own curriculum can be seen as limited as teacher and school choices are now confined to quantifying time and effort spent on the achievement of each outcome within the eight KLAs (Alford 1998).

An increasingly crowded, state/territory-imposed curriculum is observed to leave little time or space for local initiatives (Alford 1998), while school-based curriculum development is further constrained by the imposition of highly competitive assessment in the final years of secondary schooling. There is a concern that when expectations and outcomes are not developed by teachers to suit the needs of specific groups of students, then their adoption is less than ideal (Darling-Hammond 1994, cited in Griffin 1997). Many critics believe that OBE fails to address family circumstances, socioeconomic status, learning disabilities and other inequalities that do not allow for equality of educational inputs (such as curricula, resources) and therefore cannot result in equality of educational outcomes (Hargreaves & Moore 1999).

OBE presents a further dilemma for teachers as it does not address how to deal with less able students who are not able to achieve the stated learning outcomes. Teachers interviewed by Hargreaves and Moore (1999) feared that the true meaning of achieving modified aims may be misinterpreted and lead to the creation of false expectations in the minds of students, parents and future employers. Teachers felt under pressure as OBE policy asserts that all students should achieve certain outcomes at certain educational levels/stages, even though they work with students who bring a great variety of academic abilities, learning styles and rates of intellectual and emotional development to the classroom.

In addition, the complexity and number of outcome statements within the profiles of each KLA present a daunting task to teachers in relation to: planning and implementing effective learning activities; selection of appropriate resources; and assessment of achievement. Consequently, there has been some reluctance from some teachers who have less than enthusiastically embraced OBE (Warhurst 1997).

Vaguely stated and broad outcomes are also seen to place great responsibility on teachers as they attempt to translate these outcomes into actual curriculum content and classroom activities. Canadian and Australian teachers reported they would prefer to be provided with more user-friendly, specific outcomes and recommended curriculum resources so they had a clearer understanding of what was expected of them and their students, and to enable them to more effectively assist their students to achieve outcomes (Hargreaves & Moore 1999).

Conclusion

In recent years, Australia has seen an increasing focus being placed on outcome-based education. This has involved the development of performance indicators for education systems, the setting of general national goals for education, the introduction of descriptive statements for assessment and reporting frameworks for key learning areas, and the development of large scale assessment programs for monitoring education standards over time.

Outcome-based education represents a fundamental shift in education policy and practice. Outcomes are explicit, and public, representations of what society intends students to learn while they are at school and to which teachers are accountable (McNeir 1993). The extent of this shift to an outcome focus in Australia is clear from the amount and direction of recent national curriculum reform. Throughout the 1990s, in all states and territories of Australia, the notion of outcomes has become enshrined in curriculum and syllabus documents and statements. Across each of the key learning areas of the curriculum they are explicitly linked to indicators of student performance.

Through OBE influenced curriculum reform, policy-makers believe the mission of schools has been refocussed and their operations redesigned so that the student achievement of learning outcomes is the paramount consideration. Whether outcome-based education actually achieves these ends and presents a substantial reform in educational practice in the twenty-first century is the question that now needs to be addressed. Practitioners, educational researchers and the community are all stakeholders in addressing how the intention of outcome-based education is expressed in action. The central curriculum problem, that is, the gap between our intentions and resultant action, remains.

INQUIRY STRATEGIES

1. What do you understand by the terms: curriculum, syllabus, outcomes and indicators? How would you describe the relationship between these terms and what order of importance would you ascribe to them?

2. The MCEETYA discussion paper, *Australia's Common and Agreed Goals for Schooling in the Twenty First Century*, provides a concise statement of the hopes that governments have for the education of young people through schooling. In groups, break up these goals into those that are systemic and those that you consider are very school-based. Discuss how schools and systems are attempting to operationalise these goals. To what extent do you think the schools that you have experienced have achieved these goals?

3. Collect a range of articles on education from the national, state and local press. See if you can identify the different discourses about education at work in these articles. Use as a framework for your thinking the orientations to curriculum of vocational/neo-classical, liberal/progressive, and social-critical that Kemmis, Cole and Suggett (1983) identified.

4. With a focus on exit outcomes and assessment, schools and their students have become the victims of media 'panics', such as that endured by the students and teachers at Mt Druitt High School in 1998 following the release of the NSW HSC results. This school was used by the Sydney metropolitan daily newspaper, *The Telegraph*, to signify how the education system was 'failing' the students at Mt Druitt High School as they had not scored as well as their metropolitan peers. It was the students themselves, however, who the community saw as failures. Little recognition was given to the fact that many of these students had shown great resilience to even complete school due to a variety of social, socioeconomic, ethnic and racial disadvantages.

Find out what you can about this story and create a mock trial or debate the issue about who had 'failed', the system or the students. At the time of writing, the students involved had taken *The Telegraph* to court.

References

Alford, K. (1998). Redefining education to serve the economy: competencies for teachers and students. *Unicorn*, 24 (3), pp. 15–26.

Baron, M.A. & Boschee, F. (1996). Dispelling the myths surrounding OBE. *Phi Delta Kappan*, 77, pp. 574–576.

Battistini, J. (1995). From theory to practice: Classroom application of outcome-based education. *ERIC Digest*. Accession No: ED 377512 95. Accessed 28 March 2000 via infoseek. Available online: http://www.ed.gov/databases/ERIC_Digests/ed377512

Eastin, D. (1999). Getting to the heart of the matter: Education in the 21st Century. In D.D. Marsh (ed), *1999 ASCD Yearbook: Preparing Our Schools for the 21st Century*. Association for Supervision and Curriculum Development: Alexandria.

Griffin, P. (1997). OBE — Challenges and opportunities. In P. Griffin & P. Smith (eds), *Outcome-Based Education: Issues and Strategies for Schools*. Deakin: Australian Curriculum Studies Association.

Griffin, P. & Smith, P. (1997). Hindering and facilitating factors in OBE. In P. Griffin and P. Smith (eds), *Outcome-Based Education: Issues and Strategies for Schools*. Deakin: Australian Curriculum Studies Association.

Grundy, S. (1998). The curriculum and teaching. In E. Hatton (ed), *Understanding Teaching: Curriculum and the social context of schooling* (2nd edition). Sydney: Harcourt Brace.

Hargreaves, A. & Moore, S. (1999). Getting into outcomes: The emotions of interpretation and implementation. *Curriculum Perspectives*, 19 (3), pp. 1–10.

Hill, P.W. & Crevola, C.A. (1999). The Role of Standards in Educational Reform for the 21st Century. In D.D. Marsh (ed), *1999 ASCD Yearbook: Preparing Our Schools for the 21st Century*. Alexandria: Association for Supervision and Curriculum Development.

Kemmis, S., Cole, P. & Suggett, D. (1983). *Orientations to Curriculum and Transition: Towards the socially-critical school*. Melbourne: Victorian Institute of Secondary Education.

Lokan, J. (1997). 'Key' competencies for all students? Australian teachers' views and practices. *SET Research Information for Teachers*, 1 (4), pp. 1–4.

Lokan, J., Withers, G., Mellor, S., Batten, M., McQueen, J. & Carthy, I. (1995). *Literacy and The Competencies: Potential impact of competency-based approaches on literacy curricula and assessment in schools*. Melbourne: Australian Council for Educational Research.

McNeir, G. (1993). Outcome-based education. *ERIC Digest 85*, Nov 1993. Accessed 28 March 2000 via infoseek. Available online: http://eric.uoregon.edu/publications/digests/digest085

Ministerial Council for Employment, Education, Training and Youth Affairs (MCEETYA) (1998). *Australia's Common and Agreed Goals for Schooling in the Twenty First Century*. Discussion paper.

Perry, C. (1996). Learning styles and learning outcomes. *SET Research Information for Teachers,* 1 (10), pp. 1–3.

Spady, W.G. (1993). *Outcome-Based Education.* Canberra: Australian Curriculum Studies Association.

Spady, W.G. (1994). Choosing outcomes of significance. *Educational Leadership*, 51, pp. 18–22.

Spady, W.G. & Marshall, K.J. (1991) Beyond traditional outcome-based education, *Educational Leadership*, 49, pp. 67–72.

Warhurst, J. (1997). Introduction. In P. Griffin and P. Smith (eds), *Outcome-Based Education: Issues and Strategies for Schools.* Deakin: Australian Curriculum Studies Association.

Zlatos, B. (1993). Outcomes-based outrage. *The Executive Educator*, September, pp. 12–16.

12

CHAPTER

New Ways of Thinking About Assessment and Reporting

We begin this chapter with what amounts to a parable; a story which brings into sharp focus the issues surrounding the assessment and reporting of student learning. Like all good parables the narrative is not only illustrative, but draws our attention to some of the moral and ethical dimensions associated with the practices which are outlined.

Finnian's story — a good parable

Finnian is fourteen years old, she lives in Canberra and receives her schooling at home. This does not mean that Finnian is socially isolated; quite to the contrary she is active in a number of service organisations and music groups. She has lived in England and been a part of a large home-schooling network there. Finnian is used to being a self-directed learner and pursuing major projects through to their conclusion. She engages in self-assessment as she discusses her learning with her parents and is well able to identify her strengths and weaknesses. Her academic achievements are above the norms for her chronological age.

In the second half of 1999 Finnian went on a half-year exchange to the province of Baden-Württemberg in Germany. There she went to school for the first time. During her stay she sent her parents this email.

> *Hi, I want to tell you about something really weird that has happened here. We have been having tests and I have done well in all my subjects except English! I don't want to sound awful, or defensive or anything, but I know the teacher doesn't like me very much. She has a very thick accent and only goes by the book. She certainly doesn't like me to speak up in class and says that my Australian accent is too hard for everyone to understand, which is a bit odd, because most of my friends in Canberra think I have an English accent. Anyway, she had this test for us. The first part was translating from German into English. I translated it as 'she's allowed to go to the disco tomorrow' and had it marked wrong; apparently the right answer was 'she may go to the disco tomorrow'. Then we had to fill the gap in some sentences, but it worked out that we should only use words that were*

already covered in the book, so some of my more creative efforts were marked wrong as well, although they were grammatically quite correct. I think she had a copy of the correct responses and that was it! My friends sailed through. Also, some of the constructions that she teaches are really odd and I can't imagine anyone talking that way. It seems a bit ridiculous to me that I have got my worst marks in English when I know I'm pretty good at it.

Why is Finnian's story a good parable in thinking about assessment and reporting? In order to address this question we first need to ask ourselves what are the purposes of both of these activities. Romburg (1993) writes that the 'goal of assessment should be to help us educate students more effectively' (p. 104). Finnian certainly learned from this experience, but we doubt her learning was to do with improving her capabilities in written and spoken English. Instead she learned that it is probably important to know what is in her teacher's mind and reproduce for her what it is that she wants. Because of her educational experiences Finnian was not 'test prepared', but she is pretty robust, she knows her abilities and just found the whole thing 'a bit ridiculous'. As we shall see later in this chapter, poor assessment practices can have highly detrimental effects for many students as they come to believe themselves to be inadequate and incapable learners.

As to the reporting — the goal of which is to keep parents informed of their children's achievements, strengths and difficulties — Finnian's parents received a report card indicating marks and the place in class. After receiving Finnian's email they were quite prepared for her results and more amused than disturbed by her English mark. But then, they know Finnian's academic achievements very well, since they have been her principal educators. However, few parents have this privilege. They send their children to school in good faith that their teachers will be knowledgeable and professional about assessing and reporting upon their learning.

The focus of this chapter is upon new ways of thinking about assessment and reporting. A definition of authentic assessment and its implications for changing assessment and reporting practices, in particular in reference to formative assessment, will be discussed. In turn, changes in pedagogical practices, led by authentic assessment, will be proposed. As well, in the chapter, high-stakes assessment practices in the various states and territories will be addressed in relation to their consequences for teaching and learning in the senior years. Innovations in assessment and reporting will be presented as a series of case studies.

Authentic assessment

Much of the early work on authentic assessment grew from dissatisfaction with prevailing regimes of testing that dominated education in the United States. Even so, the evolving principles of authentic assessment are of great relevance to us here in Australia. Paris and Ayres (1994, pp. 7–8) drawing upon the work of Valencia, Hiebert and Afflerbach (1994) suggested authentic assessment has four features, which we have synthesised thus:

1. It is consistent with classroom practices. Students are asked questions about meaningful information and asked to solve problems that are relevant to their educational experiences.

2. Authentic assessment collects diverse evidence of students' learning from multiple sources rather than relying exclusively upon single tests or single modes.

3. Authentic assessment is designed to promote improved student learning, based upon the premise that all students are capable of ongoing improvement in their learning.

4. Authentic assessment is contextualised and takes account of local culture and experience.

To these four features we would add:

5. Authentic assessment recognises student agency in the process; it assumes that students are able and capable in understanding and evaluating their own learning.

6. Authentic assessment values error-making and misunderstanding as cues about learning, rather than as a means of labelling learners.

7. Authentic assessment is ethical assessment. It is designed to support and assist learning in ways that are not harmful to the learner.

Teachers who utilise authentic assessment are necessarily engaged in a change process. They are helping students to become more effective learners, seeking to change their learning; and they are helping themselves to become more effective teachers, seeking to change their teaching practices. Authentic assessment is learner-focused and requires a learner-focused classroom.

The following section will examine, in particular, the nature of formative assessment and the contribution it makes to student learning. Later, we shall also discuss summative assessment and the ways in which it, too, can take on authentic dimensions.

Formative assessment and its relation to learning

Formative assessment is the regular, relevant and specific feedback students receive as they engage in their learning. It enables them to apprehend what they know, understand and believe at a particular moment what directions their learning needs to take. Formative assessment takes both verbal and written forms. Teachers regularly occupy themselves in evaluating student responses in classroom interaction and providing their students with feedback to written tasks, both large and small. As well, students self-assess when they reflect upon their learning, what has been achieved and what is desired. The student is not a passive receiver of assessment, he or she is an active agent. For formative assessment to be at all useful to the learner it must be predicated upon an understanding that there is a gap between what he or she currently knows and can do and what he or she can potentially know or do. Learning is seen as incremental and socially constructed.

Convergent and divergent formative assessment

In their consideration of formative classroom assessment Torrance and Pryor (1998) identify two conceptually distinctive approaches to classroom assessment that they describe as 'convergent' and 'divergent' (p. 152). The distinction is between *whether* a student knows, understands or can do a predetermined thing and *what* it is that the student knows, understands or can do. In the former case the assessment assumes teacher-centred instructional practices, where the teacher plans and delivers the curriculum in a relatively lock-step fashion. The assessment processes are likely to be of a closed nature, governed by checklists and continuous testing. It is 'assessment *of* the child *by* the teacher' (p. 154). Divergent assessment is predicated upon a constructivist model of teaching and learning that gives the student far greater agency and emphasises understanding and high levels of learner engagement. It is appropriate to open-ended, learner-centred pedagogy. The focus is as much upon learning from mistakes and error, as it is in accumulating marks. It requires an involvement of the students in self-assessment and critique.

While there is not a suggestion that you, as teachers, would exclusively use one form rather than another, the distinction is helpful in directing you to giving real consideration to the purposes to which the assessment is to be put. As we have already indicated, formative authentic assessment is designed to support learning. In some skill development it is useful to break learning up into small, sequenced, discrete parts that can then be employed to undertake more broadly based tasks and, here, convergent assessment practices could be quite defensible. The caveat is that the processes do not result in the consistent labelling of some students as poor achievers, as this reduces both their self-esteem and motivation (Broadfoot et al. 1992, p. 6):

> Assessment which leads to labelling . . . can in certain circumstances have harmful effects on children's learning. There is much research that shows that a competitive climate such as labelling produces does not increase learning outcomes for all. Rather the already successful thrive and the less successful (always the majority) underachieve more and more as they are repeatedly discouraged by the way their efforts are judged.

Furthermore, it is important to be guarded about the implicit messages sent to students about what is worthwhile knowledge. Convergent assessment clearly assumes that there is one correct answer. If we return to the case of Finnian, her teacher had only one possible translation in mind; yet the professional translator would have it that there are many subtle and nuanced translations for any text. Today, we well understand that there is a plurality of meanings and interpretations. Students who inhabit school classrooms where convergent assessment is the dominant mode can be led to believe that the world is an uncomplicated and simplistic place. Many of our talkback radio hosts and even our politicians would wish it were so.

Take as an example the discussions conducted in recent years regarding civics education (see the report, *Whereas the People*, Civics Expert Group 1994). There is a belief that if only our school students could reel off a series of dates regarding the development of the Australian Constitution, define the distinctions between the House of Representatives and the Senate, and name the relative responsibilities of the Commonwealth and the states/territories, they would become more responsible and responsive citizens. However, when Phillips and Moroz (1999) investigated the perceptions of Western Australian students of political awareness and the characteristics of a 'good citizen' they found that students believed that attitudes and behaviours were well ahead of levels of knowledge as the most important characteristics of a good citizen. An authentic assessment procedure would use multiple strategies to tap into those attitudes and behaviours as well as examine the ways in which knowledge about our institutions might be applied.

Of course it is much more difficult to develop assessment procedures that operate divergently. Importantly, such procedures require a high level of professional judgment on the part of the teacher. How does one become a good judge of learning? Dictionary definitions of judgment speak of forming opinions, appraising and weighing up merit. In order to do these things we need first to have an understanding of what it is that we are examining. A judge of cake making has a set of criteria regarding taste, texture, appearance; a judge of dogs might examine obedience, loyalty and characteristics of the breed. A wine judge may be concerned with viscosity, colour, flavour as it strikes the front and back of the palate, and so on. To be a good judge effectively means to be a connoisseur of the thing that is being judged. Elliot Eisner (1977, 1993) has written extensively on the notion of educational connoisseurship. He argues that we have a great deal of professional knowledge about learning and that such knowledge should inform our opinions about the quality of learning and the ways in which it might be improved.

Judges, in whatever capacity, rarely work alone. They spend much of their time with their professional peers discussing and refining the ways in which they arrive at their opinions. So too, it should be the case in education. We need to work with others to improve our professional judgment. A close examination of some students' work has implications for all students' work. As well, assessing student learning becomes a means of assessing our own learning about teaching and providing for teaching and learning. In order to become good judges, who can articulate findings about learning, teachers need to be collegial. Some of the most stimulating professional conversations we have witnessed have been about judging student work in relation to learning outcomes. It is this capacity that is most denied by the exclusive employment of convergent assessment procedures.

Divergent formative assessment builds upon the development, rather than the settlement, of learning outcomes. It does not view learning as static, but rather that the learner's knowledge, understanding and competence is evolving. Various criteria may be used to support teacher professional judgment and these will take the form of descriptors of levels of achievement. Thus, students are not compared so much one with the other, but compared with a set of standards of achievement. Newmann and Archbald (1992) suggest that many schools fail to set and make transparent specific performance criteria. Effectively students are shut out from the secrets of schooling, although for them the stakes are high.

Standards of attainment and their relation to formative assessment

Defining standards is a tricky matter. Where does one set the bar — low or high? Are we talking of minimum standards or ultimate goals, personal best standards, or standards for all? Standards about what? Marzano, Pickering and McTighe (1993) have chosen to look at standards of attainment, in the first instance in relation to what they name the 'Five Dimensions of Learning', these being (pp. 1–3):

1. positive attitudes and perceptions about learning;
2. acquiring and integrating knowledge;
3. extending and refining knowledge;

4. using knowledge meaningfully;

5. productive habits of mind.

To take the last of these as an example Marzano et al. suggest that it is possible to map student development in (p. 3):

- being clear and seeking clarity;
- being open-minded;
- restraining impulsivity;
- being aware of your own thinking;
- evaluating the effectiveness of your actions;
- pushing the limits of your knowledge and abilities; and
- engaging intensely in tasks even when answers or solutions are not immediately apparent.

In their discussion of standards Marzano et al. also make connections to knowledge in the relevant subject areas. Knowledge in their view is divided into declarative knowledge and procedural knowledge. Declarative knowledge builds from specifics, which we have asserted can be assessed using convergent procedures, to generalisations, then through to concepts. So it might be said that, 'Australian electors defeated a referendum directed to the country becoming a republic in November, 1999' is a fact. The statement, 'Australians have had a tendency over the years to defeat referenda' is a generalisation. The phrase 'constitutional monarchy' is a concept. Each one requires a higher level of professional judgment in deciding that the student has the required knowledge.

Procedural knowledge can be thought about in terms of strategies or skills. Students proceed from fundamental skills to applications using efficient strategies. Too often assessment processes focus upon skills out of context, rather than on applications *in situ*. Mathematics education is a good example. As well as being capable of undertaking fundamental algorithms students need to be able to reason, design models, create and solve problems. They need to be able to respond to the *'What if . . .'* questions (Romberg 1992, p. 33).

Whether simple or complex, standards need to be explicit. They are not an end in themselves, but provide benchmarks for ongoing learning.

Formative assessment, learning, and pedagogy

We cannot emphasise enough that learning is seen as the goal of formative assessment, rather than performance to some kind of normative expectations. Newman and Schwager (1995) looked at two forms of feedback guidance. One group of students were told that the goals of the assessment were based in learning — 'this will help you to learn new things'. The second group were told the goal was their performance in comparison to others — 'how you do will help us get to know how smart you are and what kind of grade you will get'. They found that students in the latter category were more likely to seek feedback about how they looked, rather than about the task in hand.

Formative assessment requires changes in classroom practices. Black and William (1998) in their critical review of the research literature on classroom formative assessment suggest that the overall picture is one of weak practices. They identified the key weaknesses as (pp. 17–18):

■ Classroom evaluation practices generally encourage superficial and rote learning, concentrating on recall of isolated details, usually items of knowledge which pupils soon forget.

■ Teachers do not generally review the assessment questions that they use (in tests, homework and the like) and do not discuss them critically with peers, so there is little reflection on what is being assessed.

■ The grading function is over-emphasised and the learning function under-emphasised.

■ There is a tendency to use a normative rather than a criterion approach, which emphasises competition between pupils rather than personal improvement of each. The evidence is that with such practices, the effect of feedback is to teach the weaker pupils that they lack ability, so that they are de-motivated and lose confidence in their capacity to learn.

As well, it is essential that the nature of classroom interaction itself is examined in relation to formative assessment. Teacher question/student response/teacher evaluation is an enduring feature of classroom interaction. Student knowledge is built upon verbal feedback in the daily events of the classroom. Verbal feedback is not merely praising or chastising a student. Indeed, some research suggests that uncontingent or ego-involving praise may be quite counterproductive. Students value being told that their response is well received because of its particular features in relation to what is being studied or discussed. 'That's a great answer Ria' does little to either support Ria's learning or that of her peers; whereas 'Ria, that's great, because you have given us another perspective on Leonardo (da Vinci) by suggesting that he is a kind of architect building images in a particular way, thanks', tells the student specifics. Equally, and on the other side of the coin, 'put downs' contribute little to learning. 'Stupid answer, John' may be an exercise of power in the classroom; but is little else. All the same, if John is way off the mark, it is helpful to know why, 'No John, the storm can't be moving in a northerly direction if the low pressure system is here; can anyone suggest a direction based on the data?'

These examples are examples of classroom interaction that is relatively teacher-centred. We would argue that a more radical approach would be to find ways of interacting with individual learners in relation to their learning by having conversations with them about such things as the arguments or explanations they are constructing in response to a real problem they are solving. Newmann (1992) argues that assessment in social studies should focus on discourse, which he defines as the language produced by the student, rather than the language of others reproduced by the student. To work in this way in classrooms necessarily means that authentic assessment is embedded in classroom work. Other students need to be meaningfully occupied, but not necessarily involved in the given conversation. Differentiated learning tasks, small group work and peer coaching strategies, all of which we have discussed elsewhere in this book, can free teachers from 'front of stage' and provide spaces for them where they can interact meaningfully with individual students over time.

Furthermore, a learning conversation that enables the student to clarify and defend a position requires the teacher to be an interpretive listener and able to identify clues regarding the student's understanding. Reynolds, Martin and Groulz (1995) suggested that teachers can use a range of clues such as:

■ changes in the students' demeanour;

■ the student extending a concept in their own words;

- students modifying a pattern;
- students applying a pattern;
- students using shortcuts;
- students explaining; and
- students being persistent.

All of these clues require teachers who are alert and able to notice what is happening in the classroom.

Secondary schooling in most states and territories embraces students aged 12 through to 18. These are six productive years for learning; but for many students, high stakes assessment, which takes place at the end of their schooling, shapes and determines all that precedes it. It will take a considerable culture shift among students, their teachers and their parents to value formative assessment as highly as that which currently occurs as students exit secondary schooling.

High-stakes summative assessment

Unlike formative assessment, which is concerned with feedback to inform student learning and teaching practices, high-stakes assessment is of a different order. We use the phrase to refer to the summative assessment that comes as the end of a stage of learning and is used as the major criterion for entry into further education, hence the wording — for a number of students there is a great deal at stake. Indeed, this is also true for teachers. Schools are increasingly judged on their performance in public examinations and the success of their students in gaining entry into courses requiring high marks. There is not a state or territory in Australia where the reporting of final public examinations is not put in terms of particularly high or low achievements on the part of particular schools or systems (Meadmore 1995). Of course, it is also true to say that for the majority of school leavers, public examinations are not used for the purposes of gaining tertiary places, but in order to be selected for employment in an increasingly difficult and competitive market — so for them the stakes are also high.

The purpose of summative assessment is to provide normative, or comparative, information about what has been learned in specific curriculum areas. It is perceived as vital that the information is trustworthy and based upon standards that are known and understood by all of the stakeholders: students, parents, teachers, administrators, tertiary admissions bodies, and employers. Given the impact upon students' life chances, it is essential that there is public acceptability of the processes used in undertaking summative assessment. However, it is important to understand that the techniques of summative assessment, dependent as they are upon forms of measurement of student learning that will allow comparisons to be made, are themselves subject to ongoing critique and debate.

Patricia Broadfoot, whose work on assessment spans two decades, makes the following observation (1996, p. 13):

> It is now widely accepted that any kind of educational measurement can be at best only a rough estimate of particular kinds of ability; that educational assessment is as much an art as it is a science; an instrument of power as much as a source of social liberation. Despite the statistical finesse which often characterizes the processing of results and the considerable quality of research which has been directed towards improving the accuracy of

assessment, the limitations of different techniques — whether concerned with student, institutional or systemic assessment — have been extensively documented in a large number of research studies.

Each Australian state or territory has evolved its own summative assessment procedures. A browse over the web sites of the various Boards of Studies indicates that senior secondary assessment is a matter for discussion and debate across the country. Perhaps the most radical of these procedures is that which has evolved in Queensland. External examinations were abolished for secondary schools in 1971. Subsequently problems were encountered in equating the various school-based assessments such that systematic comparisons could be made regarding the achievement of various criteria. Butler (1995) examined the development of moderating strategies in senior science subjects whereby teachers could make explicit to each other their professional judgments of student achievement. The argument is made that a high level of skill is expected of the teachers and it can be attained with sufficient professional support.

The Queensland Board of Senior Secondary School Studies, (QBSSSS) discusses moderation in this way (QBSSSS 2000):

> Moderation involves contextualised teacher judgments and a system of verification of school decision-making. The aim of moderation is to ensure comparability. Students who take the same subject in different schools and who attain the same standard through assessment programs based on a common syllabus will be awarded the same level of achievement on their senior certificates.
>
> This is not to suggest that two schools who receive the same level of achievement have had the same collection of experiences or have achieved equally in any one aspect of the course, but rather it means they have on balance reached the same standard.

Moderating teachers' professional judgment of student work is also occurring in New South Wales as the New Higher School Certificate, with its standards-referenced approach, takes hold. The state is seeing the most radical shake-up of its school exit credential since the Wyndham reforms of the 1960s.

While nearly every secondary school in Australia uses the exit credentials that have been designed by that state or territory it is also the case that some independent schools have chosen to enrol their senior students in the International Baccalaureate (IB). This could be said to be a reflection of the increasing trend to globalisation referred to in the opening chapters to this book. The IB is recognised by most prestigious universities as a sufficient credential to gain entry to their courses. Thus a student who chooses the IB route can gain entry, not only to local Australian universities but those in the wider global environment. Bagnall (1995, p. 224) quotes students undertaking the IB as seeing themselves being able to study 'anywhere in the English speaking world'.

Furthermore, as Bagnall indicates the IB is a relatively rare credential and there rests its value. More and more we are seeing that education is a marketable commodity (p. 234):

> The recognition of this [that the IB is more than just a credential attached to a curriculum] by students in Australia and Canada highlights the importance of the IB as a useful 'card' in the game of global power.

The connection between student attainments in high-stakes assessment and teacher performance in assisting them in their achievements is increasingly being made within a market environment of choice and accountability as we shall see in the following section.

Assessment for teacher accountability — value adding

We have intimated throughout this chapter that the principal purpose of assessment is to inform decision-making regarding student learning: what the student is learning; how the student is learning, what the student needs to do next, and so on. We have also suggested that information about student learning should inform teacher professional learning: 'How well am I communicating?', 'How effective have I been in providing for differentiated learning?' and 'How appropriate have the tasks I have set been in determining student outcomes?', are but a few of the questions teachers can ask themselves as a result of examining student performance in assessment tasks.

Although, at this point in time, there are no league tables of results made public in the Australian context, and which we discuss later in this chapter, it is the case that teachers and schools are judged by the results they obtain. Often the comparisons are crude and take little account of the value the school has added. A school with a high proportion of students operating in a second language, who may additionally suffer socioeconomic disadvantage, and in a neighbourhood with poor ancillary facilities such as libraries and transport infrastructure, may have performed much better in value adding than the school whose students are significantly privileged.

The phrase 'value adding' is a key one in the contemporary economist's lexicon. Fundamentally the phrase applies where values, in terms of inputs and outputs, are clearly defined by markets. Crudely, the value added is the output, less the value of material input. It is an intellectual artefact useful for examining economic performance. Economists add up value added in the economy to form a summary measure of total economic activity: gross domestic product. There are three fundamental principles underlying economists' interest in value added:

1. value added is about *improvement* in the value of goods and services (to assess improvement you must have an idea of the initial attributes of a good or service, which is why economists subtract the value of material inputs from output to measure value added);

2. there is a set of *prices*, typically market-based, which signal the value of the process of transformation of such material inputs; and

3. there exists some form of *relationship* between value added and a whole host of factors, such as capital (physical and human), research and development, industrial relations, macroeconomic stability and so on.

The concept of value added and its underpinnings clearly have analogies, albeit differently expressed, for education. In school education, value adding consists of a set of improvements in student learning or in the society, arising from schooling processes. Students enter school with certain attributes, participate in the process of education and exit with a different, purportedly higher value, set of attributes.

There are some major complexities and insights which arise from the application of the economic concept of value adding to education, relating to the value of schooling, the role of the student as an 'input' (students are not merely raw materials in the same way that minerals, crops and animal products are) and the role of other factors, such as school plant, teachers' expectations and community involvement.

Information on the market value of education is missing. Even the notion of fees set by non-government schools are at best only a weak indicator of economic value, given that private schools are not-for-profit entities, receive substantial state and federal subsidies and exist in a system where people have access to public schooling at relatively low costs. So what other aspects of schooling might be treated as indicators of value? Is it the acquisition of literacy, the child minding service, the access to prestige and social networks? For whom is the service valuable? The parents? The teachers? The students? The wider community? The bureaucrats? The minister? Over what period of time? Five, ten, twenty years from now?

The links between valuable outcomes and the inputs are arguably more complex than most activities in the economy. However, if there is a predictable, stable, functional relationship between inputs and outputs, then the residual is a measure of school performance (Hill & Rowe 1996). So that for School X, with a certain proportion of students in poverty, students from language backgrounds other than English and Aboriginal students, and a profile of incoming student capabilities, we should be able to predict learning outcomes, on the basis of normalised data. If the school performs beyond this prediction it can be said to be better at adding value than a similar counterpart whose learning outcomes are less.

But, as we indicated above, and earlier, the students themselves are not the only input variables to be considered. Schools would need to take account of external data, variables that impact upon learning outside the school. These might be such things as access in the home to computers, the number and variety of print materials, travel experience, television viewing patterns, the range of languages spoken. McPherson (1994) for example, cites household size and adult composition, the educational level of parents and parents' occupations. The list could go on and on. The school itself should be considered, its location, the quality of buildings, grounds and facilities, the staff profile in terms of experience and qualifications, ancillary services, information services. Then the question arises as to how the outputs are to be measured so that comparisons can be made.

In England, results in the General Certificate of School Education (GCSE) have been used as output measures and league tables constructed with some unfortunate effects. League tables followed the *Parent's Charter* and *Education Schools Act 1992* in the United Kingdom and they were seen as a means of facilitating parental choice (Feintuck 1994). Irrespective of the value adding argument crude league tables of the relative performance of schools were published by government decree. Bagnall (1995, p. 221) quotes the Melbourne *Age* from 10 January 1995 (p. 11):

> It is claimed that publication of the tables has prompted schools at the bottom of the ladder to lift their game. In a glowing story of the 'school the league tables could not kill', the *Independent* newspaper chronicled the achievements of the Sandringham School in St Albans which two years ago 'was wallowing near the bottom of the local tables: now it holds its own among the high-performing secondary schools of this affluent town north of London'.
>
> But the feel good story of the dynamic new headmaster, the cohesive staff and the 'cheerful, purposeful and orderly atmosphere of the school' loses something of its warmth when it is revealed that the school's turnaround in performance was the result of 'an exceptionally successful operation to market itself to the middle class and high ability range'.

So why characterise the effects as 'unfortunate' rather than 'misleading'? Gewirtz, Ball and Bowe (1995) argue that school funding is based upon enrolment; thus the schools which attract large student numbers will be better endowed than those schools who attract less. At the same time students designated as more 'able' are less costly to educate than those who have learning difficulties. Thus the school which performs well on the league tables is more likely to attract larger numbers of able students, which, in turn, will cost them less to educate; while the schools which educate the remaining less talented students, have fewer and fewer resources to undertake that challenging enterprise.

As Ball noted elsewhere (1994, p. 41), the effect is to diminish what we have referred to as authentic assessment, in favour of 'unproblematised' summative examinations:

> *Complex* assessment is seen as designed to obscure. *Simple* tests are revealing. Complexity is 'soft', misleading, producer-based. Simplicity is 'hard', clear, unequivocal and common-sensical. For the restorationists (those returning to earlier times) testing is a way of differ-entiating between students and identifying 'poor' schools; for the neo-liberal wing of the New Right test results also provide the information system which they believe will drive the market in education. In part also, the restorationists' attack upon coursework and teacher assessment rests on a fundamental distrust of the teacher.

Without a doubt, teacher accountability is an important issue, both professionally and in terms of the nation's investment in schooling. But crude indicators do little to uncover the complex and demanding equity and productivity issues facing today's policy-makers. It may be the accruing of professional wisdom, through well-defended and well-judged innovative practices that will, in the end, point us to overall improvement — the carrot rather than the stick. An important measure of teacher accountability is the extent to which they provide to parents and the community valid forms of reporting.

Reporting student learning

Typically, when we think about reporting student learning we are concerned with the kinds of report cards schools send home half way through the year and at the conclusion of the year. Arrangements are made for parents to interview teachers regarding achievements and the ways in which particular learning difficulties might be being addressed. In some instances students may also be welcomed at the meetings. It is not unusual to find parents scurrying from one appointment to another, unsure of rooms and with only a very short time available for discussion. In other cases the meetings are scheduled in large halls with teachers stationed at their desks around the perimeter. Either way, it is generally a fairly unsatisfactory way of communicating the information that parents believe they need and deserve.

Time is always a huge pressure; both on the parents and the teachers. Rarely is there time for parents to present to the teachers their experiences of their children's learning at home. The process tends to be uni-directional.

Partly the problems arise from the ways in which teachers' work is normally organised in our secondary schools. Many teachers are encountering up to 150 students in one week. It is virtually impossible for them to come to know their learning in the same intimate way that parents understand their offspring. As well, there is the additional challenge produced as young secondary students move to autonomy and independence, as we discussed in Chapter 4. Many students prefer that their parents are not visible in the school setting. They want to keep school and home as separate territories. A great deal depends upon how well the student is achieving and the relationship that has built up over time between the school and the home.

Ashfield Boys' High School in Sydney (Currie & Groundwater-Smith 1989) has chosen, during its middle school years (7 and 8) to have small teams of teachers work across the curriculum with specific groups. In this way they come to know the students well. Not only through their work with them in the classroom; but through team meetings where student progress is discussed. A strategy adopted by the teams is to contact parents frequently through brief notes; often a positive observation about the way in which a particular boy has tackled a challenging task, or worked cooperatively with his peers. Parents have reported on the value of the notes in building up a picture of their sons' learning.

The developments at Ashfield Boys' High School have not come about by chance. The school has been participating in Team Small Groups (TSG) for a number of years, along with many other schools across Australia and under the auspices of the National Schools Network (White & Moore 1999). Miolin (1999) became involved in TSG as a result of his work as an Education Department Consultant in the Manjimup District of Western Australia. Along with other Australian educators he visited schools in the Cologne Holweide district in Germany and became familiar with the TSG reform. One of the most significant outcomes of the processes adopted is that teachers do become very familiar with their students' learning and can report upon that learning with confidence and authenticity.

Too often, teachers underestimate parents' concerns regarding their children's learning. After focus group discussion with parents (Groundwater-Smith & Hunter 2000), observations were made by parents regarding things that assisted good learning and things that inhibited good learning.

Good learning was seen to be assisted by:

- individual attention;
- well-paced instruction;
- observation;
- learning alongside others;
- modelling;
- having someone there when you need them;
- being given expert guidance;
- clear explanations and 'tips';
- courage (on the part of the learner);
- student confidence;
- persistence and perseverance on the part of the learner, patience and tolerance on the part of the teacher;
- shared understandings;
- talking through ideas with a capable knowledgeable person;
- enlightened communication;
- reinforcement;
- practice;
- balance and compromise;
- building on prior experience;

- being able to expand ideas creatively;
- a sound, nurturing environment;
- positive attitudes by all involved;
- hands-on activities;
- clear standards;
- recognition of achievements (even when quite small);
- opportunities to learn from mistakes; and
- necessary facilities (both human and material).

Inhibitors to good learning included fear and anxiety, particularly in relation to making mistakes and being judged as incompetent:

- At times students may be given too much information, too quickly. As a result of information overload, the learning can become confused. Lack of communication and poor communication could both contribute to poor learning. Poor communication could be manifested in inadequate or inappropriate feedback (or no feedback at all) impatience, pacing that is inappropriate (too fast or too slow) and not checking the student's level of understanding.
- Unrealistic time frames, where the learning is rushed, can lead to surface rather than deep learning. Students need to be supported in developing good time management skills and in prioritising their workload; this should not be left to chance.

With regard to assessment and reporting, the parents believed it:

- should be clear and unambiguous;
- should be based upon dialogue with parents and students; and
- should indicate specific difficulties and ways in which these are being addressed.

Clearly these parents, given the opportunity, were able to discuss their children's learning in far more enlightened ways than had been anticipated. One of the difficulties schools face is that it is often the angry and dissatisfied parent whose voice is heard. By listening to randomly selected groups of parents from across the age and ability range it was possible to demonstrate, in this instance, that parents were open to innovation and change in assessment and reporting practices.

In the concluding section to this chapter we are going to turn to some such innovative practices and ask you to consider how you might employ them and what their consequences could be for student learning.

Innovative strategies in assessment and reporting

An important contribution to innovative strategies in assessment and reporting of student learning has been made by the Australian Council for Educational Research (ACER) in its publication of the *Assessment Resource Kit* (ARK) (see Masters & Forster 1996).

Authentic assessment as an interactive process is central to the design of the ARK materials (Masters & Forster 1996) which have developmental assessment as their focus. The principal metaphor used by the ACER is the progress map; this is consistent with the statements and profiles now currently in use in Australian states and territories. Using the descriptors provided by the statements and profiles, a developmental map can be constructed and the learners' progress documented. In order to place learner's achievements on the map it is essential that teachers and learners engage in sustained interactions.

The kit pays particular attention to three major areas of documentation of student learning in support of the progress map. These are portfolio assessment, performance assessment and project assessment. Of course teachers have thought about these matters for a number of years and writers have discussed them widely. However, the ACER publication is an important one in that it provides a practical resource with examples spanning from Kindergarten to Year 12. The kit resulted from a project funded by the then federal Department of Employment, Education, Training and Youth Affairs (DEETYA) and draws upon practices across the states and territories. It has been extensively trialed and has been taken up by a number of individual schools. Below we discuss the ARK materials in relation to portfolio assessment, performance assessment and project assessment and we supplement these processes with additional information from the current literature. We then present a number of case studies where these strategies are being employed. You might like to consider how and when you could use these processes as you begin to teach.

Portfolio assessment

Portfolio assessment is founded upon teachers and students making judgments about learning based upon a rich array and variety of evidence. A number of you may have been required to keep a learning portfolio in your senior years of study at school. Some of you may even be keeping them right now during your tertiary studies. The student learning portfolio may vary quite considerably, depending on the uses to which it is to be put. It may be a collection of evidence of the progress of that student's learning over time in a specific curriculum area or more generally, or it may be a record of achievement that celebrates the student's learning and is a demonstration of that learning.

The former are best characterised as working portfolios; they are formative and diagnostic in nature. They will contain samples of work which reflect the student's development; for example, working drafts of a piece of writing as well as the final polished, published account. They may contain reflective statements made by the student regarding his or her approaches and attitudes to a specific key learning area and goals that have been set. They are an opportunity for the learner to consider their learning strategies as well as their achievements. The latter, records of achievements (RoAs), are documents that reflect the best of student work and contain finished products. Students in the expressive and performing arts in various practical subjects, such as art, have long been accustomed to presenting portfolios of their work and its development.

As yet we have seen little evidence of the keeping of electronic portfolios, but these are becoming increasingly possible using scanners and computer-linked photographic applications. With the burgeoning of computer technology it may well be that in the future students will keep their portfolios on disk rather than maintaining the hard copy; and that, when printed out, the portfolio will have considerable 'show status'. In one of the examples we offer later in this chapter, students displayed their portfolio as a Powerpoint presentation.

Whatever the medium, it is important to stress that keeping a learning portfolio as a part of authentic assessment should not become an add-on trial for teachers and their students, but should be built into the curriculum.

Finally, it should also be remembered that the portfolio is not an end in itself. It is a material demonstration of learning. Teachers and students need to guard against merely gathering bits and pieces. The selection of evidence needs to be warranted — why is something there, what has it added to the growing picture of the student's learning?

Performance assessment

While portfolio assessment is based on the artefacts of learning, performance assessment is based on the actual doing of the work, either as an independent learner, or as a member of a group. (Too often we focus only on the learning of the individual, rather than recognising the synergy created by the overall learning taking place in the group.)

The performance may be related to a specific key learning area; for example, undertaking a measurement and graphing task in mathematics; or it may be related to generic learning competencies such as problem solving, or working effectively with others. The conduct of performance assessment may be formal and planned or informal and incidental (such as the making of anecdotal notes when a particularly noteworthy behaviour occurs). Performance assessment is the demonstration of a capacity to do the work in hand, be it cognitive, creative, physical or social. The important thing about performance assessment is that it is based upon the observable, whether it be a gymnastics routine, using a computer application, managing a class debate, engaging in peer support, high jumping, resuscitating, assembling a piece of laboratory equipment or putting on a play.

As adults, most of us have already been engaged in a significant performance assessment experience when we undertook our driving test. It was not sufficient for us to demonstrate a theoretical understanding of safe and competent driving; we had to actually get behind the wheel and drive the car to the satisfaction of an examiner who had a number of criteria we were required to meet. This is a useful example to consider because it also demonstrates the concept of mastery. If one fails a driving test, one can return and take it again as many times as is required to convince the examiner that the skills of managing a car in a number of situations have been mastered.

Project assessment

Projects in the secondary school are seen as opportunities for students to be highly self-directed. Often they can identify their own topics, they research and compile information and present their work in a variety of ways: video/audio tapes, booklets, scripts, charts, collages, even CD-ROMs. Students studying society and culture in the New South Wales Higher School Certificate undertake just such a project. We talked to Kate, who had developed a project on 'Sex, Shoes and Status'. Her investigations had led her to such diverse sources as museums, folk-tales, feminism, erotica, design and technology. 'It was incredibly challenging, but I have never felt more in charge' was the way she summed up her experience.

Because teachers' work is so intense, there is a temptation to take projects and assess them away from the learning environment that produced them. How often do we see teachers struggling to their cars with great boxes of student work. For project assessment to contribute to educative assessment it is essential that some arrangement is made for the student to explain, defend and justify their work. Throughout this discussion of means for collecting evidence we cannot emphasise enough the benefits of student participation in the processes.

Students need to be encouraged to reflect upon not only what they learned, but also how they learned. It is possible to build into the project specifications a brief for students to consider how they set about the task. Again, it is a matter of connectedness, connecting the assessment to the learning in powerful ways. In planning projects it is possible to consider that they can embody a number of key learning areas and a number and variety of learning outcomes — these can be oriented to both process and product. Students can document how they went about designing and undertaking the project as well as demonstrating the substance. The teacher can be engaged not only in making a judgment about the quality of the final product, but can be involved in co-monitoring with the student the project on the way through. As Masters and Forster suggest (1996, p. 18):

> Some teachers provide a list of dates for the completion of stages of a project. Some provide progress sheets which, when completed by students, provide evidence of engagement with the task. Sometimes students are asked to track their work using a response journal or by completing a detailed checklist. Some checklists ask students to reflect on their use of resources over a period of time across projects. This strategy may assist students to see the cross-curricular skills they are applying. The evidence recorded on progress sheets, response journals and checklists can be useful in assessing students' general investigation skills.

Exhibitions

While the ARK materials do not make direct reference to the notion of exhibitions it is clear that this innovative approach to assessment is highly commensurate with the ACER processes.

McDonald (1993) has had a long association with the Coalition of Essential Schools. He recalls one of the most influential educators concerned with the Coalition, Ted Sizer, became interested in the idea of the exhibition by a 'strange route' (p. 68):

> Sizer reached all the way back to the eighteenth century in a search for an assessment mechanism that might help schools drive themselves rather than be driven. He found it in the *exhibition*, a common feature of the eighteenth century and early nineteenth century American academies, an occasion of public inspection when some substantial portion of an academy's stakeholders might show up to hear students recite, declaim or otherwise perform.

Modern exhibitions require senior students to assemble a learning portfolio and publicly defend it to their peers, parents, teachers, members of the school and broader community. Sizer has made several visits to Australia under the auspices of the National Schools Network, as have a number of Coalition of Essential Schools teachers and leaders. At the moment the intensity of time and the logistics involved make it a great challenge for schools to attempt the exhibition.

An example of a school attempting such work is to be found in a large independent girls' school on Queensland's Gold Coast. During 1997 a unit of work entitled 'Rights and Responsibilities, Work and Society' was undertaken with Year 10 students. They were required to combine two key learning areas, English and social science, to investigate the citizenship implications of a range and variety of workplaces. Teachers acted as facilitators as the students identified the particular aspect which they wished to research. The culmination of the inquiry was a presentation to a roundtable of peers, parents, teachers and community members. Each student produced a Powerpoint presentation, accompanied by a working portfolio containing: journal entries, reflections on learning, written tasks generated from class activities and critical responses to text material. Roundtable participants were asked to identify:

- areas of strength;
- areas needing improvement;
- overall features deserving praise;
- other issues which might have been covered; and
- suggested future goals.

Since each presentation took approximately 30 minutes the whole school was required to adapt its timetable over a week. This drew upon considerable goodwill across all departments in the school. The logistics were quite daunting, but it is noteworthy that only two families were not able to be represented at the roundtables. Given that a number of students were boarders from remote properties the high rate of parental attendance signified the value which was placed upon the exhibition of learning.

Multiple intelligences

Another innovative approach to assessment is now being considered in relation to the burgeoning understanding of multiple intelligences. Ever since Gardner's (1983) groundbreaking work *Frames of Mind: The Theory of Multiple Intelligences* there has been a quest to develop teaching and learning that takes account of the great variation between students in learning styles and learning preferences. He argues that two kinds of intelligence have typically been assessed and rewarded in our schools: verbal and logical/mathematical intelligences. There has been little recognition of visual-spatial, bodily-kinaesthetic, musical, interpersonal and intrapersonal intelligences in the design and implementation of assessment tasks. While schools are beginning to use assessment strategies such as concept mapping, debating, dramatic representations and so on, we could find little evidence that these are, as yet, widespread or well documented. Teachers will need to reflect carefully upon existing practices and ask themselves how cognisant they are of the learning preferences of their students and the extent to which they take account of them.

Teacher reflection

As we have observed a number of times throughout this chapter, assessing student learning can be a moment for teacher professional learning. But this will not come about by chance. Teachers need to develop strategies that will enable them to document their learning and reflect upon it. Indeed, it is possible to think about learning portfolios as being as important for teachers as they are for students (Retallick & Groundwater-Smith 1999).

Even if a teacher were not able to maintain a detailed professional learning portfolio it is possible to develop reflective practice based upon particular heuristics. For example, comparing how things are typically undertaken and how the teacher would like to change, as demonstrated in the table below.

Teacher reflection

We normally	I would love to
Mark students' homework away from the class.	Take a few students per week and mark their work in consultation with them.
Set assessment tasks within the one faculty	Work across a couple of faculties and design some integrated assessment tasks.
Teach in 50 minute blocks.	Have longer blocks of learning time, so that we can use some different assessment strategies.

In Chapters 13 and 14 we shall be discussing teacher and corporate professional learning more fully. Suffice to say here that it is at the intersection of student learning and teacher learning that growth and change can occur.

Conclusion

In this chapter we have examined assessment in its many guises. We have considered the consequences of employing limited and limiting assessment strategies. Perhaps the last word should rest with a young woman, Nadine, who has recently completed her secondary schooling and who was asked to read this chapter and comment:

> You know, I only finished school the year before last; but I have to say that I can't remember a time when a teacher sat down with me and talked about my work and my learning in the ways that you suggest. To tell you the truth, I've never really thought about how I learn. I just do it. But then, I think I'm a survivor. Maybe there were other kids who weren't.

INQUIRY STRATEGIES

1. Think about a recent moment when you learned something. It may be a skill, a social encounter, something in the workplace. What helped you to learn? What impeded your learning? How do you know that you learned something? In small groups collate your responses and ask yourselves the question: Are there some principles here for considering the relationship between assessment and learning?

2. Consider a unit of study that you are designing in your teaching area — how have you made accommodations for authentic assessment? How would you justify that the tasks that you have designed meet the conditions for authentic assessment outlined earlier in this chapter?

3. Gather up a variety of reports from different schools (some of your own, or those of your children, if you are willing to take the risk). What are the explicit messages in the reports? What are the implicit messages?

4. Arrange to interview some employers (e.g. the Human Resources Person at your local supermarket or fast food outlet). What information would they find useful regarding school leavers who are seeking employment? Are school reports helpful to them and in what way?

5. Visit the web site of your local Board of Studies. What do they have to say about assessment of student learning? What latest trends do they point to?

References

Bagnall, N. (1995). Global culture capital: the global field. In N. Bagnall (ed), *Tradition and Change.* Proceedings of the Australia New Zealand Comparative and International Education Society, Sydney: University of Sydney, pp. 221–237.

Ball, S. (1994). *Education reform: a critical and post-structural approach.* Buckingham: Open University Press.

Black, P. & William, D. (1998). Assessment and classroom learning. In *Assessment in education: principles, policies and practices,* 5 (1) pp. 7–74.

Broadfoot, P. (1996). *Education, assessment and society.* Buckingham: Open University Press.

Broadfoot, P., Dockrell, B., Gipps, C., Harlen, W. & Nutall, D. (eds) (1992). *Policy issues in national assessment.* BERA Dialogues 7. Clevedon: MultiLingual Matters Ltd.

Butler, J. (1995). Teachers' judging standards in senior science subjects: fifteen years of the Queensland Experiment. In *Studies in Science Education,* 26 (1) pp. 135–157.

Chapman, P. (1988). *Schools as Sorters.* New York: New York University Press.

Civics Expert Group (1994). *Whereas the People: Civics and Citizenship Education.* Canberra: Australian Government Printing Service.

Connell, R., White, V. & Johnston, K. (1991). *Running Twice as Hard.* Geelong: Deakin University Press.

Currie, J. & Groundwater-Smith, S. (1998). *Learning is When. . .* Milperra: National Schools Network, University of Western Sydney.

Eisner, E. (1977). On the use of educational connoisseurship and criticism for evaluating classroom life. In *Teachers College Record,* 78 pp. 345–358.

Eisner, E. (1993). Reshaping assessment in education: some criteria in search of practice. In *Journal of Curriculum Studies,* 25 (3) pp. 219–233.

Feintuck, M. (1994). *Accountability and Choice in Schooling.* Buckingham: Open University Press.

Forster, M. & Masters, G. (1996). *The Assessment Resource Kit.* Hawthorn, Vic: The Australian Council for Educational Research. (Note: some individual booklets in the kit reverse the order of authors.)

Gardner, H. (1983). *Frames of Mind: the Theory of Multiple Intelligences.* Harvard University Press.

Gewirtz, S., Ball, S. & Bowe, R. (1995). *Markets, Choice and Equity in Education.* Buckingham: Open University Press.

Groundwater-Smith, S. & Hunter, J. (2000). Whole school inquiry: evidence based practice. Paper presented to the Second CERG Conference *Change and Choice in the New Century is Education Y2K Compliant.* Sydney, 4–5 February.

Hill, P. & Rowe, K. (1996). Multilevel modelling in school effectiveness research. In *School Effectiveness and School Improvement,* 7 (1) pp. 1–34.

Marzano, R., Pickering, D. & McTighe, J. (1993). *Assessing Student Outcomes: Performance Assessment Using the Dimensions of Learning Model.* Alexandria, VA: Association for Supervision and Curriculum Development.

Masters, G. & Forster, M. (1996). *The Assessment Resource Kit.* Hawthorn, Vic: The Australian Council for Educational Research. (Note: some individual booklets in the kit reverse the order of authors.)

McDonald, J. (1993). Exhibitions: authentic assessment that points but doesn't drive. In J. Bamburg (ed), *Assessment — How do we know what they know?* Dubuque, Iowa: Kendall/Hunt Publishing Company, pp. 68–71.

McPherson, A. (1994). Measuring added value in schools. In B. Moon & A. Shelton Mayses (eds), *Teaching and Learning in Secondary Schools.* London: Routledge, pp. 328–336.

Meadmore, D. (1995). Linking goals of governmentality with policies of assessment. In *Assessment in Education,* 2 (1) pp. 9–22.

Miolin. S. (1999). Team small groups: a personal reflection. In M. Monkemeyer, A. Ratzki, H. Wubbels, B. Neiser, G. Schulz-Wensky, L. Laskey (eds), *Team Small Group: a Whole School Approach.* Sydney: Hawker Brownlow Education, pp. 191–194.

Newman, R. & Schwager, M. (1995). Students' help seeking during problem solving. In *American Educational Research Journal,* 32 pp. 352–376.

Newmann, F. (1992). The assessment of discourse in social studies. In H. Berlak, F. Newmann, E. Adams, D. Archbald, T. Burgess, J. Raven & J. Bamburg (eds), *Toward a New Science of Educational Testing and Assessment.* New York: State University of New York Press, pp. 53–69.

Newmann, F. & Archbald, D. (1992). The nature of authentic academic achievement. In H. Berlak, F. Newmann, E. Adams, D. Archbald, T. Burgess, J. Raven & J. Bamburg (eds), *Toward a New Science of Educational Testing and Assessment.* New York: State University of New York Press, pp. 71–84.

Paris, S. & Ayres, L. (1994). *Becoming Reflective Students and Teachers with Portfolios and Authentic Assessment.* Washington, DC: American Psychological Association.

Phillips, H. & Moroz, W. (1999). Research findings on students' perceptions of political awareness. In *Youth Studies Australia,* 15 (2), pp. 13–19.

Queensland Board of Senior Secondary School Studies, (2000). Website: http://www.bssq.edu.au

Retallick, J. & Groundwater-Smith, S. (1999). Teachers' workplace learning and the learning portfolio. In *Asia Pacific Journal of Teacher Education,* (27(1), pp. 47–59.

Reynolds, S., Martin, K. & Groulx, J. (1995). Patterns of understanding. In *Educational Assessment,* 3 (2) pp. 363–371.

Romberg, T. (1993). Assessing mathematics competence and achievement. In H. Berlak, F. Newmann, E. Adams, D. Archbald, T. Burgess, J. Raven & J. Bamburg (eds), *Toward a New Science of Educational Testing and Assessment.* New York: State University of New York Press, pp. 23–52.

Torrance, H. & Pryor, J. (1998). *Investigating Formative Assessment.* Buckingham: Open University Press.

Valencia, S., Hiebert, E. & Afflerbach, P. (1994). *Authentic Reading Assessment: Practices and Possibilities.* Newark DE: International Reading Association.

White, V. & Moore, R. (1999). Introducing team small group to Australia: the National Schools Network. In M. Monkemeyer, A. Ratzki, H. Wubbels, B. Neiser, G. Schulz-Wensky, L. Laskey (eds), *Team Small Group: A Whole School Approach.* Sydney: Hawker Brownlow Education, pp. 167–178.

PART FIVE

The Workplace Learning
of Teachers –
A Fresh Orientation

CHAPTER *13* Professional Development: Documenting Teachers'

Workplace Learning

CHAPTER *14* Documenting the Corporate Learning of the School Community

for School Improvement

CHAPTER *15* The Full Service School

An emphasis which we wish to make in this book is that schools are not only sites for student learning, but also places where teachers engage in substantial professional learning. Schools are workplaces for one of the largest occupational groups in the country. Teachers, as professional workers, gain knowledge from their experience. However, the knowledge which is produced often remains tacit. Schools which are generative working environments are places where teacher workplace learning is shared and critiqued.

In this section there are three chapters. The first of these examines the ways in which teachers can document and reflect upon their workplace learning. A number of different approaches to that documentation, within national projects, is presented and evaluated. The second chapter looks at the ways in which the school itself can be characterised as a learning organisation and the processes which are used for school improvement.

The concluding chapter in this section departs somewhat from the two which precede it, in that the chapter focuses upon a holistic and inter-agency approach to school improvement through the notion of the 'full service school'.

CHAPTER

Professional Development: Documenting Teachers' Workplace Learning

Teachers talk, just like students, about 'going to school'. For both groups, schools are workplaces, yet while schools are often studied for the conditions of students' workplaces as learning settings, there is not quite as much attention given to the parallel workplace of teachers. The workplace learning conditions of teachers are important since schools are workplaces for one of the largest occupational groups in any country. It is rare that the conditions for teachers' learning and continuing professional development are considered seriously. This chapter asks how teachers continue to learn, not only over the time in which they work as individual members of the profession, but also as members of a particular workplace, with shared conditions. What are the conditions under which teacher professional development is most likely to occur? What kinds of knowledge about their workplaces do teachers produce? How is this learning recorded or documented — and passed on in the form of induction programs to neophyte teachers? Examples of different approaches to promoting and documenting teachers' workplace learning will be provided, including action-research projects, Internet conferences, the National Schools Network Research Circles, national competencies for teachers, professional associations and major government reports into the Status of Teaching.

Since schools continue to change, as well as provide, continuities as a major societal institution, it is important to consider how teachers themselves, entrusted with the responsibility for the learning of young people, address the question of their own learning. This ongoing learning is often discussed among teachers as 'in-service', 'professional development' or training sessions. Sometimes there are 'cluster days', when a group of schools in an area gets together to share the planning and experience of common materials. The landscape of teachers' support for their work continues to change, as conditions for schools also change.

Teachers as continuing learner-workers: an overview history

On-the-job education has always been the norm for teachers, although much of this has necessarily been isolated, in their own classrooms. Learning on the job, with and alongside students, remains a necessary part of the evolving work. Schools, despite many and sometimes awkward continuities, have also changed over time in ways that meet the changing society and the changing make-up of the student body. Compared to last century, books in many homes can now be taken for granted; even computer access or familiarity in many homes is another kind of change that schools through their teachers are adapting to. The changing family structure and roles for schools that follow have also had to be incorporated into how teachers do their work. Professional networks have helped to ensure that this learning is not only the province of individual teachers but can enter professional conversations among teachers.

During the 1970s, the Commonwealth Government made available certain funds to state/territory employer authorities for devoting to in-service training for teachers. At that time, the teaching force was making large adaptations to cope with significantly increased numbers of students in secondary schools, greater growth of metropolitan areas and large numbers of students who spoke languages other than English as their native language. Across the different states/territories, regions and in single schools, teachers began to participate in planning for their own professional development, individually, for the whole school and across schools.

Treating schools as workplaces in which all participants needed to see their work in context led also to 'in-service' activities being directed towards the whole school. 'Whole-school' approaches to discipline, to literacy, to school evaluation, for example, all recognise the inter-relationship among any reform-directed activities. No single member of the partnership of parents, students and teachers could, by themselves and without the active support of the others, make enough difference to change current practice. In Victoria's School Improvement Plan (Ministerial Paper 2 1982), the evaluation of current school practice by the whole-school community was seen as a way of exploring how the different perspectives could contribute to new ways of framing both the problems and possible solutions. This was a difficult move for many teachers, as well as parents, requiring both sharing of expertise and a capacity to listen to feedback and suggestions that emerged from different perspectives of the problem of schooling.

In most Australian states and territories, the movement away from central syllabus prescription during the 1970s meant that many teachers had reason to collaborate with other teachers, to share their work, for quality moderation, and to gain ideas of planning for different groups of students. In-service education became a venue for teachers to document and share their work, locally, across the state/territory and sometimes even nationally. In the 1970s, parallel to the school-based curriculum development, movement also grew centrally for nationally sponsored curriculum development projects. The national science education project was the first and others followed. These projects and others sponsored by governments were important in developing major groups of interested teachers to trial and implement the curriculum developed so far. During these years, the idea of a teacher as a professional developed strongly, partly as an aspect of the industrial union struggle for better conditions of work tied to more professional concerns about the quality of student learning (Spaull

1985). (See also Chapter 3 for an exploration of the idea of teachers as professionals.)

For many teachers in recent years, there has not been a systematic attempt to ensure they are provided with adequate professional development opportunities. Indeed, some would claim that except when there are new policy initiatives, when the employing authority runs some compulsory information or implementation sessions, most professional development is left to the individual teacher to find and enrol in. With the increase in postgraduate university course fees, and the reduction of the infrastructure from state education authorities, many teachers find there is not much on offer within their budget. What used to be treated as an employer responsibility, to provide opportunities to access professional development is now treated largely as an individual responsibility. When teachers are relatively lowly paid, and many of the courses cost a significant amount, there is a growing perception among teachers that opportunities to continue to develop as a teacher are minimal. In turn, this lack of opportunity can be treated in the media or among employing authorities and governments as a way to 'beat teachers over the head' as not being professional, as not caring about standards or not being committed to their work. There have been arguments that teachers' holidays should largely be spent in professional development activities.

Such a negative portrayal of teachers as not committed to their ongoing professional improvement is countered when we recognise that teachers tend to participate strongly in activities in which they see themselves as having significant control over the direction and the processes of the activity. A number of these activities are discussed in the sections which follow, highlighting the kinds of professional development that teachers have found particularly useful. What is missing from these accounts are the case studies of schools that are innovative, where there is a strong and long-lived culture of professionalism, and where staff meetings and projects to change curriculum or school operations become the well-spring of those teachers' professional development. These accounts are largely missing because those who are involved are usually too busy participating to write them up. For some, they are so much a fact of life that they do not see anything remarkable in such an experience. For teachers, for whom it is a rare occurrence to experience quite such a constructive school environment and culture, such an opportunity is greatly valued. Many teachers can attest to the importance of such opportunities built into everyday working life – a way of approaching the work of teaching as a reflective practitioner.

The accounts below of different approaches to teacher professional development all involve some form of investigation and documentation of teachers' workplaces. They implicitly, and in some cases explicitly, argue that where teachers are enabled to investigate their workplaces their participation in workplace renewal, professional understanding and collegiality are generally increased.

First we outline the National Professional Development Program, a federal initiative with widespread funding across the country, before moving to consider some of the work of the National Schools Network in promoting teacher research through Research Circles. The initiatives around teachers as evaluators, emerging from the 1970s and early 1980s, has recently been a stronger emphasis in the field, especially in the context of school-based management.

The National Professional Development Program

The National Professional Development Program (NPDP) was a federally funded initiative established in the 1993 to 1995 triennium. It was targeted towards assisting teachers to develop greater facility to understand and use the (then new) national directions agreed for the schooling sector, especially Key Competencies, Vocational Education, Equity, Information Technology and the national Curriculum Statements and Profiles. Figures from the evaluation of NPDP suggest that in the years 1994 and 1995, over 100 000 teachers participated in some way in the NPDP (National Curriculum Services 1995), indicating a level of interest by teachers across Australia both in taking up professional development activities and their preference for a style of partnership in the activities that strongly valued teachers' own professional interests and judgment.

According to the national evaluation of the program, participants argued that good professional development should:

- be based on teachers' needs or wants;
- focus on classroom practice;
- provide support or follow-up for teachers;
- be run by high quality facilitators;
- take a variety of approaches;
- be collaborative/cooperative/collegial;
- involve active participation;
- take account of teachers in remote or rural areas;
- provide financial or other support or reward to teachers attending;
- motivate teachers, or give teachers confidence; and
- balance theory and practice.

(Adapted from Figure 4.3 National Curriculum Services 1995, p. 89,
which drew on Louden's 1994 work.)

The study concluded that there was a substantial voluntary contribution to the professional development projects where its characteristics were more in line with those criteria in terms of teacher time and access to related resources in other organisations such as professional associations, indicating the value placed on such activities by teachers.

A wide variety of projects were funded through the NPDP, including direct conduct of professional development short courses, facilitation of networks of teachers, partnership research between schools and universities, action-research projects, training of facilitators, materials production for curriculum or for professional development, and delivery through the use of information technologies. The Innovative Links project, one of those funded to promote partnership between universities and school groups, set up 'roundtables' of teachers and university colleagues to engage in research together, with newsletters and regional and national forums for teachers to present the outcomes of their research. The evaluation of the Innovative Links project found that this kind of reporting facilitated professional networking among teachers in ways that have been unusual in the profession. 'The *Innovative Links* project provided teachers with the opportunity to make their knowledge public, and to open their knowledge and practice to various forms of reflective dialogue' (Yeatman & Sachs 1995, p. 61). Clearly the opportunity provided by a national project with adequate funding was valued by both the university and school colleagues involved. Most particularly, the documentation of school-level projects to real audiences of peers was spurred on by the projects infrastructure of newsletters and forums, and assisted the motivation of teachers to engage in action-research projects at their workplace.

The National Schools Network: Research Circles

The National Schools Network (NSN) grew out of a wave of reform focussing on workplaces in the early 1990s. In the school education sector, this took the form of the National Project on the Quality of Teaching and Learning. The National Schools Network was established from that project to help teachers work together across Australia, sharing their knowledge about the links between workplace organisation, curriculum, pedagogy and assessment. It was federally funded from 1994–96, based on a national accord jointly negotiated among the systems of education, the Australian Education Union, Independent Education Union and universities and schools. The triennial funding of approximately $1.5 million provided for 16 university roundtables (attached to 100 schools) and 500 NSN schools. These funds were distributed to schools and managed through a small national secretariat. Over its years of operation, there have been various activities, including the conduct of national residential programs, the development of professional development kits, associated with national and international research, validated by teacher activists around the country, explicit attention to networking and the sponsoring of teacher-based research, usually supported by the national secretariat and member university staff.

One important development of the NSN has been the establishment of Research Circles. This work continued in new ways in the 1970s and early 1980s with emphasis on 'teachers as researchers' in movements such as action research, language and learning networks, many of which have folded under the new emphasis on accountability and management in the late 1980s and early 1990s. These latter emphases have made it more difficult to argue for the role of professional judgment among teachers. Rather, teachers have been seen as the object of other group's reforms rather than as necessary and active agents in school reform.

The NSN work with Research Circles has created room for the support and encouragement of teacher professional judgment, seen as crucial in the improvement of student outcomes and school conditions. It has resuscitated a venue for teachers to work together, sometimes in partnership with universities, on matters which they define as worth investigating. The NSN has developed a set of principles for Research Circles, which reflect this commitment to practitioner-based research, that is focussed around issues valued and defined by teachers, and which are also likely to lead to improvement in practices at the school level. Partners participating in NSN Research Circles agree to the following principles of operation (NSN, Mimeo, no date):

- 'to engage in an ongoing program examining their work organisation structures and learning in accordance with principles of research-oriented reflective practice;
- to engage in research which is informed by principles of social justice and which is

directed towards improving the learning outcomes for all students;

- to engage in research grounded in principles of collaboration and democratic research processes both in the development of research and the interpretation of data;

- to commit to principles of teacher research which give precedence to the research questions generated within the school setting;

- that the ownership of the results of the research will be jointly negotiated by the research circle;

- that the research results will be published only with the approval of participating school(s), with due acknowledgment of the contribution of members of the schools, and with respect for confidentiality where appropriate.

The principles capture some of the tensions that are often evident when teachers work with others to document their work. Sometimes, others' questions dominate the agenda, or things are published without the consent of the participants, or issues arise which are interesting but not central to improving justice and learning outcomes for students.

Research Circles which have run with NSN using these principles have covered a range of areas. In central Queensland, for example, there was one on the role of play in early childhood and another on improving middle school curriculum. Victoria has been running one focussed on science teaching and the ACT, as with several other groups, has three circles working on learning about teachers' work by looking at students' work. The results of some of these Research Circles have been published under the title *Student work: The heart of teaching* (NSN 2000).

In developing these Research Circles, the NSN has seen them as contributing to the improvement of teaching and of student outcomes, by recognising the interrelationship between teachers' work settings, in all their complexity, and their professional role as producers of knowledge about their own work. They give primacy to assisting teachers in groups to develop their research and analysis skills, and to see their work as a collegial endeavour, which occurs within particular climates for themselves and their students.

Standards-based reforms of teachers' work: the example of 'Beginning Teacher Competencies'

Another example of a focus of reform of teachers' work, and another offshoot of the National Project on the Quality of Teaching and Learning, has been the development of a national set of competencies for beginning teachers. These grew out of a move towards trying to describe the range of activities and expertise needed for teaching. The emphasis on beginning teachers linked the work of existing teachers with colleagues in Teacher Education faculties and provided a national perspective on teachers' work for the first time. As teacher education remains a state/territory responsibility under the constitution, there have been significant barriers to developing any national standards for the profession. Indeed, at the time of writing, there are only two states with formal registration requirements for entry to the profession and no national standards for exit students from pre-service courses. This makes it difficult for those applying across states/territories for entry into the profession. The competencies are performance-based, rather than benchmarked or statements of high achievement. That is, beginning teachers are asked to be able to provide evidence that they can meet the majority of indicators of these minimum competencies. The competencies grew out of documentation of teachers' work and their development brought together many of the stakeholders in teacher entry standards, especially the teacher unions, and the employer authorities.

A number of education faculties around Australia have used these as the basis of their evaluation of the work of student teachers in schools, and particularly for exit students who will be applying for teaching positions. The following table gives the overview list of competencies, which are also supported by a list of indicators for each

Beginning teacher competencies

1 Using and Developing Professional Knowledge & Values
1.1 Knows content and its relationship to educational goals
1.2 Understands the relationship between processes of inquiry and content knowledge
1.3 Understands how students develop and learn
1.4 Is active in developing and applying professional knowledge
1.5 Operates from an appropriate ethical position
1.6 Operates within the framework of law and regulation
1.7 Appreciates and values diversity, all students have a right to learn
1.8 Demonstrates professional commitment
2. Communicating, Interacting and Working with Children and Others
2.1 Communicates effectively with students
2.2 Develops positive relationships with students
2.3 Recognises and responds to individual differences
2.4 Encourages positive student behaviour
2.5 Responds to role in the team responsible for students' education
2.6 Works effectively with teachers, ancillary staff and others
2.7 Works effectively with parents and others responsible for the care of students
2.8 Communicates with school support staff, the profession and the wider community
3. Planning and Managing the Teaching and Learning Process
3.1 Plans purposeful programs to achieve specific student learning outcomes
3.2 Matches content, teaching approaches and student development and learning in planning
3.3 Designs teaching programs to motivate and engage students
3.4 Structures learning tasks effectively
3.5 Demonstrates flexibility and responsiveness
3.6 Establishes clear, challenging and achievable expectations for students
3.7 Fosters independent and co-operative learning
3.8 Engages the students actively in developing knowledge
4. Monitoring & Assessing Children's Progress and Learning Outcomes
4.1 Knows the educational basis and role of assessment in teaching
4.2 Uses assessment strategies that take account of relationships between teaching, learning & assessment
4.3 Monitors student progress and provides feedback on progress
4.4 Maintains records of student progress
4.5 Reports on student progress to parents and others responsible for the care of students

Beginning teacher competencies (continued)

---

5.   Reflecting, Evaluating and Planning for Continuous Improvement

5.1 Critically reflects on own practice to improve the quality of teaching and learning
5.2 Evaluates teaching and learning programs
5.3 Plans to meet longer-term personal and school goals
5.4 Developing professional skills and capacity

---

area of competency and its sub-components (NPQTL 1996).

Many current teachers are clear that this codification of the work of teachers does meet the range of activities which beginning teachers will need to be able to perform. They also, on many occasions, question their own capacity to meet all these requirements at more than a basic level. Entry levels to the profession have obviously grown, especially at a time when competition for jobs is high. By developing the competencies through a process of documenting what teachers actually have to do, the combined practice of many stakeholders in the work of teachers has been recognised nationally.

There are other related developments based on similar assumptions about making explicit the range and level of performance exhibited in teachers' work. These include following the USA experience of providing the opportunity for teachers to demonstrate advanced skills through a process of application for Advanced Certification as a teacher. Proposals of this kind require teachers to prepare a portfolio demonstrating how they meet a series of standards which could be said to characterise highly skilled teachers. While not all experienced teachers could fulfil these criteria, a significant proportion should be able to demonstrate their skill in this way. The criteria for the Advanced Certificate are set high to show both the teaching profession and other interested parties what accomplished teachers can achieve. The processes used in the USA National Board of Professional Teaching Standards include videoing classroom sequences and discussing them with a colleague, samples of student work and units developed by the teacher, self-reflection and change as a result of this investigation (Ingvarson 1999). Similar processes are currently being considered in Australia.

Professional associations and unions

Many teachers belong to professional associations as a means of ensuring that they engage in professional conversations and continue to update their knowledge base and skills. Some of these associations are subject-based (English, social education, history) while others are more general in their focus across the school, such as the Australian Curriculum Studies Association or the Australian Educational Administration Association. All of these associations are built on the voluntary work of members who pay a fee for joining. Some associations take on projects to raise money or to promote the profession. For example, maths, science and literacy associations have been working to investigate and develop standards for advanced teacher certification as part of a large national research project. Most associations conduct regular meetings and conferences bringing together members and others active in the field, and provide newsletters or journals to share research, policy updates, and ideas with relevance for practice. Many of these associations also bid for projects under federal or state/territory funding, as in the NPDP described above, where professional associations were one of the important partners in offering professional development for teachers.

Teacher unions also have a long history in Australia where members are represented on a range of committees and policy groups. Australian teacher unions have been concerned with professional education and further training as well as with industrial matters about conditions of work and pay. In Australia there are teacher unions in both the government and independent school sectors, with local branches, state bodies and national organisations. Like all unions, those in education both continue their representation of members' concerns and seek to shape policy and contexts in a rapidly changing world. Many of the union publications are helpful in summarising key initiatives and policy directions and in providing access to networks useful for beginning teachers. Some unions have special groups for those in their early years of teaching. All also organise regular conferences on both industrial and professional matters. Given the efforts by many different groups to reform teaching, the teacher unions have a history of participating in the formation of the guidelines so that their members' work is adequately supported. The history of teachers' unions has many lessons about the shifting issues in teachers' professional development, which are documented in their files, as well as in the living history that many teachers represent.

Participative inquiry

The names under which collegial or participative research are known vary in the literature on teacher research. Peter Reason (1988) outlines three main strands to participative inquiry: cooperative inquiry, participatory action research and action learning. For Reason, *cooperative inquiry* recognises the social nature of work. It follows that, since practice is social, then co-participants can agree to co-research an area for inquiry. The group applies their questions to their everyday life and work, immersing themselves in their context. Cooperative inquiry is concerned with critical subjectivity: the participant researchers are aware of their own perspectives and differences. *Participatory action research* is concerned with the politics of knowledge production. It is often concerned with empowerment of oppressed peoples by linking improvement of knowledge with local action. It also tends to criticise orthodox or mainstream social science for their separation from local situations and values. *Action learning* (also known as action inquiry and action science) is concerned with identifying theories that guide or inform people's behaviour. All three emphasise the importance of participation in research to have an outcome of changing lived experience *and* understanding of self and other. They differ in their emphasis — on psychological, individual/group focus or the political dimensions of the research.

The advocates of research conducted by teachers, for teachers and their schools, make many suggestions about its advantages in comparison with other forms of professional development and also in contrast with research conducted solely by those outside the situation (Reason 1988; Altrichter, Posch & Somekh 1993; Kemmis & McTaggart 1988). One major advantage of practitioner research is that such research is able to reveal the complexity of practice *in situ*. Many teachers have found that other people's research does not meet their own needs or sense of what actually happens in a school. There is a ready community with whom to discuss the findings, and interpret the results of any research. It is possible to gather rich, descriptive data as it occurs in 'ordinary' time, rather than having to set up conditions for research. Ethical problems of access to people and their practices can be minimised, as colleagues and students are more likely to trust people already responsible to others in the situation. Furthermore, such research is more likely to be action oriented, leading to results if practitioners are themselves involved.

Action-oriented teacher research: practitioner involvement

Individual teachers have often engaged in some form of systematic research on their own practice. This is how a number of innovations in teaching practice have occurred. More supportive circumstances occur when a group of teachers band together to investigate a common issue. A group activity enables others to check interpretations of information and provides a source of support if the going gets tough. One of the basic requirements for groups engaged in teacher research is the creation of a 'safe space' for discussion, for making mistakes and for building a capacity to disagree as well as develop a common language for discussing the topic. Another key issue is to ensure that students, their families and colleagues are dealt with in an ethical manner that protects them from any potential for harm, ensures their privacy and confidentiality where appropriate, and that access to people's materials and views is negotiated. Processes need to be transparent so other people know what is going on, especially how it might affect them. Failure to pay attention to these ethical dimensions of research will often lead to workplace dissatisfaction and unnecessary conflict. It can also damage relationships, careers and commitment to working together. Thus, attention to ethics is a crucial part of any research. It is obviously critical to research in a workplace where people will have to work with one another after the research and where the reasons for undertaking the research usually require group commitment to shared interpretations and shared action. A good discussion of ethics for research in educational settings has been produced by the Australian Association for Research in Education (AARE) and may be found on their web site: http://www.swin.edu.au/aare.

Some key practical ideas in action-oriented teacher research

Of course, we all 'research' informally every day: we set about finding out, checking evidence and acting on the basis of what we find. However, undertaking research and evaluation more formally requires more systematic attention to the processes of research, keeping records and checking interpretations more carefully and consciously. So while humans can be seen as 'researchful' in their orientation to the world, much of this occurs unconsciously. The process of researching aims to bring this to more explicit levels of articulation, creating findings that are able to be reflected upon by the teacher-researcher and, where it is done as part of a group, by colleagues.

Define a focus

A first step in most research undertaken by teachers is to define a focus. This might be what Wadsworth (1997) calls an 'ouch' experience — the researcher has a feeling of discomfort or contradiction between what was expected and what actually happens. The focus could also arise from something seen as a problem, a longstanding interest, a new policy or opportunity that requires a decision and new practices. Sometimes just learning how to do a new activity sparks off a researchful orientation. Examples of different foci for research might include how to work with a small group of students who seem unable to connect with the classroom activities, how to give access to the big ideas of a subject to all the students, how to involve students in building judgments about their own work, or how to work across disciplines to provide more integrated curricula.

In the Integrated Curriculum for the Middle Years Research Circle, each school in the circle had their own focus which was able to feed into a broader project on Integrated Curriculum. The focus was tailored to the specific history and interests of those at the school.

'Researchable' questions

Next, it is important to specify a particular question that can be investigated. Sometimes, examining some data or information already available will help to define the question. In the case of the Integrated Curriculum for the Middle Years group, questions were quite specific. One school wanted to answer the question 'How does integrated curriculum fit within a broad school policy framework that supports both social and academic achievement?' Another question from another school was how assessment for integrated curriculum could operate within the state-mandated statements and profiles. Another was how to support staff coming into the middle school program. Each question helped to focus the area of interest down to something manageable. According to Brennan and Hoadley (1984, p. 13) a good question will:

- be supported as important to answer by those involved;
- lead people to suggest what they would do with information;
- suggest 'collectable' sources of data;
- be answerable within a time frame;
- be concerned with educational issues, not just managerially oriented.

In some cases, an initial question will change, as more data becomes available and reflected upon. For example, the school wanting to know how to support staff coming in resulted in concerns about how to support existing staff and ensure they did not suffer burnout, as well as developing an induction process for incoming staff.

Evidence or data

Evidence needs to fit the question being asked. Often, there is already quite a lot of information available on a topic. As suggested above, examination of such data can actually lead to new questions emerging. For example, in the National Schools Network Research Circle on learning from students' work, a range of questions arose about teachers' work purely from spending time giving close attention to what the students did in their written work. None of these questions existed prior to looking at the work. Data often exists already, rather than needing to be collected specifically. After examining it, new data or further sub-sets of existing data may be needed.

There are many kinds of data that can be used in research. The three main approaches in social research involving people can usually be summarised as: asking people, observing people or gathering artefacts of the situation. A list of possible approaches is potentially enormous but common approaches in schools include:

- student work
- teacher unit plans

- timetables
- school policies
- photos
- computer logs
- videos
- diaries
- phone logs
- maps
- correspondence
- attendance records
- meeting minutes
- demographic records
- interviews
- anecdotal records
- newspaper cuttings

Among all of these and more, it is sometimes hard to choose which data gathering method is most appropriate for the situation and the question. The following questions (Brennan & Hoadley 1984, p. 15) to help choose a data-gathering method were developed to help schools conducting school-based research and self-evaluation:

- Will it help provide materials to help answer the question?
- Will it produce material which can easily be worked with?
- Does it have the potential to draw more people into the educational debate?
- Will it sensitise people to the issues, building a base for future participation?
- Can it be completed within the time frame we have set?

The questions indicate some likely problem areas that have been experienced in other research and evaluation projects. Often data is collected but is not helpful in answering the question. Or there are problems in collecting huge amounts of data that take ages to process, well beyond the resources of the people involved. It is more important to spend time analysing smaller amounts of data, and doing the analysis properly than to have large scale data that sits around awaiting analysis. If the results of the data gathering are helpful, they should be able to draw more people into a discussion of the issues seen as worthwhile to investigate. Sometimes this can be as simple as showing one student's work and its improvement (or lack of it) over time. This can sometimes convince people to do something serious that requires more time. One school whose staff had largely dismissed claims of the urgency of Year 8 students' problems was convinced to work on it where the Year 8 level of work was shown to be less competent than what the same student had produced three years earlier in Year 5.

Questions to help analyse data

It is often helpful to have a group to analyse data, even if the information has been collected by one person only. It can start quite formally or with people noticing anything that they 'read' in the data, something surprising or trends that have become noticeable. It is important to keep some form of record, however minimal, of the kinds of findings people have seen in the evidence and the arguments or reasoning that arise from the discussions. The following questions (Brennan & Hoadley 1984, p. 18) can be used as a guide for analysing data:

■ Is there anything surprising or unusual here?

■ Are there any patterns emerging?

■ Is there something we don't understand or need follow-up to get more information?

■ What are the most significant or important things to notice?

■ Which points are likely to raise debate within the school?

■ On any topic is there a noticeable difference in the data from different groups of people e.g. teachers and students, Year 7 and Year 10 or from different sources (e.g. interview and observation)?

■ Is there other material available that could help us widen our understanding of this issue?

■ In what ways can this data be presented so that it helps more people understand the issue and any positions taken on it by a range of people in the school community?

■ If we have collected data before, what changes have occurred?

■ What potential has this data to contribute to a decision in the school?

Action and communication

The links between research and action in teachers' work are usually strong: with so many other demands, research is usually undertaken because of interest or concern with a major issue. Thus, the importance of moving from research and analysis of issues takes priority in many people's approaches. That is also why action-research approaches, in which action cycles are monitored and investigated as part of the project, are popular among professions in the human services. If using an action-research methodology, action is built into the research, rather than as a separate stage at the end, and changes to the action can be done along the way. In other kinds of research, the link to action may require negotiation with others who have influence or related work in the area, and this needs to be done sensitively if the project is to result in action. If the action required is under the control of the person/s involved in the research, then that is a simpler situation. In all cases, however, the issue of reporting on the research and communicating both the processes and outcomes of the research to others needs to be handled carefully. A principle of 'transparency' for the project — making its goals, processes and outcomes open, except for protection of privacy — is helpful when it comes to the action phase involving other people. If people have been kept informed all along, then they are more likely to listen at the end of the project.

Managing a project

When undertaking a project in schools, the single most difficult commodity to find is teacher time. Thus, a project must be seen as worthwhile by those anticipated to participate and it must be well managed. The processes of management include:

■ getting things done to agreed deadlines;

■ negotiating appropriate times and access, according to ethical principles;

- communicating/keeping people informed (e.g. through staff meetings, notice-boards, inclusion of items in a newsletter);
- tracking the process;
- collecting relevant literature on the topic or methods;
- offering opportunities to reflect on progress made and re-plan;
- celebrating small milestones along the way;
- addressing any conflicts as they arise in ways which are respectful and humane;
- ensuring materials produced (e.g. newsletters, notice boards, reports, videos) are done quickly and reflect the ethical principles agreed upon among participants.

Attention to management issues can spread the load, keep people informed and ensure the project meets its deadlines. There are several functions of management: management of internal relationships; management of the research processes and analysis; management of contextual relationships; and management of administrative affairs of the project. Each needs some attention: if one is not attended to, then the other three dimensions will not be able to work as well. A small group can divide the functions of management and keep on regular agenda items for meetings. Larger groups as well as individuals will also need to develop project management skills to ensure the outcomes of the research effort are maximised.

Conclusion

Fullan and Hargreaves (1992) suggest that projects for teacher development must take into account four different elements if they are to be effective (p. 5):

1. the teacher's purpose;
2. the teacher as a person;
3. the real world context in which teachers work;
4. the culture of teaching: the working relationship that teachers have with their colleagues inside and outside the school.

In all the initiatives discussed in this chapter, there is an embedded notion of what it means to be a teacher, sometimes discussed explicitly in terms of teacher professionalism, and elsewhere in other terms. Underpinning all of them is a view that the role of teacher includes the responsibility for ongoing learning — for both the individual and for the professional group as a whole. Fullan and Hargreaves remind us of the importance of remembering that teaching is simultaneously highly personal, and highly contextualised. Documenting teachers' work, engaging in research and evaluation, and in local, state/territory and national projects are all processes that assist teachers to exhibit their commitment to building their knowledge base and professional networks. In the discussions, we have highlighted some of the issues that might be relevant to consider when thinking through the issue of beginning teachers' commitments to their own philosophy of teaching and to a developing idea of what is important to them in being a teacher.

Research and documentation at the school level does not all have to be done by teachers alone. Indeed, as several of the initiatives outlined above can demonstrate, there is much to be gained by networks of teachers working together, and by partnerships among different groups in education, including teachers, university academics, unions, employers and others. Grundy (1996), in a discussion of issues in building professional research partnerships in education, distinguished between two kinds of such partnerships: researching *for* the profession and researching *with* the profession. Both offer important resources to schools. By having workplace conditions and issues well documented, for example in the Senate Inquiry into the Status of the Teaching Profession (1998), it is more possible to discuss issues in the public arena that have traditionally remained within schools or school systems. This can be seen as research that is directed for the good of the profession and is usually carried out by those outside schools, including unions, academics and employer bodies. There can be questions, as Grundy points out, about who controls the research and whose issues are covered in the research, all of which need careful attention in management of projects and participation. The second kind of research, partnerships that involve research *with* the profession, has a further advantage of bringing together people with a direct stake in research processes and outcomes but driven by the concerns of those at the school setting. National Schools Network, for example, has this principle firmly built into its partnership research, as demonstrated earlier. The advantage of teacher participation in research is the recognition of the expertise of the teacher and the increased likelihood of translation of research into direct action at the local level.

All of these examples emphasise the importance of ongoing learning for teachers — about themselves as teachers, about their students and their changing world, about partners in the educational process, about their subject matter, and about the changing role of schools in society. Sometimes this takes the form of a focus on increasing disciplinary knowledge; at other times, the professional development is in the form of research work or collaborative activity to analyse teachers' own work. The processes suggested here can directly contribute to the skill base of teachers in engaging in educational research and improvement.

There are many barriers to teachers engaging in research in their own workplace. The most obvious is that of lack of time but there are others which emerge from the history of teachers' working conditions. Since much professional development has tended to be controlled by others, there has been strong resistance to it among the teaching profession. There remains only a small memory of other ways of organising professional development, illustrated in the examples provided in this chapter. The difficulty of working with others, in conditions which normally promote individualist responses to classroom problems, should not be underestimated. Teachers themselves, in this sense, can be their own worst enemies — they have accepted as given the isolated nature of their work, instead of building possibilities of collaborative activity and professional development. There is also a danger that some people engage in research only to justify their own position, calling into question the validity of their findings.

Despite these barriers and constraints, teachers' own participation in forms of action research or participative inquiry attests to its perceived long-term usefulness to the profession. It ensures that the educational issues of concern to teachers are addressed, in their own terms. It provides a way for teachers to update themselves professionally and produce new kinds of knowledge about their workplaces and themselves, and it recognises that successful professional activity is always under construction: practice can never be known fully. The criteria outlined in the NPDP study for good professional development provide a useful framework for teachers, individually and in groups such as professional associations, to judge the relevance and likely outcomes of their professional development.

INQUIRY STRATEGIES

1. Among teachers you have known or visited in the course of your program, what professional development opportunities have they accessed? Which have they found most valuable and why?

2. Which of the professional development initiatives discussed in this chapter are familiar to teachers you know or to you?

3. Discussion: What do you see as the main areas of pressure on teachers' ongoing commitment to professional development activities?

4. What do you think are the main issues needing professional development among inexperienced teachers? What would you yourself most value?

5. Whose responsibility is teacher professional development? What version of professionalism underpins your answer to this question?

6. What practice in schools have you seen so far that would, in your view, be most important to research or evaluate? Design a small scale research project to do this.

References

Altrichter, H., Posch, P. & Somekh, B. (1993). *Teachers Investigate their Work: An introduction into methods of action research.* London: Routledge.

Brennan, M. & Hoadley, R. (1984). *School Self-Evaluation.* Education Department of Victoria. Melbourne: Victorian Government Printing Office.

Brown, L. (1981). *Action Research: Teachers as learners.* Curriculum Services Branch, Education Department of Victoria. Melbourne: Victorian Government Printing Office.

Fullan, M. & Hargreaves, A. (eds) (1992). *Teacher development and educational change.* London; New York: Falmer Press, 1992.

Groundwater Smith, S. (1995). *Let's Not Live Yesterday Tomorrow: Curriculum and Assessment Reform in the Context of School Restructuring.* Ryde, NSW: National Schools Network.

Grundy, S. (1996). Building professional research partnerships: Possibilities and perplexities. *The Australian Educational Researcher*, 23, 1, April, 1–16.

Ingvarson, L. (1999). The power of professional recognition. *Unicorn*, 25, 2, 60–70.

Kemmis, S. & McTaggart, R. (eds) (1988). *The Action Research Planner* (third edition). Geelong: Deakin University Press.

Louden, W. (1994). *What counts as best practice?* Perth: WA Cross-sectoral National Professional Development Program (NPDP) consortium.

Ministerial Paper 2 (1982). *The School Improvement Plan.* Minister of Education. Melbourne: Victorian Government Printing Office.

National Curriculum Services (1995). *Evaluation of the National Professional Development Program.* Commonwealth of Australia, Canberra: Australian Government Publishing Service.

National Project on the Quality of Teaching and Learning (NPQTL) (1996). *National Competencies Framework for Beginning Teachers.* Leichhardt, NSW: Australian Teaching Council.

National Schools Network (2000). *Student work: The heart of teaching.* Professional Development kit. Sydney: National Schools Network.

National Schools Network (no date). *Principles of Participation in NSN Research Circles.* Mimeo. National Schools Network.

Reason, P. (1988). Human inquiry in action: developments in new paradigm research. London: Sage.

Senate Education, Employment and Training Committee (1998). *A Class Act: Inquiry Into The Status of the Teaching Profession.* Canberra: Australian Government Printing Service.

Spaull, A. (1985). *A History of Federal Teachers' Unions in Australia: 1921–1985.* Carlton, Vic: Australian Teachers' Federation.

Wadsworth, Y. (1997). *Do-It-Yourself Social Research* (second edition). Sydney: Allen & Unwin.

Yeatman, A. & Sachs, J. (1995). *Making the Links. A Formative evaluation of the first year of the Innovative Links Project between universities and schools for professional development.* Murdoch, WA: Innovative Links Project National Office.

14

CHAPTER

Documenting the Corporate Learning of the School Community for School Improvement

Schools produce masses of information. There is always an excess of 'data' in and about schools, much more than can usefully be organised to inform planning and evaluation of programs and schools. Ironically, in recent years there has been an emphasis on developing standardised forms of data about schools, teachers and most especially students, in order to check whether schools have been doing their job. This emphasis on accountability occurs, of course, in a context where the schooling budget is a large slice of public expenditure and the taxation base has been shrinking. Thus demands for greater accountability are not only because schools need monitoring for their effectiveness in spending public money but also because governments and policy-makers need ways to find out where best to cut or reallocate budgets. This is not a cynical excuse for opposing accountability measures but rather a caution about reading discussions of accountability only for their face value.

Since mass schooling was introduced, there have continued to be major waves of school reform, often couched in terms of a 'crisis' in education. Many teachers find these 'interventions' into their work stressful and counterproductive, leading to what has been called the 'predictable failure of school reform' (Sarason 1990). The latest wave of school reform has tended to be concerned with site-based management (termed 'devolution' in state systems) with an emphasis on standardised accountability, monitoring of performance of all concerned (teachers and principals as well as students), and local community representation on officially constituted school boards or councils. This chapter gives a reading of different movements of school improvement, which suggests that the local school site could be the well-spring of 'grassroots' improvement of educational practice, where the development of a 'learning organisation' allows for horizontal and mutual accountability at the local level. 'School improvement' in these terms uses the current requirements for reporting and documentation to ask questions that participants of the school community — teachers, parents and students — engage in answering together. This effectively redefines 'accountability' in terms of those who are enabled to participate in giving purpose to education.

The chapter also gives practical strategies for local documentation of learning about the school and its outcomes. The inquiry strategies will address what can be learned about students, school demography and student achievement by the rigorous conduct of principled school self-evaluation.

The chapter outlines various approaches to school reform in Australia, most of which are organised from outside the school, and extracts from those approaches some ideas of what the school as a whole might be able to do. Where the previous chapter considered how teachers are positioned in relation to efforts to reform schooling, this adds a further dimension of considering how schools themselves are positioned as part of the reforms. The reforms are discussed in a rough chronology covering the last 20 or 30 years, dividing reforms into their underpinning assumptions about how reform is meant to work.

The first group of school reform efforts we discuss here are those that focus on reforming the school from the outside, usually governmental policy measures. The discussions here are very general, provided to indicate some of the debates that have raged over the years about whether and to what extent schools can be improved. Here, the school effectiveness and school improvement debates are first covered, followed by discussion of investment in curriculum packages, improved teacher qualifications, school-based management, and testing and accountability-based reforms. The reforms 'from the outside' are then followed by discussions of reforms more internal to schools, such as school-based curriculum development, community schools, and partnerships among teachers, parents and students.

School improvement and school effectiveness debates

During the 1960s, there began to be systematic questioning of whether schools could make any difference to the educational outcomes of students. Research in both the UK and the USA into educational achievement among different groups of students seemed to show that students' socioeconomic status correlated most strongly with their levels of school achievement.

In these major research projects, the school was treated as an institution that acted on behalf of the public — and an institution worth researching. Schools were examined to see what, if any, difference they might make to different populations of students. School effectiveness studies measured the characteristics of schools that were seen to 'add more value' to what students brought with them from home. The characteristics of effective schools were listed to show other schools those features that seemed to make the most difference to students, controlling for population diversity. Each study seemed to have a slightly different version of the list, but most seem to agree with Mortimore et al. (1988) that a school exhibiting the following features is more likely to be educationally sound and assist its students to achieve at higher levels:

- purposeful leadership of the staff by the head teacher;
- the involvement of the deputy head;
- the involvement of teachers;
- consistency among teachers;
- structured sessions;

- intellectually challenging teaching;
- work-centred environment;
- limited focus within sessions;
- maximum communication between teachers and pupils;
- record keeping;
- parental involvement; and
- positive climate.

As Roger Slee and others have argued (Slee et al. 1998), the focus on such a list is often appealing. It seems to show policy-makers and practitioners alike where to put their energy for reform. There is a large 'research industry' that has been operating for over thirty years, producing enormous amounts of information about how, and to what extent, schools exhibit these characteristics. Much of the literature on effective schools is built into the approaches to school-based management and into the ways in which school accountability systems are organised. However, there is also a long tradition of criticism of school effectiveness and school improvement research. People argue strongly that such lists tend to over-emphasise the capacity of single schools to change, ignoring the fact that schools are embedded in particular contexts, about which they have little control (Angus 1993). From a teacher's perspective, too, the lists can seem totally irrelevant to the daily work of classrooms where students' school experience is largely determined. Teachers can easily be blamed for not achieving better outcomes with their students since the problems are seen to be well known. Yet, the research itself, and its massive debates about how change happens in schools, reveals how complex the problem of school change really is. Even if we know all the 'bits', we don't know how they fit together in any one place, or across schools as a whole.

'Teacher-proof' curriculum packages

After the Russians put the space ship *Sputnik* up into the sky in 1957 — ahead of the USA — many in government and community in that country blamed losing the 'space race' on the quality of education, specifically in the sciences. There was a great deal of money spent on developing major science curriculum packages, developed by the best scientists of the day, to put into all schools to improve the nation's scientific capacity. In Australia, too, the first major national curriculum package to be developed was the Australian Science Education Project. Australia also imported a number of American curriculum products in physics and biology, for example, to ensure that Australian students got access to the best scientific education available.

For many in schools, the new packages provided wonderful resources, at a level not seen before. Schools were accustomed to working to a state-set curriculum, often at syllabus level. Some school inspectors boasted that they knew what page of the textbook students would be using across the state at a particular time of the day! The move to develop curriculum materials packages was in keeping with that dominant practice, in that the syllabus was set outside the school, and teachers were supposed only to implement what had been decided elsewhere. However, the proliferation of packages meant that there were materials to choose among, and this built the capacity of teachers to design curriculum to suit the interests and ability of their students from among the materials on offer.

Improved teacher qualifications

A further contributor to improving the quality of education has been the focus on improving the quality and qualifications of teachers. While the 1960s and 1970s saw a shortage of teachers, which too often resulted in putting any adult — any adult 'warm, upright and breathing' (as the saying was at the time) — in front of a class, this was also a time which saw strong moves towards building teacher registration and increased minimum qualifications for teachers. Importing teachers from overseas, especially from North America, was a favoured response from employers faced with a lack of teachers, but at the same time, there was strong support for the improvement of teacher status and expertise by insisting on qualifications and upgrading of existing qualifications.

While many primary teachers had only one or two years training, this moved to three years and in the late 1980s there was a suggested base line of four-year qualifications for all teachers. This brings them into parity with secondary teachers, who usually have a three-year specialist degree prior to their education qualification. While this level of qualification is not yet universal in Australia, it has fast become the norm. In many overseas countries, the teacher qualification occurs as a master's degree after the primary degree in another area. This has also begun to be seen in Australia.

The pressure to increase teacher qualifications has many sources. First it is seen to increase the knowledge base of teachers at a time when the 'knowledge-based economy' and the 'information age' are seen as prominent characteristics of the current era. This is then to benefit the students, who have access to teachers who have greater knowledge in a wider range of areas than was previously the case. There is also a rationale that a better qualified teaching force is more likely to win public respect for the task of teaching, and improve its status as an occupational group. The school improvement dimension of these rationales has often been supported by employing authorities, anxious to demonstrate the contribution of their sector to national economic and social goals. Clearly, teachers who have significant areas of knowledge about which they are passionate, and better levels of pedagogical content knowledge, are most likely to contribute to their students' capacities to produce knowledge themselves.

The most recent of these debates concerns a series of reforms known generally as 'standards-based reforms'. In this set of reforms, there are included a range of activities, such as standards for teacher registration, standards for beginning teachers and probation, standards for giving advanced certification to recognise excellent teachers, and standards for promotion. Some of these 'standards' are based on demonstrating performance, often codified in the form of competencies. The Beginning Teacher Competencies, discussed in Chapter 3 on teachers' work, are of this kind (NPQTL 1996). Another set of standards are seen to apply to courses. These may apply to pre-service qualifications, in the form of proposals for national accreditation of teacher education programs, occurring already in some areas of the USA and under discussion in Australia (Adey 1998), or such standards as are applied to teacher qualification and professional development 'upgrades', for example in special education, or literacy teaching. A third approach uses standards to define what counts as an excellent teacher and proposes standards for advanced certification to support the ongoing learning of teachers. This approach is currently under discussion in Australia (Ingvarson 1999) and is already in place in the USA. In the early years of your own teaching career, it is highly likely that the place of standards-based reforms of this kind will be hotly contested.

Accountability, testing and assessment-based reforms

Changing the kinds of assessment and accountability used in schools has also been a favourite way to control the work that goes on there. The rationale seems to be that assessment — and testing regimes in particular — will give teachers and students the extra incentive to work harder, to aim higher and to work towards new approaches to curriculum that have been introduced. This is not to imply that the older approaches to assessment were good, merely that when new forms of assessment are introduced, they are usually part of a reform to shift what happens in schools. The motivation of reformers is not what is at stake here — on the whole, reformers are genuine in their commitment to improving schools. Rather, what is at stake is the assumption that the way to organise the desired change is through monitoring the results. It is assumed that if assessment changes the curriculum will also follow and students' achievement will rise. (Chapter 12, on new forms of assessment and reporting, can also be read with this assumption in mind!)

Similar assumptions seem to operate in relation to the introduction of new forms of accountability. The underlying idea that people will work differently — and harder — if someone is looking at them has at its core the fact that, for many students, schools are compulsory and it is unofficially presumed that students (and staff) might not be there if not for the compulsory aspect. Staff and students are seen to need incentives, and the negative incentive of accountability is seen as the best means to achieve that. Again, we are not arguing here that there is no purpose for accountability. Obviously, when schools are performing a public function for the society, there needs to be a means by which the rest of society can see the extent to which schools that function well are performing.

However, there are ways in which certain forms of reform through accountability can interfere with the operations of schools. Too much testing or public reporting can detract from the capacity of those in schools to do their core work appropriately. The crucial question that needs to be asked when any new form of accountability is proposed is: Will the new form of accountability or testing add to the capacity of teachers to teach, students to learn, or society to support schools to do their job better?

Reforms in school governance and management

In the last two decades, there has been an increased emphasis in state school systems around the Anglo-American world on policies of devolution, in which schools take on more management responsibilities. In many cases, this has meant local management of budgets as well as the development of educational policies that meet statewide guidelines but are also tailored to the local setting. Most schools will now have publicly audited statements of accounts, a strategic plan, a mission statement, school policy documents, and operational plans. Depending on their size and resources, the school may well have these published in a glossy format, but most will have documents of this kind associated with the principal's office, the school council and its sub-committees, and its educational committee. State and Catholic schools will have a regular form of school review to check on the progress of these documents, and to redesign future directions for the school.

For beginning teachers, the documentation of the school's goals and priorities, as well as its educational policies, can provide a useful induction process. It also orients the teacher new to the school to particular features of the school community and the pressures experienced by the school from broader contexts.

There are many different opinions about the effectiveness of the move towards greater levels of school-based management. For some, it brings state systemic schools more into line with practice in the private schools, and gives local flexibility in planning. For others, it means a large increase in workload focused on management but no real capacity to meet local needs because of the increased and standardised accountability requirements that also take time. For others still, moves to school-based management are a signal of greater democracy or community participation in schooling, while for others they signal a concern for management at the expense of educational issues. Some consider this a defacto privatisation of the public system, in a time of decreasing funding for schooling, whereas for others it is treated as a lessening in the dead hand of bureaucratic control and a freeing up of available resources.

The hope underpinning many of the reforms involving school-based management include a commitment to changing habits of schooling that have been systematised over a century and a half of public, mass schooling. The goal is to ensure there is enough local flexibility to maximise the use of resources and to build new practices that do not require a whole system to shift along with the school. There is probably some truth in all interpretations but, as with all shifts in power relations, there is likely to be continued contestation about the practices and effects of school governance and school-based management.

All the reforms outlined above can be said to have originated or been sponsored outside the school. There have also been numerous reforms that have emerged from the school-site. Sometimes these have been officially supported by education departments and recognise the importance of the local site in building new ideas. In the following sections the reforms associated with school-based curriculum development, community schools, school-based curriculum policy, teachers as researchers and democratic school partnerships are discussed briefly.

School-based curriculum development

School-based curriculum development (SBCD) remains in some forms throughout Australia. Since the demise of the centrally prescribed syllabus — during the 1960s and early 1970s, in most states and territories — schools have become an important site for the development of curriculum. The debates around this approach have been much stronger in Australia, the UK and the USA, for example, than in European traditions where the teacher is presumed to be the primary source of curriculum tailored for that teacher's students. The initial moves towards school-based curriculum development emerged from the massive expansion of secondary education in Australia, combined with a large influx of non-English speaking immigrants as part of the school population. Many schools with large populations of migrant students, alongside those with larger populations of working-class students staying on at school, found that their traditional approaches to curriculum would not work with their new students. Staff found they had to develop quite different content, teaching methods and assessment in order to meet the needs of their students.

During the 1970s, when there was a significant infrastructure of support for schools, many schools found themselves able to develop curriculum materials and syllabuses. However, many also suggested that there was not so much a 'school'-based curriculum but an individual teacher-based curriculum, open to the idiosyncrasies of individuals rather than being a whole-school effort. Others have also suggested that SBCD was only ever partially implemented in most states/territories and piecemeal in its development, making it easier for schools to be controlled from outside, while paying lip-service to local development (Prideaux 1993). Much of the work of schools in curriculum in recent years depends primarily on teachers being able to translate policy guidelines into curriculum approaches and daily planning. The question for all teachers is the extent to which this is really able to be achieved locally.

Community schools

There have been some very famous schools that stand out against the bulk of schools for their different approaches to students, curriculum and the purposes of schools. Some are associated more with their founder, like A.S. Neill's 'Summerhill', while others, such as the Montessori schools, have built a small alternative band of schools around the world that embody different assumptions about how children learn best.

During the 1970s in Australia, a number of school systems allowed the establishment of small, community-based schools. Some of these started with groups of students and their parents disaffected with the mainstream education approaches, and staffed by teachers who were interested in alternative forms of education. The alternative approaches to education varied according to the philosophy of the school, and might at any one time include more student choice in curriculum, the removal of age-cohorts as the basis of school organisation, better relations with communities, foregrounding community languages or more democratic relations among students and staff.

Many of these schools, however, disappeared for what seem to be two main reasons. The first is that as these schools became known in their community for caring relationships with students, students with a wide range of social, emotional and academic problems flocked to them. This tended to mean that the surrounding schools had a 'safety valve' for their unwanted or difficult students, so that the community school was treated as a problem 'dumping ground', while the mainstream school could continue with existing practices without having to adapt to a wide range of students. The influx of students into the small community schools — often only a hundred or less students — meant that these schools could not pursue their educational aims but had to spend more and more time working on intractable problems produced by other schools, and in liaison with welfare and social agencies. Their educational alternatives often became lost in the process, with a lessening of commitment by those involved to achieve those alternatives, especially staff.

The second main reason for the ending of the community-based schools is the downsizing of funding to schools. Smaller schools, under the strict financial reckoning forced by reductions in budgets, could not demonstrate efficiency and received less favourable treatment from the state/territory employing authorities in terms of staffing, buildings and policies. Some of the aspirations of these alternative schools may have been pursued by smaller private schools in recent years. However, the cost of running such small, community-based schools seems prohibitive to many parents. In addition, the current context of the competitive, market-driven focus on outcomes is not supportive of alternative educational approaches. Only a very few community-based or small-scale experimental education school settings continue to exist in Australia.

Partnerships among teachers, students and parents

While there has been much discussion of partnerships between schools and the community, interaction between schools and their communities has largely been on terms set by the state or by practices established for businesses. In most government school systems, there is a formal school board or council which advises or has responsibility for oversight of school funds and school policies. Private schools have similar bodies with formal responsibilities for school governance. In some schools, this board or council acts more like a board of directors of a company, whereas in others, it acts in an advisory role to the principal. In some schools and systems, parents have a major role in driving school policy, while in others there is more emphasis on managing the money and the school's image.

School councils and parents and citizens groups (P&C) have a long history in public education in Australia. In many instances, the council or P&C have taken a strong lead in raising funds for the school, often enabling it to stay open or to offer improved programs and facilities than would otherwise be the case. Yet their role does not have to be restricted only to fundraising. Many schools have had a strong and close relationship with their school community through the P&C. In many rural areas, the P&C provides continuity as young teachers come and move on through the school. Where the teachers rely on the parents as carriers of the community ethos, and reminder of past curriculum practices and achievements, the school is likely to continue to play an important role in building its community. Where, however, there is a 'stand-off' between the professionals and the community, with administration and teachers emphasising their expertise, there is less likely to be close relations with the parents through a P&C or school council. These organisations may well continue formally but the usual signs of poor relationships appear — difficulty in attracting office bearers, in-fighting and lack of open discussion or knowledge of what happens in the school. There is no real partnership, more a set of demarcation disputes.

School-based management seems to promise that local decision-making will involve all concerned. However, unless there is a real power sharing, and recognition of the different expertise brought to the table by all the players, then it is unlikely to make a difference to the school and its operations. A real partnership between teachers and parents, for example, would acknowledge that the parents are expert about their own children and about the community they come from. Parents also understand much about the reality of students' expectations of the future, their life and job aspirations and about the broader economic, political and social conditions in which the students are expected to operate. Teachers really need access to this knowledge if they are to work effectively with students, and to help make the school an important centre and resource for the community of students. Teachers' knowledge of curriculum, of their students from a perspective different to parental knowledge, and of content as well as the wider world, is also a resource for communities.

However, too often, even with good relations between teachers and parents, schools leave out a crucial partner in the educational process — the students themselves. In secondary schools, it is not enough for teachers and parents to act in the best interests of students, to act on their behalf. Part of the educational message that must emerge from secondary schools is the central role of the learner as a partner in education. Students, by the time of entry into secondary schools, are already socialised into the institution of schools. They also have basic skills in literacy and numeracy, even if some are seen as not quite skilful enough for secondary school purposes. However, the 'basics' have already been achieved in the primary years. The secondary years need to build on these achievements. Yet the role of students in the secondary years is often relegated to the sidelines.

If students were treated as real partners in their own education, they would need to participate in the discussions on evaluating the school, its policies and outcomes. They would also need to be actively engaged in major decision-making on curriculum, across the school and inside classrooms. Roger Holdsworth (1993) has pointed out for many years that real student participation in the school requires participation in school governance, in organising themselves as a student body and in classroom curriculum decision-making.

Pearl and Knight (1999) argue that the development of citizenship skills is a crucial dimension of schooling ignored far too often in favour of narrow approaches to work and skills. They include as necessary parts of citizenship a study of history and democratic citizenship, cooperative learning and problem-solving, a focus on important personal and social problems and development of citizenship through action and reflection. It is the last that is often forgotten. If there is to be real action and the capacity to reflect on action, then schools need to offer plenty of opportunities for students to experience democracy in action. This may take the form of an SRC, a support group for student representatives on the school council/board, regional or district student forums.

Changing relations of power in schools to explore real partnerships among teachers, parents and students is a major challenge for schools. It will require serious and long-term activity, with much of the onus on teachers to demonstrate they are serious about working with parents and students. Without such work, student alienation from schooling is likely to increase, especially in the high school years. Teachers also have to 'reconceptualise' curriculum if students are to take up their partnership role in schools.

School reform?

The discussion of school reform approaches suggests that there are no easy solutions to changing schools. Yet we are constantly surrounded by efforts to change schools, from governments, media, and employing authorities. In schools, too, the lived experience of schools keeps suggesting ways in which we might need to change schools to be more satisfactory workplaces for students and for teachers. The existence of these challenges to reform schools can provoke excitement among some but cynicism in others who have become weary of demands for change. There is plenty of evidence that most approaches to reform fail because they do not address the underlying relations between teachers and students and between schools and the society.

Fullan and Hargreaves (1992, p. 4) cite Pink's barriers to effective innovations in schools:

1.   an inadequate theory of implementation, including too little time for teachers to plan for and learn new skills and practices;

2.   district tendencies towards new skills and practices;

3.   lack of sustained central office support and follow-through;

4.   underfunding the project or trying to do too much with too little support;

5.   attempting to manage the projects from the central office instead of developing school leadership and capacity;

6.   lack of technical assistance and other forms of intensive staff development;

7.   lack of awareness of the limitation of school administrator knowledge about how to implement the project;

8.   the turnover of teachers in each school;

9.   too many competing demands or overload;

10. failure to address the incompatibility between project requirements and existing organisational policies and structures;

11. failure to understand and take into account site-specific differences among schools;

12. failure to clarify and negotiate role relationships and partnerships involving the district and the local university — which in each case had a role, albeit unclarified.

This list can be turned into a set of questions to act as a checklist a school can work through regarding whether a particular proposed reform is worth pursuing, or how it might be changed to be more likely to have an impact.

Documenting schooling: by whom and for what?

This chapter started with the observation that schools produce masses of information. Clearly, from the overview of school reform efforts discussed above, much more information is available about schools from the outside as well as inside them. The issue facing schools is what to do with all this information. Information alone, as the truism reminds us, does not make a difference. In this final section of the chapter, we work from the idea that focused evaluation, involving wide participation of the school's community, provides an important way to make sense of the school in its context and in its specific practices.

There are many misapprehensions about evaluation and many competing definitions and approaches to its practice. One simple definition is 'undertaking systematic learning in order to understand and improve the practices in a situation'. Too often, evaluation is seen as an event, occurring at the end of a process of implementation. However, evaluation does not have to be interpreted in this way. It is not necessarily for 'finding out' what is happening, nor does it merely provide 'information' for decisions. It is also possible to use evaluation as a tool to build a community that

works together, both to understand and to develop better ways to act in education —
that is, evaluation can also focus on improving the practice which is under investigation.
If the warnings about reform are to be taken seriously, then the importance of
participation in evaluation cannot be overstated.

People who work together to explore how a practice works, how effective it is, and
what else might be done, engage in important learning activities. Evaluation is thus a
way for the school community to learn about itself. It is thus important to ensure that
those who draw reflections or conclusions from evaluation are supported to make those
conclusions informed and worthwhile. As noted in Chapter 3, on teachers' work, this
won't then be undertaken lightly, as everyone is busy, we only evaluate those things we
really want to know. To think of evaluation as an integral part of the planning and
implementation of new initiatives is particularly helpful in situations when, as in the
case of social justice, there are no tried and true approaches that are already available for
a school to 'implement'. New approaches have to be tried out, not just re-hashes of old
recipes. In most cases, schools cannot afford to wait until the end of a long trial period
before discovering whether or not the changes they have implemented are worthwhile
or not. They need to keep adjusting the practices as they go. Ongoing evaluation makes
this process of constant adjustment possible.

Conclusion

Chapter 13, on documenting teachers' work, gave a number of practical examples of
how to organise data, questions to ask, and ways to manage a project, all of which apply
to evaluation that is community-based and action-oriented. Evaluation is a specific
form of research, usually one that is easily connected to action that could arise from the
questions being asked. A school might begin with questions about the social justice
implications of existing practices. Another might just begin to explore new curriculum
offerings to attract the students who find school unattractive. Another might explore
the future job aspirations of students and do a 'reality test' about possible destinations
from school. If students, teachers and parents cooperate about setting the agenda of
important questions for evaluation, then there is likely to be commitment to
participation in the processes of evaluation, and the outcomes of the evaluation are also
likely to be acted upon.

This version of action-oriented, community-based evaluation is also a way for the
school-community to make sense of those masses of information the school produces
and which surround the school. No single group or person can ever hope to 'get on top
of' this material. Evaluation activities that are connected to an action outcome help to
set the boundaries of what is needed in terms of information. Often, such evaluations
can be built into the school curriculum so that students receive credit for the work they
put in to the evaluation. This not only ensures that the debates are fruitful but also
provides real 'arms and legs' for the work of evaluation. The documentation of the
school and its context, or the documentation of the practices and effects of practices on
students and teachers, can thus become a key tool for reflection by those directly
engaged in the work of schools.

INQUIRY STRATEGIES

1. Interview a teacher who has been teaching for some years and discuss their experience with some of the reforms discussed here. Which did they personally experience? What is their view of their relative successes and failures?

2. Which reform movements to improve schools are currently popular among governments, teacher unions and in the schools in which you experience the practicum? In what ways do these appear to take on board the criticisms of reform? What are their assumptions about the problems of improving schools?

3. Which standards-based reforms are currently being discussed in the media or current teacher union/professional associations? How do you position yourself on these proposals?

4. What is your experience of or observation about participation in school governance? How is this similar to or different from current school system policies about governance and school-based decision-making? What skills might you need to acquire to participate better in school decision-making?

5. What areas of schooling in your most recently visited school seem most in need of local evaluation? How might this be best pursued?

References

Adey, K. (1998). *Preparing a Profession: Report of the National Standards and Guidelines for Initial Teacher Education Project.* O'Connor, ACT: Australian Council of Deans of Education.

Angus, L. (1993). Sociological analysis and educational management: The social context of the self-managing school. *British Journal of Sociology of Education* 15, 1, pp. 79–91.

Fullan, M. & Hargreaves, A. (1992). *Teacher Development and Educational Change.* London & New York: Falmer Press.

Holdsworth, R. (1993). Student participation: A decade of unfinished business. In David L. Smith (ed), *Australian Curriculum Reform: Action and Reaction*, pp. 87–96. ACT: Australian Curriculum Studies Association.

Ingvarson, L. (1999). The power of professional recognition. *Unicorn*, 25, 2, pp. 52–70.

Mortimore, P., Sammons, P., Ecob, R. & Stoll, L. (1988). *School Matters: The Junior Years.* Salisbury: Open Books.

National Project on the Quality of Teaching and Learning, (NPQTL) (1996). *National Competencies Framework for Beginning Teachers.* Leichhardt, NSW: Australian Teaching Council.

Pearl, A. & Knight, T. (1999). *The Democratic Classroom: Theory to Inform Practice.* New Jersey: Hampton Press.

Prideaux, D. (1993). School based curriculum development in the 1990s: Learning from the mistakes of the 1970s. In Alan Reid & Bruce Johnson (eds), *Critical issues in Australian Education in the 1990s.* Adelaide: Painters Prints.

Sarason, S. (1990). *The Predictable Failure of Education: Can we change course before it's too late?* San Francisco: Jossey-Bass.

Senate Education, Employment and Training Committee (1998). *A Class Act: Inquiry into the Status of the Teaching Profession.* Canberra: Australian Government Printing Service.

Slee, R., Weiner, G. with Tomlinson, S. (eds) (1998). *School Effectiveness for Whom? Challenges to the School Effectiveness and School Improvement Movements.* London: Falmer Press.

15
CHAPTER

The Full Service School

Teachers often complain that they can't do their work because the students are not 'ready' to learn, as if there is a clear demarcation about what counts as 'teaching' and what counts as 'welfare'. This chapter makes that divide somewhat more problematic than a demarcation dispute between different professionals. It works from the assumption that students are whole people who cannot necessarily devote themselves to study when other areas of their lives or selves are in disarray. There is no nice, neat dividing line between the 'student' part of a person and the other parts; teachers do have to teach 'whole people', not just subject matter. As the Disadvantaged Schools Program showed from the early 1970s (Connell, White and Johnston 1991), schools which work *with* communities offer a stronger chance of making a difference educationally to students than those which concentrate only on teaching or where there are beliefs that many students cannot really learn. It is in the context of making an educational difference that the challenges of working with other professionals and local communities are explored in this chapter on 'full service schools'.

The 'full service school' (FSS) is a concept that has received significant practical attention in the USA (Dryfoos 1994) and recently in Australia where a number of pilot schemes have been put into place. The Federal Government has followed these pilots with interest, and has made available special funding for full service school projects associated with students at risk for the triennium 1998–2000, as part of changes to its youth policies, especially to youth allowances (see http://www.detya.gov.au). In practice, there are several models of full service schools and communities but most share the idea that schools can be a centre for the development of community and also remain the logical site for linking services needed by students and their families. The idea raises questions that teachers have long debated, particularly the relative emphasis on 'welfare' and curriculum in teachers' work. It also brings to the fore questions of the relations among different groups of professionals, each of which defines the 'problem' differently, but who might, together, work with students and their families to address people and their issues holistically. This chapter will outline different approaches to cross-agency cooperation in the human services, around schools and their communities, and give examples of Australian cases where such initiatives have occurred. It also returns to issues explored earlier in the book by considering the clash of different professions, and the demographics of different communities for whom 'full service schools' might be the best option for achieving coordinated service from agencies, including schools. Young people can be seen as active participants in their own lives, including education and other services. The full service school can provide opportunities for the enactment of young people's citizenship in the design of their own services. Perhaps this might be the way schools in the future look?

Why would 'full service schools' arise?

Full service schools have arisen for several reasons. First, where schools and their communities are faced with long-term, structural problems such as unemployment, poverty, ill health, and/or drug cultures, young people often face intractable problems which have lifelong consequences. The problems are complex and cannot be addressed by a single agency working in isolation, such as a school. Schools do not have the expertise or resources to properly work with some of the inter-linked issues that need to be addressed. Second, the idea of full service schools arose at a time when fiscal constraints on government funding meant that many services were downsized or dismantled, leaving an acute shortage of professionals to provide a range of human services. Thus 'full service schools' is a way to make maximum use of whatever services are available. Third, where community problems are complex and services in poor supply, many young people face a set of issues that may get in the way of their schooling. Since school is compulsory and the institutions of schools already exist in most areas, the school appears as a logical focus for coordinating the development and delivery of a wide range of services for young people and their communities. Some even prefer to talk about the term 'full service community', where all services are integrated and organised according to forms of community development (ACEE 1996).

The Federal Government's FSS program identified a number of what they have termed 'risk factors' for young people in not completing school to Year 12. In an advertisement for a tender to evaluate the program, these were identified as (DETYA: http://www.detya.gov.au, 1999):

- lack of school 'connectedness';
- involvement in drug and alcohol usage;
- disability/mental illness;
- involvement in violence, offending, early school leaving, truancy and challenging behaviours;
- being indigenous or from non-English speaking background;
- lack of resilience;
- suicidal ideations;
- coming from long-term unemployed families;
- social and geographical isolation;
- teenage parenthood; or
- are members of a family where these risk indicators are present.

Pat Thompson (1999) asks 'What is the problem for which this program (FSS) is the answer?' She sees the problem as lying in the education sector's enmeshment in what she calls a 'rhetoric of risk'. Schools have been caught up in labelling students — at risk — and even most of our concerns about equity among students help to frame the problem. She argues that failing to follow a holistic path will produce solutions that ultimately fail those very students we intend to assist. The Australian Centre for Equity through Education, which has taken a leading role in promoting the concept of full service schools and communities, argues that FSS provides a means for assisting those students who have been systematically marginalised in the social, economic and educational arenas to break the cycle of poverty, poor educational achievement and social disempowerment (Mukherjee 1997). Thompson and Mukherjee give priority to those students who have been systematically failed by the schools that were established to help them learn. These schools, often treated as 'ghetto' schools, are in need of the range of services that can address the interlinked problems experienced in their communities, of which education is only one. The schools, health services and community welfare groups all demonstrate that a single service cannot address the problem singly — thus giving rise to the concept of and the practice of the FSS. However, both Thompson and the ACEE see that FSS will only work where there is local community and student participation in arranging which services will be linked in and how they will be organised.

Bob Connell (1986 in Connell et al. 1991, pp. 281–5) some years ago discussed five aspects of poverty needed to understand how education is deeply implicated in any attempt to redress long-term effects. These include:

- low income;
- economic dependence (especially vulnerability to unforeseen crises, even where waged);
- exclusion from social resources (collective assets of a city, for example);
- damaging environments (for example, housing situated near polluted areas); and
- cultural marginalisation.

What poverty most obviously means to a school is that the community is unlikely to be able to resource its school well. In the current climate, with school-based management, local fundraising is both important and necessary even to the running of a school. Yet the other dimensions of poverty may be more insidious. Poverty is usually associated with poor health, insecure access to housing, and young people are often needed to work as a contribution to the family's resources. Of particular interest in this chapter is the lack of access or networking with professionals needed in times of crisis. Most professionals (including teachers) do not live in the communities that serve the poorest schools. Thus, even their informal knowledge is not easily accessible; nor is there enough first-hand knowledge by professionals of the conditions of daily life of the people they are there to serve. Often the service itself is under-funded and can target only a part of what it sees needing to be done.

Where a student attends a school in a poor area then, in comparison with students with better resources and a history of health in the community, they are less likely to use their share of public educational resources. In addition, a student who does not complete Year 11 and 12, for example, or go to university or TAFE, is 'giving' their share of these areas of most expensive education to others who are already more advantaged in terms of health, employment opportunities, economic safety nets and access to education. Poor people actually use a lot less educational resources than those already better off. In rural areas, lack of access to services such as education, health or counselling, and to employment prospects has led the Human Rights and Equal Opportunity Commission (HREOC) to explore these issues on behalf of young people through considering them a question of basic human rights.

Full service schools have tended to develop in areas where problems are significant: this gives a sense of urgency and commonality of purpose, providing that added impetus to many different groups to join together to organise in alternative ways. This does not mean, however, that FSS ought to be restricted only to areas where problems are already serious. As we have noted elsewhere in the book, adolescent alienation is a significant issue for students from all backgrounds, and schools are in need of significant reworking to become intrinsically worthwhile for all associated with them. Perhaps FSS will provide one of the key directions for future school and community reform.

Full service schools: examples

There is no single model of a FSS. There are even many different terms that are used when the idea of 'full service schools' is discussed. Other terms people might use include: health promoting schools, healthy cities, integrated support services, co-located services, school-linked services, school-based services for youth, child-serving institutions and inter-agency support services, among others. Schools and communities have often initiated the move towards some form of community-led, linked services in Australia, although elsewhere, such as in the USA, the health sector has often had a leading role in developing the new ideas and practices. Since school communities look very different, we would expect to see really obvious differences among the versions of FSS that operate in different settings.

In giving a small range of examples of full service schools, it is important to recognise that these represent only a small sample of what has been seen as possible and desirable to the present time. Many other initiatives are underway, exploring new kinds of relationships, new practices and new roles for young people and their communities. That is partly what the 'movement' towards FSS aims to develop: local responses that fit local issues. Lori Beckett (1997) sees the commonality among the projects as 'a concern to address our children's and adolescents' real lived experience', and Kirner (1996) points to a philosophy of equity underpinning FSS initiatives, particularly the interest in linking economic and social goals for both government and for community action.

Indigenous student projects

The 1994 National Review of Education for Aboriginal and Torres Strait Islander Peoples argued that Aboriginal peoples and Torres Strait Islanders continue to be the most educationally disadvantaged groups in Australia. They drop out of secondary school at a much earlier age than non-indigenous students and therefore only a small percentage of indigenous students begin tertiary studies or further training. As a result, they do not have access to their percentage of resources spent on higher levels of education, nor to the economic and cultural benefits that accrue from participation in further education and training. While the causes of this low participation are many, formal and informal suspensions, exclusions and expulsions may explain at least some of the low rates of retention to Years 10, 11 and 12 of young Aboriginal and Torres Strait Islander students. What is particularly of concern to those in indigenous communities is the link between low participation in school and participation in the juvenile justice system, often with dire consequences.

There are a number of FSS projects specifically directed towards Aboriginal and Torres Strait Islander students. The *Keeping our Kids at School* Project was developed by a collaborative partnership between the National Aboriginal Youth Law Centre, the National Children's and Youth Law Centre with the Australian Centre for Equity through Education (ACEE). This project set out to document the often hidden and informal suspensions, absenteeism and rates of real participation in schools. They also developed case studies of school practices that appear to contribute to the over-representation of Aboriginal and Torres Strait Islander students in suspension, exclusion and non-participation figures. Without such documentation, it becomes difficult to understand how services, including schools, contribute to the problem. In addition it is important to be able to take knowledge about how services work together in specific areas to see if they work in other regions (ACEE 1996).

A metropolitan example of an Indigenous Australian FSS project comes from Redfern in Sydney. There, school and community leaders got together and pointed to a need for safe and regular transport to school for their children. A local community bus service was organised to call at designated places around the suburb, supporting attendance of students and thus encouraging school participation, as a necessary prerequisite for achievement.

Another metropolitan Indigenous Australian FSS initiative occurred in Melbourne, where the East Preston Area Pilot is located at Northland Secondary College, which has the highest secondary enrolment of Koorie students in Victoria. Many of the students also had a history of interrupted schooling, juvenile justice problems and homelessness. Activities undertaken as part of the project include:

- individual counselling and family support;
- curriculum development;
- a breakfast program;
- a recreation program;
- community projects, including the development of a code of practice about student use of the local shopping centre, negotiated with security guards;
- local agencies' network for student referrals and documentation; and
- a student housing submission so Year 11 and 12 students who are homeless have a place to live that is administered by the school.

Davies and Peut in their report of the project in 1996 discussed the importance of close links between school personnel and the project, with a mix of activities including academic redirection, a whole-school approach to student welfare and flexibility in timetabling, supported by teams of teachers working with the same group of students. Koorie community members worked closely with and in the school so that the young people had a range of support people and could not 'fall between the cracks', unseen until too late. The mix of academic and community welfare, decided upon by those affected, has been much more effective than school or community initiatives alone in keeping students at school, addressing social and economic issues and reducing the effects of homelessness.

Homeless students

In 1994 MacKenzie and Chamberlain conducted a week-long census of homeless young people showing a total of known homeless secondary school students of 11 000, with an estimate of 25 000 to 30 000 secondary students experiencing homelessness sometime during a school year (MacKenzie & Chamberlain 1995). They found that 61 per cent of schools had homeless students during census week and the majority of schools had homeless students at some stage during the year. For many young people, becoming homeless means they can no longer attend school, an almost certain indicator of poor long-term economic and personal life chances. A number of schools, under a number of different programs including School to Work Transition, Students at Risk and more recently FSS, have made support programs for homeless students a priority, breaking that cycle at an early stage, rather than waiting for students to become part of a culture of homelessness.

Schools that try to support homeless students need to link a number of agencies for financial, physical, health, social and peer forms of support. Sometimes the problems homeless students want dealt with are very basic and practical. Somewhere to shower, to store clothes and school equipment, and access to uniforms or other required equipment are often high on the list. Many of these very basic level needs can be provided by a careful school without infringing privacy or confidentiality, or involving anyone other than the students themselves. Others require assistance to deal with substance abuse, personal safety and places to live. In several FSS programs, schools have helped with submissions for community-based housing, food and clothing support, while acting as a referral centre for other services.

Rural youth

Many studies of young people in the bush identify factors that affect their participation in society. Lack of access to transport precludes many young people from access to education and further training as well as from jobs, part-time work or socialising outside the family. This often means that rural young people, unlike some of their metropolitan counterparts, are unable to participate in part-time paid work when at school, an opportunity which many regret is unavailable. This lack of access to opportunities also means that there is less income individually and in the family. The consequences of low cash flow and transport is heavily compounded by loss of services or inadequate services. Often, a young person finds a service and the agency changes its name or the staff member relocates or the service is restructured. This lack of continuity is a problem identified in the HREOC (Human Rights and Equal Opportunity Commission) inquiry into educational access in rural areas.

Health, welfare and education are often good partners in regional and rural settings to coordinate the services for young people. The Roma Interagency team project explores the possibilities of providing integrated support to young people who are at risk in their regular learning environments. They want to maximise the links between agencies, and avoid duplication of services while gaps remain in other areas. The team of different agencies focused on middle school years in particular. A different kind of project occurred in Wide Bay, Queensland, an area with one of the highest rates of unemployment and low socioeconomic resources in Australia. There a project was established to enhance and extend the operation of their Child and Adolescent Management Forum that worked with membership from a number of agencies and the northern schools of the region.

In such programs, students and their families are able to have coordinated access to whatever services there are. Where services do not exist, there is a place to document the need and to lobby government and other agencies for their provision. Funding groups are much more likely to provide further services in places where projects not only have demonstrated need, but also an existing infrastructure to supervise the initiation of new or extended services.

Anti-bullying programs

There is a growing level of agreement that one-to-one behaviour management and counselling programs do not address the underlying problems of powerlessness and lack of purpose for many students, around which much conflict arises in the school setting and elsewhere. In anti-bullying programs, there has been a strong emphasis on developing an institution-wide process for dealing with issues as a whole-school community with responsibility to and for one another. Anti-bullying programs usually provide a level of training for young people as mediators and for all students in ways of dealing with feelings of inadequacy, fear, anger and confusion that do not result in physical or emotional abuse. Variations of anti-bullying programs include peace promotion, peer mediation for young people, and conflict resolution training. Often such programs bring together teachers, church groups, counsellors, youth workers and community leaders.

The anti-bullying programs often allow students themselves to be part of the solution to their problems. They also focus on issues of power and provide a model for how small groups in communities can introduce small-scale projects, which can escalate into broader forms of community participation. The presence of bullying is often used as an indicator of organisational and community health, appearing in a school which might otherwise treat its presence only in terms of 'behaviour management'. By naming bullying in its range of forms, conflict can be dealt with constructively, and in ways that pay due attention to the inter-linked problems that can give rise to it. Students learn a range of personal and group strategies and build the health of the school as a community to deal with conflict, spilling over into curriculum and student participation in school governance.

Young children at risk: the FAST program

The FAST program stands for Families And Schools Together (McDonald et al. 1997). It starts from the assumption that early intervention involving a range of agencies working in collaboration with families is a good way to avoid students who show up as 'at risk' at school. A 'FAST Collaborative Team' includes among its ten members a family representative (often from a previous program), the school, a family support agency and a drug and alcohol agency and other volunteer groups. The program targets children 4–9 years old and their families and works through a regular set of meetings where families talk with and listen to one another. There are weekly multiple family meetings run at the school, facilitated by the team, and parent-run follow-up meetings for two years. Participation is voluntary. The program draws on research in family development, substance abuse, school–home cooperation, and community development. There are incentives such as transport, a meal, childcare, and adult company. In coaching the parents to assist their children, FAST organises structured activities focusing on families working together, including family meals, children's activities, special play, and special sessions. They focus on building resilience in family members and positive relationships, rather than labelling families as dysfunctional.

The impact on participating families and their children is closely monitored and evaluated using statistically significant instruments. Parents and teachers report significant increases in student achievement and decreases in behavioural problems. What is also important for the longer-term improvement is that there is usually stronger parental involvement in schooling, with 86 per cent of parents liking the FAST program (Sayger and McDonald 1999). The collaboration between the school, families and other agencies is the key feature of this program. If family functioning is supported, this reduces stress for all involved. As the program acts as a support network for each family for up to two years, this program focuses not on providing services but on enabling the parent to be empowered to strengthen their own support for their children. The longer-term evaluations suggest that parents themselves benefit, not only children. By working early to prevent educational failure, and by working collaboratively with families, the parents themselves and the agencies learn to work together in a supportive way. A number of schools across Australia have already found that the benefits contribute to a cooperative school and community, with educational benefits for the children.

Issues in considering the challenge of FSS

In the sections which follow, a number of key issues are addressed, which both support the directions of many of the examples given above of FSS in operation and pose a number of challenges that will be experienced in practical and ethical terms if FSS initiatives are put into place. There are clear issues of whether students, in vulnerable positions in a compulsory institution such as the school, will have any control over their use of or range of services operating. There are similarly issues of expertise and how different professionals might work together. There are also questions about whether indeed the political will might exist to ensure coordination of services rather than giving in to demarcation disputes across existing services. Dryfoos (1996) noted a number of developments but also key barriers that have been experienced where schools and communities attempt to link services. These include funding, governance, controversy and 'turf wars', especially over using school buildings for other purposes, and the problem if there are poor levels of continuity of personnel. In the following sections, we provide some discussion starters to consider issues that arise if and when attempts are made to put full service schools and communities into practice.

Professional demarcation disputes?

Professional groups are trained to define problems from a single perspective. Thus what may appear to a teacher as a learning problem might appear to a social worker as a family dysfunction, or to a community worker as a matter of racism, or to a police officer as a criminal possibility. Many initiatives that attempt to bring together different agencies often get caught up in how each defines the problem. Quite often funding is tied to each definition, and solutions are seen as agency-specific, rather than involving other agencies. Indeed, integrated or linked services often have trouble in being adequately accountable to each of the contributing agencies' head offices, as data are collected differently by each.

Marquart and Konrad (1996) found many examples of this kind of problem in their evaluations of FSS and linked services in the USA. They pointed out the need to clarify a number of dimensions around which services could be linked and around which decisions could be made about the level and kind of integration desired to occur. They suggest that partners, stakeholders, target populations, goals, program policy and legislation, governance and authority, service delivery system models, planning and budgeting, financing, outcomes and accountability, licensing and contracting, and information systems and data management are all areas around which services might be integrated. The level of integration they saw was on a continuum from information sharing and communication, through cooperation and coordination, through to collaboration, consolidation and full integration. The intensity of the integration tends to bring out more problems but may have a stronger effect for the recipients of the services.

However, one of the problems that tends to occur under such conditions is that the professionals spend a lot of time fighting amongst themselves. The people who have least influence on what happens are those whom the services are supposed to benefit. Susan Robertson and Quentin Beresford discuss problems in coordination of youth affairs in terms of a 'politics of non-decision-making' (1996, p. 23). Their study of coordination in Western Australia considered the tensions between different levels and agencies that stopped effective coordination of services from occurring. They argued that their evidence suggested that (p. 23) 'in an era of restricted resources and heightened competition within the public sector, agencies are pushed to more clearly define their boundaries'.

Many teachers simply have not got the time away from their classrooms and schools to engage in this kind of turf warfare. The accountability pressures on schools and the pressures of working with large numbers of students every day are such that teachers need to define their work tightly. Yet, where students who are least provided for in schools are not really included in the outcomes of schooling, there has been occasion for teachers and community members to work to redefine boundaries with other agencies. If there is a chance to work together for the improvement of students' life chances, then many teachers will take up the challenge of FSS. Many of the examples of FSS projects have shown there to be improvements not only in health and welfare outcomes but also in school achievement levels. The inter-dependence of issues thus becomes more clearly a rationale for the work associated with FSS. The funding made available through cooperation can clearly benefit students and their families.

Range of outcomes

The question of the extent to which student outcomes are improved is critical for the long-term survival of initiatives that favour the linking of services. Muirhead (1996), in his overview of the Queensland Interagency Teams Project, suggests that there are a series of inter-linked outcomes that ought to emerge from full-service schools and similar initiatives that are posited on cooperative service. These outcomes are for students, families, service providers, communities, schools and agencies. The student outcomes he looks for require service operation so that (p. 99):

- students are stabilised during their schooling and are able to maintain attendance;
- enable more effective teaching and learning;
- proactive steps [are taken] to help prevent and solve major issues;
- [there is] unrestricted eligibility of young people to all services;
- each young person has access to a wider variety of support personnel rather than the guidance officer or liaison officer;
- [there is] a wide array of prevention, treatment and support services that are comprehensive in scope;
- [there is a] comprehensive service system that ensures that children, young people and families actually receive services they need (e.g. a single point of contact characterised by a structure for case management and service collaboration).

Such efforts in inter-agency work to ensure student and school outcomes that are supportive and enable learning outcomes to occur in a broad context of life support. Unless there is the linking of outcomes in educational terms as well as community, health and welfare terms, then most schools will not be able to justify their participation. However, early evaluations of outcomes from projects involving schools seem to suggest that there is sufficient inter-linking of outcomes to make it worthwhile. (Evaluations of the FSS program funded by DETYA (Department of Education, Training and Youth Affairs) are still underway at the time of writing. The Australian Centre for Equity through Education is conducting major evaluations for DETYA and should be able to provide documentation and resources for further consideration of these issues.)

'Us' and 'them'

Another set of problems for the challenge posed by the existence of full service school initiatives comes out of the need to change relationships between schools and their communities. Pat Thompson reminds us that (1996, p. 32):

> Most people do not want to be labelled; to be a 'them' for whom 'we' will provide. They resent being described as 'the other' by well-meaning service providers, and 'framed' as deficient, inferior or inadequate.

As a response to these framings, Thompson has developed a checklist of questions (pp. 32–3) to ask in schools moving to include other services. These are set out below.

Words

How is our additional service described in the school literature, in the stories we tell in the staffroom, in the official reports we write, in the conference papers we deliver? Can these be summarised as creating 'otherness'? How many of these words stick to the people who use the service?

Confidentiality

How public is the use of the service? Are people made visible in waiting rooms or on lists in offices and staffrooms?

Is there any consequence for individuals or families after using the service? Is it positive or negative?

What is the difference between sharing essential information about a student or family and invasion of privacy? Is this an implicit or explicit policy? Who has made this policy and in whose interests is it?

Support versus control

Are we assisting people to make decisions for themselves? Or are we telling them what to do — control through advice?

Do we operate a double standard and refuse to acknowledge that the people with whom we are working can make choices and mistakes, just as we do?

Do we use disapproval, threats of withdrawal of support?

Is this institutionalised into policy or financial audit procedures?

Getting off

Are we creating a dependency model, where our rationale for being or for continued employment is dependent on people continuing to need us?

Do we revel in horror stories and discussions about the 'victims' . . . [you should have seen the one I saw yesterday] . . .

Do we want to take people home [and keep them as 'pets']?

Do we stop doing our jobs because we believe we can't do them 'until something is done'?

Power

Are we a charity or are we interested in empowering, getting people to take charge of their own lives?

Do we ask ourselves who has the problem? For example, do we ask 'if this was our problem what would it be? If this was a learning problem, what would it be?'

Who decided this service was necessary?

What are our links with the community? What is our involvement in community programs and plans? How does this service link with others?

Whose vision of the future is being enacted?

Who is the public for our public service and how are we accountable to them?

Do we have structures to get feedback and do we actively seek it out?

Do we make sure that people have access and understand relevant information they need in order to take charge of their own situation — both individually and collectively?

Do we assist people to analyse and generalise about their situation?

Do we structure management committees so recipients of services can not only attend but make real decisions using real money?

Are the service recipients part of the problem or the solution?

Are we committed to doing ourselves out of a job and so we have a plan to make this happen?

Will this service make a difference? What?

How else could this be achieved?

Who else could or should do it?

If someone else should, how can I make it happen?

These questions are very confronting, especially for groups such as teachers, health workers, community and welfare workers who see so much despair and cynicism, yet continue to want to make some difference to the communities they serve. Yet they are really important questions, especially for a service such as a school. Whose interests do we really serve? Are the practices organised for schools amenable to flexible response to local community initiatives?

The questions remind us of the significant investments that most of us make in our own jobs, but force us to question the extent to which our ethic of service is really serving the interests of those we espouse to serve. These are important ethical, political and cultural questions. There is no necessarily 'right/wrong' answer to them, but their underlying assumptions have certain features in common.

Community and student empowerment

Among most of the FSS-type initiatives, there is usually a strong commitment to community empowerment, to ensure that programs meet their identified needs and to ensure there is a growth of skills and networks in the community itself, not located only among the professional service providers. Part of Pat Thompson's challenging questions is the matter of real control of services. The expert-driven model, which assumed that one or other group of experts would make decisions on behalf of the communities they served, has been shown to be patronising of its participants and inadequate in long-term solutions. Thompson, in another paper (1999), argues that the answers to the questions she raised above lie in developing other versions of what might count as a good society.

Many projects under the banner of FSS tend to blame either the children or their parents for their lack of capacity to make a difference. Sometimes the deficit view of the community is strong enough to get in the way of being able to take parents and students as serious partners in the reform of schools.

Paul Heckman, an educator from Arizona in the USA, has taken a very different view of the need for cooperation if any solution to the problem is to be long-term. What are the conditions in schools for ideas and practices to change? In his view, unless parents and students are directly involved then the changes will only be cosmetic. He argues that (1996, p. 5), 'all families, irrespective of their economic well-being have powerful knowledge and resources inside them. They do not have deficits, even though they may be economically poor'. He continues with the view that 'if someone does something for another person, they are undermining that person's capacity to act on their own behalf and to use the knowledge and resources they have'. Through a process of weekly dialogue sessions, teachers, students and their parents together invent practices and activities to develop and build on knowledge and skills in their local area. After school care programs for Native Americans in one school community are now built on traditional indigenous knowledge and histories (Heckman and Peacock 1995, p. 46). In another project, students on neighbourhood walks with their teachers noted the number of vacant lots and rubbish on those lots. This became the focus for a community clean-up based on student research, with parents cooperating with the teachers to take the matter to local government authorities.

Students are often the last group to be allowed to participate in deciding the services they need and how they are to be accessed. Well-meaning parents, teachers and other professionals, according to some students, might well be seen as 'ganging up' on them to fit a mould decided already.

Lori Beckett in her keynote address to the 1997 FSS conference run by the ACEE, argued that schools need to 'engage [with] social issues and give students the experience of working on them through the experiences of critical reflection, social negotiation, and the organisation of action'. Such an approach to FSS makes central the role students themselves take up in understanding the social context in which they live. For this to work, FSS can be integrated into the curriculum. Secondary students in particular are well positioned to be able to explore their community and themselves. As a focus for school and curriculum development, FSS provides a practical focus for understanding governance issues — indeed for addressing most of the barriers to inter-agency cooperation raised by Marquart and Konrad above. A critical study of local services can be linked to integrated curriculum that might include all key learning areas.

Conclusion

It is hard to move outside the traditional role for schools and teachers. Yet it is precisely that move which FSS invites teachers to make. There are already plenty of indicators that schools in their current embodiment are not able to do their job adequately. FSS suggests that, with greater cooperation across agencies, and with the active participation of students and their families, educational outcomes can be improved and student life chances in the longer term also improved. It may thus be worth the effort to explore such options rather than giving in to the cynical and deficit view that nothing can really change. It is still too early to tell whether full service schools and communities make enough of a difference by themselves, or whether additional reform efforts will be needed. However, in an evolving field, the options are important to explore and contribute to the reinvention of school–community practices. Beginning teachers who do not come with the full paraphernalia of socialisation into what is expected of teachers and schools may thus play an important role in this reinvention.

INQUIRY STRATEGIES

1. Taking Thompson's checklist of questions for schools contemplating new and/or linked services, answer the questions in relation to the school structure itself at a school where you have been either as student or as student teacher or perhaps as parent.

2. In two different schools you are familiar with, compare and contrast the ways in which poverty and educational advantage and disadvantage are seen in the school.

3. What problems can you envisage would face a homeless student in successful participation at school? What changes would a school need to make in order to support homeless students?

4. Compare the rationales offered by Heckman's approach to school community participation and that offered by the FAST program. How do they take similar and different stances on the role of families?

5. Students' roles in understanding their own needs and those of their community can place teachers in a difficult ethical position. What issues can you envisage coming up for a new teacher when opening up discussion on these? How might you safeguard both the students and yourself in such a setting?

References

ACEE (Australian Centre for Equity through Education) (1996). Full service schools. *Equity Network*, vol 2, no 2, May, p. 1 (ISSN 1323-9767).

ACEE (Australian Centre for Equity through Education) (1999). http://www.ozemail.com.au:80/~

Beckett, L. (1997). Full service schools in Australia. Keynote address. *Making It Work: The Next Steps.* Sydney: ACEE.

Chamberlain, C. & MacKenzie, D. (1998). *Youth Homelessness: Early Intervention and Prevention.* Leichhardt, Sydney: ACEE.

Connell, R.W., White, V. & Johnston, K.M. (eds) (1991). *'Running Twice as Hard': The Disadvantaged Schools Program in Australia.* Geelong: Deakin University.

Davies, F. & Peut, A. (1996). Schools as a site for early intervention, school-based young homeless pilots. In Australian Centre for Equity through Education, *School and Community action for Full Service Schools: Making it Work. The views of education, health, and community service practitioners presented at a national conference on full service schools.* Sydney: ACEE.

Department of Education, Training and Youth Affairs (2000). Full service schools for students at risk. Web site: http://www.detya.gov.au

Dryfoos, J. (1994). *Full Service Schools: A revolution in health and social service for children, youth and families.* San Francisco: Jossey Bass.

Dryfoos, J.G. (1996). Full-service schools. *Educational Leadership*, 53, 7, p. 18.

Heckman, P. (1996).Connecting schools and communities through educational reinvention. In Australian Centre for Equity through Education, *School and Community action for Full Service Schools: Making it Work.* The views of education, health, and community service practitioners presented at a national conference on full service schools. Sydney: ACEE.

Heckman, P. & Peacock, J. (1995). Joining schools and families in community change: a context for student learning and development. *New Schools, New Communities.* 12, 1 (Fall) pp. 46–51.

Kirner, J. (1996). A turning point conference. In Australian Centre for Equity through Education, *School and Community action for Full Service Schools: Making it Work. The views of education, health, and community service practitioners presented at a national conference on full service schools.* Sydney: ACEE.

MacKenzie, D. & Chamberlain, C. (1995). The national census of homeless school students. *Youth Studies Australia*, 14, 1, pp. 22–28.

Marquart, J.M. & Konrad, E. (eds) (1996). *Evaluating Initiatives to Integrate Human Services.* American Education Association. San Francisco: Jossey-Bass.

McDonald, L., Billingham, S. Conrad, T., Morgan, A. Payton, N. & Payton, E. (1997). Families and schools together (FAST): integrating community development with clinical strategies. *Families in Society: The Journal of Contemporary Human Services.* (March-April) pp. 140–155.

Muirhead, B. (1996). State and Local Interagency Work in Queensland. In Australian Centre for Equity through Education, *School and Community action for Full Service Schools: Making it Work. The views of education, health, and community service practitioners presented at a national conference on full service schools.* Sydney: ACEE.

Mukherjee, D. (1997). Full service schools: linking schools and communities. Paper presented at the annual conference of the Australian Association for Research in Education. Brisbane, December.

Robertson, S. & Beresford, Q. (1996). Coordination in youth affairs: the politics of non-decision-making. *Australian Journal of Public Administration 55,* (March) 1, pp. 23–32.

Sayger, T.V. & McDonald, L. (1999). Evaluation for Australian FAST schools. Report #3, Melbourne: FAST International Inc.

Thompson, P. (1996). An education perspective: cooperation, coordination and collaboration . . . but for what? In Australian Centre for Equity through Education, *School and Community action for Full Service Schools: Making it Work. The views of education, health, and community service practitioners presented at a national conference on full service schools.* Sydney: ACEE.

Thompson, P. (1999). *Against the Odds: Developing school programmes that make a difference for students and families in communities placed at risk.* Sydney: ACEE.

Ethical Accountability

CHAPTER *16*   Ethics and Responsibilities in the Education Profession

Τhis final section in the book has one chapter. But it is by no means a postscript. We are asking you to consider very carefully what it is to be a responsible member of the teaching profession. We argue that teaching is first and foremost a moral activity which carries a range of accountabilities: accountability to self and the profession; accountability to our students; accountability to their parents; and, accountability to the wider community and society.

Those choosing to become teachers need to be aware that ethical dimensions attach to every aspect of teachers' work. The basic rubric of professional ethics is to minimise harm. We need to be aware that our actions should not damage those we teach or those who are around us.

In this final chapter we offer the example of the code of ethics which has been published by early childhood educators and ask you how this code might relate to practice in our secondary schools and colleges.

Teaching is a public activity whose purpose is not only to enhance the life chances of our individual students, but also to make a contribution to the wider society. We congratulate you upon having chosen to become a teacher, one of our society's most demanding and satisfying professions.

PART SIX

16
CHAPTER

Ethics and Responsibilities in the Education Profession

Being a teacher is not a private occupation. Rather, as the Senate Inquiry into the Status of the Teaching Profession noted in 1998, teachers' work operates under the glare of the public spotlight, often in ways that bear little relation to the daily work of teachers. During pre-service education, it might sometimes appear that becoming a member of the profession is mainly a matter of passing the subjects and the practicum experience in schools. The qualification, once attained, is the pathway to the profession. While this certainly has some truth to it, there are other, perhaps more subtle, ways in which teachers become members of their profession. And, since the work continues to change, there is never a fixed, static group with whom one 'belongs': the profession changes, and so do we as individuals. In this chapter, we begin to bring together some of the themes of the book, particularly the wide range of activities which go into the work of the teacher. They are discussed first in terms of ethical issues at stake in being a teacher, followed by discussions about the broad responsibilities of teaching, highlighting some of the ethical dimensions involved in this wide and disparate range of tasks and skills required.

Ethics and teaching

Most of us are accustomed to being responsible for ourselves, for making decisions and choices, and living with the consequences. We know ourselves, at least in part, by the kinds of values and ethical stances we take on a particular issue. Yet when it comes to teaching, the ethics of the situation are not just a private matter. This is a common issue in the so-called 'human services' — those areas of work which are primarily people-oriented. It is not quite enough to 'be a good person' to be a good teacher. Rather the scope of our ethics have to be more than just personal, encompassing something of the collegiality of working with others. As teachers we act on behalf of our society, working in an institution which is perhaps the only common societal institution most people know. Our ethics in this arena cannot only be a matter of private 'choice' because our work so strongly effects the lives of other people.

Ethical matters are in the public eye, and have been for over a decade now. Witness the recent John Laws/Alan Jones debacle about conflict of interest and the assumption that 'truths' should be told in the media without even the perception of the influence of money. Witness the disgust at the 1980s entrepreneurs who invested money in takeovers and asset-stripped companies to make profits, wrecking many companies and jobs in the process. Witness the Queensland Government being replaced, with a Criminal Justice Commission established as a watchdog for corruption in the public sector, after public airing of potential and actual wrongdoing. Witness the Woods Royal Commission in New South Wales and the pressure to open up the hidden issue of paedophilia. In such a highly volatile context, it is important to think about ethics carefully. That's clearly what many people have done in recent years, developing codes of ethics as well as codes of practice in different professions. What the contextual issues remind us, however, is that taking ethical stances, even privately, is strongly informed by a public context, usually mediated to us. We learn about ethics as public matters which, as a society or a group within that society such as a profession, we explore.

In the profession of teaching, as in other areas of action, most ethical matters have been translated into customary practices that help to guide our actions based on common assumptions about what is right, what is a better way to define an issue or decide what to do. Ethical codes have developed as a way to make more explicit the tacit understandings and values seen to underpin the practice of a profession or group. The codes are a way of defining shared stances and making public statements about what is seen to be right, and the proper way to approach practice. There have been debates about the extent to which codes of ethics can be anything more than a set of broad rules which do not safeguard people. There are also those who point to the importance of the process of developing codes of ethics as a way to promote debate and raise consciousness about the ethical dilemmas involved in professional practice (Preston 1994; Stonehouse & Creaser 1991).

The problem for us as ethical beings is that we do not live in a homogenous world. This is not just a recent phenomenon: there have always been differences which are treated with suspicion. There has been a creation of the 'Other' as someone to be regulated, treated as deviant, punished, and held up as an example. Schools, for many people, are the organisations where young persons are to be disciplined into knowing their place in the world, finding out what counts as a 'good' or 'normal' person, at least in terms of assessment. This role for the schools in inducting students into this framework has often been a problem in situations where there is a diverse community, where there are different class-based, cultural, religious or social conventions that open up the question of the extent to which schools are 'common', public institutions. What do we do, as ethical persons, when the values are not shared in our community? Do we act as if we were right and others are necessarily wrong? Do we assume that there are necessarily universal values which underpin the role of schools and our work as teachers? How much diversity can exist without the growth of chaos?

There are no easy answers to questions such as these. Clearly, in an Australian context, our legal system provides some guidance about the limits of what can be expected. But it is never enough only to be 'legally right' if we want to act ethically; that usually results in treating every situation as if it was a technical matter to be adjudicated. Nor is it enough to plead ignorance. That is called the 'Nuremberg defence', after the trials of war criminals from Nazi Germany: 'Please sir, I didn't know what was going on'. Part of our job is to be informed and to work, as far as possible, to teach as well as possible, within the domains laid out for us as part of a public institution. There are some tensions that can never be resolved satisfactorily, that can only be worked towards in the situation where they arise, preferably in concert with others involved, but sometimes as an individual. In the following section, we raise some of the kinds of ethical dilemmas that face teachers during the course of their work; new issues and new spins on old issues emerge all the time. Yet we do not live on 'ethical tightropes' every minute of the day. Usually such matters are dealt with as part of customary practice. As new teachers, you have to explore whether these customary ways need to be brought out and re-examined, in the light of new understandings in the society or in relation to your own personal ethical concerns.

The table below provides a copy of the code of ethics developed by the Australian Early Childhood Association (AECA). It was developed by a national working party consisting of Anne Stonehouse (Convenor), Margaret Clyde, Barbara Creaser, Lyn Fasoli, Barbara Piscitelli, and Christine Woodrow, and was adopted by AECA in 1990. While some may argue that some of the aspects of this code are relevant only to children from birth to eight years old, we believe it captures much of what is central to the work of teaching. Specific wording may be modified or additional areas considered, but the core issues are recorded. It is a fine example of a code of ethics in the field of education.

The Early Childhood Code of Ethics

Adherence to this code necessarily involves a commitment to:
- View the well-being of the individual child as having fundamental importance.
- Acknowledge the uniqueness of each person.
- Consider the needs of the child in the context of the family and culture, as the family has a major influence on the young child.
- Take into account the critical impact of self esteem on an individual's development.
- Base practice on sound knowledge, research and theories, while at the same time recognising the limitations and uncertainties of these.
- Work to fulfil the right of all children and their families to services of high quality.

i. In Relation to Children, I will:
1. Acknowledge the uniqueness and potential of each child.
2. Recognise early childhood as a unique and valuable stage of life and accept that each phase within early childhood is important in its own right.
3. Honour the child's right to play, in acknowledgment of the major contribution of play to development.
4. Enhance each child's strengths, competence, and self-esteem.
5. Ensure that my work with children is based on their interests and needs and lets them know they have a contribution to make.
6. Recognise that young children are vulnerable and use my influence and power in their best interests.
7. Create and maintain safe, healthy settings which enhance children's autonomy, initiative, and self-worth, and respect their dignity.
8. Help children learn to interact effectively, and in doing so to learn to balance their own rights, needs, and feelings with those of others.
9. Base my work with children on the best theoretical and practical knowledge about early childhood as well as on particular knowledge of each child's development.

The Early Childhood Code of Ethics continued

10.   Respect the special relationship between children and their families and incorporate this perspective in all my interactions with children.
11.   Work to ensure that young children are not discriminated against on the basis of gender, age, race, religion, language, ability, culture, or national origin.
12.   Acknowledge the worth of the cultural and linguistic diversity that children bring to the environment.
13.   Engage only in practices which are respectful of, and provide security for, children and in no way degrade, endanger, exploit, intimidate, or harm them psychologically or physically.
14.   Ensure that my practices reflect consideration of the child's perspective.

ii. In Relation to Families, I will:

1.   Encourage families to share their knowledge of their child with me and share my general knowledge of children with them so that there is mutual growth and understanding in ways which benefit the child.
2.   Strive to develop positive relationships with families which are based on mutual trust and open communication.
3.   Engage in shared decision-making with families.
4.   Acknowledge families' existing strengths and competence as a basis for supporting them in their task of nurturing their child.
5.   Acknowledge the uniqueness of each family and the significance of its culture, customs, language and beliefs.
6.   Maintain confidentiality.
7.   Respect the right of the family to privacy.
8   Consider situations from each family's perspective, especially if differences or tensions arise.
9.   Assist each family to develop a sense of belonging to the services in which their child participates.
10.   Acknowledge that each family is affected by the community context in which it operates.

iii. In Relation to Colleagues, I will:

1.   Support and assist colleagues in their professional development.
2.   Work with my colleagues to maintain and improve the standard of service provided in my workplace.
3.   Promote policies and working conditions which are non-discriminatory, and that foster competence, wellbeing and positive self-esteem.
4.   Acknowledge and support the use of the personal and professional strengths which my colleagues bring to the workplace.
5.   Work to build an atmosphere of trust, respect and candour by:
      – encouraging openness and tolerance between colleagues;
      – accepting their right to hold different points of view;
      – using constructive methods of conflict resolution; and
      – maintaining appropriate confidentiality.
6.   Acknowledge the worth of the cultural and linguistic diversity which my colleagues bring to the workplace.
7.   Encourage my colleagues to accept and adhere to this Code.

iv. In Relation to the Community and Society, I will:

1.   Provide programs which are responsive to community needs.

The Early Childhood Code of Ethics continued

2. Support the development and implementation of laws and policies which promote the wellbeing of children and families, and which are responsive to community needs.
3. Be familiar with and abide by laws and policies which relate to my work.
4. Work to change laws and policies which interfere with the wellbeing of children.
5. Promote cooperation among all agencies and professions working in the best interests of young children and families.
6. Promote children's best interests through community education and advocacy.

v. In Relation to Myself as a Professional, I will:

1. Update and improve my expertise and practice in the early childhood field continually through formal and informal professional development.
2. Engage in critical self-reflection and seek input from colleagues.
3. Communicate with and consider the views of my colleagues in the early childhood profession and other professions.
4. Support research to strengthen and expand the knowledge base of early childhood, and where possible, initiate, contribute to, and facilitate such research.
5. Work within the limits of my professional role and avoid misrepresentation of my professional competence and qualifications.
6. Work to complement and support the child-rearing function of the family.
7. Be an advocate for young children, early childhood services, and my profession.
8. Recognise the particular importance of formal qualifications in early childhood studies, along with personal characteristics and experience, for those who work in the early childhood profession.
9. Act in the community in ways that enhance the standing of the profession.

(Australian Early Childhood Association web site: http://www.aeca.org.au/code.html)

To develop a code of ethics represents a significant investment by the members of that organisation, developed by a group working on behalf of a national professional association, with extensive consultation processes across its members. The AECA emphasises the importance of understanding the vulnerability of young people from birth to about aged eight years. The preamble of the code underscores the point that no code of ethics can replace the work needing to be done or resolve all the conflicts that necessarily arise in the course of working life:

> A code of ethics is not intended to, and could not possibly, provide easy answers, formulae, or prescriptive solutions for the complex professional dilemmas they face in their work. It does provide a basis for critical reflection, a guide for professional behaviour, and some assistance with the resolution of ethical dilemmas.

The invitation to reflect, to consider one's own position and the responsibilities to others that arise from being a member of a professional group, is a crucial dimension of working as a teacher. 'Reflective teaching' has a long history and in recent years has grown a large literature discussing ways in which teachers might enhance their reflection as professional workers with responsibilities with and for young people.

What is particularly interesting in the AECA code of ethics is the way the focus for ethical action is divided up, covering a general set of principles, to which members commit themselves, and five areas of responsibility for ethical action:

1. children
2. families
3. colleagues
4. community and society
5. self as a professional.

This set of sections demonstrates the diversity of areas of practice required for a professional. Most importantly, it includes treatment of the self as a part of the code of ethics. This is important because focussing only on relations with others does not provide enough support for the conditions under which a professional can conduct their own work with dignity, respect and effectiveness. There may be particular emphases to this section that are most relevant to beginning teachers, building their capacities to act ethically in their work. Examples of this might include familiarising themselves with legislative and ethical frameworks, and ensuring there is time for professional development.

A broader ethical framework outside the boundary of the profession is also important to consider: teachers work in connection with a wider range of other groups, and often as part of public sector organisations. The ethical framework for all public sector organisations has become much more overt in recent years, particularly as a response to Royal Commissions and scandals. It is useful to compare and contrast the principles developed by the AECA with those from a state government authority. The ACT Government (2000) has a code of ethics which all teachers, like other public employees, are expected to follow (http://www.act.gov.au/government/publications/psms/1ethics.htm). These include a set of values and principles, such as:

- taking reasonable care and skill;
- impartiality;
- probity (honesty and integrity);
- courtesy and sensitivity;
- service to the public;
- anti-harassment;
- unlawful coercion;
- compliance with legal provisions;
- compliance with lawful directions;
- avoiding conflicts of interest;
- avoidance of improper advantage of position or information;
- unauthorised comment — public comment that might be taken as an official view;
- avoiding improper use of territory property;
- avoiding waste and extravagance;
- reporting fraud, corruption and maladministration.

Teachers in the ACT system are expected to be familiar with the relevant parts of the legislation and to ensure that their behaviour complies with these broad parameters. Other professional and unskilled workers are also expected to work within this ethical framework. Similar provisions apply in other states and territories in Australia. Such formal statements provide a guide to areas of professional action and broad orientations to what are formally agreed ways to behave.

There is no national code of ethics for teachers other than early childhood teachers. This is partly because there is no single national body covering all teachers. The closest is the teachers' union, the Australian Education Union, which covers the majority of teachers except those in private schools. The Australian Teaching Council, as a group established with reference to all educators in all sectors from early childhood to universities, had such a code of ethics on its agenda but it was abolished in 1996 and no group has been in a position to develop a code further at this time. This may be an area of action that beginning teachers might well participate in during their early working life.

Conclusion

The dimensions of teachers' work that have been explored throughout this book might centre on the classroom, but they have been shown not to be confined just to the classroom. This is sometimes difficult for a beginning teacher to recognise, given the pressures and the central importance of performing well in the classroom. Our book has argued across its chapters for the interdependence of different aspects of the teachers' role. Teaching involves many different practices as part of understanding the learning process, the institution of the school, relations with colleagues and the influences of broader contexts on the classroom, school and broader teaching profession. The beginning teacher will obviously take time to become familiar with the range of practices involved even within a single school, but they are also in an important position to 'read' the context of schools in a way that might be different to others who have been acculturated into schools for longer. What is key to recognise here is the way that the context of schools continues to shift, but in many cases what happens inside them does not shift alongside those broader changes. New teachers can thus be a gift to the school staff in bringing different questions to bear on the problems of teaching practice.

It is dangerous to treat learning new practices mainly as getting on top of a technical problem. This is to reduce the complexity too much. Equally, it is important not to be paralysed with indecision about what to do. Teaching requires teachers to act every minute of every day. Setting aside a time for reflection regularly, with others if at all possible, is an important way to bring these two extremes into some kind of balance.

The AECA sub-headings can be important here. You can ask yourself, how the work you are doing contributes to the principles outlined in the first section of that document. Reflection on these dimensions helps to bring to the surface your own unexamined assumptions about what it is to be a teacher, your own values and priorities, and expectations of yourself and others. To consider the effects of your actions on students, you might clarify particular critical incidents that you have taken part in, or observed around the school. For instance, you might take the AECA first heading and find examples around the school which appear to be contravened by existing practice. Or you might better understand the pressures on schools and the problems for colleagues if you frame up questions about how teachers relate to colleagues and see how these fit with the standards in the AECA code of ethics. Such invitations are not designed to call the ethical standards of you and your colleagues into question but to understand how the ethical dimensions of collegiality have been understood.

Relations with families are often more fraught in the secondary years than in the primary years. How might you balance your responsibilities to keep parents informed with the students' privacy? How do families whose children systematically receive poor grades relate to the school? Is it possible for them to feel it is a 'public' institution in which they might have a say? Such ethical questions bring out the problem that ethical questions often involve making judgments about the balance of others' interests. How might others be involved in contributing to decisions that affect them? This question is most obvious around issues of assessment but is also part of how classroom relations, curriculum content, and future pathways need to be addressed.

Sometimes the beginning teacher is in the best position to raise issues such as these, not only to help themselves to develop better as teachers but also to help other professionals work through the practices that are taken for granted in schools. Framing some of these issues as *questions* can be a fruitful way of focussing attention to the underlying ethical issues. For example, raising the question 'Is it ethical to use grades? or 'What are the ethical aspects of our weekly assembly and end of year awards?' may be a better way to engage teachers in the complex issues involved in the educational decisions that have been made. Often practices have become habits in schools for reasons that have become lost in the mists of time. By framing issues as including an ethical dimension, it may be possible to explore more quickly the inter-connections of all the dimensions of teaching with colleagues.

The work of teachers is necessarily going to raise ethical issues because education is centrally a matter of values. If teachers continue to question themselves and their work, and work with students to help them do the same, this will develop a society in which high standards of ethics and ethical debates are seen to be 'normal'. In a fast changing context, developing a language and capacity to explore these issues is an important set of skills and expertise for all citizens.

INQUIRY STRATEGIES

1. Examine the AECA code of ethics. What would need to be changed for this to apply to secondary schools? What might stay the same?

2. Find examples of codes of ethics or codes of practices that apply in your state/territory and/or for other professional groups. How are these similar or different to those that might apply to the work of teachers specifically?

3. Take the national Beginning Teacher Competencies in Chapter 13 and list out ethical issues that might arise for each competency and sub-competency.

4. Discuss some of the ethical dimensions of a particular situation in which you have found yourself as a student teacher or have observed first-hand in a school.

5. What do you see as the ethical issues in grading students competitively? How are these different when considering grades used on standardised tests?

References

Australian Early Childhood Association 2000, http://www.aeca.org.au/code.html

ACT Government, 2000,
http://www.act.gov.au/government/publications/psms/1ethics.htm

Preston, N. (1994). *Ethics for the Public Sector: Education and Training.* Sydney: Federation Press.

Senate Education, Employment and Training Committee (1998). *A Class Act: Inquiry into the Status of the Teaching Profession.* Canberra: Australian Government Printing Service.

Stonehouse, A. & Creaser, B. (1991). A code of ethics for the Australian early childhood profession: Background and overview. *Australian Journal of Early Childhood,* 16 (1).

Index

Aboriginal education, 67, 266–8
  and adolescence, 62
  bilingual, 179
  literacy levels, 180, 183
  literacy programs, 183–4
  pre-invasion, 19–20
accountability, 192, 279
  assessment of, 216–18
  literacy levels and, 182
  of schools, 249, 253–4
  see also ethics
ACT Government code of ethics, 286–7
action-oriented teacher research see teacher
  research (for professional development)
active learning model (online education), 153–4
adolescence, 40, 53, 62–3
  background to, 56–7
  bio-psychological processes, 57–8
  defined, 55–6
  identity development, 60–2
  school/teacher roles, 62
  self-esteem, 60–1
  youth subcultures, 59–60
  see also youth studies
Advanced Skills Teachers (ASTs), 42
advertising (globalisation of), 9
'age of adolescence', 56
agency cooperation see full service schools
alcohol and drugs, 11, 61
anti-bullying programs, 269
assessment, 208
  authentic, 208–9
  formative, 209–11
  International Baccalaureate (IB), 215
  of teachers, 216–18
  outcome-based education (OBE), 197–8
  parents' views, 220
  practices alienating students, 74
  report card writing, 103–4
  standards and, 211–12, 215
  summative assessment, 214–15
assessment-based school reform, 253
assessment strategies, 220
  Assessment Resource Kit (ARK), 220–1
  multiple intelligences, 224
  performance assessment, 222
  portfolio assessment, 221–2
  project assessment, 222–3
  teacher learning portfolios, 224–5

'at risk' students, 70, 264–5
Australia's Common and Agreed Goals for Schooling
  in the Twenty First Century, 191–2
Australian Association for Research in Education,
  240
Australian Centre for Equity through Education,
  265, 272
Australian Council for Adult Literacy (ACAL), 181
Australian Council for Educational Research
  (ACER), 220
Australian Early Childhood Association (AECA)
  Code of Ethics, 283–5, 287
Australian Language and Literacy Policy, 179–80
Australian Science Education Project, 251
Australian Teaching Council (ATC), 135, 287
Australian Technology Park (ATP), 6
autonomy
  adolescents and, 53, 218
  school education policies, 18, 169
  teacher, 41, 47
Award restructuring, 42–5

'Balkanisation', 23, 99
beginning teachers/student teachers, 287–8
  competency standards, 135–40, 236–8, 252
  expectations, 142–3
  isolation of, 144
  school adviser relationships, 131–2
  schools'/universities' expectations of, 134–5, 254
  self-evaluation, 142, 242
bilingual education, 179
Birmingham School, 59
blue-collar workers, 8
boredom (alleviating student), 116–17
Bourke, Governor, 18
'bricolage', 39
bullying, 269

campus-based teacher education, 144–5
case studies see communication dilemmas;
  examples/scenarios
change, 20
  challenge of, 11–12
  economic, 3, 8
  resistance to, 37–8
  technological, 1–2, 4–7, 10, 20
  within society, 3–5, 11, 56
  workplace, 5–6, 8
  see also school reform

Charles Sturt University, Wagga Wagga
    practicum report, 136–40, 160
class distinctions (working), 69–71
    language of learning and, 72
    student attitudes, 70–1
    worker categories, 8
classroom
    communication conventions, 90–1
    conflict, 95–6
    interaction and assessment, 213
    interaction and technology, 155–6, 169
    management, 91–3, 95–8, 146–7
    transformation, 21–2
classroom practices, 77–8, 82, 118
    formative assessment and, 212–14
    modifying for information technology, 158–9
    theory and, 145–7, 200
Coalition of Essential Schools (US), 27, 29
codes of ethics, 282–3
    ACT Government, 286–7
    early childhood, 283–5
    see also ethics
collaboration
    classroom, 119
    staff, 99, 101–2
    technology and student, 156
communication, 89–90, 105
    action-research and, 243–4
    classroom conventions, 90–1
    extending student participation, 119–21
    initiating, response, follow-up (IRF), 119
    Internet, 121, 177–8
    language of learning, 72
    literacy teaching, 184–5
    online education, 153–4
    parent/caregiver, 102–4
    report card writing, 103–4
    staff, 98–102, 130
    subject area, 115
    teacher–student start-up plan, 92–3
    teacher–student, 90–8, 119
    with the community, 104–5
communication and information technology
    (CIT), 153, 156
communication dilemmas
    classroom management, 97–8
    pre-existing patterns, 92–3
    report writing, 103–4
    student–teacher confrontation, 95–6
    teacher–student friendship, 93–4
    teacher isolation, 100–1
    see also examples/scenarios
community-based schools, 255–6
community–school relationships, 77, 79
    communication, 104–5, 256–7

full service schools (FSS), 264–5, 274–5
competency
    developing student, 115–16
    'generic', 195
    key areas of, 24–5
    standards for beginning teachers, 135–40,
        236–8, 252
    teachers', 23, 134, 182
Competitive Academic Curriculum (CAC), 23
computers, 10
    as a resource, 121–3
    Internet revolution, 152
conflict
    full service school cross-agency, 270–1
    intergenerational, 59
    student–teacher, 95–6
'continuous socialisation', 58–9
'contrived collegiality', 99, 101
'critical literacy', 178–9
cross-curriculum teaching, 28
cultural disadvantage, 68
    see also socioeconomic status
cultural pluralism, 192
curriculum, 21–2, 251–2
    alienating students, 74–5
    'cyberspace', 152
    'default option', 23
    exit outcomes, 195, 197, 199
    future learning paradigm, 25–6
    'hidden', 71–2
    information technology, 156–7
    interpretations of, 193–4
    'key competencies', 24–5
    middle years, 27
    NSN effect upon, 44
    orientations of, 194
    overcrowding, 27
    reform, 195–7
    science in the, 251–2
    social, 11
    see also outcome-based education
Curriculum and Standards Framework (Victoria),
    199

data-gathering methods, 242
    see also teacher research (for professional
        development)
delinquency, 63, 77, 176
    see also adolescence
demographics (teacher), 35, 45
Department of Education, Training and Youth
    Affairs (DETYA), 56
    full service schools and, 272
devolution, 249, 253–4
Disadvantaged Schools Program, 263

disempowerment of students, 72–4
diversification (amongst teachers), 35
'drop-outs', 75–7, 182
drugs and alcohol, 11, 61
Durkheim, Emile, 74

economic change, 3, 8, 20
education, 21
    disempowering students, 72–4
    equity in, 265–6
    foundations of, 24
    governments' role, 198–9
    history of, 18–20, 36–7
    impact upon social inequality, 68, 265–6
    liberal progressive, 22, 194
    lifelong, 5, 24–5
    socially unequal outcomes, 69–70
    stages of development, 19
    value adding, 216–18
    see also curriculum; online education
educational disadvantage, 67–8
    full service schools (FSSs) addressing, 264–5
    homelessness, 75–7, 268
    indigenous peoples', 266–7
    information technology and, 167–8
    locational disadvantage, 7–8, 167, 181–2,
        266, 268
    overcoming, 77–80
    programs addressing, 80, 183–4, 266–9
    resource distribution and, 265–6
    student alienation, 70, 74–5
    students' teacher resistance, 72–4
educational goals, 111
    achieving, 112
    twenty-first century, 191–2
ethics, 134, 279, 281–2
    ACT Government code, 286–7
    beginning teachers and, 287–8
    codes of, 282–3
    early childhood code, 283–5
    in teachers' research, 239–40
    teacher–student 'friendship', 93–4
    see also accountability
ethnicity, 4–5, 45, 63, 67, 72–3, 75, 78, 118, 192
evaluation
    school, 258–9
    self, 142, 242
    see also assessment
Eveleigh Locomotive Workshops, 5–6, 8
examples/scenarios
    adults' view of school, 16–17
    assessment and reporting, 207–8
    classroom management, 147
    ethnicity, 4–5
    homeless students, 76

HSC history course and technology, 164–5
Indigenous Australian FSS initiative,
    267–8
legal studies and technology, 163–4
mathematics and technology, 162–3
negotiating practicum learning goals, 140–1
practicum report form, 136–40
student participation, 120
student teacher–colleague, 133
student teacher–school adviser, 132
technology in the classroom, 158–61
theories of practice, 146–7
see also communication dilemmas
exit outcomes (curriculum), 195, 197, 199

Families And Schools Together (FAST)
    program, 269–70
family life
    home computers and, 10
    patterns, 56
    role in successful education, 77, 79, 288
    television (impact on), 9
    see also parents and learning
final assessment, 214–15
Finn review, 24
'Five Dimensions of Learning', 211–12
'Fordism', 41
formative assessment, 209, 212–14
    convergent/divergent, 209–11
    standards and, 211–12
friendship (teacher–student), 93–4
full service schools (FSSs), 263–4, 275
    anti-bullying programs, 269
    checklist, 272–4
    cross-agency conflict, 270–1
    educational equity and, 265–6
    Families And Schools Together (FAST)
    program, 269–70
    homeless student initiatives, 268
    Indigenous student initiatives, 266–8
    outcomes, 271–2
    rural education initiatives, 268–9
    students' role in, 274–5
future (the), 4, 20
    curriculum for, 22–6
    learning paradigm, 25

gender
    differentiating Aboriginal education, 20
    literacy levels and, 183–4
    structuring student opportunity, 75
    teacher–student relationships and, 93–4
    teaching demographic, 45
'generic competencies', 195
global mass media, 9

globalisation, 3, 192
    domestic impact, 9
    literacy levels and, 176–7
    workplace impact, 5–6, 8
'gold-collar workers', 8
government
    codes of ethics for teachers, 286–7
    education responsibility, 198–9, 236
    full service school (FSS) program, 264–5
    reshaping education, 192, 263
Guttenberg literacy, 177

'hidden curriculum', 71–2
Higher School Certificate
    assessment, 215
    history course and technology, 164–5
    online, 160–1
home computers, 10
homeless students, 75–7, 268
Human Rights and Equal Opportunity
    Commission (HREOC), 181–2, 266, 268

identity development (adolescent), 60–2, 68
illiteracy, 176
    see also literacy
indigenous student education, 62, 67, 266–8
    bilingual, 179
    literacy levels, 180, 183
    literacy programs, 183–4
    pre-invasion, 19–20
individualism (teacher), 99
industrial age (the), 5–6
information technology, 6, 26
    demands upon teachers, 165–7
    teachers adapting to, 153, 156–7
initiating, response, follow-up (IRF)
    communication, 119
input-driven curriculum, 195–6, 199
in-service training, 232
    see also professional development
intelligence (multiple), 224
intergenerational conflict, 59
    see also youth studies
International Baccalaureate (IB), 215
Internet
    as a resource, 121
    literacy and the, 177–8
    NSW HSC and the, 160–1
    online education, 153–4
    project sites, 162
    revolution, 152
interpreting literacy, 165–6, 177–9, 187
interpreting the curriculum, 193–4
interpreting text, 185

K-12 syllabus reform, 195
key competencies, 24–5
key learning areas (KLAs), 198–9, 202
knowing that/knowing how, 23–6
knowledge (as a commodity), 6
knowledge-based labour market, 7–8
knowledge-based society, 4, 7

labour market changes, 5–6, 8, 56
language
    bilingual education, 179
    social class and, 72
    Standard Australian English (SAE), 179–80
learner-centred classrooms, 21–2
learning
    as a social process, 112–13, 123
    communities, 101–2
    cross-curriculum, 28
    dimensions of, 211–12
    do-it-yourself, 39
    foundations, 24
    language of, 72
    paradigm (future), 25–6
    parents' views on, 219–20
    prism, 110, 112
    programs, 20
    theories of, 109–12
    'what' and 'how' of, 25, 109–10
    see also educational goals; technology in
        the classroom
legal studies and technology, 163–4
lesson plans, 111
liberal/progressive curriculum orientation, 194
life chances, 68–9
    literacy levels and, 180–2
    summative assessment and, 214
literacy, 175, 187
    'critical', 178–9
    debates on standards, 175–6
    dimensions of, 176
    interpretation of, 165–6, 177–9
    levels and gender, 183
    levels, 180–2
    programs, 183–4
    socioeconomic status and, 180, 182
    sociocultural understanding of, 166
    teaching strategies, 184–6
    tests, 182–3
locational disadvantage, 7–8, 167, 181–2, 266, 268

marginalised groups
    adolescents in, 62
    homeless people, 75–7, 268
    indigenous people, 67, 180, 183, 266–8

rural youth, 7–8, 160, 167, 181–2, 266, 268–9
Maricopa Roundtable, 153
mass schooling, 41–2, 176, 249
mathematics and technology, 162–3
Mayer committee, 24
media
    against teachers, 37
    effects upon teaching, 121
    global, 9
    portrayal of adolescence, 56
    reporting literacy levels, 175–7
mentoring, 101
middle years schooling, 21, 26–9
    literacy levels and, 180–2
Ministerial Council on Education, Employment,
    Training and Youth Affairs (MCEETYA), 191
mistakes (teachers'), 34–5
Montessori schools, 255
Mt Druitt High School, 203
'multi-literacies', 177
multimedia
    as a resource, 118, 121, 155
    literacy, 165–7, 177
multiple intelligences (assessment and), 224

National Professional Development Program
    (NPDP), 234–5
National Project on the Quality of Teaching
    and Learning (NPQTL), 42–5, 135, 235
National Review of Education for Aboriginal
    and Torres Strait Islander Peoples, 266
national school system, 18
National Schools Network (NSN), 25, 43–4
    Research Circles, 235–6, 241
non-English speaking backgrounds (NESB),
    4–5, 62, 232, 254
    and bilingual education, 179
NSW HSC On-Line, 160–1
NSW Ministerial Advisory Council on the Quality
    of Teaching and Learning, 135
'Nuremberg defence', 282–3

online education, 153–4
    gender issues of, 167–8
    HSC history course, 164–5
    legal studies, 163–4
    mathematics, 162–3
    NSW HSC, 160–1
Outback Satellite Education Trial, 160
outcome-based education (OBE), 23, 173, 192,
    202
    approaches to, 196–7, 199
    assessment techniques, 197
    benefits, 199–200

    criticisms, 201–2
    curriculum models, 195–6
    exit outcomes, 195, 197, 199
    key learning areas (KLAs), 198–9, 202

Palmerston North Girls' High School (NZ), 158–9
parent/caregiver communication, 102–4
parents and citizens (P&C) groups, 256
parents and learning, 219–20, 288
    Families And Schools Together (FAST)
        program, 269–70
pedagogy alienating students, 74–5
performance assessment, 222
portfolio assessment, 221–2
post-compulsory schooling, 8–9, 24, 40
poverty and education, 68, 70, 167, 265
practicum (the), 127, 281
    competency standards, 135–40
    learning goals, 134–5
    negotiation case study, 140–1
    negotiation, 133, 147
    nomenclature, 130
    purpose of, 128
    report forms, 135
    self-evaluation, 142, 242
    staff relations and, 130–3, 143
    student expectations of, 142–4
    teacher education and, 129–30
primary school transition, 26–7
production-line schooling, 41–2
productive pedagogy, 80–2
professional associations, 238–9
professional development, 231, 244
    beginning teacher competencies, 135–40,
        236–8
    history of, 232–3
    National Professional Development
        Program (NPDP), 234–5
    National Schools Network (NSN), 235
    NSN Research Circles, 235–6
    participative inquiry, 239–40
    teacher qualifications, 252–3
    see also teacher research (for professional
        development)
professionalism, 47–8
programs addressing educational disadvantage, 80,
    183–4, 266–9
progressive education, 22
project assessment, 222–3
project management (research), 243–4
project sites (Internet), 162
Protestant opposition to national system, 18
puberty, 57
    see also adolescence

public accounts (of schools), 253–4
  see also school reform
public intellectuals, 38

qualifications (teacher), 252–3, 281
  see also professional development
Queensland Board of Registration, 135
Queensland Board of Senior Secondary School
  Studies (QBSSSS), 215

'realms of knowledge', 23
'reflective teaching', 225, 285
relationships, 21, 256–7
  community–school, 77, 79, 104–5, 264–5,
    274–5
  practicum, 130–3
  school reform and, 256–7
  schooling and inequality, 70–1, 80, 265–6
  staff, 98–102
  student teacher–school adviser, 131–2
  teacher–community, 104–5
  teacher–parent/caregiver, 102–4
  teacher–student, 10, 81, 90–3, 95–6
  see also communication dilemmas
religion (school development affected by), 18, 20
reporting, 218–19
  parents' views, 220
  report card writing, 103–4
  see also assessment strategies; communication
research *see* teacher research (for professional
  development)
Research Circles (National Schools Network),
  235–6, 241
resources, 121–3
  inequitable distribution of, 265–6
  transforming classrooms, 22
  see also online education; technology in
    the classroom
River Oaks Public School, Ontario, Canada,
  159–60
Roman Catholic support for national system, 18
rural families social disadvantage, 7–8, 167, 181–2,
  266, 268

salary, 37, 42
'Sandstone Curtain', 7
'scaffolding', 118–19
school advisers, 131–2, 143
school board/council, 256
school curriculum *see* curriculum
school-based curriculum development (SBCD),
  254–5
school-based management, 253–4, 256
school-based professional development, 101–2, 105
school education policies

autonomy, 18
  for adolescents, 53–4
  outcome-based education (OBE) and, 197–8
school funding, 192, 216–18, 263
'school knowledge', 113–14
school practices
  alienating students, 74–5
  for success, 79, 250–1
school reform, 250–1, 253, 259
  barriers to, 257–8
  community-based schools, 255–6
  devolution, 249, 253–4
  evaluation, 258–9
  power sharing, 256–7
  qualification quality and, 252–3
  school-based curriculum development (SBCD),
    254–5
schools
  adult view of, 16–17
  areas for change, 20
  community-based, 255–6
  'conventional', 77
  culture of, 130
  de-institutionalising, 21–2
  expectations of, 15, 19
  history of, 18–20
  lack of change, 15–17
  parent feedback and, 219–20
  staff relationships, 98–102
  successful, 77–80
  value adding, 216–18
  see also full service schools (FSSs);
    accountability
secondary school transition, 26–7
self (concept of), 60
self-evaluation, 142, 242
Senate Inquiry (status of teaching), 37, 245, 281
social atlases, 7
social engineering, 10
social inequality, 68
  indigenous people, 67, 180, 183
  rural youth, 7–8, 167, 181–2, 266, 268
social process (of learning), 112–13, 123
social reproduction, 67–71
  'hidden curriculum' aiding, 71–2
social responsibility, 46–8
socially critical curriculum orientation, 194
society, 3–5, 11, 20
  influences upon adolescents, 58
  locational disadvantage, 7–8, 167, 181–2,
    266, 268
  working class disadvantage in, 69–71
  workplace changes, 5–6, 8
sociocultural groups pedagogical needs, 81
sociocultural influences

global mass media, 9–10
home computers, 10
technology, 1–2, 4–7
upon adolescents, 58
socioeconomic status, 8, 63, 67–8, 70, 75
literacy and, 180–3
student achievement and, 201, 216, 250
staff meetings, 130
staff relationships, 98–102
Standard Australian English (SAE), 179–80
standards-based reforms, 252–3
standards-referenced assessment, 211–12, 215
strategies
assessment, 220–5
classroom technology, 156–7
literacy teaching, 184–6
middle school education, 27–8, 105
successful school practice, 79, 250–1
Street Kids Access Tertiary Education (SKATE), 75–7
Stromlo High School middle school innovation, 27–8, 105
student alienation, 21–2, 70
disempowerment, 73–4
educational practices and, 74–5
student-centred classrooms, 159–60
assessment and, 209–10
student–teacher relationships, 81, 93–4
see also teacher–student relationships
student teachers/beginning teachers, 287–8
competency standards, 135–40, 236–8, 252
expectations, 142–3
isolation of, 144
school adviser relationships, 131–2
schools'/universities' expectations of, 134–5
self-evaluation, 142, 242
students
'at risk', 70, 264–5
from working class backgrounds, 69–71
homeless, 75–7, 268
indigenous, 19–20, 62, 67, 179–80, 183–4, 266–8
'resilient', 79
rural, 7–8, 160, 167, 181–2, 266, 268–9
work force preparation of, 15, 19
students'
backgrounds and classroom participation, 117–18
boredom (alleviating), 116–17
definition of teachers, 33–4
educational resistance, 70–2, 74
opportunities structured, 75–6
subject matter participation, 117–19
views on teachers' mistakes, 34–5
subject-based departments, 23–4, 99, 113

middle-years schooling and, 27
subject matter
approaches to, 113–16
'knowing how'/'knowing that' components of, 114
knowledge building, 113
motivating learning, 116–17
student participation, 117–19
Summerhill school, 255
summative assessment, 214–15
see also assessment

teacher-centred classrooms, 2, 21–2, 29
assessment and, 210, 213
information technology and, 159–60
teacher education, 144–5, 244
learning portfolios, 224–5
qualifications, 252–3
reflection, 225, 285
technology and, 156–7
theory and practice, 145–7
see also practicum; professional development
teacher research (for professional development), 240, 244–6
analysing data, 242–3
defining a focus, 240–1
defining specific questions, 241
evidence and data, 241–2
project management, 243–4
teacher–student communication, 119–21
see also communication
teacher–student relationships, 90–1
conflict, 95–6
social distance, 10, 93–4
start-up plans, 91–3
technology and, 156
teachers
as public intellectuals, 38
assessment of, 216–18
demographics, 35
diversification amongst, 35
expectations of, 3, 46, 134–5, 161
new technologies and, 10
popular culture and, 10
social responsibility, 47–8, 282–3
status of, 37
students' definition of, 33–4
women, 45–6
see also teacher education; vocation (teaching as a)
teachers'
backgrounds and classroom participation, 117–18
competence (challenge to), 23
isolation, 100–1, 144

professional associations, 238–9
reflection, 225, 285
roles with adolescents, 62
salary, 37, 42, 46
unions, 239
workplace reform, 44
see also professional development; teacher
    education
teaching and learning prism, 110, 112
teaching practices, 77–8, 82, 118
    formative assessment and, 212–14
    modifying for information technology,
        158–9
    theory and, 145–7, 200
teaching work force
    demographics, 35
    perceptions of, 45–6
    women within, 45
technological change, 1–2, 4–7, 10, 20, 151–2
technological literacy, 178
technology in the classroom, 154–5
    benefits/drawbacks, 154, 158, 168
    case studies, 158–61
    curriculum integration, 158–60
    interaction and, 155–6, 169
    modifying teacher practice for, 159
    project work and, 161–2
    teachers adapting to, 152–3
    see also Internet; online education
television (impact of), 9
testing
    literacy, 182–3
    school reform, 253
    summative assessment, 214–15
    see also assessment; assessment strategies
theory and practice, 145–6, 200
    case study, 146–7
Torres Strait Islanders *see* indigenous student
    education
transitional stages
    primary to secondary school, 26–7

to adolescence, 55, 57–8, 63
unions, 239, 287

value adding (education), 216–18
vocation (teaching as a), 36–8, 45–6, 229, 279
    emotional work, 40–1
    intellectual work, 38–9
    work organisation, 41–2
    see also accountability; ethics
vocational/neo-classical curriculum orientation, 194
Vygotsky, Lev, 114–15, 118

web (the) *see* online education
web sites
    ACT Government codes of ethics, 286
    ethics in research, 240
    history study, 165
    HSC online, 161
    legal study, 164
    Murder Under the Microscope, 163
    Norfolk Island Central School, 162
    project sites, 162
    Sefton High School, 162
white-collar workers, 8
women dominating teaching, 45–6
work force (knowledge-based), 7–9
working class
    educational outcome for, 69–70
    student attitudes, 70–1
    worker classification, 8
workplace changes (general), 5–6, 8
workplace literacy, 178

young people *see* adolescence; youth studies
Youth Research Centre, 56
youth studies, 56–7
    conflict theorists, 59
    functional approach to, 58–9
    youth and power, 60, 72–3
    see also adolescence
youth subcultures, 59–60